2000

SYSTEMATIC TEACHING STRATEGIES

SYSTEMATIC TEACHING STRATEGIES

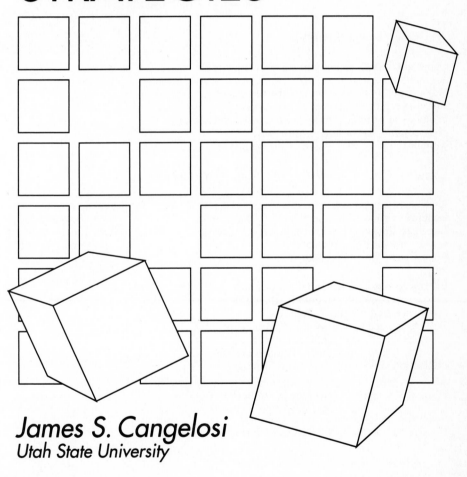

James S. Cangelosi
Utah State University

Longman
New York & London

Systematic Teaching Strategies

Copyright © 1992 by Longman Publishing Group.

Longman, 95 Church Street, White Plains, N.Y. 10601

Associated companies:
Longman Group Ltd., London
Longman Cheshire Pty., Melbourne
Longman Paul Pty., Auckland
Copp Clark Pitman, Toronto

Executive editor: Raymond T. O'Connell
Development editor: Virginia L. Blanford
Production editor: Ann P. Kearns
Text design adaptation: Anne M. Pompeo
Cover design: Joseph DePinho
Text art: Elaine Campanella; Pompeo Designs
Production supervisor: Richard C. Bretan

Library of Congress Cataloging-in-Publication Data

Cangelosi, James S.
   Systematic teaching strategies / James S. Cangelosi.
       p.   cm.
   Includes bibliographical references.
   ISBN 0-8013-0633-7
   1. Teaching.   I. Title.
LB1025.3.C36   1992
371.1′02—dc20   91-29017
                                                 CIP

1 2 3 4 5 6 7 8 9 10-HA-9594939291

To Amanda

Contents

Chapter 8   Theory into Practice: Nancy Fisher, First-Year High
School Teacher   **334**

Preface

Some teachers design and orchestrate learning experiences leading students to acquire enriching abilities, skills, and attitudes that serve the students throughout their lives. The practice of some other teachers takes students through misguided, time-wasting experiences resulting in missed learning opportunities, misconceptions, and a distaste for academic pursuits. Whether you choose to be an exemplary or a malpracticing teacher, you will have a profound, life-long impact on every one of your students. Assuming you prefer that impact to be enriching rather than debilitating, you need to develop your own abilities to apply systematic teaching strategies that have been proven to be effective in classrooms at every grade level.

Systematic Teaching Strategies is designed to help you, as an elementary, middle, or secondary school teacher, successfully utilize proven systematic approaches so that your students eagerly acquire enriching abilities, skills, and attitudes. To succeed, you must design and conduct both inquiry and direct instructional lessons in ways that motivate students' cooperation and make use of accurate assessments of their progress. This book integrates those aspects of instruction in nine chapters:

Chapter 1, "Being a Teacher," points out the complexities of teaching and introduces a five-stage model that serves as an advanced organizer for the more specifically focused chapters that follow.

Chapter 2, "Defining Learning Goals," demonstrates how to define the subject matter content and learning levels on which your lessons are to focus.

Chapter 3, "Designing Lessons," demonstrates how to sequence and design lessons that lead your students to achieve the learning goals you set for them.

Chapter 4, "Managing Student Behavior," suggests and illustrates methods for establishing a classroom climate that is conducive to learning, gaining and maintaining students' cooperation in the classroom, and efficiently dealing with student off-task behaviors.

Chapter 5, "Engaging Students in Learning Activities," demonstrates how to design, organize, and conduct different types of learning activities (e.g., interactive lecture sessions, questioning and discussion sessions, cooperative task-group sessions, independent work sessions, and homework) in ways that motivate students to be attentive and to eagerly cooperate with you and with each other.

Chapter 6, "Assessing Student Achievement," introduces fundamental measurement and evaluation principles and demonstrates how to develop and use tests that provide feedback for guidance in designing lessons and valid data for judging student progress.

Chapter 7, "Theory into Practice: Dustin Manda, First-Year Elementary School Teacher," affords you the opportunity to vicariously experience the thoughts, plans. classroom activities, decisions, disappointments, and successes of an elementary school teacher as he attempts to implement the suggestions from Chapter 1–6 of this text.

Chapter 8, "Theory into Practice: Nancy Fisher, First-Year High School Teacher," walks you through the first year of a beginning teacher as she attempts to apply systematic teaching strategies at the high school level as did Dustin Manda at the elementary school level.

Chapter 9, "Looking Ahead," is intended to stimulate your thinking about the current movement to reform classroom teaching practice and to reflect on your own professional role in that movement.

Systematic Teaching Strategies is an unusual book in that research-based principles for teaching are not only presented, but also demonstrated via realistic classroom-based examples and contrasted with examples that violate the principle. Furthermore, topics (e.g., defining learning goals, designing lessons, motivating student cooperation, and evaluating achievement) are integrated throughout using 119 vignettes that follow teachers' thoughts, actions, and reactions as they design, organize, conduct, evaluate, and redesign lessons. The book is structured to utilize the same type of research-based teaching strategies that it suggests you use with your students. In other words, (a) inductive approaches with carefully orchestrated examples are used to lead you to discover principles, (b) direct instructional strategies are incorporated in the presentations to expose you to information and techniques, and (c) deductive structures are used to lead you to apply the principles and techniques. Throughout the text, comprehension strategies are used to introduce technical terms and advanced organizers.

Such an approach necessitates that some topics that are isolated from one another in other teaching methods texts be integrated throughout this text. For example, the model for specifying learning outcomes that is introduced in Chapter 2 is utilized throughout subsequent chapters. Thus, suggestions for how to design and conduct an inquiry lesson are linked to the appropriateness of inquiry instructional strategies depending on the learning level targeted by the lesson's objective.

Each of the book's examples and vignettes reflects aspects of actual events, but they are presented herein with fictitious names, locations, and institutions. Circumstances, actions, and situations are likely to appear familiar to any reader acquainted with the realities of schools, but any similarities among names, locations, and institutions alluded to in these scenarios and examples are strictly coincidental.

As an aid to professors who incorporate *Systematic Teaching Strategies* into their course, an *Instructor's Manual* is available from Longman. The manual contains (a) suggestions for taking advantage of the book's features in a variety of course structures, (b) a detailed sample syllabus, including a sequence of class-meeting activities and assignments, (c) a variety of lesson-planning and lesson-critique forms, and (d) sample midterm and final examinations with scoring criteria and forms for each.

I am particularly grateful to the numerous, but proportionally rare, teachers who have demonstrated that research-based approaches are practical in realistic classroom situations. They are the people who provided me with the bases for the examples, without which I could not have written a book utilizing inductive and deductive teaching strategies.

The manuscript was expertly reviewed by Rodolfo Vilaro, of Northeastern Illinois University, Chicago; Deborah Brown, of Friends University, Wichita, Kansas; and Donna Mertens, of Gallaudet University, Washington, D.C.

Elaine Campanella's prodigious art talent injected life into the vignettes and examples scattered throughout the book. Debra Allan provided preliminary sketches for a number of the illustrations. Ray O'Connell, Ann Kearns, Laura McCormick, and Virginia Blanford are among the competent, personable professionals at Longman Publishing with whom I was privileged to work. To my best friend, Barb Rice, I extend my sincerest appreciation for her support, counsel, and expert copyreading.

Note on Terminology

Each profession has its own terminology. There are *general usage terms*, which are words and symbols with conventional meanings listed in standard dictionaries that are understood by people both within and outside the profession. With respect to the education profession, *friend*, *brown*, and *sing* are examples. There are also *special usage terms*, which are words and symbols from the general vocabulary that take on esoteric meanings when used in certain contexts within the profession. In the education profession, *objective*, *conceptualization*, and *inquiry lesson* are examples. Then there are *technical usage terms*, which are words and symbols that have meaning only within the context of the profession. In education, *with-itness*, *synectics*, and *construct validity* are examples.

Due to the spiral organization of this text, many educational *special usage terms* (e.g., *teaching unit*, *learning goal*, *exploratory activity*, *direct instruction*, *cooperative learning activity*, *transition time*, and *inductive questioning*) are used before they are operationally defined. For example, the goals of this book are defined by objectives appearing at the beginning of each chapter. Special usage terms (e.g., *Cognitive: conceptualization*) in parentheses following each objective help clarify its meaning. But these terms are not defined and explained until Chapter 2. Up to the point where special usage terms are operationally defined in the text, please interpret them as general usage terms. In other words, to comprehend this text, the vague general meanings are adequate until the special definitions are provided. Technical terms (e.g., *synectics*) are avoided until they are defined (e.g., on page 113).

CHAPTER 1

Being a Teacher

GOAL OF CHAPTER 1

The intent of this chapter is to increase your awareness of the complexities of teaching and your role as a professional teacher. Furthermore, a five-stage model is introduced that serves as an advanced organizer for the more specifically focused chapters that follow. In particular, Chapter 1 is designed to help you

1. explain why teaching is an extremely complex art, requiring teachers to contend with and manipulate a number of variables (*Cognitive: conceptualization*)
2. describe instruction and the roles of teachers within the framework of the five stages of teaching (*Cognitive: conceptualization*)
3. explain some of the many ways in which students vary—variations you will need to consider whenever you practice the art of teaching (*Cognitive: comprehension*)
4. define and explain the meanings of the following terms: *school curriculum, course curriculum, curriculum guidelines, teaching unit, learning goal, learning objective, lesson, learning activity, formative evaluation, summative evaluation, instructional supervision, peer coaching, mentor teacher, research-based, systematic teaching strategy, preservice teacher, inservice beginning teacher,* and *inservice experienced teacher* (*Cognitive: comprehension*)
5. list some of the noninstructional professional responsibilities of teachers (*Cognitive: simple knowledge*)
6. explain how the art of teaching is dependent on the science of teaching (*Cognitive: conceptualization*)

THE COMPLEX ART OF TEACHING

Jay Santiago at Work

Your work as a classroom teacher begins long before you meet your first student. One teacher's preparations for an upcoming school year is reflected in Vignette 1.1:

VIGNETTE 1.1

As a teacher at Malaker Middle School, one of Jay Santiago's many responsibilities is to design and conduct a general science course for a class of 28 sixth-grade students. The school district's curriculum guide indicates that the course should include basic work in life, physical, earth, and health sciences. Before the beginning of the school year, Jay organizes the course into 12 teaching units with 2 additional units possible if time permits.

In light of his evaluations of the students' needs, prior experiences, aptitudes, interests, and prior achievements, he establishes a goal for each unit and develops a general plan for leading students to accomplish that goal within a practical time frame. He plans, for example, to devote about 3 weeks to the following goal for one of the physical science units, "Laws of Motion":

> Students explain the effects of Newton's three laws of motion, gravity, and friction on speed and acceleration and apply their understanding of these effects in real-world situations.

It's only August, and the unit isn't scheduled to be taught for another 10 weeks. Thus, he doesn't yet formulate specific objectives leading to that goal nor design specific lessons for the unit. Jay's experiences have taught him that during the weeks leading up to that unit, he will learn things about the students and unanticipated events will occur that are likely to change his mind about any specific lesson plans he makes this far ahead of time. However, he does develop general strategies for this and the other 13 units so that the course will flow smoothly from one unit to the next with students' goal achievement dependent on their achievement of previous goals. Jay also must anticipate his needs for specific instructional materials and equipment far enough in advance to have them ready when the unit commences.

Thus, Jay sketches out his general strategies for accomplishing each of the unit goals. He anticipates beginning Unit 5, "Laws of Motion," with hands-on, exploratory activities leading students to formulate their own hypotheses. More direct instructional activities are visualized to teach process skills after those initial conceptual-level experiences. For the end of the unit, he thinks that inquiry lessons leading to application-level learning would be appropriate. After completing this *long-range planning* phase of teaching, not only for the science course, but for all of the courses he will be teaching, Jay organizes his classroom, prepares materials, secures equipment, and devises procedures that will facilitate his plans. For example, in many of his units (e.g., Science Unit 5), he intends to use both cooperative learning activities in small-group sessions as well as direct instructional activities in large-group sessions. Thus, he arranges the classroom in a way that will accommodate efficient transitions between those two types of sessions.

Decisions are made regarding such matters as how to establish, teach, and en-

---

VIGNETTE 1.1 (continued)

force rules of conduct for maximizing student engagement in the learning activities, discouraging disruptions, and securing a healthy and safe learning environment. Jay formulates procedures for taking care of administrative matters, establishing classroom movement patterns, distributing materials, utilizing school resources, and communicating with parents. He also enters into collaborative arrangements with colleague teachers (e.g., helping one another deal with behavior management problems and coordinating teaching units).

Only after such extensive long-range planning and work organizing for the year does Jay feel ready to meet his students on opening day.

Short-range planning and designing lessons in detail are ongoing responsibilities throughout the school year. For example:

VIGNETTE 1.2

Eight weeks have elapsed since the opening day of school. Jay's science course is in the early stages of Unit 4, "The Structure of Matter." Now he's ready to design the details of Unit 5, "Laws of Motion," which he anticipates beginning in two weeks. It's 5 P.M. as Jay sits at his desk with the science course textbook, the syllabus he developed in August, notes he's accumulated over the past eight weeks, and the computer he utilizes to write lesson plans. He ponders Unit 5's goal:

Students explain the effects of Newton's three laws of motion, gravity, and friction on speed and acceleration and apply their understanding of these effects in real-world situations.

Deliberating carefully and utilizing techniques described in Chapter 2 of this book, he defines this goal with a sequence of 12 objectives that specify the exact science topics for students to learn and the levels at which they are to learn each. Exactly what should they be able to explain, remember, apply, and so forth by the end of the unit is enumerated. Jay then formulates a lesson plan for each objective. For example:

One objective is for the students to discriminate between speed and acceleration. To help them achieve this, Jay decides to take the students outside onto a sidewalk with equally spaced parallel lines as shown in Figure 1.1. He will then have one student operate a remote-controlled toy car along the sidewalk at a constant rate while others record the number of lines the car crosses in a 10-second time frame. After repeated trials using different students and speed settings, the class will engage in similar, but modified experiments. In these subsequent experiments, the students controlling the car will vary the throttle setting during the runs while other students use stopwatches to clock how long it takes the car to pass from one line to another. In other trials, controllers will also change the direction of the car (i.e., turning or backing it up). The data students gather from the experiments are to be used in a subsequent class session in which Jay plans to use inductive questioning

(continued)

VIGNETTE 1.2 (continued)

Figure 1.1. Mr. Santiago Teaching Students to Discriminate between Speed and Acceleration

strategies to lead the students to discover the differences between speed and acceleration and articulate a definition for each.

Another objective is for students to remember the definitions for *speed* and *acceleration*. For this objective, Jay plans to display the definitions articulated in the lesson for the previous objective and direct the students to write them in the "Science Word Glossary" section of the notebook he requires them to keep. Then he will frequently have students repeat the definitions as the concepts of speed and acceleration are discussed in subsequent lessons for other objectives (e.g., an objective for students to explain the effects of friction and gravity on the speed of a moving body).

Jay also devises plans for keeping students motivated and on-task during the lessons and for maintaining an almost continuous flow of feedback on students' progress so that he can modify lesson plans accordingly. Finally, he outlines a blueprint for a test to be used in evaluating how well students will have achieved the goal upon completion of the unit.

Jay implements the unit plan when the class is done with Unit 4 using feedback and making changes as necessary (Vignette 1.3).

VIGNETTE 1.3

As planned, Jay devotes 14 school days to Unit 5. However, more time than planned was spent on the lesson for the first objective because students seemed so enthusiastic about the initial activities that they raised questions and developed hypotheses that extended beyond speed and acceleration issues. This led Jay to bring in some ideas on Newton's laws of motion sooner than he had planned. Thus, he expanded the lesson to include at least parts of three other objectives. He made up for the time by eliminating some of the activities that were planned relative to Newton's third law (i.e., for every force there is an equal and opposite force). The feedback he received during the first three lessons influenced his decision to put more emphasis on other aspects of the unit and less on the third law of motion.

Mr. Santiago Uses Strategies to Keep Students on Task and Engaged in Learning Activities

The enthusiasm students displayed in the initial lesson seemed to provide momentum that maintained high levels of cooperation throughout the unit. There were, however, several isolated incidences of disruptive behaviors with which Jay had to contend. Nedra, for example, twirled around the stopwatch she was using during the first lesson even after Jay indicated that the action was disturbing the work of

(continued)

VIGNETTE 1.3 (continued)

others and the watch might become damaged. He then directed her to surrender the watch, step back from the group, and to continue timing the car as before, but without benefit of the watch (i.e., she was to count, "one thousand one, one thousand two, . . .," silently to herself).

On the thirteenth day he administered the unit test and used the results in evaluating the success of the unit and in assigning each student a grade. Answers to test items and test results were reviewed on the last day of the unit.

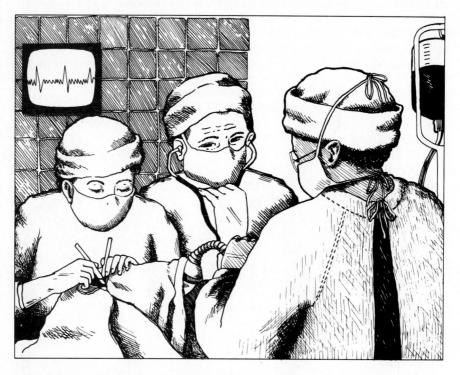

Teaching Isn't Brain Surgery; Teaching Is Far More Complex

The Stages of Teaching

Classroom teaching is not brain surgery; teaching is far more complex. Brain surgery involves (a) organizing and preparing the setting for the diagnosis and treatment of patients; (b) diagnosing a patient and determining the need for surgery; (c) designing, planning, and preparing the surgical procedure; (d) conducting the surgery (with assistance) and monitoring the patient's progress; and (e) evaluating the success of the operation and follow-up for possible further treatment. The stages of teaching parallel those of brain surgery; however, unlike the brain surgeon, the teacher does not have the luxury of working with only one client (i.e., student or patient) at a time. Typically, a teacher deals with about 30 students at a time. Whereas the brain surgeon can focus on one aspect of one patient at a time (e.g., removing an intraaxial neoplasmic tumor from the occipital lobe) while others (e.g., an anesthesiologist) focus on other variables (e.g., the patient's respiratory rate), the teacher (usually working alone) is expected to concurrently concern himself with 30 or so students regarding a myriad of variables (e.g., self-images, aptitudes, motivations for learning, prior achievements, attention levels, interest in the lesson's content, long-range goals, moment-to-moment objectives, and disruptive behaviors).

Consider Jay Santiago's work in Vignettes 1.1, 1.2, and 1.3. Before the school year began, Mr. Santiago designed not only the general science course, but also the other courses he's assigned to teach. He engaged in long-range planning, organized the classroom, gathered and prepared learning and teaching materials, and anticipated equipment needs in light of how he planned to conduct the courses.

Having organized the courses into teaching units, he spent considerable time throughout the year assessing students' needs and determining objectives for up-coming units. Lessons are then designed to help students achieve those objectives. This unit planning includes strategies for maintaining students on task during the lessons, monitoring their progress, and evaluating achievement of unit goals.

Each lesson is comprised of specific learning activities that he designs and conducts in ways that depend on daily feedback from interactions with students and observations of their work and behaviors.

Teaching, for Mr. Santiago and you, is a complex art that involves five general stages, depicted in Figure 1.2: (a) course design, long-range planning, and organ-

Figure 1.2. Five Stages of Teaching

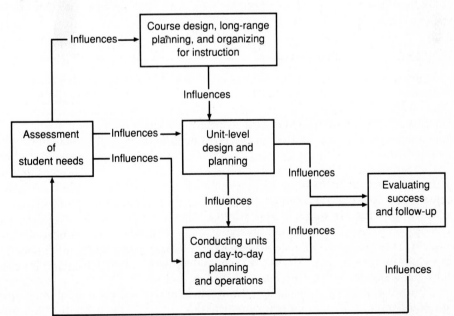

izing for instruction; (b) assessment of student needs; (c) unit-level design and planning; (d) conducting units and day-to-day planning and operations; and (e) evaluating success and follow-up.

Course Design, Long-Range Planning, and Organizing for Instruction

Curricula. Your responsibilities as an elementary, middle, or secondary school teacher begin well before the opening day of the school year. During this initial stage of teaching, you establish the direction for the *curriculum* your students will experience. A *school curriculum* is a system of planned experiences (e.g., coursework, school-sponsored social functions, and contacts with school-supported services—for example, the library) designed to educate students. A *course curriculum* is a sequence of teaching units designed to provide students with experiences that help them achieve specified learning goals (Cangelosi, 1991, pp. 135–136).

Prior to the Opening of the School Year. You don't enjoy complete control over curricula because there are mandated guidelines to follow and constraints on resources. Most importantly, you do not select your students. However, within certain bounds, you make a myriad of decisions that influence curricula and set the stage for the school year. For example, see Mr. Santiago's plans and arrangements in Vignette 1.4.

The many decisions Mr. Santiago made in this first stage of teaching were influenced by his understanding of how to most effectively practice the art of teaching for his students under the given circumstances. Subsequent chapters of this book are intended to provide you with suggestions and stimulate your thinking about how you can best practice your art with your students in whatever circumstances.

Assessment of Student Needs

The sample curriculum guidelines displayed in Figure 1.3 indicates that the general science course should be designed to, among other things, help sixth-graders "identify laws governing motion" and "explain how motion is produced." Apparently, the panel of teachers and instructional supervisors who wrote these guidelines believed that sixth-graders have a need to understand some ideas relative to motion. Prior to the opening of school, Mr. Santiago determined that his sixth-graders should learn to explain the effects of Newton's three laws of motion and apply their understanding of these effects in real-world situations. Any acceptable justification for setting a particular goal for students to achieve reflects concern for what the students *need* (Cangelosi, 1982, pp. 9–16; Ryan & Cooper, 1988, pp. 180–181). Thus, during the initial stage of teaching, you must anticipate students' needs in order to establish goals for the teaching units of your courses. In Vignette 1.5 (p. 13), Mr. Eicho's anticipation of student needs influences how he organizes for instruction.

With the opening of the school year, you begin to interact with students and are, thus, provided with continuing opportunities to assess their needs rather than

VIGNETTE 1.4

Mr. Santiago's supervisors (e.g., the principal) expect him to attend to the school district's curriculum guidelines for sixth-grade general science as he designs the course. But the curriculum guidelines (see, e.g., Figure 1.3) only provide broad parameters for course content and a list of goals students are to achieve. The guidelines do not specify the particular student skills, abilities, and attitudes comprising each goal, nor do they dictate how Mr. Santiago should go about helping students achieve them. Although limited by the availability of resources (e.g., one set of textbooks and a $475 budget for supplies), burdened (see Figure 1.4) by other re-

CORE STANDARDS FOR GENERAL SCIENCE—LEVEL 6
Page 2

STANDARD 06-03	Students will identify and describe fundamental ideas, principles, vocabulary, procedures, and applications of physical science.

Goals

06-03-01. Identify laws governing motion
06-03-02. Explain how motion is produced
06-03-03. Investigate different types of matter
06-03-04. Describe the fundamental structure of matter
06-03-05. Identify and compare different forms of energy

STANDARD 06-04	Students will explain fundamental principles, and structures of earth science—especially those associated with meteorology and geology.

Goals

06-04-01. Demonstrate relationships between rocks and minerals
06-04-02. Describe the structure of the earth (crust, mantle, and core)
⋮

Figure 1.3. Excerpt from District Curriculum Guide for Sixth-Grade General Science

First-Semester Schedule

Class	Period	Assignment	Room	Course Credits per Semester
Homeroom	8:30–8:45	Seventh-grade rap	125	———
1st–3rd	8:45–11:50	Seventh-grade core cluster (integrated science, social studies, language arts)	125 127 133	1.5
Lunch–1	11:55–12:20	Lunch supervision	lunchroom	———
Lunch–2	12:25–12:50	Planning	———	———
4th	12:55–1:50	Sixth-grade general science	125	0.5
5th	1:55–2:50	Planning	125	0.5
6th	2:55–3:45	Sixth-grade general science	125	0.5
Announcements	3:45–3:50	———	125	———

Figure 1.4. Mr. Santiago's Year-Long Teaching Assignment

(continued)

VIGNETTE 1.4 (continued)

MALAKER MIDDLE SCHOOL CALENDAR
Mary Frances Lambert, Principal

School year begins Thursday, August 20, and ends Friday, June 4.

Th/8/20–F/8/21: Orientation meetings for new teachers in the district
M/8/24–T/8/25: Opening conferences, faculty meetings, teacher workdays
W/8/26: Orientation day for sixth-graders
Th/8/27: First full day of class—beginning of first semester
M/9/7: Holiday—Labor Day
F/10/23: Teacher preparation day (no classes)
M/10/26: Parent conferences (no classes)
Th/10/29–F/10/30: State teachers association convention (no classes)
Th/11/26–F/11/27: Thanksgiving holidays
M/12/21–F/1/1: Winter holidays
Th/1/15: Last day of first semester
F/1/16: Parent conferences (no classes)
M/1/18: Holiday—Martin Luther King, Jr., Day
T/1/19: First day of second semester
M/2/15: Holiday—Presidents' Day
M/3/15: Parent conferences (no classes)
Th/4/8–F/4/9: Spring break holidays
T/4/27–Th/4/29: Standardized testing days
T/6/1: Last day of classes
W/6/2–F/6/4: Teacher workday

Figure 1.5. Malaker Middle School Year Calendar

Figure 1.6. Mr. Santiago's Classroom before He Modified It to Fit His Needs and Those of His Students

VIGNETTE 1.4 (continued)

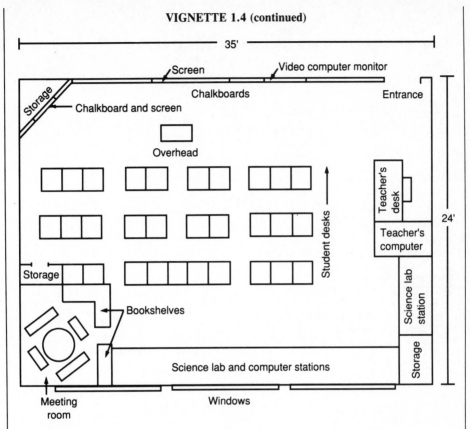

Figure 1.7. Mr. Santiago's Classroom Arrangement for Large-Group Meetings

sponsibilities, operating within a fixed time and space frame (see Figure 1.5 and Figure 1.6), and having to accommodate 28 students, Mr. Santiago exercises considerable freedom in how he designs the course, plans for the year, and organizes and equips his classroom. Such decisions are a function of his anticipation of students' needs, interests, attention spans, prior achievements, and behavior inclinations as well as a function of his unique teaching style.

For example, his decision to organize the course into 12 to 14 teaching units was influenced by the curriculum guidelines, the sequence of topics in the textbook, the fact that 35 teaching weeks are available, and his prior experiences. He's learned from those experiences that he needs at least 2 weeks to conduct a typical teaching unit, but that sixth-graders' interests in a topic tend to wane if the unit extends much beyond 3 weeks. To accommodate flexible grouping arrangements he anticipates using throughout the year and because his style of managing student behavior requires him to quickly move with ease from one point in the room to any other, he rearranges the classroom for opening day as indicated by the diagrams in Figures 1.7 and 1.8.

(continued)

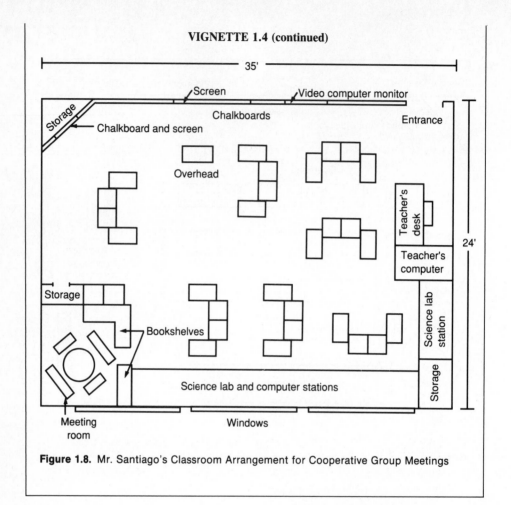

VIGNETTE 1.4 (continued)

Figure 1.8. Mr. Santiago's Classroom Arrangement for Cooperative Group Meetings

VIGNETTE 1.5

Mr. Eicho is preparing for the courses he will be teaching his second-graders in the upcoming school year. Examining the tentative schedule he's worked out to this point (see Figure 1.9), he thinks:

"This schedule is pretty close to what worked well for me last year. I can always modify it as I get to know these students. But it's nice to stick pretty close to one schedule for at least the first half of the year because the students are more likely to maintain a nice cooperative work routine that follows a predictable pattern. At this age they generally need to anticipate how long they're expected to work before they get to change activities. It helps me teach them to pace themselves.

Figure 1.9. Mr. Eicho's Tentative Schedule for His Second-Grade Class

8:30 A.M.	Sharing and community meeting
8:45 A.M.	Reading
9:30 A.M.	Citizenship
10:00 A.M.	Recess
10:15 A.M.	Mathematics
11:00 A.M.	Science
11:45 A.M.	Lunch and recess
12:30 P.M.	Language usage and communications
1:30 P.M.	Health and physical education (MWF), music (T), and art (TH)
2:30 P.M.	Wrap-up and community meeting

"On the other hand, I'd like to integrate the courses more than I did last year. Students need to associate reading, math, citizenship, science, and so forth—like applying what's learned in math to citizenship problems. Having the courses scheduled in separate blocks like this discourages integrative activities.

"So does this mean I should alter this schedule and have larger blocks that combine courses? . . . The only times I don't control are the 11:45 to 12:30 lunch period and the 1:30 to 2:30 health and physical education/music/art period when the specialists take over and I supposedly get a break. . . .

"So, how do I take care of both their need to have a predictable schedule and their need to integrate content from the various courses? . . . Rather than tamper with the schedule and make it too complicated to explain to them and their parents, I'll keep the schedule as is and integrate topics by coordinating lessons from the different courses. The time slots will stay distinct, but they'll still apply what they're learning in one course during activities for another."

Even though he has yet to meet with his class and assess entry achievements of individual students, he knows enough about second-graders in general to anticipate that he will have to be prepared to deliver a wide range of reading and mathematical instruction to accommodate various students' achievement levels. He thus organizes the classroom to facilitate flexible group activities so that sometimes the class will be organized as a single large group whereas other times students will work in small cooperative groups or engage in individual activities. His initial arrangement is depicted in Figure 1.10. He also determines procedures for governing movement, talk,

(continued)

VIGNETTE 1.5 (continued)

and noise within the room and for such mundane matters as use of the drinking fountain, the rest room, equipment, and materials. These determinations are made out of concerns for what students *need* to be doing throughout the year.

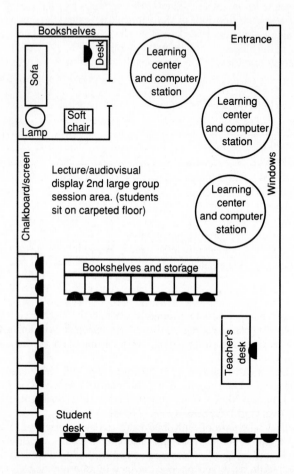

Figure 1.10. Mr. Eicho's Classroom Arrangement (*Source*: From *Classroom Management Strategies: Gaining and Maintaining Students' Cooperation* [p. 174] by J. S. Cangelosi, 1988, White Plains, NY: Longman. Adapted by permission.)

simply anticipating them. This second stage of teaching, *assessment of student needs*, becomes an integral part of the other stages as your decisions regarding exactly how to define learning goals with specific objectives, how to design lessons that lead those students to achieve the objectives, and how to engage individual students in the lessons' learning activities all depend on your assessments of their needs. For example:

VIGNETTE 1.6

Like most high school mathematics teachers, Ms. Begin planned and conducted teaching units so that lessons followed a consistent pattern (Jesunathadas, 1990):

1. She identified the skill students were to gain from the upcoming lesson (e.g., "Today, we're going to learn how to use the uniform motion formula."). Typically, the skill required students to memorize a fact, symbol or vocabulary meanings, or steps in a sequential process (i.e., algorithm).
2. With the aid of an overhead projector she displayed and stated what the students were to remember (e.g., "The formula is *rate × time = distance*.").
3. She then demonstrated the skill with two textbook examples ("For example, if a car travels at the rate of 45 miles per hour and we wanted to know how far it will get after 3.5 hours, we would substitute 45 for rate and . . .").
4. She responded to questions students raised about the steps in the two examples she worked for them.
5. Ms. Begin assigned textbook exercises similar to the two in the demonstration. Students worked on the exercises independently as she circulated among them providing individual guidance. The students were directed to complete the assignment for homework.
6. The following day, Ms. Begin either displayed or had student volunteers display homework exercises with which some students indicated they experienced difficulties.
7. Later, they were tested on the skills, and Ms. Begin used the results of the test to decide whether to move on to the next lesson immediately or to reteach the skill.

However, recently Ms. Begin noted that students who demonstrated a skill during one unit failed to apply that skill in other units or to situations in which problems deviated the least bit from those in the textbook. Also, most students seemed to forget what they memorized shortly after they were tested on it. For example:

During the lesson on the uniform distance formula, Cynthia successfully worked textbook exercises and word problems dealing with auto, train, and plane travel. But when Mr. Begin confronted her with a problem involving how long it would take her to walk between her home and school, she never thought to use the formula. Several units later, Cynthia and other students failed to see any relation between the *rate × time = distance* formula and *rate × principal × time = interest* formula although the two formulas are based on the same fundamental principle of multiplication.

Concerned that her students' *need* to be able to apply what they learn to their

(continued)

VIGNETTE 1.6 (continued)

own lives and to relate content from one unit to another, Ms. Begin read journal articles (e.g., Schoenfeld, 1988) and books (e.g., Cangelosi, 1992) explaining how to structure units and lessons so that students not only memorize mathematics, but also understand and apply it to their own real worlds. Consequently, she began to include not only skill-level objectives in her units, but also conceptualization- and application-level objectives. As suggested by her readings, she restructured her units so that they began with discovery lessons that led students to understand why content worked as it does (e.g., students discovered for themselves that *rate × time = distance* rather than simply being told of the fact). She began following these discovery lessons with the type of skill lessons she had used previously and then completed units with application-level lessons that fulfilled students' need to apply content to their own lives—not only to textbook word problems.

Variables on Which Students Differ

Virtually every teaching decision you make is impacted by your assessments of students' needs. Those assessments are complicated by the extreme variation among students regarding their needs. Each student is a unique individual. A minute proportion of the variables on which you can expect your students to differ are alluded to in this section.

Interest in Learning. You are interested in teaching your students, but you will be disappointed if you anticipate they will all be equally interested in learning. Children's and adolescents' interests in what schools offer them range from obsessive avoidance to obsessive pursuit. Major challenges of teaching include (a) motivating otherwise disinterested students to learn and (b) preserving and fostering the enthusiasm of those who are already motivated to learn.

Self-Confidence. Some students view learning tasks as opportunities to acquire new abilities and skills. Others approach learning tasks as competitive situations in which their existing abilities and skills are challenged. Unlike the latter group, the former are not burdened with fears that their mistakes will be ridiculed, so they are willing to pursue perplexing tasks and to learn from their mistakes. The amount of effort students are willing to invest in a learning task is not only dependent on the value they recognize in the task, it also depends on their perception of the likelihood they will successfully complete the task (Ames & Ames, 1985). Problem solving, discovering relationships, analyzing academic content, and interpreting communications are cognitive tasks requiring students to work through perplexing moments. Those who are not confident in their own abilities tend to stop working on the task as soon as they become perplexed; more confident students tolerate perplexity longer and are more likely to continue with the task.

Perception of What Is Important. Adults tend to value schools as vehicles for preparing their children for the future. "Study hard and you'll be able to get a good job and make something of yourself when you're grown!" a parent tells a child. However, most of your students are far more concerned with succeeding as children or adolescents than with succeeding as adults (Goodlad, 1984, pp. 75–81). Today seems more important than tomorrow. Thus, many of your students will need to recognize immediate benefits in what you're trying to teach them before they are motivated to learn from you. There is tremendous variation among what students consider immediately beneficial. For example, some students want to please their parents with their accomplishments; others find peer approval over their appearance far more important. There are those who seek satisfaction within themselves and do not depend on outside approval. Still others seek material rewards for their efforts. In any case, students are driven by a unique combination of motives based on a variety of things they find important.

Attitude toward School. Some of your students will greet you as their friend, expecting to benefit from the experiences you provide. Others arrive with little regard for how you might help them, and view you as an authority figure who interferes with what they would prefer to be doing.

Aptitude for Reasoning. Consider the following exchange as it occurred in Mr. Santiago's general science class:

VIGNETTE 1.7

Mr. Santiago and one of his students, Oral, are sitting on the classroom floor facing one another about 12 feet apart. Mr. Santiago slides a book toward Oral; the book stops about 3 feet short of Oral.

MR. SANTIAGO: Describe what just happened, Oral.

ORAL: You slid that book toward me, but it didn't reach me.

MR. SANTIAGO: Why didn't it reach you?

ORAL: Because you didn't push it hard enough.

MR. SANTIAGO: But what stopped it?

ORAL: Nothing; it stopped on its own.

MR. SANTIAGO: Was there some kind of force that slowed down the book's motion until it stopped?

ORAL: No, nothing.

MR. SANTIAGO: What does Newton's First Law of Motion say about an object in motion.

ORAL: That it will stay in motion in a straight line at constant speed, unless a force acts on it to move it or change its motion.

MR. SANTIAGO: Was the book in motion traveling in a straight line?

ORAL: Yes.

MR. SANTIAGO: What force caused it to stop?

ORAL: There wasn't any; it stopped by itself.

MR. SANTIAGO: But what about Newton's First Law of Motion? Do you believe it?

(continued)

VIGNETTE 1.7 (continued)

ORAL: Of course. An object remains in motion until some force stops it or changes its direction.

MR. SANTIAGO: Did that law apply to our sliding book? Does it explain why the book stopped?

ORAL: Sure!

MR. SANTIAGO: Then was there a force acting on the book's motion to cause it to stop?

ORAL: No, it stopped on its own—by itself.

Mr. Santiago throws up his hands in frustration.

The success of Mr. Santiago's lesson depended on Oral's ability to reason deductively about an abstract principle. Such reasoning, as well as other reasoning processes (e.g., inductive), is quite arduous for some preadolescents and adolescents, but presents no difficulty for others. Whether you teach elementary, middle, or secondary school students, you will have to contend with a wide range of students' abilities to use various reasoning processes.

Sometimes people try to convert a complex theory into a few simple rules for teaching practice. For example, some naively interpret Piaget's stages of cognitive development (summarized in Table 1.1) to mean that no student under 11 can learn so-called "abstract" subjects such as algebra, but through a "magical" maturing process they should be able to do so with little difficulty after 15 (Engelmann, 1971; Furth & Wachs, 1974; Smedslund, 1977). In truth, many children under the age of 11 successfully reason with abstractions (Baroody, 1989; Kouba, 1989), whereas some over 15 struggle terribly (Schoenfeld, 1985, pp. 11–45).

An oversimplified version of another theory, *left and right hemispheric learning* (Quina, 1989, pp. 425–431) suggests that students are either left-brain learners or right-brain learners. Supposedly, left-brain learners have an easier time with mathematics and science tasks because they are better able to cope with the "cold" logic of abstract reasoning, whereas right-brain learners are more inclined to "warmer" aesthetic pursuits such as art, music, and creative writing. In truth, subjects like mathematics and science are not the cold and exacting technical endeavors that they are often presented to be and there are logical and technical aspects to subjects such as art, music, and creative writing. In general, the subjects you teach have both left-brain and right-brain functions and you need to provide experiences that appeal to both sides of the brains of all students (Grady, 1990).

Prior Achievement. Look at the initial chapters of a textbook designed for any upper grade level (e.g., 3 or 11). Note how the book begins with remedial material that overlaps the content of books for prior grades. Apparently, the author(s) recognized that having been exposed to content in prior courses does not guarantee that content was learned by all students. Most of your students will have failed to learn some content at a learning level you consider prerequisite for what you want to teach them. However, learning gaps will vary from student to student. Furthermore, many students, although lacking some remedial skills and abilities,

TABLE 1.1. Piaget's Stages of Cognitive Development

	General Description	Age Level
Sensorimotor	The child progresses from instinctual reflexive action at birth, to symbolic activities, to the ability to separate himself from objects in the environment. He develops limited capabilities for anticipating the consequences of his actions.	0 ½ 1 1½ 2
Preoperational	The child's ability to think becomes more refined during this period. First, she develops what Piaget calls preconceptual thinking, in which she deals with each object or event individually but is not able to use symbols, such as words, to deal with problems. During the latter half of this period, the child develops better reasoning abilities but is still bound to the here-and-now.	2½ 3 3½ 4 4½ 5 5½ 6 6½ 7
Concrete operational	At this stage, the child develops the ability to perform intellectual operations—such as reversibility, conservation, and placing in order by number, size, or class. His ability to relate time and space is also maturing during this period.	7½ 8 8½ 9 9½ 10 10½
Formal operational	This is the period in which the person learns to reason hypothetically. She is able to function for the first time on a purely symbolic, abstract level. Her conceptualization capacities have matured.	11 11½ 12 12½ 13 13½ 14 14½ 15

Source: From J. W. Santrock, *Adolescence* (2nd ed., p. 140). Copyright © 1984 by W. C. Brown, Publishers, Dubuque, Iowa. All rights reserved. Reprinted by permission.

will have already acquired understanding of some advanced topics you are expecting to introduce to them. Your assessments of students' needs will detect differences among their motor skills as well as cognitive learning. Of particular concern to most teachers are differences in students' communication skills. Most teaching strategies depend on students' being able to both receive messages (e.g., by listening and reading) and send messages (e.g., by speaking and writing).

Experiences on Which You Can Build. Different students bring vastly different backgrounds to your classroom. Participating in sports, caring for younger children, repairing motors, raising gardens, working in a salaried job, traveling, experiencing major family upheavals, playing music, suffering from illnesses, and raising animals are only a minute proportion of the types of students' experiences to which you can relate the things you teach. Ms. Begin, for example, assessed students' experiences and interests and took advantage of them in designing learning activities for her algebra students:

VIGNETTE 1.8

Ms. Begin thinks to herself as she plans a lesson on solving first-degree open sentences: "Before demonstrating methods for solving these algebraic sentences, I should first have them analyze some application-level problems. Let's see, what kind of word problems does the textbook offer? . . . Looks like the right kind of problems, but not very motivating for these ninth-graders. I could rewrite them so the mathematics stays the same but the situations are more in line with their interests. Okay, the first one reads:

> An exotic tribe has a rule that the number of guards protecting the tribe must be at least one-tenth of the number in the tribe less 50. According to this rule, how many tribespeople can be protected by 40 guards?

"Great! An exotic tribe, [sarcastically] just what my students can identify with! To what should I make this relate? Something where one number depends on another. Phil has experience racing dirt bikes, maybe I could do something with the relation between tire size and power, instead of guards to tribespeople. Oh, I've got it! At least a dozen of the kids love to go to rock concerts. I'll change the guards to security people for a concert and the tribespeople become the concert goers. I've got to work this out. . . . Okay, here's the problem:

> The number of security guards working at rock concerts depends on the number of people expected to be in attendance. One rule of thumb stipulates that the number of security guards must be at least one-tenth of the number of concert goers less 50. According to this rule, how many people can attend a concert with 40 security guards?

"But I don't know if that rule is at all realistic. It doesn't make any more sense to me than the one for the exotic tribe. . . . Oh, another brilliant idea! Naomi is always reading those rock magazines. I'll bet she could be our resource person for coming up with the rule. There's bound to be something about that in her magazines. This is perfect! Naomi hates math, but this time she can be the one to provide the formula we plug into the word problem.

"Okay, I'll make this next one relate to something different. Let's see . . ."

Adapted with permission from *Teaching Mathematics in Secondary and Middle School: Research-based Approaches* (pp. 7–8) by J. S. Cangelosi (1992), New York: Macmillan. Copyright © 1992 by Macmillan Publishing Company.

Home and Social Life. Children and adolescents are under continual domestic and social pressures. The parenting of your students will range from supportive to neglectful, healthy to abusive, and constant to absent. For most students peer acceptance is of paramount concern (Charles, 1989, pp. 70–87; Dreikurs, 1968). Some have friends who encourage their pursuits of learning and cooperation with your efforts. Others may perceive that they risk acceptance of those whose friendship they value most by being studious and cooperative with you. Although it is important that you understand the pressures and influences with which your students live, please keep two things in mind (Cangelosi, 1992, p. 10):

1. Each student is a unique individual. Do not apply the aggregate results from demographic studies in judging individuals. For example, as a group, Japanese children tend to value academic activities more than Western children (Allen, 1988), but that doesn't mean that any particular student from a Japanese family will be more motivated toward learning than a student of non-Asian heritage. Nor will any one student living in an inner-city housing project be any more inclined to abuse drugs than one from a suburb.
2. If students live with disadvantages (e.g., abusive parents) that does not mean they cannot control their own behaviors nor should it imply that you should expect less from them (Cangelosi, 1988a, pp. 25–33; Glasser, 1986). Variations in home and social life create differences among students regarding such matters as how much time they have to devote to schoolwork, whether or not they have a place conducive to doing homework, and whether or not you can depend on their parents' cooperation.

Cultural Background and Ethnicity. Schools in the United States serve a pluralistic society bestowed with multiethnic, multicultural communities. Unless you teach in a particularly isolated school setting, your classes are likely to be characterized by cultural and ethnic diversity. Prior to the 1940s, advocates of "Americanization" influenced school curricula. They supported the notion of the existence of an American culture based on the mores of northern Europeans and believed minorities should reject their own cultures and assimilate into the dominant American culture (Cubberley, 1962, pp. 488–489). A competing philosophy that dominated curriculum development into the 1970s viewed American society as a "melting pot." Melting pot advocates embraced cultural and ethnic diversity as a source of strength. They believed an American culture could be built, not by forsaking the values and customs of various minorities, but by fusing them into a new, stronger civilization (Krug, 1976, pp. 7–12; Winitzky, 1988). Today, the idea of *cultural pluralism* prevails among shapers of school curricula:

> Cultural pluralism, as currently defined, rejects the racism of Americanization and also rejects the conception of a single culture emerging from the melting pot. Culture pluralism instead, while acknowledging the existence of a dominant American culture, also recognizes the strength and permanence of its subcultures. In Kallen's (1924) conception, minority groups should accept the common elements of the dominant culture but should be constantly interacting with it and injecting into it new elements, to the benefit of all. The melting pot metaphor, with its implications of homogeneity, has now been replaced with the salad metaphor, in which each ingredient is distinct and valued by itself, while at the same time contributing to the whole, and bound together with a common "dressing," that is, the dominant culture. (Winitzky, 1988, p. 204)

You take advantage of cultural and ethnic diversity among your students by employing principles of multicultural education. Multicultural education is an interdisciplinary approach to curriculum that emphasizes (a) recognition of the strength and value of cultural diversity, (b) development of human rights and respect for cultural diversity, (c) legitimation of alternate life choices for people, (d) social justice and equal opportunity for all, and (e) equitable distribution of power among members of all ethnic groups (Sleeter & Grant, 1987).

Some teachers implement a *topical approach* to multicultural education by devoting special lessons to the history, customs, accomplishments, and personalities of various cultures and ethnic minorities. Recently published textbooks tend to include inserts or addenda dealing with such topics. Although this approach is favored over ignoring pluralism, it has been criticized because of its tendency to focus on differences rather than similarities among groups and to leave students with nothing more than fragmented information rather than appreciations and understandings (Winitzky, 1988). Consistent with the principles underlying this book is the *integrative approach* to multicultural education. With the integrative approach subject matter content associated with cultural pluralism is incorporated continually throughout almost all lessons. A mathematics teacher, for example, might select sample problems examining differential treatment of various minority groups in an application lesson on permutations and combinations. While designing lessons for improving elementary school students' language arts skills, a teacher could select reading and writing assignments that emphasize the accomplishments of personalities of various ethnic backgrounds. Examples of teachers using this integrative approach appear throughout this book (e.g., Vignette 3.23). Another strategy is to select and develop instructional material that casts minority as well as majority people in a wide range of roles. The examples you use for your lessons, including choice of names for characters, can foster healthy attitudes among students and help minority students feel more at home in your classroom.

Students in culturally and ethnically homogeneous classrooms (e.g., all rural white or all urban black) may lack needed opportunities interacting with persons culturally different from themselves. Integrating multicultural topics throughout lessons in such situations helps fill a critical void. References on multicultural education are included in the "Suggested Reading" section near the end of this chapter.

Use of Drugs. Inadequate study skills, boredom, lack of confidence, fatigue, hyperactivity, and nonacademic interests are just some of the many factors that can hinder students' willingness to engage in learning activities. Being either high or depressed from drugs at school or when trying to study is just one more factor that hinders students' academic work (Cangelosi, 1990a, pp. 64–66). Special mention of drug use is included here, not because that factor is any more pervasive than others, but because its influence seems to be increasing at an alarming rate among students of all ages (Elam, 1989; Towers, in press) and information on how to deal with students who abuse drugs has recently become available (see, e.g., Cangelosi, 1988a, pp. 245–255; Rogers & McMillin, 1989; Towers, 1987).

Special Needs. Although you may not be a special education teacher, you can expect to have a few students mainstreamed into your classes whose special needs have been formally identified. Included among the labels are "learning disabled," "hearing impaired," "hard of hearing," "blind," "visually handicapped," "orthopedically impaired," "behaviorally disordered," "emotionally handicapped," "gifted," and "multihandicapped" (Ryan & Cooper, 1988, pp. 211–218). The number of such exceptional students mainstreamed into "regular" classrooms increased dramatically since the U.S. Congress passed the Education for All Handicapped Children Act of 1975 (i.e., P.L. 94–142). P.L. 94–142 mandates that free, appropriate public education be available to all handicapped students between the ages of 3 and 18, that they be educated to the maximum extent possible, and that their education take place in the "least restrictive" learning environment. For handicapped students, an Individualized Education Program (IEP) is to be designed collaboratively by their special education and regular classroom teachers, parents, and the students themselves. The IEP is a description of the student's individualized curriculum including statements of learning goals, prescriptions for educational services related to those goals, timelines for delivery of those services, and a delineation of the assessment procedures to be used for placement decisions and evaluation of the program's success. Coolican (1988) stated:

> It is important to realize that handicapped children are often socially ignored or even ridiculed by their nonhandicapped peers (see Sabornie, 1985). Teachers of mainstreamed students should therefore attempt to establish positive attitudes toward the handicapped and to encourage appropriate interactions between their disabled and nondisabled students. For example, students in a class that includes a hearing-impaired child could be taught the manual alphabet (for "finger spelling") and rudimentary sign language. To further reduce social isolation of mainstreamed students, teachers might develop a social skills training program or, if necessary, a self-care program. Such a program could be developed with the assistance of the handicapped student's special education teacher.
>
> Many of the educational needs of handicapped children are similar to the needs of other students in your classrooms. As a result of improved identification and placement procedures, emphasis is being directed toward each child's educational characteristics. This could eventually prove to be a useful way of assessing all learners. In addition, the classroom teacher is in a key position to recognize those students who have special needs. A comprehensive diagnosis, however, is not the classroom teacher's responsibility, but that of specialized personnel in the school system. You should be prepared to communicate learners' problems and work cooperatively with the professionals assigned to diagnose disabilities and prescribe treatments. (p. 216)

References on working with students identified as having special needs are included in the "Suggested Reading" section near the end of this chapter. Besides contending with these students' special needs, you can be assured that your so-called "normal" students also vary considerably in their abilities to hear, see, perform mental tasks, control their emotions, concentrate, and perform physical tasks. For example, it is estimated that at any one point in time, 25 percent of students with "normal" hearing are suffering a temporary hearing loss (e.g., because of an infection) serious enough to interfere with their ability to follow an oral presentation (Berg, 1987, pp. 22–38).

How to go about anticipating students' needs prior to interacting with them and assessing needs during and following interactions with students is addressed throughout this book.

Unit-Level Design and Planning

Teaching Units. Each course is organized into *teaching units*. Figure 1.11 lists the teaching units Mr. Santiago plans for his middle school science course, Figure 1.12 lists the units for Mr. Eicho's second-grade language and communications course, and Figure 1.13 lists those for Ms. Begin's algebra I course.

1. Plant Cells and Organisms	8. Electricity
2. Animal Cells and Organisms	9. Geology
3. Reproduction	10. Meteorology
4. Structure of Matter	11. Human Anatomy
5. Laws of Motion	12. Human Physiology
6. Energy	13. Preventing Diseases
7. Sound and Light	14. Treating Diseases

Figure 1.11. Titles of the Teaching Units Mr. Santiago Plans for His Middle School General Science Course

Each teaching unit consists of (a) a learning goal, (b) a set of specific objectives that define the learning goal, (c) a planned sequence of lessons each consisting of learning activities designed to help students achieve specific objectives, (d) mechanisms for monitoring student progress and utilizing feedback in the design of lessons, and (e) a summative evaluation of student achievement of the learning goal.

The Learning Goal. The *learning goal* is the overall purpose of the teaching unit. It is stated to indicate what students are expected to learn if the teaching unit is successful. For example, Mr. Santiago's learning goal for his fifth unit from Figure 1.11 is for students to explain the effects of Newton's three laws of motion, gravity, and friction on speed and acceleration and apply their understanding of these effects in real-world situations. Mr. Eicho determined the following learning goal for Unit 5 from Figure 1.12 to be for students to empathize with their reader and focus on getting a specified message across as well as improving their writing mechanics (e.g., handwriting, spelling, and sentence structure). Ms. Begin's Unit 7 goal from Figure 1.13 is for students to understand why certain factoring algorithms work and how to use them in problem solving.

The Set of Specific Objectives That Define the Learning Goal. The learning goal provides direction for designing the teaching unit by identifying the overall student outcome. However, teaching is a complicated art. Taking students from where they are at the beginning of the unit to where you've decided they need to be at the end of the unit involves a complex of different learning stages requiring varied teaching strategies. For students to achieve the learning goal they must acquire a number of specific skills, abilities, and/or attitudes. Thus, the learning goal is defined by a *set of specific objectives* each indicating a particular skill, ability, or attitude that is a necessary, but insufficient, component of learning-goal

Figure 1.12. Titles of the Teaching Units Mr. Eicho Plans for His Second-Grade Language Usage and Communications Course

1. Saying What You Mean	8. Conversing
2. Listening to What Is Said	9. Making Speeches
3. Understanding What People Mean	10. Writing Stories and Skits
4. Getting People to Understand	11. Producing Skits
5. Writing So People Understand	12. Poetry
6. Persuading People	13. Creative Communications
7. Writing for Fun	

1. Algebra and Its Language
2. Numbers and Arithmetic Operations
3. Operations on Rational Numbers
4. Algebraic Inequalities
5. Powers
6. Polynomials
7. Factoring Polynomials
8. Quadratic Equations
9. Algebraic Functions
10. Extending Functions
11. Systems of Open Sentences
12. Extending Powers and Radicals
13. Extending Quadratics
14. Operations with Rational Polynomials
15. Extending Work with Rational Polynomials
16. Special Functions with Natural Numbers
17. Extending What You've Learned

Figure 1.13. Titles of the Teaching Units Ms. Begin Plans for Her High School Algebra I Course

Goal: Students explain the effects of Newton's three laws of motion, gravity, and friction on speed and acceleration and apply their understanding of these effects in real-world situations

A. Discriminate between speed and acceleration
B. State definitions for *speed, acceleration, force, mass*, and *distance*
C. Measure the speed of moving objects
D. From either observations of a moving object or utilizing sufficient data, determine whether the object is or isn't accelerating
E. Explain Newton's first law of motion
F. State Newton's first law of motion
G. Explain the effects of friction and gravity on the speed of a moving body
H. Explain Newton's second law of motion
I. State Newton's second law of motion
J. Explain Newton's third law of motion
K. State Newton's third law of motion
L. Given a real-life problem, determine whether or not any combination of Newton's first three laws of motion apply to the solution of that problem and if so formulate a solution to the problem using that combination

Figure 1.14. Objectives Mr. Santiago Used to Define Unit 5's Learning Goal (from Figure 1.11)

achievement. The combination of the objectives equals the learning goal. Figures 1.14, 1.15, and 1.16 indicate how Mr. Santiago, Mr. Eicho, and Ms. Begin each defined a learning goal with a specific set of objectives.

Chapter 2 is intended to help you define each goal of your teaching units with an appropriate sequence of specific learning objectives.

The Planned Sequence of Lessons. The paramount components of each teaching unit are the *lessons* you design and conduct for the purpose of achieving the stated objectives and, thus, the learning goal. Each lesson consists of *learning activities*. For example, Mr. Santiago engaged his students in Unit 5's lessons over a three-week period to help them achieve Objectives A through L (listed in Figure 1.14) as follows:

A. The lesson for Objective A included the following learning activities:
   1. The students conduct the experiment with the remote-controlled toy car as described in Vignette 1.2.

Goal: Students empathize with their reader and focus on getting a specified message across as well as improving their writing mechanics (e.g., handwriting, spelling, and sentence structure)

A. Approach a writing task via the following procedure:
  1. describe the targeted readers
  2. summarize the principal message to be communicated
  3. outline a plan for writing
  4. write the piece
  5. read the piece
  6. edit the piece
  7. rewrite
B. Willingly accept constructive criticism about their own writing
C. Write with a specified purpose in mind
D. Utilize writing mechanics appropriate to the writing task

Figure 1.15. Objectives Mr. Eicho Used to Define Unit 5's Learning Goal (from Figure 1.12)

Goal: Students understand why certain factoring algorithms work and how to use them in problem solving

A. Explain how factoring polynomials can facilitate problem solving
B. Translate the meaning of the following terms in the context of communications relative to algebraic polynomial expressions: *factor, prime factorization, greatest common factor, difference of squares, perfect square trinomial,* and *prime polynomial*
C. Explain why the distributive property of multiplication over addition can be used to express a polynomial in factored form
D. Factor polynomials expressible in the form $ax + ay$
E. Explain why polynomials expressible in the form $a^2 - b^2$ can be expressed in factored form as $(a + b)(a - b)$
F. Factor polynomials expressible in the form $a^2 - b^2$
G. Explain why polynomials expressible in the form $a^2 + 2ab + b^2$ can be expressed in factored form as $(a + b)^2$
H. Factor polynomials expressible in the form $a^2 + 2ab + b^2$
I. Explain why some polynomials expressible in the form $ax^2 + bx + c$ (where x is a real variable and a, b, and c are rational constants) can be expressed in factored form as $(dx + e)(fx + g)$ (where d, e, f, and g are rational constants) and others cannot
J. Given a polynomial expressible in the form $ax^2 + bx + c$ (where x is a real variable and a, b, and c are rational constants), determine if it can be expressed in factored form as $(dx + e)(fx + g)$ (where d, e, f, and g are rational constants) and, if so, do so
K. Write and use computer programs to execute the algorithms alluded to in the previous objectives
L. Given a real-life problem, explain how, if at all, factoring polynomials can be utilized in solving that problem

Figure 1.16. Objectives Ms. Begin Used to Define Unit 7's Learning Goal (from Figure 1.13)

2. Utilizing data collected in the experiment, Mr. Santiago engages the students in an inductive questioning/discussion session leading them to describe differences between speed and acceleration and formulate a definition for each.
3. For homework, students develop similar experiments, but these do not involve land vehicle travel.

4. In cooperative learning groups, students share the experiments they devised for homework and relate them to each other and to the definitions for speed and acceleration they formulated the previous day.
5. Each group reports to the class as a whole and in a questioning/discussion session the class decides to further refine their definitions.

B. The lesson for Objective B is described near the end of Vignette 1.2.

C. The lesson for Objective C includes the following learning activities:

1. In an interactive lecture session, Mr. Santiago demonstrates how to measure the speed of one of the students walking the length of classroom by using a tape measure and stopwatch. He then demonstrates the process, but this time he measures the speed of a videotape playing in the classroom videocassette recorder (VCR). The VCR counter replaces the tape measure this time.
2. Following Mr. Santiago's directions, students list the steps common to both of Mr. Santiago's measurements (i.e., for the walking student and for the moving videotape) in an independent work session. They then work several textbook exercises determining speed from given data.
3. For homework, students measure speeds for three different moving objects using various instruments to measure time and distance. For each measurement, they describe the process they used and report the results in a paragraph.
4. The homework results are reviewed in class. Mr. Santiago makes sure that students have the process accurately described in their notebook.

D. . . .
 ⋮
L. The lesson for Objective L includes the following learning activities:

1. Mr. Santiago conducts a deductive questioning/discussion session in which students are confronted with three problems. Two of the problems are solved by applying Newton's first two laws of . . .

Mechanisms for Monitoring Student Progress and Utilizing Feedback in the Design of Lessons. When you plan a teaching unit you design its lessons. However, because teaching is such a complex art, you need to routinely monitor students' progress throughout the unit. The feedback from your assessments of their progress should determine the pace of lessons and influence the design of learning activities. This is part of the ongoing assessment of students' needs. Assessments of students' progress you make for purposes of guiding the design and conduct of teaching units are referred to as *formative evaluations* (Cangelosi, 1990b, pp. 2–6). Part of unit planning includes devising ways to collect data for formative evaluations of student achievement.

A Summative Evaluation of Student Achievement of the Learning Goal. As a teacher, you are expected to make periodic reports to communicate to students, their parents, and your supervisors how well your students are achieving learning goals. Consequently, most teaching units terminate with a test of students' achievement of the learning goal. Your judgments of students' success are referred to as *summative evaluations* (Cangelosi, 1990b, pp. 2–6). Chapter 6 focuses on techniques for developing and interpreting valid measures of student achievement for both formative and summative purposes.

Conducting Units and Day-to-Day Planning and Operations

Well-designed units are of little value if the teacher fails to conduct them as planned or fails to utilize formative feedback in making moment-to-moment, on-the-spot decisions (e.g., Mr. Santiago's decisions in Vignette 1.3). When people generally think of teachers teaching, they visualize the teachers interacting with students, orchestrating learning activities, managing student behaviors, and over-seeing classroom operations. These processes, along with daily planning, com-prise the fourth stage of teaching, *conducting units and day-to-day planning and operations*. How to (a) develop daily plans (e.g., the one illustrated in Figure 7.13), (b) conduct learning activities so that students are cooperatively engaged in them as you planned, (c) effectively respond to student off-task behaviors, and (d) efficiently manage day-to-day classroom operations are the principal concerns of Chapters 4, 5, 7, and 8.

Evaluating Success and Follow-Up

The summative evaluation you make at the end of each unit you conduct indicates how well your students achieve the unit's goal. Such evaluations have implications for both the students and you. Students who failed to achieve the goal well enough to proceed to subsequent units need some sort of follow-up lessons to alleviate the deficiencies. Students attaining advanced levels of achievement for one unit may profit from accelerated work in the next. Furthermore, the success of the unit to some degree reflects the effectiveness of your own teaching performances. This fifth stage of teaching, *evaluating success and follow-up*, leads you to reflect on your own teaching performances and how you might modify your strategies in the future. How to evaluate your own instructional effectiveness is attended to in Chapters 6, 7, and 8.

Other Professional Responsibilities

Besides the aforementioned *instructional responsibilities* embedded in the five stages of teaching, there are also other professional responsibilities that you will be expected to meet as a teacher.

Participating in School-Level Governance and Management. As a member of a school faculty your responsibilities go beyond your own classroom. Ordinarily, teachers are expected to contribute their ideas regarding the school policies and operations. This is a primary function of faculty and departmental meetings.

Serving as Instructional Supervisor to Other Teachers. Instructional supervision is collaborating with teachers to help them enhance their effectiveness with students (Cooper, 1984, pp. 1–2). Two of the more promising and flourishing models for improving instruction are *peer coaching* (Bang-Jensen, 1986; Brandt, 1989; Chrisco, 1989; Raney & Robbins, 1989) and *mentoring* (Duke, Cangelosi, Knight, 1988; Stallion, 1988). Peer coaching involves two or more teachers sharing ideas and providing formative feedback on one another's teaching (e.g., by making classroom observations) (Swartz & Perkins, 1990, pp. 198–203). Mentor teachers work with beginning teachers to help them through their first few years. If you are fortunate enough to work in a school where such instructional supervision programs are in place, you will be expected to contribute to the effectiveness of other teachers.

Representing Your Profession and School in the Community. Schools as well as the community of professional educators depend on the lay public for support. How laypersons perceive the school and the profession is at least partially a function of their contacts with teachers. You gain needed support by modeling professional behaviors and asserting yourself whenever educational issues are raised in public forums.

Maintaining Quality Control within the Profession. Our profession is represented by dedicated, highly competent teachers as well as unethical fools (Bridges, 1986). As a member of the former category, be a protagonist for professional reforms that encourage excellence and eliminate malpractice.

Contributing to the Growth of Your Profession. Take advantage of your teaching experiences, professional literature, and professional societies to increase your own knowledge base and the knowledge base of the profession about teaching. You can conduct action research projects in your own classroom that suggest ways to improve how we teach. Share what you learn and gain from the findings of others through professional journals (e.g., *Arithmetic Teacher*, *The Clearing House*, *Delta Pi Epsilon Journal*, *Elementary School Journal*, *Journal of Physical Education*, *Recreation and Dance*, *Journal of Research in Music Education*, *The Reading Teacher*) and books and through your participation in professional societies (e.g., American Educational Research Association, International Reading Association, National Council of Teachers of Mathematics, National Science Teachers Association).

These "other" professional responsibilities are vitally important, but because teaching is a complex art, this book only deals with instructional responsibilities (i.e., the five stages of teaching).

THE COMPLEX SCIENCE OF TEACHING

Teaching: An Art and a Science

Art is the *power* to perform certain actions that have been learned via study and experience (Merriam Webster, 1986, p. 122). Thus, by expertly performing the five stages of teaching you are performing an art. Ryan and Cooper (1988, p. 450) stated, "Teaching can be considered an art because teachers must improvise and spontaneously handle a tremendous number of factors that interact in often unpredictable and nonsystematic ways in classroom settings." Teaching is too complex to be a purely technical activity governed by recipes and formulas (Gage, 1985). However, to devise more effective ways of practicing the art, teaching is the subject of systematic study. Thus, teaching is also *science* (Ryan & Cooper, 1988):

To speak of teaching as a purely spontaneous, intuitive, ineffable, or totally un-predictable activity is not helpful for teachers who hope to improve their teaching artistry.

Science may not be able to systematize the complexities of teaching and provide absolute guidance for teachers as they balance the demands of subject matter, students' needs, and their own instructional strategies, to name just a few of the classroom variables; but research can provide a scientific basis for the art of teaching. In Gage's (1985) words, "At least, a scientific basis consists of scien-tifically developed knowledge about the relationships between variables." Such a basis prepares the teacher-artist for the range of relationships among teaching practices and student achievement of various educational objectives. As artists, teachers make instrumental use of the research on these relationships, even if they are only weak generalizations to accomplish the artistry of moving a unique classroom of unique students toward intended learning. (p. 450)

Scientific research for the purpose of improving teaching occurs on two lev-els: (a) action research by classroom teachers and (b) formal research dissemi-nated via scholarly publications.

Action Research Conducted by Practicing Teachers in Their Own Classrooms

In their quest to improve their own performances and to be better prepared to exchange ideas with colleagues, many teachers experiment with contrasting strategies and techniques and compare outcomes. For example, Ms. Olson con-ducts a cooperative group session in Vignette 1.9.

VIGNETTE 1.9

An article by Slavin (1988) spurred Ms. Olson's interest in using cooperative learning activities in which students learn from one another working on specified tasks in small groups. To gain insights into how she might utilize cooperative learning strate-gies with her own fourth-grade class, she reads more about the topic (e.g., from Ornstein, 1990, pp. 422–431 and from the section "Engaging Students in Cooperative Task-Group Sessions" in Chapter 5 of this book) and participates in an in-service workshop (Edwards, 1990).

Although now convinced of the values of cooperative learning activities and knowledgeable on how to use them, she worries that her students will display far more disruptive off-task behaviors during such activities than they normally do dur-ing the large-group and independent work sessions she's used to conducting. She's simply not ready to commit a major share of her instructional time to cooperative learning activities if the consequences are an increase in off-task behaviors—no matter what the academic benefits might be.

To help her resolve the question, she experiments with the lessons in a writing unit by conducting six comparable learning activities over a two-week period so that two of the activities use large groups, two are independent work sessions, and two involve cooperative small groups. To compare the three types of activities relative to levels of student cooperation and on-task behaviors, she videotapes the sessions

VIGNETTE 1.9 (continued)

Ms. Olson Conducts Action Research in Her Classroom

with a camcorder stationed on a tripod in the rear of the room. To reduce the effects of being videotaped on the students' behaviors during the experimental sessions, she videotaped class sessions during the previous week so the students would be used to having the camcorder in the classroom.

    After the six experimental sessions are complete, she views the videotapes, carefully counting incidences of student off-task behaviors and noting evidence of student cooperation. Her comparisons reveal no major differences in students' cooperation and on-task behaviors according to the type of activity. She also gains insights as to what she might do to improve her classroom management techniques. She concludes that as long as cooperative learning activities are carefully planned and orchestrated, students are just as likely to be on-task as they are during other types of learning activities. Thus, she plans to include more cooperative group activities in subsequent units.

Formal Research Disseminated via Scholarly Publications

Formal research, as it is commonly defined, examines phenomena that extend beyond the confines of a particular individual or setting. The idea of *generalizability* of explanations or answers to heretofore unanswered questions is central to conventional definitions (Cangelosi, 1991, p. 197). For example, "Research is systematic inquiry aimed at obtaining generalizable knowledge by testing claims about the relationships among variables, or by describing generalizable phenomena (Worthen & Sanders, 1987, p. 23). "Research is the manner in which we attempt to solve problems in a systematic effort to push back frontiers of human ignorance or to confirm the validity of the solutions to problems others have presumably resolved" (Leedy, 1985, p. 4). "Research is a detailed and systematic attempt, often prolonged, to discover or confirm through objective investigation the facts pertaining to a particular problem or problems and the laws and principles controlling it" (Wolman, 1989, p. 92).

Formal research studies on teaching contribute to the understanding of what constitutes effective instruction and how instruction can be more effective. Here are three examples in the area of *course design, long-range planning, and organizing for instruction*:

> For purposes of teaching isolated skills, research findings suggest that courses should be designed so that content is sequenced into small, fragmented segments with easier skills preceding more difficult-to-learn skills (Bowden, 1991; Joyce & Weil, 1986, pp. 317–336; Stallings & Stipek, 1986, pp. 738–746). However, whenever course goals include students being able to integrate different skills and creatively apply content, the simpler-to-more-difficult sequence is not always advisable. For example, the process for multiplying two fractions with unlike denominators (e.g., $7/8 \times 5/6 = 35/48$) is simpler than the one for adding fractions with unlike denominators (e.g., $7/8 + 5/6 = 41/24$). But students are better able to interrelate the two processes, and thus apply them, if they learn the more difficult addition process first and are then led to discover the multiplication process as a special case of addition (Cangelosi, 1992, pp. 17–18).
>
> Teachers' long-range planning efforts and how they organize for instruction prior to the beginning of a school year are directly related to how well students cooperate during the year (Arends, 1988, pp. 87–155).
>
> Classrooms organized similar to the one depicted in Figure 1.7 tend to establish a more rigid learning environment than those shown in Figures 1.8 and 1.9 (Evertson, 1989).

Examples in the area of *assessment of student needs* include:

> Teachers whose goals attend to both content and student behaviors tended to be more responsive to students' needs than those who have strictly content-oriented goals (e.g., "Fourth-grade students are aware of fundamental aspects of the U.S. Constitution, its history, and its influence on them today and can apply constitutionally based principles to everyday situations" as opposed to "Fourth-grade students will learn about the U.S. Constitution") (Housner & Griffey, 1985).
>
> Students' readiness to learn to apply a relationship (e.g., Newton's first law of motion) depends on them first conceptualizing it (i.e., being able to

explain why the relationship exists) (Shuell, 1990). Thus, teachers should assess whether or not students adequately conceptualize a relationship before attempting to teach students to apply it.

To maximize formative feedback from tests of students' achievement, the tests should include three types of items: (a) moderately difficult items to which between 25 percent and 75 percent of the students respond correctly, (b) easy items to which at least 75 percent of the students respond correctly, and (c) hard items to which less than 25 percent of the students respond correctly (Cangelosi, 1982, pp. 99–100; Cangelosi, 1990b, pp. 53–54; Hambleton & Swaminathan, 1985, pp. 33–50, 225–253; Hoffmann, 1975).

Examples in the area of *unit-level design and planning* include the following:

If a unit's goal is for students to be able to apply certain content, then the unit's objectives should generally be sequenced so that conceptualization-level learning occurs prior to memorization-level learning (Bourne, Dominowski, Loftus, & Healy, 1986, pp. 2–195).

Direct instruction is appropriate for memorization-level and skill-level objectives (Rosenshine, 1987) whereas inquiry instruction is appropriate for conceptualization-level instruction (Joyce & Weil, 1986, pp. 25–68).

Examples in the area of *conducting units and day-to-day planning and operations* include the following:

Teachers markedly increase the probability that students will be on-task during learning activities by providing students with explicit directions for the activities using unmistakable body language (e.g., eye contact, facing students with shoulders square, and in close proximity to the students) (Jones, 1979).

Students are far more likely to respond cooperatively to teachers who communicate using assertive, descriptive, and supportive language than they are to teachers who use passive or hostile, judgmental, and nonsupportive language (Cangelosi, 1988a, pp. 82–110; Canter & Canter, 1976; Ginott, 1972; Gordon, 1974).

Students are far more likely to attentively engage in a lecture session when lecturers move about the room purposefully using their position to cue students' thinking (e.g., in the manner illustrated by Vignette 5.3) than to lecturers who either pace aimlessly or stand rigidly in one spot (Quina, 1989, pp. 140–143).

Examples in the area of *evaluating success and follow-up* include the following:

Typically, students judge what their teachers' expect them to achieve by the level of the test items teachers use for summative evaluations. Thus, students tend to learn at the same level as they are tested (Stiggins, 1988).

Students' standardized achievement test scores per se do not provide valid data relative to the effectiveness of those students' teachers' instructional effectiveness (Cangelosi, 1991, pp. 11–12; Medley, Coker, & Soar, 1984, pp. 29–51). Such scores are too dependent on factors that teachers do not control (e.g., students' prior achievements, aptitudes, family influences, and temperaments) (Lamb & Thomas, 1981; Soar, Medley, & Coker, 1983). Often, the tests are not relevant to the more important goals that the teachers have set for their courses (Cangelosi, 1982, pp. 343–351; 1990b, pp. 178–184).

RESEARCH-BASED, SYSTEMATIC TEACHING STRATEGIES

A *strategy* is "a plan, method, or series of maneuvers or stratagems for obtaining a specific goal or result" (Random House, 1984, p. 1298). You continually formulate and use strategies as you teach—strategies for gaining students' cooperation that affect how you organize courses, materials, and your classroom, strategies for assessing students' needs and determining learning objectives, strategies leading students to achieve a specified objective, strategies for regaining a student's attention who has drifted off-task during a learning activity, and strategies for evaluating how well students have achieved a unit goal. A teaching strategy is *research-based* if evidence from action or formal research studies suggest that the strategy has a higher likelihood of succeeding in the given situation than alternative strategies.

Each teaching situation you confront is unique, so your strategy of choice cannot be pulled from a cache of proven research-based strategies. You must invent unique strategies as you teach. However, the science of teaching is advanced to the stage that your judgments about strategies can be guided by research-based principles (e.g., direct instruction is appropriate for skill acquisition, but not for conceptualization—Rosenshine, 1987; Joyce & Weil, 1986, pp. 25–68). The subsequent chapters of this book are intended to provide you with ideas for formulating teaching strategies consistent with research-based teaching principles.

But teaching is a complex art. A cleverly devised research-based strategy for assessing student needs and a cleverly devised research-based strategy for designing lessons do not result in successful instruction unless the lessons lead to achievement of learning objectives that meet student needs. In other words, the strategies used in different stages of teaching need to be interlinked (Dick & Carey, 1985):

A . . . contemporary view of the instructional process is that instruction is a systematic process in which every component is crucial to successful learning. The perspective is usually referred to as the systems point of view. . . . A system is technically a set of interrelated parts, all of which are working together toward a defined goal. The parts of this system depend on each other for input and output, and the entire system uses feedback to determine if its desired goal has been reached. . . .

The result of using the systems view of instruction is to see the important role of all the components in the process. They must all interact effectively. . . . And it is clear that there must be both an assessment of the effectiveness of the system in bringing about learning, and a mechanism to make changes if learning fails to occur. (pp. 2–4)

Too frequently, teaching strategies are learned in isolation so that a teacher applies research-based strategies at each stage of teaching, but fails to adequately interrelate the stages (Duke, Cangelosi, & Knight, 1988). For example:

VIGNETTE 1.10

In one of her teaching methods courses, Blanca Aroya learned strategies for formulating learning objectives, designing and conducting a variety of learning activities (e.g., lectures and cooperative group sessions), and managing student behavior. However, when she began student teaching, she discovered she didn't know how to interlink the strategies into a system so that how she managed student behavior depended on the type of learning activity, which depended on the type of learning objective.

Teaching strategies need to be *systematic*. This text deals with systematic, rather than isolated teaching strategies, thus its contents are presented in a spiral rather than a linear fashion.

YOU AS A PROFESSIONAL TEACHER

As you move from novice to expert teacher, your professional career unfolds in four phases—the first three relatively brief, the fourth, hopefully, quite lengthy: (a) *Preservice teacher prior to either engaging in student teaching or serving a year-long internship*, (b) *student teacher or intern teacher*, (c) *inservice beginning teacher, and* (d) *inservice experienced teacher.*

As a preservice teacher you are involved in your college or university teacher preparation program. From the program's content area (e.g., history, science, and literature) and professional education (e.g., social foundations of education, learning theory, general methods, measurement and evaluation, classroom management, and special methods) courses and experiences (e.g., pre-student-teacher or pre-intern working in classroom field sites) you gain prerequisite abilities, skills, and attitudes needed to *learn* to be a successful teacher.

It is a sobering thought to realize that people cannot learn to teach until they try to teach. While you may collect the tools to be a teacher (i.e., the prerequisite abilities, skills, and attitudes to apply research-based, systematic strategies), actual teaching experience provides the means for learning to effectively use those tools (Cangelosi, 1991, pp. xv–xvi). For most, this experience begins in earnest when they either engage in full-time student teaching or serve as an intern responsible for courses for a full complement of students. This second phase of your career provides you opportunities to learn from both successes and failures with supervisory help of a cooperating teacher.

By accepting a faculty position with a school you become an inservice teacher. The first two years you're considered a *beginning teacher.* Expect some of the more exciting, frustrating, eye-opening, exhausting, edifying experiences of your life to occur during those beginning years. The vast majority of teachers experience their most significant, career-threatening frustrations and challenges during the first two or three years of their professional careers (Lanier & Little, 1986, pp. 560–562). Beginning teachers are more likely than veteran teachers to leave the profession in favor of nonteaching occupations (Duke, Cangelosi, & Knight, 1988). Their situation is different from that of their experienced colleagues in many ways. They are adapting to a new career and working environment; they do not have a wealth of professional experiences on which to base decisions; they have not proven to themselves that they can survive in the classroom; they have yet to establish a reputation among students, parents, colleagues, and administrators; and they do not enjoy the security of having earned tenure (available in most states to experienced teachers).

Although security with one's self and position is a virtual requisite to effective teaching performance, beginning teachers are generally occupied with feelings of doubt and fear of inadequacy (Glickman, 1985, pp. 157–159). There can be little wonder why beginning teachers, as a group, are less effective in the classroom than their experienced counterparts (Clark & Peterson, 1986, pp. 278–281). Particularly troublesome areas for beginning teachers are problems related to classroom management and discipline, acquiring needed instructional materials, assessing student work, interacting with parents, and organizing curricula (Arends, 1988, p. 530; Stallion, 1988).

The picture is, of course, not all bleak. Most recognize that the beginning teaching experience provides a period of immeasurable growth and personal accomplishment. The excitement and hard-earned successes with students are worth the exhausting days and frustrating, but enriching, failures. The abilities, skills, and attitudes you acquire from your preservice experiences will serve you well. Furthermore, mentoring programs for beginning teachers are proliferating and succeeding in an increasing number of school districts around the United States and in other countries. Such programs provide for expert, experienced teachers to collaborate with beginning teachers providing support, counsel, suggestions, and colleagues with whom ideas can be shared and critiqued. In general, beginning teachers in mentoring programs experience less frustration and feel more successful than beginning teachers who are not provided with these services (Stallion, 1988).

With the completion of their beginning teaching experiences, most teachers reflect on those first two years as invaluable. Typical comments include: ''I wouldn't trade the experience for anything!'' ''The most fulfilling thing I've ever done!'' (Duke, Cangelosi, & Knight, 1988). However, it is during the start of your years as an experienced teacher that you can expect the ''success-to-frustration ratio'' of your teaching experiences to rise dramatically.

SELF-ASSESSMENT EXERCISES FOR CHAPTER 1

The self-assessment section for each chapter provides exercises to (a) help you evaluate your achievement of the chapter's objectives so that you can identify your areas of proficiency and the topics you need to review and (b) reinforce and extend what you've learned from the chapter. An ulterior purpose of these exercises is to encourage you to articulate your thoughts about systemic teaching strategies in both writing and oral discourse. Understanding is enhanced through such activities (Beyer, 1987, pp. 191–216; Cangelosi, 1988c).

Here are the exercises for Chapter 1:

I. Observe with a colleague a lesson conducted by an inservice teacher in a classroom. Preferably, the teaching speciality (e.g., primary grade, upper elementary, health and physical education, industrial arts education, special education, secondary social science, or secondary English) of both your colleague and the teacher whom you observe is the same as yours. The observation should last about an hour. Independent of one another, you and your colleague are to each (a) select two students and discreetly focus your attention on them, (b) describe the activities within the classroom and each of the two students' apparent involvement in those activities, and (c) assess how the activities affected each student (e.g., What do you think they learned? How might their attitudes have been influenced?). Distinguish between effects on each student that are related to the teachers' objectives for the activities or lesson and effects that might be considered side-effects or incidental outcomes. After the observation period, write out a report of your findings and exchange it with your colleague (who is also engaging in this exercise). Compare the two reports and discuss observed differences in the students that might have influenced them to respond differently to the classroom activities.

II. Interview a student who is in a grade level or taking a course that falls within your teaching specialty. Raise the following questions (adjusting the wording to fit the comprehension and attention level of the student):

    A. If no one required you to attend school, would you choose to go to school? Why or why not?

    B. What courses (subjects, activities, topics, etc.) do you think help you the most? Why?

    C. What courses (subjects, activities, topics, etc.) do you think help you the least? Why?

    D. What courses (subjects, activities, topics, etc.) do you enjoy most? Why?

    E. What courses (subjects, activities, topics, etc.) do you enjoy least? Why?

    F. If you were a teacher, how would you teach?

    Record the interview responses, and if you obtain the student's permission to share them, compare the responses you got to those of a colleague who also completes this exercise with another student.

III. Interview an experienced teacher who works within your teaching specialty. Raise the following questions:

    A. For you, what are some of the more enjoyable and satisfying aspects of being a teacher? Why?

    B. For you, what are some of the less enjoyable and more frustrating aspects of being a teacher? Why?

    C. What do you know now about teaching and the teaching profession that you didn't know when you were a preservice teacher? How did you learn these things?

    D. Other than delivering instruction, what other professional responsibilities do you have as a teacher?

    E. What do you do to prepare your courses and organize your classroom before the start of each school year? How has the process changed since your first year as a teacher?

    F. Other than what you've already told me, what lessons did you learn from your first year as a teacher?

    G. What advice and suggestions do you have for me and for others who aspire to be professional teachers?

Record the interview responses, and if you obtain the teacher's permission to share them, compare the responses you got to those of a colleague who also completes this exercise with another teacher.

IV. Acquire (e.g., by borrowing them from a teacher or from a curriculum library) a set of instructional materials for a course you anticipate teaching at some point in your career. The materials might include a teacher's edition of a student textbook and a curriculum guide. Suppose that these are the adopted materials for a course you are assigned to teach. Now, begin to design the course by: (a) determining a sequence of units for the course, (b) listing each unit by name, (c) indicating how much time your class would devote to each unit, and (d) stating the learning goal for each unit. Have colleagues critique your work and discuss with them your rationale for the design. Your rationale should have some scientific basis (i.e., research-based).

V. Write a one-page essay explaining why, at least according to this textbook, teaching is both an art and a science. Exchange your paper with that of a colleague; compare the papers for differences and similarities.

VI. Figure 1.2 depicts five stages of teaching. Label each of the following instructional activities according to which stage or stages (it could be more than one) of teaching subsume(s) it:

    A. Determining the overall goal for a teaching unit

    B. Defining the learning goal of a teaching unit with a set of specific objectives

    C. Designing a lesson for a specific learning objective

    D. Deciding whether or not a student is ready to move on to the next objective during a learning activity

    E. Responding to a student's disruptive behavior during a learning activity

    F. Deciding whether or not one student is displaying a behavior pattern that should be modified

    G. Determining how well students achieved the goal of a unit

    H. Deciding who is ready to move on to the next unit

    I. Organizing the classroom prior to the beginning of a school year

    J. Deciding how to sequence the content for an upcoming course

    K. Reflecting back on a completed unit and deciding what to do differently next time

    L. Making specific plans for tomorrow's learning activities

    M. Presenting a lecture

    N. Assigning homework

Compare your responses to those listed in the next paragraph. Discrepancies between two responses may be a consequence of differences in interpreting the descriptions of the aforementioned activities or they may be caused by some misunderstanding about the five-stage teaching model. Resolve any discrepancies in discussions with others who also completed this exercise.

If we use "1st" for *course design, long-range planning, and organizing for instruction,* "2nd" for *assessment of student needs,* "3rd" for *unit-level design and planning,* "4th" for *conducting units and day-to-day planning operations,* and "5th" for *evaluating success and follow-up,* the responses are: A: 1st & 2nd; B: 3rd and 2nd; C: 3rd & 2nd; D: 4th and 2nd; E: 4th & 2nd; F: 4th and 2nd; G: 5th & 2nd; H: 5th & 2nd; I: 1st & 2nd; J: 1st & 2nd; K: 5th & 2nd; L: 4th & 2nd; M: 4th & 2nd; N: 4th & 2nd.

SUGGESTED READING

ABOUT THE COMPLEX ART AND SCIENCE OF TEACHING AND TEACHING AS A PROFESSION

Dunkin, M. J. (1987). Teaching: Art or science? In M. J. Dunkin (Ed.), *The international encyclopedia of teaching and teacher education* (p. 19). Oxford: Pergamon Press.

Goodlad, J. I. (1984). *A place called school.* New York: McGraw-Hill.

McLaren, P. (1989). *Life in schools: An introduction to critical pedagogy in the foundations of education.* New York: Longman.

Reynolds, M. C. (Ed.). (1989). *Knowledge base for the beginning teacher.* Oxford: Pergamon Press.

Ryan, K., & Cooper, J. M. (1988). *Those who can, teach* (5th ed.). Boston: Houghton Mifflin.

Smith, B. O. (1987). Teaching: Definitions of teaching. In M. J. Dunkin (Ed.), *The international encyclopedia of teaching and teacher education* (pp. 11–15). Oxford: Pergamon Press.

Zumwalt, K. K. (Ed.). (1986). *Improving teaching: 1986 ASCD yearbook.* Alexandria, VA: Association for Supervision and Curriculum Development.

ABOUT CURRICULUM DEVELOPMENT

Brandt, R. S. (Ed.). (1988). *Content of the curriculum: 1988 ASCD yearbook.* Alexandria, VA: Association for Supervision and Curriculum Development.

McNeil, J. D. (1990). *Curriculum: A comprehensive introduction* (4th ed.). Glenview, IL: Scott, Foresman/Little, Brown.

Resnick, L. B., & Klopfer, L. E. (Ed.). (1989). *Toward the thinking curriculum: Current cognitive research: 1989 ASCD yearbook.* Alexandria, VA: Association for Supervision and Curriculum Development.

ABOUT PROVIDING FOR INDIVIDUAL NEEDS OF STUDENTS AND MAINSTREAMING

Biklen, D. (1985). *Achieving the complete school.* New York: Teachers College Press.

Bos, C. S., & Vaughn, S. (1988). *Strategies for teaching students with learning and behavior problems.* Boston: Allyn & Bacon.

Sabornie, E. J. (1985). Social mainstreaming of handicapped students: Facing an unpleasant reality. *Remedial and Special Education, 6,* 12–16.

Wolery, M., Bailey, D. B., Jr., & Sugai, G. M. (1988). *Effective teaching: Principles and procedures of applied behavioral analysis with exceptional students.* Boston: Allyn & Bacon.

ABOUT MULTICULTURAL EDUCATION

Davidman, L. (in press). *Teaching with a multicultural perspective across the curriculum: A comprehensive approach to effective instruction.* New York: Longman.

Grant, C. A., & Sleeter, C. E. (1989). *Turning on learning: Five approaches for multicultural teaching plans for race, class, gender, and disability.* Columbus, OH: Merrill.

Johnson, D. W., Johnson, R. T., Tiffany, M., & Zaidman, B. (1984). Cross ethnic relationships: The impact of intergroup cooperation and intergroup competition. *Journal of Educational Research, 78,* 75–79.

Sleeter, C., & Grant, C. (1987). An analysis of multicultural education in the United States. *Harvard Educational Review, 57,* 421–444.

TAKING WHAT YOU'VE LEARNED TO THE NEXT LEVEL

Fully aware of the complexities of teaching and your role as a professional teacher, turn your attention to a paramount activity of the third stage of teaching: *Defining a unit's learning goal with a set of specific objectives.* Research-based strategies and techniques for doing so are emphasized in Chapter 2.

Defining Learning Goals

GOAL OF CHAPTER 2

This chapter provides a model for clarifying the learning goal for each of your teaching units, delineating the subject matter content and the learning levels you expect students to achieve with that content. Chapter 2 will help you

1. specify the *content* of each objective you set for your students, categorizing it as either a (a) concept, (b) specific, (c) relationship, or (d) process (*Cognitive: application*)
2. specify the *learning level* (i.e., what you will teach students to do with the content) of each objective as either (a) cognitive: simple knowledge; (b) cognitive: knowledge of a process; (c) cognitive: comprehension; (d) cognitive: conceptualization; (e) cognitive: application; (f) cognitive: creativity; (g) psychomotor: voluntary muscle capability; (h) psychomotor: ability to perform a specific skill; (i) affective: appreciation; and (j) affective: willingness to try (*Cognitive: application*)
3. define and explain the meanings of the following terms: *objective's content, learning level, concept, specific, subordinate concept, relationship, fact, conventional relationship, rational relationship, process, cognitive, knowledge level, simple knowledge, knowledge of a process, intellectual level, comprehension, conceptualization, application, creativity, psychomotor, voluntary muscle capability, ability to perform a specific skill, affective, appreciation,* and *willingness to try* (*Cognitive: comprehension*)
4. Define the learning goal for each unit you teach, using a set of objectives that clarify exactly what students are expected to achieve (*Cognitive: application*)

LEARNING GOAL

The Purpose of a Teaching Unit

The first step in designing a teaching unit is to determine and articulate its purpose (i.e., to state its learning goal). *Teaching* is helping students achieve learning goals. Each teaching unit is designed to provide students with experiences that lead them to reach the unit's goal. Figure 2.1 lists examples of titles of teaching units along with their respective learning goals. The teachers who formulated these seven goals need to further clarify for themselves what they mean by goal achievement before they are in a position to design lessons that target the appropriate content and learning levels. For example:

> Exactly what does the kindergarten teacher mean by "associates"? Is the goal for the student to make the *b*-sound when seeing the letter *b*? Or is it to distinguish the *b*-sound while listening to a variety of sounds? Chances are the teacher would like for the unit to accomplish both in addition to some other skills. A listing of those more specific skills would help clarify what appears to be a well-stated, appropriate learning goal.
>
> The goal for the second-grade classroom-conduct unit seems appropriate and

Figure 2.1. Examples of Teaching Unit Titles and Goals

The Sounds of b, d, *and* g (kindergarten language arts);

    Goal: Associate the appropriate consonant sounds with the letters *b, d,* and *g*

Classroom Conduct (second-grade citizenship):

    Goal: While in the classroom, display respect and consideration for the rights and feelings of others

U.S. Constitution (fourth-grade social studies):

    Goal: Are aware of fundamental aspects of the U.S. Constitution, its history, and its influence today

Surface Area (sixth-grade mathematics):

    Goal: Efficiently solve real-life problems that require finding sizes of surface areas

Reading Persuasive Essays (ninth-grade English):

    Goal: Critique essays written to sway readers' opinions

Food Webs (high school biology):

    Goal: Understand the fundamental elements and operations of food webs

Weight Training Maintenance Programs (high school physical education):

    Goal: Plan and follow a weight-lifting program for maintaining muscle strength provides some direction for lessons, but definitions of *respect* and *consideration* vary. Once those terms are clarified, what would the teacher consider an appropriate "display" of respect and consideration for the rights and feelings of others?

Regarding the fourth-grade social studies goal, just how "aware" is the student expected to become? Just how much detail regarding "aspects," "history," and "influence" should the lessons cover?

How complex should the problems addressed by the sixth-grade unit be? What geometric shapes should be included? What does the teacher mean by the term *real-life*? It may be that real-life, like *surface area*, is a well-defined specialized term among professional mathematics teachers and, thus, needs no further clarification.

For what points and using what criteria should the student critique the essays for the ninth-grade English unit? In what medium (e.g., written or oral discourse) should critiques be communicated? How sophisticated should the essays be? What range of topics will the essays cover?

For the high school biology goal, what cognitive or mental activity is targeted by the term *understands*? Does "fundamental elements and operations of food webs" clarify the content of the unit well enough in the mind of the biology teacher?

How advanced should the plan developed in the physical education unit be? Does student achievement depend on how well they develop a personalized plan for themselves or should the concern only be for general principles? How much of the goal involves being able to design strength programs (i.e., cognitive behavior)? How much emphasis is on the student's willingness to follow a program (i.e., affective behavior)? How much emphasis is on the student's muscles responding to programs (i.e., psychomotor behavior)?

The Need for Specificity

The learning goal indicates what you intend for your students to gain from a teaching unit. Just how should the unit's lessons be designed so that students will achieve the goal? Before answering that question, the goal needs to be defined in greater detail so that both its *content* and the *learning levels*, which students must display to reach the goal, are spelled out. You provide that detail by defining the goal with a set of specific objectives.

A SET OF OBJECTIVES

The seven teachers who formulated Figure 2.1's learning goals detailed the content and indicated the specific skills, abilities, or attitudes their students are to display with that content by listing objectives (A, B, C, etc. for each goal) as displayed in Figures 2.2., 2.3, 2.4, 2.5, 2.6, 2.7, and 2.8.

The Sounds of b, d, *and* g

Goal: Associate the appropriate consonant sounds with the letters *b, d,* and *g*

Students' achievement of this goal depends on how they:
A. explain the general relation between a word's letters and how that word "sounds" (*Cognitive: conceptualization*)
B. identify the appropriate letter by sight on hearing the consonant sound for *b, d,* or *g* (*Cognitive: simple knowledge*)
C. attempt to sound out the beginning sounds of words that begin with either *b, d,* or *g* (*Affective: willingness to try*)
D. know how to vocalize the appropriate consonant sound when prompted to make the sound for *b, d,* or *g* (*Cognitive: knowledge of a process*)
E. vocalize the appropriate consonant sound when prompted to make the sound for *b, d,* or *g* (*Psychomotor: ability to perform a specific skill*)

Figure 2.2. Goal and Objectives for a Kindergarten Language Arts Unit

Classroom Conduct

Goal: In the classroom, display respect and consideration for the rights and feelings of others

Students' achievement of this goal depends on how they:
A. refrain from littering the classroom floor (*Affective: willingness to try*)
B. if a classmate expresses a need for help, attempt to help, providing that they are able and that such help is acceptable to the teacher (*Affective: willingness to try*)
C. refrain from interrupting others speaking in the classroom (*Affective: willingness to try*)
D. take care not to damage or waste the property of classmates (*Affective: willingness to try*)
E. refrain from stealing from classmates (*Affective: willingness to try*)
F. minimize borrowing from classmates (*Affective: willingness to act*)
G. express appreciation to classmates for being helpful (*Affective: willingness to try*)
H. avoid physically contacting classmates in a way that would cause them pain or discomfort (*Affective: willingness to try*)
I. want classmates to succeed in their efforts to learn (*Affective: appreciation*)

Figure 2.3. Goal and Objectives for a Second-Grade Citizenship Unit

U.S. Constitution

Goal: Are aware of fundamental aspects of the U.S. Constitution, its history, and its influence today

Students' achievement of this goal depends on how they:
A. state that the purpose of the Constitution is to provide a general plan for governing the United States (*Cognitive: simple knowledge*)
B. list the general parts of the original Constitution as the Preamble and seven articles (with the subject of each article) (*Cognitive: simple knowledge*)
C. list facts from the following: In 1787, 43 people wrote the Constitution in a four-month-long Constitutional Convention in Philadelphia. Forty of the 43 signed the document on September 17. The Bill of Rights was added in 1791. (*Cognitive: simple knowledge*)
D. explain George Mason's, Edmund Randolph's, and Elbridge Gerry's reasons for refusing to sign the document (*Cognitive: comprehension*)
E. explain the general provisions in the Bill of Rights (*Cognitive: comprehension*)
F. explain at least four amendments that have been added since the Bill of Rights (*Cognitive: comprehension*)
G. describe the general process for amending the Constitution (*Cognitive: knowledge of a process*)
H. given a description of a well-publicized current issue, determine what, if any, bearing the Constitution has on the resolution of that issue (*Cognitive: application*)
I. believe that the Constitution serves a valuable purpose (*Affective: appreciation*)

Figure 2.4. Goal and Objectives for a Fourth-Grade Social Studies Unit

Surface Area

Goal: Efficiently solve real-life problems that require finding sizes of surface areas

Students' achievement of this goal depends on how they:
A. discriminate between the surface area of a figure and other quantitative characteristics of that figure (e.g., height and volume) (*Cognitive: conceptualization*)
B. explain why the area of a rectangle equals the product of its length and width (*Cognitive: conceptualization*)
C. state the formula for the area of a rectangle (*Cognitive: simple knowledge*)
D. given the dimensions of a rectangle, compute its area (*Cognitive: knowledge of a process*)
E. explain how the formula for the area of a right triangle can be derived from the formula for the area of a rectangle (*Cognitive: conceptualization*)
F. given the dimensions of a right triangle, compute its area (*Cognitive: knowledge of a process*)
G. explain how the formula for the area of a right cylinder can be derived from the formula for the area of a rectangle (*Cognitive: conceptualization*)
H. given the dimensions of a right cylinder, compute its surface area (*Cognitive: knowledge of a process*)
 I. when confronted with a real-life problem, determine whether or not computing a surface area will help solve that problem (*Cognitive: application*)

Figure 2.5. Goal and Objectives for a Sixth-Grade Mathematics Unit

Reading Persuasive Essays

Goal: Critique essays written to sway readers' opinions

Students' achievement of this goal depends on how they:
A. distinguish between examples and nonexamples of each of the following: fact, opinion, evidence, conclusion, and rationale (*Cognitive: conceptualization*)
B. state the definitions of the following: *persuasive essay, fact, background information, opinion, evidence, conclusion, rationale,* and *critique* (*Cognitive: simple knowledge*)
C. from reading an essay (with the sophistication level of a *Newsweek* or *Sports Illustrated* article), separately summarize the author's conclusions and the evidence supporting those conclusions (*Cognitive: comprehension*)
D. express and defend a personal value judgment about the validity of an argument presented in an essay (*Cognitive: application*)
E. formulate both supporting and counterarguments to those expressed in persuasive essays (*Cognitive: creativity*)

Figure 2.6. Goal and Objectives for a Ninth-Grade English Unit

Food Webs

Goal: Understand the fundamental elements and operations of food webs

Students' achievement of this goal depends on how they:
A. list the fundamental elements of a food web (*Cognitive: simple knowledge*)
B. distinguish examples of food webs from other mechanisms within an ecosystem (*Cognitive: conceptualization*)
C. state the definitions of the following terms: *food web, pyramid, biomass, tertiary consumer, secondary consumer, primary consumer, producer,* and *decomposer* (*Cognitive: simple knowledge*)
D. given a description of interlinking food chains, sketch the resulting simplified food web (*Cognitive: knowledge of a process*)
E. given a description of an example of a food web, predict the impact of each of a number of possible disruptions to that web (*Cognitive: application*)

Figure 2.7. Goal and Objectives for a High School Biology Unit

Weight Training Maintenance Programs

Goal: Plan and follow a weight-lifting program for maintaining muscle strength

Students' achievement of this goal depends on how they:
A. on hearing the name of a major muscle group, point to the location of that group on their own body (*Cognitive: simple knowledge*)
B. describe the steps for executing a flat bench press, military press, leg press, calf raise, tricep pull-down, standing curl with curl bar, seated lat pull-down, and behind-the-neck press (*Cognitive: knowledge of a process*)
C. demonstrate the correct procedures for executing a flat bench press, military press, leg press, calf raise, tricep pull-down, standing curl with curl bar, seated lat pull-down, and behind-the-neck press (*Psychomotor: ability to perform a specific skill*)
D. in the weight room, display consideration for the other students, use the equipment in a safe manner, and put weights in their proper places after using them (*Affective: willingness to try*)
E. explain the fundamental relations among (a) weight work, (b) rest, (c) nutrition, and (d) muscle strength (*Cognitive: conceptualization*)
F. design a personal weight-training program for maintaining overall, balanced muscle strength (*Cognitive: application*)
G. follow a plan for maintaining students' overall, balanced muscle strength (*Affective: willingness to try*)
H. when using correct techniques, complete eight repetitions of: (a) Flat bench press 75 percent of own body weight, (b) military press 33 percent of own body weight, (c) leg press 125 percent of own body weight, (d) calf raise 150 percent of own body weight, (e) tricep pull-down 15 percent of own body weight, (f) curl 10 percent of own body weight, (g) lat pull-down 60 percent of own body weight, and (h) behind-the-neck press 5 percent of own body weight (*Psychomotor: voluntary muscle capability*)

Figure 2.8 Goal and Objectives for a High School Physical Education Unit

THE CONTENT SPECIFIED BY AN OBJECTIVE

The Need to Classify Content

Each objective should specify a *content* so that you clearly know what subject matter topics students are to learn. For example, Objective A listed in Figure 2.8 specifies names and locations of muscle groups as content. Objective B's content includes exercise processes; Objective E's includes certain relationships among three concepts—weight work, rest, and nutrition.

As indicated in Chapter 3, the strategy for helping students achieve an objective depends on, among other factors, the type of content specified by the objective. Thus, before designing a lesson for helping students achieve a particular objective, you need to classify its content. Four classifications of content addressed herein are (a) *concept*, (b) *specific*, (c) *relationship* (both logical and conventional), and (d) *process*.

Concept

Look at your present location. Begin listing each individual thing you can see, hear, feel, touch, or taste right now. Like you, the things I'm sensing in my present location are far too numerous to list completely. Before becoming too bored to continue, here's what I managed to list:

1. the computer keyboard I'm using at the moment
2. my computer printer
3. the multicolored pencil box my daughter Amy made for me
4. the stapler on my desk
5. my desk
6. the book shelf in front of me
7. my copy of the blue book entitled *Psychology for the Classroom*
8. my copy of the burnt orange book entitled *Archimedes' Revenge: The Joys and Perils of Mathematics*

    .
    .
    .
    .
    .
    .

 99. the spectacles on my face
100. my guitar
101. the watch on my left wrist
102. my left foot
103. my right foot

    .
    .
    .
    .
    .

848. the photograph of Allison taped to the corner of my maroon disk file box
849. my son Casey's drawing of a surfer taped to the wall
850. my daughter Amanda's drawing of a cat taped to the wall
851. that dull grey, oddly shaped, odorless, thing on the floor that appears to be made of soft plastic and is about 12 centimeters across

    .
    .
    .
    .
    .

1310. the dry taste in my mouth right now
1311. the sound of a truck passing on the street outside
1312. that itchy feeling on my left hand
1313. the fatigue I'm experiencing as a consequence of making this list
1314. my decision to terminate this list

Our real world is composed of *specifics* we detect with our empirical senses. Specifics are far too numerous for us to efficiently deal with or think about each as a unique entity. Thus, we categorize and subcategorize specifics according to certain commonalties or attributes. The categories provide a mental filing system for storing, retaining, and thinking about information. The process by which a person groups specifics to form a mental category is referred to as *conceptualizing*. The category itself is a *concept*.

The tedious task of listing 1,314 specifics I detected from my present location was greatly facilitated by the fact that most of the things listed had conventional names associated with categories (i.e., concepts) both you and I recognize (e.g., "book," "desk," and "guitar"). You've never seen my guitar, but you have a reasonable idea as to what the 100th item on the list is because you've seen other guitars. On the other hand, the 851st item did not fit any concept for which I know a conventional name (other than "thing," and that's not very informative). Thus, more words were used to describe the 851st listing than for others that fit preconceived categories (e.g., book).

Instead of listing each unique item, I could cluster examples of the same concept (e.g., books) and report them as a set. It would require a higher level of thought on my part, but the task would not be nearly as tedious and you would be provided with a more convenient list to read. One-of-a-kind specifics (e.g., I have only one guitar) would still be listed as a singular entity. Compare the following list to the original one:

1. computer-related equipment
2. office supplies and furnishings
3. about 400 books
4. a dozen bookshelves
5. me
6. children's artwork and photographs
7. office space confined to a typically structured 12-by-13-ft. room
8. my guitar
9. other personal items
10. several objects for which I have no conventional name
11. sounds from outside
12. some uncomfortable feelings
13. the thoughts in my head

Of the 13 items in the list, 10 refer to more than one specific thing. Thus, those 10 items are *concepts*. Three, namely, the fifth (me), the seventh (a fixed amount of space), and the eighth (my one guitar), each refer to a single unique entity. Thus, each of those three is a *specific*.

Return to the seven sets of objectives listed in Figures 2.2–2.8. Objective A from Figure 2.5 specifies *surface area of a figure* as the content about which students are to learn. *Surface area of a figure* is a *concept* because there is more than one such surface area. In fact, there are infinite surface areas (e.g., the surface area of the page you are now reading and the surface area of your own body). Each concept is defined by attributes, that is, characteristics that all examples of that concept possess. Any surface area, for example, is a quantity that reflects the size of a two-dimensional, flat portion of an object. *Food web*, the content specified by Objective B from Figure 2.7, is also a concept. Food web refers to any complex of food chains in an ecological community. There are, of course, many different food webs, but each shares a common set of attributes (e.g., a collection of decomposers).

Concepts are, of course, not the only type of content specified by objectives. Objective B from Figure 2.4 focuses on the Preamble and the seven articles of the U.S. Constitution. There is only one preamble to the U.S. Constitution and each of the seven articles is unique. Thus, for that unit, Objective B's content consists of *specifics*, not concepts. A specific can be an example of a concept (e.g., the *U.S. Constitution* is an example of a *government document*). Furthermore, one concept can be subsumed by another (e.g., *mammal* is a type of *animal*). A concept (e.g., mammal) that is subsumed by another concept (e.g., animal) is *subordinate* to the concept that includes it.

Examine the following list to (a) determine which entries are concepts and which are specifics, (b) identify, for each specific, those concepts on the list for which it is an example, and (c) identify subordinate relationships among the concepts:

1. 48.09
2. geographic feature
3. number
4. negative number
5. teacher
6. lake
7. surgeon
8. former baseball player
9. Lake Ontario
10. professional occupation
11. the book you are now reading
12. college textbooks
13. baseball hall of famer
14. book
15. geometric figure
16. the rectangle determined by the four corners of the page you are now reading
17. rectangle
18. Jackie Robinson
19. triangle
20. You
21. The very last teacher, other than yourself, with whom you spoke
22. Person

Compare how you grouped the 22 items to the following:

1. 48.09: a *specific* that is an example of the concept listed as item 3
2. geographic feature: *a concept*
3. number: *a concept*
4. negative number: a *concept* that is subordinate to item 3
5. teacher: a *concept* that is subordinate to item 10 if considered a position; a *concept* that is subordinate to item 22 if considered the being who also serves as a teacher
6. lake: a *concept* that is subordinate to item 2
7. surgeon: a *concept* that is subordinate to item 10 if considered a position; a *concept* that is subordinate to item 22 if considered the being who also serves as a surgeon
8. former baseball player: a *concept* that is subordinate to item 22
9. Lake Ontario: a *specific* that is an example of the concepts listed in items 2 and 6
10. professional occupation: a *concept*
11. the book you are now reading: a *specific* that is an example of the concepts listed in items 12 and 14
12. college textbook: a *concept* that is subordinate to item 14
13. baseball hall of famer: a *concept* that is subordinate to items 8 and 22
14. book: a *concept*
15. geometric figure: a *concept*
16. the rectangle determined by the four corners of the page you are now reading: a *specific* that is an example of items 15 and 17
17. rectangle: a *concept* that is subordinate to item 15
18. Jackie Robinson: a *specific* that is an example of items 8, 13, and 22
19. triangle: a *concept* that is subordinate to item 15
20. you: a *specific* that is an example of item 5 and 22 (and possibly 7 (if you also happen to be a surgeon) and 8 (if you're a former baseball player)
21. the very last teacher, other than yourself, with whom you spoke: a *specific* that is an example of items 5 and 22 (and possibly 7 and 8)
22. person: a *concept*

Specific

The content specified by learning objectives usually involves abstract ideas or processes that extend beyond a single specific. Specifics are, however, the components of abstractions and provide examples from which students conceptualize and develop process skills. Occasionally, you may want to focus a unit on a particular specific such as one entitled "The U.S. Constitution" or "Jackie Robinson."

Relationship

A *relationship* is a particular association either (a) between concepts, (b) between a concept and a specific, or (c) between specifics. Unlike a concept or a specific, a relationship is denoted by a complete statement. The following are examples of relationships:

Students have varying interests. (A relationship from a concept, namely, *student*, to another concept, namely, *varying interests*)

Todd loves playing the guitar. (A relationship from a specific, namely, *Todd*, to a concept, namely, *guitar*)

You are reading this book right now. (A relationship from a specific, namely, *you*, to another specific, namely, *this book*)

The content specified by most of the seven sets of objectives from Figures 2.2–2.8 are relationships. Objective A from Figure 2.2, for example, specifies the following relation between two concepts: *The letters in a word affect the sound of the word.* Objective B specifies three relationships between pairs of specifics, such as: *The letter* b *triggers the sound "bah," "buh,"* and so forth.

Relationships that can be discovered by reasoning are referred to as *rational relationships.* The formula for computing the area of a rectangle (i.e., length × width = area) is an example of a rational relationship because there is logic and reason behind the existence of the relationship. One can discover why it works. The content of Objective E from Figure 2.8 focuses on effects of varying combinations of weight work, rest, and nutrition on muscle strength. These are examples of rational relationships.

Relationships are *conventional* if they are established through tradition or agreement. The association between the letter *b* and its sounds is an example of a conventional relationship. Relationships associating a word with an idea or definition are conventional. For example, the Pythagorean theorem is a rational relationship (i.e., one can use reason to discover $c^2 = a^2 + b^2$ for any right triangle with hypotenuse c and legs a and b). However, the following relationship is conventional: The expression $c^2 = a^2 + b^2$ is called the *Pythagorean theorem.*

Relationships that are true are referred to as *facts.*

Process

A process is a step-by-step method by which a task is completed. Processes depend on relationships. For example, the process for computing the area of a rectangle is based on the relationship, *length × width = area.* A number of processes are specified by objectives for our seven units. For example, both Objectives D and E from Figure 2.2 are concerned with a process for vocalizing consonant sounds. Objective G from Figure 2.4 specifies the process by which the Constitution is amended. Objectives D, F, and H from Figure 2.5 focus on processes for computing surface areas. The definition of the goal from Figure 2.8 includes Objectives B, C, D, F, G, and H specifying certain exercise procedures, safety procedures, and regimens to be followed or designed.

Other Ways of Classifying Content

Having only four content categories (i.e., *concept, specific, relationship,* and *process*) is insufficient for all objectives. An objective may specify a content that involves a complex of relationships and processes. Objective D from Figure 2.6, for example, specifies *the validity of arguments presented in essays* for content.

That includes a multitude of interrelated relationships. Each teaching specialty area (e.g., English, health and physical, early childhood education) contains its own specialized content-related terms. Draw from your teaching field's specialized language to expand on the four-category scheme presented here.

THE LEARNING LEVEL SPECIFIED BY AN OBJECTIVE

The Need to Classify Learning Levels

Compare the following five objectives for similarities and differences:

A. Given an addition fact (i.e., a statement of the sum of any two one-digit whole numbers—e.g., 3 + 8 = 11) and a set of at least 18 objects, demonstrate the fact by counting (*Cognitive: knowledge of a process*)
B. Given an addition fact, explain why the fact is true (*Cognitive: conceptualization*)
C. State the addition facts (*Cognitive: simple knowledge*)
D. Believe that time can often be saved by using addition facts instead of counting when solving real-life problems (*Affective: appreciation*)
E. When confronted with a real-life problem, determine whether or not using addition facts will help solve the problem (*Cognitive: application*)

All five objectives deal with what primary grade teachers refer to as "the addition facts." For content, Objective A specifies a process for demonstrating each addition fact. The content for the other four objectives is the set of addition facts; each fact is a relationship. In spite of the similarity among the objectives' content, no two of the objectives are alike. How do they differ? The objectives differ in the way the student is to think about and deal with addition facts. Objective A is concerned with the students remembering a process for demonstrating the facts. Objective B focuses on the student understanding why each relationship is true (e.g., can verbally explain why 5 + 4 = 9). By achieving Objective C, the student can recall each fact from memory. Objective D is not focused on the student's ability with addition facts, but rather the student recognizing value in being able to use the facts. Students' ability to decide when to make use of their knowledge of the facts in real-world situations is the target established by Objective E.

In summary, each objective differs from the other four in the *learning level* it specifies. Just as an objective's content influences your teaching strategies (e.g., you teach about addition facts differently than you teach about the U.S. Constitution), so should your strategies depend on the objective's learning level.

Learning Domains

You are in no position to design appropriate lessons until you've identified the learning levels of the targeted objectives. Thus, it is crucial for you to formulate each objective so that there is no doubt about the intended learning level.

Familiarity with one of the published schemes for classifying objectives according to their specified learning levels will help you clarify your own objectives.

The scheme presented in the remainder of this chapter is adapted from a variety of sources (Bloom, 1984; Cangelosi, 1980; Cangelosi, 1982, pp. 90–95; Cangelosi, 1990b, pp. 7–19; Cangelosi, 1992, pp. 57–68; Guilford, 1959; Harrow, 1972; Krathwohl, Bloom, & Masia, 1964).

Learning levels are traditionally classified into three domains: *cognitive, psychomotor*, and *affective*.

If the intent of an objective is for students to be able to do something mentally (e.g., remember a fact or deduce a method for solving a problem), the learning level falls within the *cognitive domain*.

If the intent of an objective is for students to develop some physical attribute (e.g., muscle flexibility) or physical skill (e.g., manipulate a pencil well enough to form legible letters), the objective falls within the *psychomotor domain*.

If the intent of the objective is for students to develop a particular attitude or feeling (e.g., a desire to read or willingness to attempt a task), the learning level falls within the *affective domain*.

Most of what is taught in schools target student behaviors that fall within all three domains. For example:

VIGNETTE 2.1

Ms. Dorsey is helping Jorge, one of her kindergarten students, to print uppercase *A*'s accurately. She must teach him the cognitive skill of knowing how to form an *A*. But Jorge will not learn to print *A*'s unless he is willing to try to form the letter correctly. But even if he knows how and wants to do so, he won't be able to print *A*'s unless he possesses the necessary psychomotor skills to control a pencil.

Ms. Dorsey should make distinctions among the cognitive, psychomotor, and affective components of the skill she's teaching Jorge. To be successful, her strategies must differ according to which one of the following objectives is being taught:

A. Recite the steps for printing an uppercase *A* (*Cognitive: knowledge of a process*)
B. Attempt to follow directions for printing an uppercase *A* (*Affective: willingness to try*)
C. Manipulate a pencil well enough to follow the steps for printing an uppercase *A* (*Psychomotor: ability to perform a specific skill*)

COGNITIVE OBJECTIVES

Knowledge-Level and Intellectual-Level Cognition

There are two types of objectives that specify learning levels in the cognitive domain: (a) *knowledge level* and (b) *intellectual level*. An objective requiring students to *remember* some specified content is knowledge level. An objective requiring students to *use reasoning to make judgments* relative to the specified content is intellectual level.

Knowledge-Level Cognitive Objectives

It is important to distinguish between *simple knowledge* and *knowledge of a process* learning levels because of the differences between how achievement of two types of knowledge-level objectives occurs (as explained in Chapter 3) and is assessed (as explained in Chapter 6).

Simple Knowledge. An objective requiring students to remember a specified response (but not a multistep sequence of responses) to a specified stimulus is at the simple knowledge level. As indicated by the label *Cognitive: simple knowledge*, 8 of the 50 objectives listed in Figures 2.2–2.8 specify the simple knowledge learning level. Here are additional examples:

> Match names of capital cities with their respective states (*Cognitive: simple knowledge*)
> State the quadratic formula (*Cognitive: simple knowledge*)
> Match each of the following schematic symbols with the appropriate electronic device:

> (*Cognitive: simple knowledge*)

These three objectives, like all simple knowledge objectives, indicate responses for students to remember when presented with certain stimuli. The stimulus in the first is the name of a state (e.g., Idaho); the response is the capital city (e.g., Boise).

Knowledge of a Process. An objective requiring students to remember a *sequence of steps in a procedure* is at the *knowledge-of-a-process* level. As indicated by the label *Cognitive: knowledge of a process*, 7 of the 50 objectives listed in Figures 2.2–2.8 specify the knowledge-of-a-process learning level. Here are additional examples:

> Compute the product of any two-digit whole number by any one-digit whole number (*Cognitive: knowledge of a process*)
> Describe the procedures for safely lighting a Bunsen burner in the biology lab (*Cognitive: knowledge of a process*)
> Given a recipe from a cookbook, describe how to adjust the amount of ingredients according to the number of people to be served (*Cognitive: knowledge of a process*)

Knowledge-of-a-process objectives are concerned with students knowing how to execute the steps in methods for finding answers or accomplishing tasks. You know the answer to the question, "What is 9 + 3?" without figuring it out, so you have achieved a simple-knowledge objective dealing with addition facts. However, unless you are quite unusual in this regard, you don't know the answer to the question, "What is 378 + 85?" What you do know is how to execute the steps in a procedure for finding the sum of any two whole numbers such as 378 and 85. This latter skill is indicative of your achievement of a knowledge-of-a-process objective. The process, not the final outcome, is the focus of strategies for helping students achieve knowledge-of-a-process objectives.

Intellectual-Level Cognitive Objectives

Intellectual-level cognitive objectives require mental behaviors that go beyond the use of memory. Four types of intellectual learning levels are considered herein: (a) *comprehension*, (b) *conceptualization*, (c) *application*, and (d) *creativity*.

Comprehension. *Comprehension-level* objectives focus on students' being able to extract and interpret meaning from expressions. There are two types of comprehension-level objectives depending on whether the objective specifies a particular message (e.g., Article I of the U.S. Constitution) to be understood or a type of communication mode (e.g., American Signed English) from which messages are to be understood:

1. *Comprehension of a message.* Of the four objectives labeled *Cognitive: comprehension* in Figures 2.2–2.8, three, Objectives D, E, and F, from Figure 2.5 are concerned with students' interpreting particular messages. Objective F, for example, is not so concerned with students' remembering amendments to the Constitution as it is with students' interpreting what amendments say. Here are three other examples:
   - Explain in their own words the definition of "absolute value of a real number" as expressed in the algebra textbook (*Cognitive: comprehension*)
   - Explain in their own words each of the five "Rules for Conduct" posted in the classroom (*Cognitive: comprehension*)
   - Summarize the major points expressed in the videotape program "Crack Cocaine" (*Cognitive: comprehension*)
2. *Comprehension of a communication mode.* Objective C listed in Figure 2.6 is concerned with students being able to extract meaning from a certain type of essay, not just from a particular essay. Thus, it is an example of a *comprehension of a communication mode* objective. Such objectives focus attention on the students' facility to receive messages via a particular mode. The mode is specified with the objective's content. Here are examples:
   - Summarize the major points of simple stories told by their classmates (*Cognitive: comprehension*)
   - From comparing two weather maps appearing on consecutive days in a newspaper, explain changes in the weather from one day to the next (*Cognitive: comprehension*)
   - After reading a simple computer program written in BASIC, illustrate the logic of the program with a flowchart (*Cognitive: comprehension*)

Conceptualization. A *conceptualization* objective requires students to use *inductive reasoning* (as explained in Chapter 3) to either (a) distinguish examples of a particular concept from nonexamples or (b) discover why a particular relationship exists. Thus, there are two types of conceptualization objectives, those that specify a concept as content and those that specify a relationship:

1. *Conceptualization of a concept.* Six objectives in Figures 2.2–2.8 carry the *Cognitive: conceptualization* label. Three of them, Objective A from Figure 2.3, Objective A from Figure 2.6, and Objective B from Figure 2.7, specify *concepts* for content. To help demonstrate what is meant by distinguishing between examples and nonexamples of a concept, consider the experiences of one infant.

VIGNETTE 2.2

Josh is an infant who feels the warmth and movement of his mother when she nurses him. He hears the sounds emanating from her. Josh's father holds him and Josh experiences some of the same sensations as when he is near his mother. The house cat rubs by Josh and Josh notices that the cat is motile and reacts to Josh's touch in a fashion similar to his parents' reactions. Josh has some toys, but none of them feel warm and vibrating the way his parents and cat feel. His toys do not move by themselves, nor do they breathe. In time, Josh encounters numerous other entities including humans, dogs, furniture, spiders, clothing, food, paper, and plants. Although Josh does not know conventional names for his categories, he categorizes and classifies what he encounters in many ways. For example, he associates humans, cats, dogs, and possibly some other creatures together and places clothes, toys, furniture, and some other things in another separate category. Thus, Josh is developing a concept of what?

When Josh begins to discriminate between things that are alive and things that are not, he is inducting the concept of an animate being. Please notice that Josh discovers this and a myriad of other concepts long before he knows conventional names for the concepts. When Josh possesses only a relatively low level of achievement regarding *conceptualizing living things*, he may only classify his mother, father, and cat as being alive. It will take years before he discovers that a tree or oyster have the *attributes* of being alive.

Persons such as Josh experience concrete examples (i.e., *specifics*) and begin to identify similarities among some of those examples. They use *inductive reasoning* to realize that those similarities, called *attributes*, distinguish examples of the concept from nonexamples (Kelley, 1988, pp. 263–367).

Examples of conceptualization-of-a-concept objectives include:
- Distinguish between verbs and other types of words in a sentence (*Cognitive: conceptualization*)

- From a description of the policies and operations of the government of a hypothetical state, determine whether or not that government is democratic and explains why (*Cognitive: conceptualization*)
- Distinguish between examples of an aerobic exercise and examples of other types of exercises (*Cognitive: conceptualization*)

2. *Conceptualization of a relationship.* The following are examples of objectives concerned with students' discovering why certain relationships exist:

- Explain why the product of 0 and any whole number is 0 (*Cognitive: conceptualization*)
- Explain why the price of a product depends on the demand for that product (*Cognitive: conceptualization*)
- Explain how the principle of negative reinforcement affects human behavior patterns (*Cognitive: conceptualization*)

Application. An *application* objective requires students to use deductive reasoning to decide how to utilize, if at all, a particular concept, relationship, or process to solve problems (Kelley, 1988, pp. 169–254). Here "solving problems" is used broadly referring to situations in which students determine strategies for addressing questions or completing tasks. By achieving an *application-level* objective, students can determine whether or not the content specified by the objective is appropriate to use in formulating a solution to problems they confront. Five objectives listed in Figures 2.2–2.8 are labeled *Cognitive: application.* Here are three other examples:

When the solution to a problem requires the measurement of a length, select a measurement unit (e.g., millimeter or kilometer) that is convenient for the given situation (*Cognitive: application*)

During an oral discourse, adjust language to the audience so that listeners find expressions palatable rather than offensive (*Cognitive: application*)

From observing the symptoms of a person in distress, and from considering the availability and accessibility of other means of help, determine whether or not cardiopulmonary resuscitation (CPR) should be initiated (*Cognitive: application*)

Sometimes teachers confuse knowledge-of-a-process objectives with application objectives. Compare the previous objective to the following one:

Demonstrate appropriate procedures for administering CPR to a person displaying a need for CPR (*Cognitive: knowledge of a process*)

Both objectives deal with the administration of CPR. But the application objective requires students to *decide when* to use the procedure, whereas the knowledge-of-a-process objective requires students to *remember how to execute the procedure.* As explained in Chapter 3, there is quite a difference between designing lessons for application-level achievement and lessons for achievement at the knowledge-of-a-process level.

Creativity. What is the fifth term in the infinite sequence 0, 5, 10, 15, . . . ? Most persons who comprehend the question reason that the fifth number should be 20.

They recognize the arithmetic sequence of uniformly increasing multiples of five beginning with 0. Such a response requires *convergent thinking* because such thinking produces the expected answer. But suppose a student's thinking *diverges* from the usual pattern as in the following example:

VIGNETTE 2.3

Ms. Strong: What is the fifth term in the infinite sequence 0, 5, 10, 15, and so forth?

Willie: 26.

Ms. Strong: Why 26?

Willie: Because each number is different from a perfect square by exactly 1 following this pattern:
Willie writes:
$$0 = 1^2 - 1$$
$$5 = 2^2 + 1$$
$$10 = 3^2 + 1$$
$$15 = 4^2 - 1$$

Willie: So, the pattern repeats with *n*-squared minus 1 followed by 2 *n*-squared plus 1 for *n* equal to 1, 2, 3, and so on.

Adapted with permission from *Teaching Mathematics in Secondary and Middle School: Research-based Approaches* (pp. 67–68), by J. S. Cangelosi (1992), New York: Macmillan. Copyright © 1992 by Macmillan Publishing Company.

Willie's divergent reasoning justifies "26" for the fifth term just as well as convergent reasoning justifies "20." *Divergent thinking* is reasoning that is *atypical* and produces an acceptable, but unanticipated, response. Do not confuse divergent thinking with the thinking of the student in Vignette 2.4:

VIGNETTE 2.4

Ms. Strong: What is the fifth term in the infinite sequence 0, 5, 10, 15, and so forth?

Brenda: 17.

Ms. Strong: Why 17?

Brenda: I don't know. Did I guess it right?

Brenda's unanticipated answer does not appear to be the result of divergent thinking.

An objective that specifies *creativity* as its learning level requires students to *think divergently to originate ideas, hypotheses, products, or methods.* The condition of originality is met as long as the creation is novel to the students themselves. A student, for example, displays achievement at the creativity learning level by "originating" a proof to a theorem even if that proof had been previously developed. However, the student must design the proof without knowledge of the earlier work.

Objective E from Figure 2.6 is labeled (*Cognitive: creativity*). Here are three other examples:

Originate a novel game for their second-grade classmates so that (a) the game is dissimilar to any game to which the students have previously played and (b) winning depends on how well teammates cooperate with one another (*Cognitive: creativity*)

Generate novel hypotheses about angle constructions using a straightedge and compass and either prove or disprove them (*Cognitive: creativity*)

Reorganize objects in a room to stimulate novel movement and interaction patterns for those working in the room (*Cognitive: creativity*)

PSYCHOMOTOR OBJECTIVES

The Nature of Psychomotor Behavior

I *know* how to shoot a basketball as well as anyone in the world. None of the great professional players, present or past (e.g., Michael Jordan) *knows* how to shoot any better than me. I've studied the mechanics of basketball shooting and learned the techniques great shooters use to be so accurate. However, I don't actually shoot a basketball nearly as well as the typical high school player. In truth, I've achieved the cognitive knowledge-of-a-process skill so that now I know how to shoot and am quite capable of describing to others how they should shoot to be accurate. But I lack the necessary *psychomotor capabilities and skills* to be able to consistently *execute* what I know how to do. It's not that the great shooters know more than I do. It's that their muscles and neural networks are better conditioned to carry out what their minds know to do. Psychomotor objectives focus on students' abilities to execute physical tasks as they cognitively know the tasks should be executed.

Strategies for teaching the steps in a process differ from those for training their bodies to efficiently execute the process, so you should differentiate between the cognitive and psychomotor aspects of tasks. Thus, the physical education teacher who formulated the objectives listed in Figure 2.8 separated Objective B, dealing with knowing how to execute certain weight-training exercises from Objective C, dealing with being able to actually do them. As indicated in Chapter 3, teaching for such interrelated objectives (e.g., B and C) should often be carried out concurrently (i.e., students learn the steps as they physically try to execute them). However, as the teacher, you need to keep the two separated in your mind because as you coach students through a process, you respond to formative feedback relative to what students *know* differently from feedback relative to what they are *physically capable* of doing.

Psychomotor objectives are categorized as either (a) *voluntary muscle capability* or (b) *ability to perform a specific skill*.

Voluntary Muscle Capability

A voluntary-muscle-capability objective requires students to use their bodies to perform physical work within certain specified parameters (e.g., time, weight, and distance). The content of voluntary-muscle-capability objectives should be specified so that the muscle groups to be trained and the types of capabilities are clarified. Here is one way general muscle capabilities can be classified:

> *endurance*, which is the ability to sustain an activity
> *strength*, which is the ability to oppose physical resistance
> *flexibility*, which is the range of motion in joints
> *agility*, which is the ability to respond to stimuli quickly and smoothly
> *speed*, which is the ability to reduce the amount of time it takes to move from one physical point to another

One of the 50 objectives listed in Figures 2.2–2.8 is labeled *Psychomotor: voluntary muscle capability*. Three other examples are:

> Increase flexibility in both hands to maximize the distance between points (e.g., on a piano keyboard) that can be simultaneously reached by the thumb and little finger of the same hand (*Psychomotor: voluntary muscle capability*)
> Increase cardiovascular endurance so that a two-mile jog can be sustained (*Psychomotor: voluntary muscle capability*)
> Increase speed at which hamstrings flex and quadriceps extend the knees (*Psychomotor: voluntary muscle capability*)

Ability to Perform a Specific Skill

An ability-to-perform-a-specific-skill objective requires students to *utilize voluntary muscle capabilities in executing a specified physical process*. The content of the ability-to-perform-a-specific-skill objective should be specified so that the physical process to be executed is clarified. Objective E from Figure 2.2 and Objective C from Figure 2.8 are labeled *Psychomotor: ability to perform a specific skill*. Here are three other examples:

> Manipulate a pencil well enough to follow the steps for printing an uppercase A (*Psychomotor: ability to perform a specific skill*)
> Execute a legal tennis serve without faulting 7 out of 10 times (*Psychomotor: ability to perform a specific skill*)
> Focus eyes on printed lines of text (e.g., from a primary reader) so that one line at a time is viewed from left to right followed by the next line, again moving from left to right (*Psychomotor: ability to perform a specific skill*)

AFFECTIVE OBJECTIVES

Unlike cognitive and psychomotor objectives, *affective* objectives are not concerned with students' abilities with content, but rather with their attitudes about content. All nine objectives listed in Figure 2.3 are in the affective domain because the learning goal focuses on students' values and what they are willing to do, not on what they are able to do. The affective domain consists of two learning levels: (a) *appreciation* and (b) *willingness to try*.

Appreciation

Students achieve an objective at the appreciation level by *believing that the content specified in the objective has value*. Objectives I from Figure 2.3 and Objective I from Figure 2.4 carry the *Affective: appreciation* label. Other examples include:

> Believe that learning how to read will be personally beneficial and rewarding (*Affective: appreciation*)
> Prefer to formulate own algebraic open sentences when solving word problems rather than having the sentence set up by someone else (*Affective: appreciation*)
> Would like to maintain a healthy diet (*Affective: appreciation*)

Achievement of an appreciation-level objective requires students to hold certain beliefs, but does not require them to act on those beliefs.

Willingness to Try

Students achieve an objective at the willingness-to-try level by *choosing to attempt a task specified by the objective*. By believing that an understanding of systems of linear equations can help them solve problems they care about, students have achieved at the appreciation level. But to learn content at the willingness-to-act level, students would have to act on that belief (e.g., by trying to learn how to read). Figures 2.2–2.8 list 11 objectives with the *Affective: willingness to try* label. The following are other examples:

> Attempt to formulate own algebraic open sentences when solving word problems before turning to someone else to set them up for (*Affective: willingness to try*)
> Follow the "Eight Cardinal Rules of Safety" while in the science lab (*Affective: willingness to try*)
> When presented with an opportunity to abuse drugs, refuse to abuse drugs (*Affective: willingness to try*)

USING THE SCHEME FOR CLASSIFYING LEARNING LEVELS

You are in no position to design lessons for a teaching unit until you have defined the unit's goal in terms of objectives, each of which clearly specifies the targeted content and learning level. The scheme for classifying objectives according to learning levels (summarized in Figure 2.9) provides you with a mechanism for:

1. organizing your thoughts about how you want your students to interact with subject matter content

Cognitive Domain

I. Knowledge level
   A. Simple knowledge
   B. Knowledge of a Process
II. Intellectual level
   A. Comprehension
   B. Conceptualization
   C. Application
   D. Creativity

Psychomotor Domain

I. Voluntary muscle capability
II. Ability to perform a specific skill

Affective Domain

I. Appreciation level
II. Willingness to try

Figure 2.9 Learning-Level Categories

2. clarifying and communicating the cognitive, psychomotor, or affective level targeted by each objective

The learning level you intend for even a well-written objective may not be communicated clearly until you actually label the objective according to the scheme. Consider, for example, the following objective:

Explain Newton's third law of motion

Does the teacher who formulated the objective intend for students to (a) recall an explanation to which they were previously exposed (simple knowledge), (b) explain what the the statement, "For every force, there is an equal and opposite force" means (comprehension level), (c) discover why the law holds (conceptualization level), or (d) originate a proof of the law (creativity level)? Attaching a learning-level label to the objective would clarify the matter (e.g., Explains Newton's third law of motion, *Cognitive: comprehension*). You are advised to label objectives you formulate so that there is no question regarding the learning level you plan to target.

SELF-ASSESSMENT EXERCISES FOR CHAPTER 2

I. Select the one response to each of the following multiple-choice items that either completes the statement so that it is true or accurately answers the question:
   A. Which one of the following is a concept?
      a. December 10, 1968
      b. 10 hours, 14 minutes, 19 seconds
      c. A point in time

B. Which one of the following is a specific?
   a. the letter Q
   b. a communication symbol
   c. a letter of the English alphabet
C. Which one of the following is a relationship from a specific to a concept?
   a. Ernest Hemmingway wrote books
   b. Books are written by people
   c. George Bush succeeded Ronald Reagan in the White House
D. Which one of the following is a relationship between two specifics?
   a. Groceries can be quite expensive.
   b. Many people enjoy living in trailer parks.
   c. Angel Enriques doesn't live in a trailer park.
   d. Fangduo Len lives at 821 Eugene Street.
E. Which one of the following is a relationship between two concepts?
   a. The people who live in Washington, DC
   b. Many politicians are lawyers.
   c. One of the more influential politicians in the world
   d. Jupiter is a planet.
F. Which one of the following is a fact?
   a. Oil is the most important source of energy in the world today.
   b. Washington, DC, the capital of the United States
   c. $8 + 3 = 25$.
   d. Jupiter is a planet.
G. Which one of the following is a conventional relationship?
   a. Aerobic exercise increases cardiovascular endurance.
   b. Tobacco contains nicotine.
   c. The first letter of the first word of a sentence should be capitalized.
   d. The first letter of the first word of a sentence
H. *A learning goal* is a concept that is subordinate to which one of the following concepts?
   a. what a student achieves if the unit alluded to in Figure 2.8 is successful
   b. one of the things teachers determine during the first of the five stages of teaching
   c. a learning objective
   d. the fundamental principles of pedagogical theory on which teaching strategies should be based
I. Students' computational proficiency depends on their achievement of what type of learning objective?
   a. appreciation
   b. conceptualization
   c. application
   d. knowledge of a process
J. The content of comprehension-level objectives is likely to involve a _____..
   a. concept
   b. communication
   c. process
K. Students learn the meaning of shorthand symbols by _____.
   a. inductive reasoning
   b. deductive reasoning
   c. being informed
   d. creative invention
L. Which one of the following learning levels requires intellectual-level reasoning?
   a. application

    b. voluntary muscle capability

    c. knowledge of a process

M. Simple knowledge-level objectives are _____.

    a. affective

    b. cognitive

    c. intellectual

    d. knowledge of a process

N. Willingness to do something is subsumed by which of the following domains?

    a. cognitive

    b. affective

    c. psychomotor

O. A learning objective requiring students to *know* the steps in a physical activity is _____.

    a. cognitive

    b. psychomotor

    c. affective

P. A learning objective requiring students to use reasoning is _____.

    a. cognitive

    b. psychomotor

    c. affective

Q. A cognitive objective requiring students to make decisions that go beyond what they remember is _____.

    a. knowledge of a process

    b. simple knowledge

    c. affective

    d. intellectual

R. Which one of the following types of objectives requires students to reason deductively?

    a. knowledge of a process

    b. appreciation

    c. application

    d. conceptualization

    e. comprehension of a communication

S. When a teacher conducts a lesson targeting an affective learning objective, that teacher is attempting to get students to _____.

    a. understand their own values

    b. understand the values of others

    c. be able to recognize values

    d. embrace values

T. By writing her name in legible cursive, Nancy displays achievement of an objective with cursive writing as a content and _____ as a learning level.

    a. cognitive: comprehension of a communication

    b. psychomotor: ability to perform a specific skill

    c. cognitive: conceptualization

U. By writing her name in legible cursive, Nancy displays achievement of an objective with cursive writing as a content and _____ as a learning level.

    a. affective: willingness to try

    b. cognitive: beyond application

    c. cognitive: applications

V. By writing her name in legible cursive, Nancy displays achievement of an objective with cursive writing as a content and _____ as a learning level.

    a. cognitive: comprehension of a communication

      b. cognitive: conceptualization

      c. cognitive: knowledge of a process

W. By accurately translating the American Signed English of a hearing-impaired person into spoken English, Jan displays achievement of an objective with American Signed English as the content and _____ as a learning level.

      a. knowledge of a process

      b. conceptualization

      c. comprehension of a communication

X. What cognitive level of achievement does Juan display by accurately computing the quotient of 55.087 and .09669?

      a. simple knowledge

      b. knowledge of a process

      c. conceptualization

      d. application

    Compare your responses to the following: A-c, B-a, C-a, D-d, E-b, F-d, G-c, H-b, I-d, J-b, K-c, L-a, M-b, N-b, O-a, P-a, Q-d, R-c, S-d, T-b, U-a, V-c, W-c, X-b.

II. Reexamine Figure 1.14's objectives. Although the wording of the objectives doesn't totally communicate exactly what Mr. Santiago had in mind (i.e., he didn't label the learning levels), infer his intentions by analyzing each to (a) identify its content, (b) categorize the type of content as either a concept, specific, relationship, process, or some combination of these, and (c) categorize the cognitive learning level according to the scheme depicted in Figure 2.9. After completing this task, compare your responses to those of Table 2.1; however, keep in mind that differences may be due to ambiguities in the phrasing of the objectives.

III. In your response to Exercise IV for the self-assessment exercises for Chapter 1, you listed a number of learning goals for teaching units. Select one of those goals and then

TABLE 2.1. Content and Learning Levels Specified by Figure 1.14's Objectives

Objective	Content	Type of Content	Learning Level
A	Speed and acceleration	Concept	Conceptualization
B	Definition of *speed, acceleration, force, mass,* and *distance*	Relationship	Simple knowledge
C	Measurement of speed	Process	Knowledge of a process
D	Measurement of acceleration	Process	Knowledge of a process
E	Newton's first law of motion	Relationship	Comprehension*
F	Newton's first law of motion	Relationship	Simple knowledge
G	Effects of friction and gravity on speed of a moving body	Relationship	Conceptualization
H	Newton's second law of motion	Relationship	Comprehension*
I	Newton's second law of motion	Relationship	Simple knowledge
J	Newton's third law of motion	Relationship	Comprehension*
K	Newton's third law of motion	Relationship	Simple knowledge
L	Newton's first three laws of motion	Relationship	Application

* If Mr. Santiago intends for his students to understand the meaning of these three laws as stated, then "comprehension" is the appropriate label. However, if the intent is for the students to discover these laws for themselves (a far more ambitious objective), then the label should read "conceptualization."

define it by formulating a set of objectives. Make sure you label the learning level of each objective using the scheme outlined in Figure 2.9. Compare your work on this exercise to someone else's.

SUGGESTED READING

Bloom, B. S. (Ed.). (1984). *Taxonomy of educational objectives: The classification of educational goals, book I: Cognitive domain*. New York: Longman.

Bloom, B. S., Hastings, J. T., & Madaus, G. F. (1971). Defining educational objectives. In *Handbook on formative and summative evaluation of student learning* (pp. 19–41). New York: McGraw-Hill.

Harrow, A. J. (1974). *A taxonomy of the psychomotor domain: A guide for developing behavioral objectives*. New York: McKay.

Kelley, D. (1988). *The art of reasoning*. New York: Norton.

Krathwohl, D., Bloom, B. S., & Masia, B. (1964). *Taxonomy of educational objectives, the classification of educational goals, handbook 2: Affective domain*. New York: Longman.

TenBrink, T. D. (1990). Instructional objectives. In J. M. Cooper (Ed.), *Classroom teaching skills* (4th ed., pp. 51–83). Lexington, MA: Heath.

TAKING WHAT YOU'VE LEARNED TO THE NEXT LEVEL

Now that your can proficiently define learning goals by formulating objectives that specify both the targeted content and learning level, turn your attention to questions regarding:

1. How to sequence a unit's objectives so that students efficiently achieve them
2. How should a unit's lessons be designed so that learning activities are appropriate for both the content and learning level of each objective.

CHAPTER 3

Designing Lessons

GOAL OF CHAPTER 3

This chapter explains how to design lessons for research-based teaching units; Chapter 3 will help you

1. use research-based strategies to define each of your learning goals with a *sequence* of objectives (*Cognitive: application*)
2. explain the meanings of the following terms: *direct instruction, inquiry instruction, inductive reasoning, inductive learning activity, psychological noise, mnemonics, overlearning, literal comprehension, interpretive comprehension, error pattern analysis, deductive reasoning, deductive learning activity,* and *synectics* (*Cognitive: comprehension*)
3. given a group of students with whom you are familiar and an objective appropriate for those students that specifies (a) content with which you are familiar and (b) an *affective* learning level, design a lesson that will help those students achieve the objective (*Cognitive: application*)
4. given a group of students with whom you are familiar and an objective appropriate for those students that specifies (a) content with which you are familiar and (b) a *conceptualization* learning level, design a lesson that will help those students achieve the objective (*Cognitive: application*)
5. given a group of students with whom you are familiar and an objective appropriate for those students that specifies (a) content with which you are familiar and (b) a *simple-knowledge* learning level, design a lesson that will help those students achieve the objective (*Cognitive: application*)
6. given a group of students with whom you are familiar and an objective appropriate for those students that specifies (a) content with which you are familiar and (b) a *comprehension* learning level, design a lesson that will help those students achieve the objective (*Cognitive: application*)

7. given a group of students with whom you are familiar and an objective appropriate for those students that specifies (a) content with which you are familiar and (b) a *knowledge-of-a-process* learning level, design a lesson that will help those students achieve the objective (*Cognitive: application*)
8. given a group of students with whom you are familiar and an objective appropriate for those students that specifies (a) content with which you are familiar and (b) an *application* learning level, design a lesson that will help those students achieve the objective (*Cognitive: application*)
9. given a group of students with whom you are familiar and an objective appropriate for those students that specifies (a) content with which you are familiar and (b) a *creativity* learning level, design a lesson that will help those students achieve the objective (*Cognitive: application*)
10. given a group of students with whom you are familiar and an objective appropriate for those students that specifies (a) content with which you are familiar and (b) a *voluntary-muscle-capability* learning level, design a lesson that will help those students achieve the objective (*Cognitive: application*)
11. given a group of students with whom you are familiar and an objective appropriate for those students that specifies (a) content with which you are familiar and (b) an *ability-to-perform-a-specific-skill* learning level, design a lesson that will help those students achieve the objective (*Cognitive: application*)

SEQUENCING THE OBJECTIVES OF A TEACHING UNIT

Reexamine the seven sets of objectives listed in Figures 2.2–2.8; note the various learning levels for each unit. The objectives from Figures 2.2, 2.5, 2.6, and 2.7 are listed in the approximate order in which they should be taught. Here is a rough rule of thumb for sequencing objectives—especially for units whose goals emphasize application-level learning:

> Lessons for objectives specifying any particular concept or relationship are sequenced so that (a) *conceptualization*-level learning occurs first, (b) followed by *knowledge-* and *comprehension*-level learning, and (c) culminating in *application*-level learning.

Here are some general principles to keep in mind:

> *Ordinarily, the name for a concept or relationship should not be introduced before students have been engaged in learning activities for conceptualizing that concept or relationship.* Memorizing words to attach to a concept or relationship before that concept or relation is understood is meaningless for most students.
> *Comprehension objectives relative to certain messages (e.g., the Preamble to the U.S. Constitution) or to certain communication modes (e.g., use of the summation notation Σ) should be taught before conducting learning*

activities that depend on those messages or communication modes. Students experience considerable difficulty following lessons in which teachers either (a) assume they understand messages they've yet to comprehend or (b) communicate via modes they've not learned to use.

Ordinarily, the statement of a relationship should not be memorized before students are engaged in learning activities for conceptualizing the relationship. Memorizing a relationship (e.g., the product of two negative integers is positive) is far more meaningful after students have discovered why the relationship exists.

If creativity or affective objectives are targeted by a unit, then learning activities for them are ordinarily scattered throughout the unit. Both creative and affective behaviors are usually acquired by experiences that extend over the entire course of a unit rather than tending to appear near the beginning (as with conceptualization learning), the middle (as with comprehension and knowledge levels), or the end (as with application).

Students need to develop prerequisite voluntary muscle capabilities and acquire knowledge of relevant processes before they are ready to successfully learn a specific psychomotor skill.

Students are ready to engage in learning activities for application-level objectives relative to a particular relationship only after they have conceptualized the relationship and acquired relevant comprehension- and knowledge-level skills (e.g., how to execute processes based on the relationship).

The sequence in which Jay Santiago taught for the objectives listed in Figure 1.14 is summarized in Vignette 3.1:

VIGNETTE 3.1

Mr. Santiago conducted Unit 5 so that he helped students achieve Objective A (i.e., conceptualize speed and acceleration) before using knowledge-level lessons on conventional definitions for some related terms (i.e., Objective B). Then he taught them knowledge-level processes for measuring speed and acceleration (i.e., Objectives C and D). He then moved on to an intellectual-level lesson on the Newton's first law of motion (i.e., Objective E), followed by a knowledge-level lesson for students to remember it (i.e., Objective F).

The pattern continued for the second and third laws, and the unit culminated with an application-level lesson leading students to be able to apply content they conceptualized, comprehended, and memorized to solve real-world problems.

INTEGRATING BOTH INQUIRY AND DIRECT INSTRUCTION INTO TEACHING UNITS

Inquiry Instruction

Inquiry instructional methods utilize learning activities that lead students to formulate their own answers to questions and discover solutions to problems. When you conduct this type of activity, your responsibility is to provide appropriate structures, leading questions or tasks, and guidance that stimulate productive student thought. Lessons based on inquiry methods are appropriate for *intellectual-level cognitive objectives* and for *affective objectives* (Gagne, 1985, pp. 301–319; Hunkins, 1989, pp. 157–167; Joyce & Weil, 1986, pp. 25–69).

There are, of course, numerous strategies for designing and conducting learning activities for inquiry instruction. Strategies and the sequencing of the activities should depend on the content and learning level of the lesson's objective (e.g., whether the level is conceptualization of a relationship or application of a process). Specific strategies and activity patterns are explained and illustrated in the five sections of this chapter devoted to lessons for affective and intellectual-level cognitive objectives.

Direct Instruction

Direct instructional methods utilize learning activities that follow a familiar, straightforward pattern: (a) Students are informed of the skill they are to acquire; (b) the skill is explained or information is provided to the students; (c) the skill is demonstrated with examples; (d) students practice the skill with examples from an assigned exercise; (e) students are provided corrective or reinforcing feedback on their work.

Lessons based on direct instructional methods are appropriate for *knowledge-level cognitive objectives* and for *psychomotor objectives* (Arends, 1988, pp. 362–385; Joyce & Weil, 1986, pp. 317–336).

Complementary Methods

Should you employ inquiry or direct instructional methods? The relative advantages and disadvantages of each have been debated in research-based and rationally based, as well as emotionally based, arguments. Inquiry instruction is referred to as "haphazard," "unstructured," and "without direction" by its detractors. Actually, in the hands of expert teachers, inquiry instruction uses far more complex structures than direct teaching. But unlike lessons based on direct instruction, the intricate structures of inquiry lessons are nonlinear and thus, more difficult for a casual observer to detect.

Generally speaking, statements of objectives at the knowledge or psychomotor levels are easier for laypersons and the less-sophisticated professional educators to comprehend than are statements of objectives at the intellectual or affective levels. Thus, they sometimes think of direct instruction as being more goal-oriented than inquiry instruction. Actually, expert teachers have very clear objectives in mind as they design and conduct inquiry lessons.

People sometimes criticize direct instructional methods as being "cold and inhuman," "only concerned with the trivial," and "boring for students." Knowledge-level and psychomotor skill acquisition may seem colder, less human, less important, and more mundane than learning to "appreciate," "conceptualize," and "apply to real-life situations." However, it takes fundamental knowledge and skills to put intellectual-level and affective learning to use (Arends, 1988, pp. 363–364). Furthermore, direct instructional learning activities need not always be boring for students. Expert teachers use games, pacing, and motivational devices to foster students' enthusiasm for some of the more mundane aspects of school curricula (See, e.g., Vignette 5.13).

Should you employ inquiry or direct instructional methods? The outcomes of inquiry instruction (i.e., intellectual-level and affective learning) and the outcomes of direct instruction (i.e., knowledge-level and psychomotor learning) are interdependent, so you have no choice but to integrate both types of instructional methods into your teaching repertoire.

LESSONS FOR AFFECTIVE OBJECTIVES

Appreciation

When you teach for an *appreciation* objective, you are attempting to influence students' preferences, opinions, or desires regarding content specified by the objective. Students who learn to *value* content are intrinsically motivated to increase their skills and abilities with it and, thus, achieve the cognitive or psychomotor objectives you establish for the unit.

Telling students about the importance and value of what you want to teach them is generally ineffectual as a learning activity for an appreciation objective. For example:

VIGNETTE 3.2

Mr. Mena realizes that if his history students appreciate the value of understanding certain events in the history of the U.S. Congress, they will be more receptive to achieving the cognitive objectives of his unit on congressional activities between 1901 and 1935. Thus, his initial objective for the unit is for students to:

> Recognize the advantage of being able to relate congressional activities during the first 35 years of the 20th century to today's current issues (*Affective: appreciation*)

In an attempt to achieve that objective, he tells the class: "Today, people, we're going to begin studying the important work of Congress between 1901 and 1935. We need to learn about that so we can extend our abilities to deal with today's problems. You enjoy debating current issues that affect each of us. Once you understand events from the past, you'll be better able to deal with today's problems and understand how we got where we are today—for better or worse."

In general, students do not learn to appreciate something by being told what they enjoy or will find important (Cangelosi, 1988a, pp. 89, 130–138). Rather than wasting time with lip service for his appreciation-level objective, Mr. Mena should integrate learning activities for the appreciation objective into lessons for his cognitive objectives so that:

1. the first few examples used to introduce the content involve situations in which most students have already demonstrated an interest.
2. initial tasks to which the content is applied are selected so that the value of the new concept, specific, relationship, or process is readily demonstrated. For example:

   If the content is the formula for computing rectangular areas (i.e., $A = l \times w$), then which one of the following tasks would better demonstrate the advantages of having such a formula?

   A. Find the area of the following rectangle:

   B. Find the area of the following rectangle:

   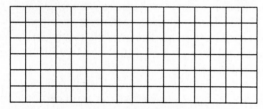

   It is just as easy to count the unit squares to find the area of the 4-by-2 rectangle as it is to use the area formula. The value of the formula is apparent for the task of finding the area of the 16-by-6 rectangle, because, with the formula, students only need to count the number of units on two edges rather than all 96 squares.
3. whenever the unit's learning goal requires the introduction of a new concept or relationship, students discover the concept or relationship for themselves. Achievement of conceptualization objectives normally requires students to be engaged in inductive learning activities in which they work toward such discoveries. These types of activities have the added benefit of developing in students a feeling of ownership in the content. Mr. Santiago's students are more likely to appreciate relationships about speed and acceleration because he led them to discover the relationships for themselves in the lesson described in Vignette 1.2.

Note how learning activities for an appreciation-level objective are integrated with those for cognitive objectives in Vignette 3.3:

VIGNETTE 3.3

Ms. Borg realizes that if her history students appreciate the value of understanding certain events in the history of the U.S. Congress, they will be more receptive to achieving the cognitive objectives of her unit on congressional activities between 1901 and 1935. Thus, her initial objective for the unit is for students to:

Recognize the advantage of being able to relate congressional activities during the first 35 years of the twentieth century to today's current issues (*Affective: appreciation*)

VIGNETTE 3.3 (continued)

In deciding how to achieve that objective, she makes a number of observations of her students to identify current issues that concern them. She decides to focus on the following problems:

Should marijuana be legalized?
What should the federal government do about unemployment?
What should Congress do to ensure the rights of ethnic minorities?
Does the United States need an Equal Rights Amendment?
What should the federal government do about the abortion issue?
What should Congress do to combat pollution?

Ms. Borg builds the lessons of the unit around these six current problems. One sequence of learning activities is as follows:

1. Ms. Borg assigns each class member to one of six task groups (according to her perceptions of individual student interests and who tend to work co-operatively with whom). One group, consisting of six students, is directed to "research" the first problem concerning the legalization of marijuana. These students are to examine how Congress handled the prohibition of al-cohol in the first 30 years of the twentieth century and then relate those "lessons of history" to the current question about marijuana. Specifically, the group is directed to explain Congress's rationale for repealing prohibition, including the benefits and consequences of the repeal, and to identify both similarities and differences between the alcohol prohibition issue in the earlier era and the marijuana issue today. Each of the other five task groups re-searches one of the other five problems in a similar fashion.
2. Ms. Borg provides each task group with an organizational structure within which to operate, a list of resources from which to acquire information, a list of deadlines for specific subtasks, and directions for reporting findings to the rest of the class.
3. To obtain an overall picture of the climate within which the Congress op-erated from 1901 to 1935, and thus to better compare the problems of that time with those of the present, each student is directed to read a textbook chapter about the 1901–1935 period.
4. Each task group receives a schedule for making periodic progress reports.
5. After each task group presents its final report, class members who were not part of the reporting group debate and vote on the task group's proposals about dealing with the current problem.

Cooperation in the Classroom: Students and Teachers Together, Second Edition, pp. 22–24, by James S. Cangelosi, copyright 1990, National Education Association. Reprinted with per-mission.

Which of the two attempts, Mr. Mena's or Ms. Borg's, is more likely to achieve the appreciation-level objective? Mr. Mena attempted to get his students to recognize the value of content by telling them about its value. But telling is not teaching. Ms. Borg's plan focused her students' attention on problems that are very real to them and they are interested in solving. Her lessons did not divorce history from students' current concerns.

Ms. Borg was concerned with the appreciation objective as well as her cognitive objectives, consequently she carefully chose initial examples that hold students' attention. Once she had them working on a problem, the content to be taught (i.e., congressional activities between 1901 and 1935) appeared as a useful problem-solving tool.

Willingness to Try

Even though students have learned to appreciate certain content, they still may not attempt to work vigorously with it because they lack confidence that they will successfully use it in situations they find meaningful. Until they have accumulated experiences successfully using content, they tend to be reluctant to pursue problem solutions in the manner Ms. Borg plans in Vignette 3.3.

Willingness-to-try objectives, such as the following one, require learning activities similar to appreciation objectives:

> Attempt to use their reading skills to locate information about issues of personal concern (*Affective: willingness to try*)

But to take students from appreciation to willingness to try, you must select problems or tasks for them that are interesting enough to maintain their attention, but easy enough for them to experience success. Keep the following in mind:

> *Until students gain confidence in their abilities and in the benefits of working on perplexing tasks, most of the tasks you assign them should be such that they will feel successful before becoming frustrated.* As their confidence builds, you gradually work in more perplexing and challenging work.
>
> *The more a task relates to what already interests students, the more students tend to tolerate perplexity and frustrations before giving up.* It is quite a challenge for you to have to judge that fine line between interest and frustration.
>
> *Achievement of willingness-to-try objectives requires a learning environment in which students feel free to experiment, question, hypothesize, and make errors without fear of ridicule, embarrassment, or loss of status.* Chapter 4 contains ideas to help you create such an environment in your classroom.
>
> *By presenting students with problems requiring applications of previously acquired skills and abilities (e.g., from prior units), students not only maintain and improve on earlier achievements, you also provide additional opportunities for them to succeed with content.* As explained in a subsequent section of this chapter, achievement of application-level objectives requires that students be confronted with both problems to which the content of the objective applies as well as problems to which content from previously achieved objectives is applicable. These application-level learning activities provide students with experiences with success because they include opportunities for them to apply previously learned content.

LESSONS FOR CONCEPTUALIZATION OBJECTIVES

Challenging but Critical to Teach

Designing lessons for conceptualization objectives will tax your understanding of your students, pedagogical principles, and the content specified by your objectives. Coming up with the choice examples, problems, and leading questions necessary to stimulate students to abstract concepts and discover relationships is challenging to say the least. However, once students have conceptualized a concept or relationship, it becomes much easier to teach them related content at other levels (e.g., knowledge of a process or application). For example, regarding the following three objectives, students who have achieved Objective A are more likely to achieve, and retain, Objectives B and C than are students who have not achieved Objective A:

    A. Explain why heating one area of the human body tends to increase circulation to that body part whereas cooling that area tends to decrease circulation to that part (*Cognitive: conceptualization*)

    B. State the following rule relative to treatment of sprains in human joints: Cold packs should be applied to the sprained area during the first 48 hours following the trauma; heat should be applied after the initial 48 hours (*Cognitive: simple knowledge*)

    C. Based on a description of how a joint was traumatized and the observable symptoms, prescribe an appropriate course of action for treating the injury (*Cognitive: application*)

The failure of many students to develop healthy attitudes, skills, comprehension-level abilities, and application-level abilities in various content areas are well publicized (e.g., Dossey, Mullis, Lindquist, & Chambers, 1988; "U. S. Teens Lag," 1989). Many of these failures can be traced to conceptual gaps in their learning (Ball, 1988; Becker, 1986, pp. 171–219; Bourne, Dominowski, Loftus, & Healy, 1986, pp. 125–195, 235–311; Garner, 1990; Shuell, 1990). Such gaps are hardly surprising in light of the fact that many teachers never even consider conducting conceptualization-level lessons (Jesunathadas, 1990; National Council of Teachers of Mathematics, 1991).

Inductive Reasoning

In order to conceptualize students must *reason inductively* (Bourne, Dominowski, Loftus, & Healy, 1986, p. 17). *Inductive reasoning is* generalizing from encounters with specifics. It is the cognitive process by which people discover commonalties among specific examples and the process that leads them to formulate abstract categories and generalizations. Students use inductive reasoning in the following examples:

VIGNETTE 3.4

Over the past month, Terri has encountered variables in her psychology, chemistry, and mathematics courses. During that time, she has noticed differences and similarities among those variables. Although she never made a conscious effort to do so, she has begun to create a dichotomy between two types. The first type includes variables such as *aptitudes people have for learning, temperature fluctuations,* and *all real numbers between two specific real numbers* (e.g., -2 and 14.2448). The second type includes variables such as *different types of emotional disorders, atomic numbers of chemical elements,* and *all the whole numbers between two specific whole numbers* (e.g., 4 and 117).

Terri thinks of the first type as more difficult to deal with because, as she says, "It's too packed in to list two things that are next to one another." Terri has apparently begun to form the concept of *continuous data* and the concept of *discrete data.* She does not, however, know the concepts by those names.

VIGNETTE 3.5

After completing a homework assignment in which she used a protractor to measure the angles of six triangles her teacher drew on a worksheet, Desiree looks at the resulting six triples: (90°, 45°, 45°), (75°, 62°, 41°), (30°, 60°, 90°), (142°, 15°, 23°), (60°, 60°, 60°), and (33°, 30°, 120°).

She thinks: "Anytime there's a big angle, the other two are small." She then attempts to draw a triangle with two "big" angles and finds it is impossible. Curious about the phenomenon, she measures the angles of 11 different triangles determined by concrete objects in her surroundings (e.g., two edges of a container). She then thinks: "The sum of the degrees of the angles of *any* triangle is about 180."

VIGNETTE 3.6

Several years ago, when his father took him to a hospital emergency room to have a cut treated, Eric noted that the man who stitched the cut was referred to as "Doctor" and the woman who also tended to his wound was called "Nurse." From various office visits, he remembers female nurses giving him shots and taking his temperature whereas men called "doctors" visited with him for shorter periods of time. Now that he's in kindergarten, he hears his teacher say, "Sometimes when we get sick, we need a doctor to help us get well. *He* needs a nurse to help *him*; *she*'ll be the one to . . ." Eric thinks to himself, "A man who works with sick and hurt people is a doctor. A woman who does that is a nurse."

In Vignette 3.4, Terri organized specific variables into two categories, thus abstracting two concepts. Desiree formulated a hypothesis from her experiences with specific triangles, thus abstracting a relationship. As illustrated by Eric, sometimes inductive reasoning can lead to a generalization that can be disproven with a counterexample (e.g., an encounter with a male nurse or female physician). But, disproving the conclusion does not discredit the reasoning.

Facilitating Conceptualization-Level Learning

An *inductive learning activity* is one that *stimulates students to reason inductively*. Such activities are used with a seven-stage lesson for conceptualization-level learning:

1. *Task confrontation*. If the objective's content is a concept, then students are presented with a task requiring them to sort and categorize specifics. For a relationship, the task is to solve problems.
2. *Task work*. The students work through the task. The teacher orchestrates the activity, managing the environment and providing guidance, but allowing students to complete the task themselves.
3. *Reflection on work*. For a concept, students explain their rationales for categorizing the specifics as they did. For a relationship, students analyze the process by which problems were addressed or solved. The teacher raises leading questions, stimulates thought, and clarifies students' expressions.
4. *Generalization*. For a concept, concept-attributes (i.e., what sets examples of the concept apart from the nonexamples) are pointed out and the concept identified. For a relationship, a common pattern utilized in problem solutions is identified and a relationship hypothesized.
5. *Articulation*. The concept is defined or the statement of the relationship is agreed on.
6. *Verification*. For a concept, the definition is tested with examples (which should fit) and nonexamples (which should not fit). For a relationship, attempts are made to produce a counterexample for the statement. Further verification is pursued depending on the teacher's judgment of the situation. The level of verification can vary from (a) a "seems to work—intuitively clear" approach, to (b) a failure to produce counterexamples approach, to (c) the type of formal proof that's conventional in mathematics and science.
7. *Refinement*. The definition of the concept or the statement of the relationship is modified in light of the outcome of the verification stage. Prior stages are reengaged as judged necessary by the teacher.

Conceptualizing Concepts

Concept Attributes and Psychological Noise. One aspect of designing lessons for conceptualization objectives that teachers find particularly difficult is formulating appropriate examples and nonexamples for students to categorize (Cangelosi, 1988b). As you determine sets of examples and nonexamples to present to students, attention to two ideas is critical:

1. *Concept attributes*. All examples of a particular concept share a common set of attributes. The attributes define the concept. A *felony*, for example, is any grave criminal offense usually punishable in the United States by

at least one year in prison. Thus, the attributes of the concept *felony* are (a) crime, (b) considered serious under the law (as opposed to a misdemeanor), (c) illegal, and (d) possibly punishable by a year or more in prison. Any specific that does not meet these four requirements is not an example of a felony (e.g., Susan drives an automobile without a current license; John steals a piece of gum from a grocery store; or Frank watches a soccer game on television). Similarly, any specific with all four defining attributes is a felony (e.g., Blaine sells a large quantity of cocaine to Vanessa or Inez embezzles $3,600 from the bank where she's employed).

2. *Psychological noise.* A characteristic of an example of a concept that is *not* an attribute of the concept is *psychological noise*. For instance, Inez's embezzlement of $3,600 from the bank where she's employed is an example of the concept *felony*. But besides the attributes of a felony, that act had other characteristics (e.g., *$3,600* was stolen, an *employer* was victimized by an *employee*, the perpetrator is a *woman*, and it is a *federal* offense) that distinguish it from other felonies. Those *other* features of this particular example are *psychological noise* with respect to the concept of felony. Psychological noise is any feature of an example of a concept that distinguishes the example from other examples of the same concept.

As you select examples and nonexamples for your concept-attainment lessons, you will need to be aware of the role played by psychological noise so that noise facilitates rather than hinders learning. Vignette 3.7 gives a simple illustration.

Note how Mr. Edwards manipulated examples to control for psychological noise. Had Stacy immediately categorized by number on seeing Figure 3.1, Mr. Edwards would have moved to a noisier situation (e.g., Figure 3.3) where the noise varies more among the examples. But because she experienced difficulty with Figure 3.1, he reduced the noise by moving to Figure 3.2. In any case, Stacy eventually needs to recognize similarities and differences in number even in high noise situations because the real world is quite noisy.

In general, how well students conceptualize a concept is dependent on the how well they learn to distinguish between psychological noise and concept attributes when classifying examples. Distinguishing between examples and nonexamples in high noise situations is indicative of a higher conceptual achievement level than when the distinction is made in low noise situations.

Incorporating the Seven Stages into a Concept Lesson. In Vignette 3.8 (pp. 80–88), note how the teacher plans and orchestrates each of the seven stages and utilizes both concept attributes and psychological noise.

Conceptualizing Relationships

As for conceptualizing concepts, lessons for conceptualizing relationships require inductive activities involving the seven stages on page 77. After conducting a brief simple knowledge lesson so students remember the definitions for *opinion* and *fact* they formulated in Vignette 3.8, Mr. Landastoy leads students to conceptualize a relationship in Vignette 3.9 (pp. 89–90).

VIGNETTE 3.7

Mr. Edwards is using inductive questioning strategies with individual kindergarten students to help them conceptualize *number*.

He displays Figure 3.1 to Stacy and asks her, "Which two groups are alike?" Stacy, pointing to sets A and B, replies, "These." Mr. Edwards: "Why?" Stacy: "Because they're not round like the other." Mr. Edwards: "Thank you. Now, can you see a way that this group of round things is like one of the other groups?" Stacy: "No, it's different."

Mr. Edwards shows Stacy Figure 3.2. Which of these two groups are alike?" Stacy points to A and C and says, "Because they have the same amount." Mr. Edwards: "Thank you. Now, let's go back and look at this one again. Mr. Edwards displays Figure 3.1 again and the activity continues.

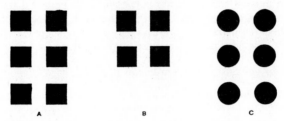

Figure 3.1. Which Two Groups Are Alike?

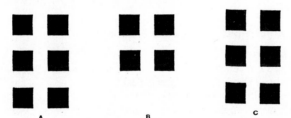

Figure 3.2. Examples Used by Mr. Edwards with Less Variability of Psychological Noise than Figure 3.1

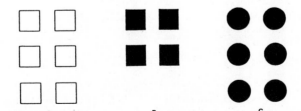

Figure 3.3. Examples with Greater Variability of Psychological Noise than Figure 3.1

Adapted with permission from *Teaching Mathematics in Secondary and Middle School: Research-based Approaches* (p. 84), by J. S. Cangelosi (1992), New York: Macmillan. Copyright © 1992 by Macmillan Publishing Company.

VIGNETTE 3.8

As Mr. Landastoy designs the initial lesson for a unit on critical reading he plans to conduct for his seventh-grade language arts class, he thinks, ''This first objective is the key to the whole unit. All others depend on it. It says:

> Distinguish between examples of *opinions* and *facts* expressed in an essay and explain the defining attributes of each concept (*Cognitive: conceptualization*)

''So the learning level is *conceptualization* and the content consists of the concepts *opinion* and *fact*. That means inductive learning activities beginning with task confrontation sorting through examples and nonexamples of each. The first thing I've got to do is come up with just the right examples of opinions and of facts for them to ponder. The facts can serve as nonexamples for the opinions and vice versa— better also toss in some items that are nonexamples of both. I'll start with a list of opinions and then match each with a fact that's similar regarding psychological noise. I don't want them to abstract the noise as part of the concept. . . .''

With further thought, he develops the following three lists:

Examples of opinions and nonexamples of facts:

1. Birds are beautiful.
2. Birds are meticulously clean animals.
3. People should not kill birds.
4. Chicken tastes good.
5. Birds of prey help farmers.

Examples of facts and nonexamples of opinions:

1. Some birds have brightly colored feathers.
2. *Compton's Encyclopedia* (1987, Vol. 3, p. 242) states, ''Birds keep their beautiful plumage spotlessly clean and neat.''
3. Ducks are killed by hunters.
4. Chicken meat is sold in grocery stores.
5. Many birds of prey eat mice.

Nonexamples of both opinions and facts:

1. Birds with feathers
2. Care of the feathers
3. Shotguns, duck blinds, duck calls, decoys, and camouflage clothes
4. Fried chicken
5. Vultures, eagles, hawks, and owls

He thinks, ''The common psychological noise of *birds* will make the defining attributes of the two concepts easier to pick out when they sort through the list. On the other hand, I'd better include some not relating to birds or else there's the danger that they'll limit their concepts of opinions and facts to 'bird-content' only. . . . But then, I want them to be able to apply their conceptualization to reading essays, and essays typically are focused on a single topic, like birds or whatever. . . . I'll limit this initial list to birds, and then make sure subsequent lists used in the lessons include much different topics like music, friendships, exercise, current events—stuff like that.'' Using his computer word-processing program, Mr. Landastoy mixes the 15 items, obtaining the list shown in Figure 3.4.

VIGNETTE 3.8 (continued)

Directions: Separate this list of 15 items into two lists of 10 and 5 items. In other words, what 5 items are like each other, but different from the other 10? Display your answer by filling the blanks with letters on the form at the bottom.

A. Birds are beautiful.
B. Ducks are killed by hunters.
C. Birds with feathers
D. Birds are meticulously clean animals.
E. *Compton's Encyclopedia* (1987, Vol. 3, p. 242) states: "Birds keep their beautiful plumage spotlessly clean and neat."
F. Fried chicken
G. Many birds of prey eat mice.
H. Care of the feathers
 I. Chicken tastes good.
J. Birds of prey help farmers.
K. Vultures, eagles, hawks, and owls
L. Chicken meat is sold in grocery stores.
M. Shotguns, duck blinds, duck calls, decoys, and camouflage clothes
N. Some birds have brightly colored feathers.
O. People should not kill birds.

Group of 5:	Group of 10:
___ ___ ___ ___ ___	___ ___ ___ ___ ___ ___ ___ ___ ___ ___

Figure 3.4. The Initial Tasksheet Mr. Landastoy Uses in a Conceptualization Lesson

He thinks, "I'll distribute copies of this list in a large-group session and direct them to organize the 15 items into three sets of 5 each—telling them to group those that are alike. . . . With some guidance during a questioning sessions, they should have an easy time separating the 5 nonstatements from the other 10, but I'm afraid that sorting out the opinions from the facts will take a long time. There's bound to be umpteen different ways they can dichotomize besides fact from opinion. That'll get us into a lot of other concepts I really don't want to have to deal with! . . . I know! I'll direct them to form two groups from the original 15—cne group of 10, the other 5. They should handle that pretty quickly and then we can make the clear distinction that this lesson deals with *kinds of statements*, not just anything—that's good—it'll help define the universe with which we'll be working! . . . Okay, so after they've teased out the 10 statements from the list, I'll hit them with the second tasksheet—then use that one in a second large-group questioning session."

He prepares the tasksheet shown in Figure 3.5 and designs the rest of the learning activities for the lesson.

Figure 3.5. The Second Tasksheet Mr. Landastoy Uses in a Conceptualization Lesson

Directions: Examine the 10 statements. How are those in Column I like each other but different from those in Column II? How are those in Column II alike but different from those in Column I? Write your answer in the first box after the two columns. Wait for directions from Mr. Landastoy before writing in the second or third boxes.

(continued)

VIGNETTE 3.8 (continued)

Column I	*Column II*
Birds are beautiful.	Some birds have brightly colored feathers.
Birds are meticulously clean animals.	*Compton's Encyclopedia* states: "Birds keep their beautiful plumage spotlessly clean and neat."
People should not kill birds.	Ducks are killed by hunters.
Chicken tastes good.	Chicken meat is sold in grocery stores.
Birds of prey help farmers.	Many birds of prey eat mice.

Box for 1st conjecture:

```

```

Box for 2nd conjecture:

```

```

Box for 3rd conjecture:

```

```

Figure 3.5. (Continued)

On the first day of the unit, Mr. Landastoy gives the students seven minutes to silently follow the directions for the initial tasksheet. As they work, he circulates about the room unobtrusively noting how different students fill in the blanks. Figure 3.6 displays a sample of their responses.

After seeing that each of the 28 students has at least something written in the blanks, he engages the class in a questioning/discussion session. From their previous experiences in such sessions under Mr. Landastoy's supervision, the students have learned that whenever he calls on someone and says "keep it going," the following procedures are in effect until Mr. Landastoy interrupts with "excuse me":

One student at a time has the floor. Anyone wanting to speak raises a hand to request the floor from the student who is speaking.

VIGNETTE 3.8 (continued)

Walter

Group of 5:	Group of 10:
C H N A E̶ (E)	B D G̶(I) F G J K L M O

Aalafua

Group of 5:	Group of 10:
C G̶(F) H M K	A B D E G I J L N O

Julie

Group of 5:	Group of 10:
C F H K M	A B D E G I J L N O

Lavar

Group of 5:	Group of 10:
S I J L a	O N M K B C D E F H

Carol

Group of 5:	Group of 10:
O M L B I	__ The rest of them __ __ __

Figure 3.6. Sample Student Responses to Figure 3.4's Tasksheet

MR. LANDASTOY: I'll use the overhead projector to display the letters for your group of 5 as you read them to the class, Walter.

WALTER: C, H, N, A, E.

MR. LANDASTOY: What do you think Walter had in mind when he lumped these 5 together, Habebee? Keep it going.

HABEBEE: C, H, and N have to do with feathers; A and E don't. Okay, Pete.

PETE: E is about feathers. Isn't that what 'plumage' or whatever is? Walter.

WALTER: A is feathers too, 'cause birds are beautiful because they have feathers.

MR. LANDASTOY: Excuse me. Anyone else who lumped these same 5 together raise your hand. . . . I see Lawanda and Karen did also. . . . Read yours while I write them down, Lavar.

LAVAR: G, I, J, L, A.

MR. LANDASTOY: You have the floor, Samone; keep it going.

(continued)

VIGNETTE 3.8 (continued)

SAMONE: Lavar's are just like mine, except I had O instead of A because I was thinking of all the good things birds do for us, so we should never kill them. Lavar.

LAVAR: But 'People should not kill birds' is not something birds do for people—being beautiful is.

MR. LANDASTOY: Excuse me. Let's hear Julie's big 5.

JULIE: C, F, H, K, M.

MR. LANDASTOY: Raise your hand if you have the same 5 as Julie. . . . Nine of you picked those 5! Wow! What's so special about those 5, Aalafua? Keep it going.

AALAFUA: Those are the only 5 without periods at the end; they're—

SAMONE: Oh, yeah—I didn't see tha—

AALAFUA: Hey, I still have the floor. The other 10 are sentences; these 5 aren't. Karen.

KAREN: But we were supposed to look at what each one *said*, not whether or not they're sentences.

MR. LANDASTOY: Excuse me. Read A for me, Karen.

KAREN: Birds are beautiful.

MR. LANDASTOY: What did that *tell* us about birds, Samone?

SAMONE: That they're beautiful.

MR. LANDASTOY: Read B, Karen.

KAREN: Ducks are killed by hunters.

MR. LANDASTOY: What did that tell us about ducks, Lawanda?

LAWANDA: Hunters kill them.

MR. LANDASTOY: Read C, Karen.

KAREN: Birds with feathers.

MR. LANDASTOY: What does that one tell us about birds, Mark?

MARK: Birds with feathers.

MR. LANDASTOY: What about birds with feathers, Mark?

MARK: Birds have feathers.

MR. LANDASTOY: Does it actually say birds have feathers? Mark, keep it going.

MARK: It says "birds *with* feathers," so that's what it means. Julie.

JULIE: C, F, H, K, M only list things or they don't really tell us anything about anything. "Birds with feathers can fly" that would say something! But just "birds with feathers" that's not a complete sentence! Okay, Erin.

ERIN: Ostriches have feathers and they don't fly!

JULIE: That's not the—

MR. LANDASTOY: Excuse me. I'm thinking of a word that starts with an *S*. And it's not "sentence," but Julie reminded me of it when she said "complete sentence." What word do you think I have in mind? . . . Shen.

SHEN: Is it "statement"?

MR. LANDASTOY: A, B, D, E, G, I, J, L, N, and O are *statements*. The other 5 are not. I've taken those 10 *statements* and organized them into two groups on this tasksheet that I'm distributing right now. . . . You have seven minutes from right now to follow the directions in this sheet.

VIGNETTE 3.8 (continued)

The class works on Figure 3.5's tasksheet as Mr. Landastoy walks about the room reading what various students write and cuing them to remain on task. Figure 3.7 (p. 86) provides a sample of the responses he noted.

Mr. Landastoy begins the questioning session by asking Robert to read his response.

ROBERT: Mine's not right because the second one in column II ought to be in column I.

MR. LANDASTOY: Why?

ROBERT: Well at first, I thought the ones on the left were sort of what people thought, but the ones on the right have the one about birds keeping their plum-things-or-whatever spotlessly clean, and all that and that's what people think too. You can't prove that.

MR. LANDASTOY: Robert's made a point I want us to come back to in just a few minutes after we've heard from a few more. Just read yours in order without discussion yet, Dalphia, Aaron, and Aalafua. . . . Go, Dalphia!

DALPHIA: Do I have to:? . . . Okay, I put—I don't know if this is right—I put, 'Both columns have statements. The first ones are what different people believe. The other ones are sort of what we know.' That's not it, is it?

AARON: . . . Most of the ones on the left are shorter than the ones on the right.

AALAFUA: The statements in the second list are things that are true and there's more detail. The statements in the first list are not certain and they're like opinions or judgments.

MR. LANDASTOY: Both Dalphia and Aalafua called the items on both lists something. What did they both call them? . . . Samone.

SAMONE: Statements.

MR. LANDASTOY: So we're comparing two groups of statements. . . . And what was it that Aaron said was different about the two groups, Rick?

RICK: I didn't hear him.

MR. LANDASTOY: Ask someone who did and then keep it going.

RICK: Uhh, Walter.

WALTER: He said the ones on the right were longer, but they aren't all longer. What I had was that the ones in column I are maybe true, but the ones in column II are always true except the second one.

MR. LANDASTOY: Excuse me. That brings us back to Robert's conjecture. He also said the second one in column II is not a fact. . . . Okay, Shen, keep it going.

SHEN: You've got to read the whole statement. It doesn't just say birds keep their beautiful plum-things clean and so forth; it says *Compton's Encyclopedia* says that. It may not be a *fact* that birds do that, but it is a fact that the encyclopedia said that. So that one belongs in column II, not column I! . . . Karen.

KAREN: That's pretty picky. What's the difference? Aalafua.

AALAFUA: It's picky, but still true. You could check every one of the statements on the right and prove them to be right or wrong. But the ones on the left are just what people think, not know right or wrong for sure!

(continued)

VIGNETTE 3.8 (continued)

<u>Lawanda</u>

Box for 1st conjecture:

> There's more detail in Column II. Column I's more general — like birds are beautiful. Column II says how they are beautiful.

<u>Chen</u>

Box for 1st conjecture:

> Column II's statements are definite. Things we know are true. Col. I's statements may vary or may not always be true.

<u>Robert</u>

Box for 1st conjecture:

> column I has what people ~~just good~~ think. Column II has more like facts except for the 2nd one. That's a judgment and should be in Column I.

<u>Walter</u>

Box for 1st conjecture:

> Some of the ones in column I are true some of the time, like chicken tastes good. Chicken taste good to some people not for other people. The ones in Col. II are always true except that birds keep their plumage spotlessly clean. ~~Some don't like my parakeet.~~

<u>Aaalafua</u>

Box for 1st conjecture:

> THE STATEMENT IN THE 2ND LIST ARE THINGS THAT ARE TRUE ~~THEY DON'T ALWAYS~~ THERE'S MORE DETAIL OR TO THE POINT ARE NOT. CERTAIN   THE STATEMENTS IN THE 1ST LIST ~~MAKE A NOT SURE~~ AND THEIR LIKE OPINIONS ARE JUDGEMENTS

Figure 3.7. Sample Student Responses to Figure 3.5's Tasksheet

VIGNETTE 3.8 (continued)

MR. LANDASTOY: Excuse me. I want Lawanda to read hers.

LAWANDA: There's more detail in column II. Column I's more general—like birds are beautiful. Column II says how they're beautiful.

ERIN: Aw, that's—

MR. LANDASTOY: Pardon me, I have the floor. . . . Lawanda, like Aaron and some of the others that I read—you were one, Lenora—referred to the details of column II—column II sort of explaining why some people might believe some of the statements in column I. . . . Keep that thought in mind; you'll need it for the lesson we'll have tomorrow. . . . What's the thought to keep in mind for tomorrow, Rick?

RICK: That the stuff in column II is more like details that—I don't know—tell people something about column I—something like that.

MR. LANDASTOY: Thank you. . . . Now, everyone take three minutes to write in another conjecture. This time, formulate a conjecture that's in agreement with Shen's and Aalafua's. Of course there's no one right answer to this. But what they said is what I had in mind when I first devised this exercise. So make this conjecture your guess as to what I have in mind when I made up these two groups. . . . Go!

Two minutes later:

MR. LANDASTOY: Read yours in order: Walter, Nancy, and Erin.

WALTER: Column I has what some people believe is true. Column II has things that are definitely true.

NANCY: The first ones are only opinions; the second ones are things for sure.

ERIN: It's the same as theirs. . . . Okay, the first column has beliefs, judgments, what people say—that sort of stuff. The second one has things you read in books—stuff that's not just what people say.

MR. LANDASTOY: How about a label for the kinds of statements on the left and another for the kinds of statements on the right? . . . Nancy.

NANCY: Opinions and facts.

MR. LANDASTOY: Everyone, write the word *opinion* at the bottom of your task-sheet. Now, define it in your own words. You've got one and a half minutes. . . . Write it. . . . No, Shen, there's no time to use the dictionary—at least not yet. Use your own words. . . . Okay, now do the same, except this time the words is *fact*. Define *fact*. You've got only one minute for this one.

Mr. Landastoy then leads a discussion in which several students share their definitions and the class agrees on the following: "An *opinion* is a statement of someone's judgment or belief and no one knows whether or not it's really true." "A *fact* is a statement that everybody knows is true."

Figure 3.8's tasksheet is assigned for homework. The following day, a sharing of homework responses stimulates a discussion over the issue of whether or not an opinion can also be a fact. The class agrees that if an opinion is shown to be true it becomes a fact, but many opinions can never become facts—either because they are false or because they are a matter of individual taste. In light of this discussion, Mr. Landastoy guides the class to refine their previous definitions so they read as

(continued)

VIGNETTE 3.8 (continued)

Directions: Analyze the items in the following list. Put an "F" by each that is a *statement of fact*, an "O" by each that's an opinion, and an "X" by each that is neither.

A. _____ The United States is a great country.

B. _____ The 50 states of the United States.

C. _____ The United States is in North America.

D. _____ Jackie Robinson is in Baseball's Hall of Fame.

E. _____ Jackie Robinson should be in Baseball's Hall of Fame.

F. _____ Jackie Robinson is not in Baseball's Hall of Fame.

G. _____ Jackie Robinson should not be in Baseball's Hall of Fame.

H. _____ Baseball's Hall of Fame, Cooperstown, NY

I. _____ If the sum of two numbers is 17 and one of the two numbers is 8, the other number is 9.

J. _____ $8 + 9 = 17$.

K. _____ $9 + 8 = 37$.

L. _____ $(2 + 4) \div (23 - 17 + 11)$

M. _____ Mr. Landastoy is my teacher.

N. _____ I enjoy doing this tasksheet.

O. _____ I'm working on this tasksheet right now.

P. _____ Doing this tasksheet is a good learning experience for everyone in the class.

Q. _____ Mr. Landastoy told me that he's happy I'm in his class.

R. _____ According to page 24 of my English textbook, "Writing poems helps us say what's in our hearts."

Figure 3.8. The Third Tasksheet Mr. Landastoy Uses in a Conceptualization Lesson

follows: "An *opinion* is a statement that someone judges or believes to be true." "A *fact* is a statement that can be proven to be true."

The lesson did not proceed exactly the way Mr. Landastoy had anticipated. However, he is quite pleased with the outcomes. He was surprised that the students struggled as much as they did with the first tasksheet. He had expected them to quickly notice the five items without periods at the end. On the other hand, they identified the difference between statements of opinion and statements of fact more readily than he had anticipated. The activity with the second tasksheet went smoother than expected. He's especially pleased that the reflection session based on the second tasksheet provided a perfect lead into a subsequent conceptualization lesson he plans for the unit. He decides to play upon Lawanda's first conjecture on the second tasksheet (see Figure 3.7) during an upcoming conceptualization lesson on the relationship between opinions expressed by authors and the facts they use to support those opinions.

VIGNETTE 3.9

Mr. Landastoy designs a lesson for the following objective:

Explain why readers are more likely to agree with authors' opinions if those authors present a factual basis for the opinions (*Cognitive: conceptualization*)

To begin the *task confrontation* stage, he assigns Figure 3.9's tasksheet as homework for 14 of the 28 students and Figure 3.10's tasksheet for the rest of the class.

Directions: Read the following essay and circle each statement of opinion expressed by the author:

The Right Person for the Job
by Mary Smith

In less than a week, the voters of this county will elect a new sheriff. There should be no doubt that George Baxter is the right person for the job, not Dexter Thomas. Mr. Baxter is fair-minded, but firm. He has the experience and expertise to manage the high office of sheriff efficiently and in the best interest of all our citizens.

Mr. Thomas is an honest, hard-working individual, but he does not have the administrative skills to run the sheriff's office the way George Baxter will. Furthermore, Mr. Baxter has a far better background in police work. The streets of this county will be secure with George Baxter in office. The voters need to ask themselves, "Will we sleep better at night knowing our sheriff is an experienced law enforcement officer like George Baxter or if the office is in the hands of a pure politician like Dexter Thomas?"

The future well-being and security of this county is in the hands of its voters. Frankly, we can't do any better than George Baxter. Be smart, taxpayers, vote for the right person for the job—George Baxter for sheriff.

Figure 3.9. The "Smith"-Essay Tasksheet Mr. Landastoy Assigned for Homework

Directions: Read the following essay and circle each statement of opinion expressed by the author:

THE RIGHT PERSON FOR THE JOB
by Susan Jones

In less than a week, the voters of this county will elect a new sheriff. George Baxter is the right person for the job, not Dexter Thomas. Mr. Baxter demonstrated that he is a fair-minded, but firm law officer. During his 12-year administration as associate superintendent of the city police force, the number of felony arrests resulting in convictions increased by 30 percent while the number of arrest-releases due to improper police procedures dropped by 60 percent! In 1992, the Multiethnic Civil Rights Action Group cited his achievements with their "Outstanding Public Service Award."

Mr. Thomas, though an honest, hard-working individual, hasn't been involved in police work since he was a deputy sheriff back in 1985. Since that time, Mr. Thomas has managed his family dry cleaning establishment and served two terms on the county school board. Compared to George Baxter, Mr. Thomas falls short on both police experience and the administrative experience and expertise to manage the high office of sheriff in the best interest of all our citizens. Mr. Baxter holds a university degree in business administration and law enforcement.

George Baxter is the right person for the job!

Figure 3.10. The "Jones"-Essay Tasksheet Mr. Landastoy Assigned for Homework

(continued)

VIGNETTE 3.9 (continued)

He actually wrote the two essays himself so that both would express the same opinions about a hypothetical situation with which students would not have prior knowledge. "Jones's" essay provides factual bases for the opinions expressed; "Smith's" doesn't provide any facts.

The next day in class, those that read Smith's essay are split into two cooperative task groups of 7 students each. Similarly, the 14 who read Jones's essay are split. Mr. Landastoy assigns specific responsibilities to members of each group (e.g., one student chairs the group, another keeps the group on task, and another serves as scribe) and then directs each group as follows: (a) Debate the opinions expressed in the essay, (b) agree to a group position regarding each of the author's opinions, and (c) prepare for the rest of the class a five-minute oral report on the group's position.

Thirty-five minutes later the four reports have been presented and Mr. Landastoy conducts a questioning/discussion session in which the students reflect back on the group's work. The session culminates with the following point emerging from the class:

> Jones managed to convince readers of her opinions much more successfully than Smith because Jones provided facts to support her opinions whereas Smith did not provide any facts.

For homework, the students compare several more essays. The next day, Mr. Landastoy uses leading questions to get them to express the general relationship specified in the lesson's objective. However, their final, refined statement of the relationship is worded differently from the wording in Mr. Landastoy's objective—but the two are equivalent.

LESSONS FOR SIMPLE-KNOWLEDGE OBJECTIVES

Facilitating Reception and Retention through Direct Instruction

Students achieve conceptualization objectives by making decisions about information (e.g., classifying it or identifying patterns in procedures for acquiring information). On the other hand, students achieve simple knowledge objectives by accurately *receiving* and *retaining* information. Reception and retention is accomplished through a five-stage *direct instruction* process:

1. *Exposition.* Students are exposed to the content they are to remember. For example:

VIGNETTE 3.10

Mr. Santiago's sixth-graders have already conceptualized *speed* and *acceleration*. Now he wants them to recall the definition whenever they hear or see the words. Thus, he devises a lesson for the following objective:

State definitions for *speed* and *acceleration* (*simple knowledge*)

VIGNETTE 3.10 (continued)

As part of a homework assignment, he directs students to copy the definitions from the textbook and into the glossary they maintain in their notebooks. The next day, he displays the definitions on the overhead screen, reads them, and asks the students to check the accuracy of the copies of their glossaries.

---

2. *Explication*. The students are provided with an explanation as to just how they are to respond to the content's stimulus. For example, Mr. Santiago tells his students, "Anytime you see or hear the word *speed*, you are to think, 'the distance an object moves in a certain period of time.' And for *acceleration*, think 'any change in an object's speed or direction.'"

3. *Mnemonics. Mnemonics* is a word derived from *Mnemosyne*, the name of the ancient Greek goddess of memory. The word means *aiding the memory* (Bourne, Dominowski, Loftus, & Healy, 1986, p. 98). For some, but not all, simple knowledge objectives, you might consider providing students with mnemonic devices to enhance retention. Mnemonic devices have proven to be effective in helping students remember *new* information (Joyce & Weil, 1986, pp. 89–96). I, for example, informed you about the derivation of mnemonics as an aid to helping you remember the definition. Thus, that was a mnemonic aid. However, unless you were already familiar with the goddess Mnemosyne, my mnemonic device is not likely to be very effective. The most effective mnemonic devices link the new information to be remembered to something already familiar to the student. For example:

> To help students remember that "whole numbers" refers to {0, 1, 2, . . .}, whereas "counting numbers" refers to {1, 2, 3, . . .}, a teacher says, "The set of whole numbers is the one with the '*hole*' in it. The hole is the zero."

Usually, it isn't necessary to use mnemonics for remembering relationships that students already conceptualize. Mnemonic devices are more helpful for recalling conventions that are not logically connected to content students have already conceptualized.

4. *Monitoring and feedback*. The accuracy with which students recall what they are supposed to have memorized is monitored. Correct responses are positively reinforced and errors corrected. For example:

VIGNETTE 3.11

Theresa asks Mr. Santiago, "What does the book mean when it says the car *decelerated*?" Mr. Santiago: "Hmm, decelerated, that's an interesting word. What's *acceleration* mean?" Theresa: "Something about how fast the car goes." Mr. Santiago: "What's the definition of the word *acceleration*?" Theresa: "I don't know." Mr. Santiago: "Look it up in the glossary in your notebook." . . . Theresa: "It says, 'Acceleration is any change in an object's speed or direction.' Is that right?" Mr. Santiago: "Absolutely. Now, recite the definition to me without looking in your book." Theresa: "Acceleration is any change in an object's speed or direction." Mr. Santiago: "Exactly. Now, let's look at the word *deceleration*. . . .

---

5. *Overlearning.* Students *overlearn* by continuing to practice recalling content even after they have memorized it. Overlearning increases resistance to forgetting and facilitates long-term retention of information (Chance, 1988, pp. 221–222). For example, even after the completion of the unit in which he introduced the terms *speed* and *acceleration*, Mr. Santiago continues to confront students with tasks requiring them to use their knowledge of the meaning of the terms.

A Five-Stage Lesson for a Simple Knowledge Objective

The lesson in Vignette 3.12 includes the five stages leading to simple knowledge-level learning.

VIGNETTE 3.12

Ms. Bohrer conducts a lesson for the following objective:

> List the defining attributes of mammals (*simple knowledge*)

Using Figure 3.11's overhead transparency slide to illustrate her words, she tells the third-grade class, "A *mammal* is any *animal* that has a *backbone*, . . . is *warm-*

Figure 3.11. Ms. Bohrer's Overhead Transparency for Simple Knowledge Lesson on Mammals

VIGNETTE 3.12 (continued)

blooded, . . . has some body *hair*, . . . and its females have what are called *mammary glands* for feeding milk to their babies. . . . I'm going to repeat the five things that are true about mammals. First, a mammal is an *animal*—like a snake, spider, fish, bird, bear, whale, human-being, or dog, but not like a tree, weed, or rock. . . . Second, a mammal has a *backbone*—like a snake, fish, bird, bear, whale, human-being, or dog, but not like spider or worm. . . . Third, a mammal is *warm-blooded* like a bird, bear, whale, human-being, or dog, not like a snake or fish. . . . Fourth, a mammal has body *hair* like a bear, whale, human-being, or dog, not like a bird or fish. . . . And fifth, mammal mothers can feed their babies milk from their bodies using *mammary* glands, like those of a bear, whale, human-being, or dog, not like a bird, lizard, fish, and all other things that are not mammals. . . . Now, take one more look at the overhead screen and get these five things planted in your minds. Then I'm going to turn it off and check to see which ones we remember. . . . Off we go. List one for me, Don." Don: "Warm-blooded." Ms. Bohrer: "Another, Eva." Eva: "Milk from mothers and—" Ms. Bohrer: "Thank you. Another, Deliah. . . .'"

The recitation continues for another 30 seconds and then Ms. Bohrer displays Figure 3.11 again and says, "Any time you hear the word *mammal*, I want you to think of these five things—animal, backbone, warm-blooded, hair, and mother's milk or mammary glands. . . . Also, anytime you observe a creature that has the five characteristics, think what? . . . Okay, all together." Most of the class: "Mammal."

For a mnemonic device, Ms. Bohrer says, "To help me remember the word *mammal*, I think of 'mother's milk from *mammary* glands' as I picture my cat nursing her kittens." She holds up a large picture of a mother cat nursing kittens

Ms. Bohrer Using a Mnemonic Device

(continued)

VIGNETTE 3.12 (continued)

"I've Got a Mammal in Here. Silently Think to Yourself What You Know About It."

and then directs one student to tack it on the bulletin board. She completes this stage of the lesson with, "Three *m*'s: mother, milk, mammary just like in the word *mammal*.

Ms. Bohrer then brings out a closed box, holds it up, and directs the class, "I've got a mammal in here. Silently think to yourself what you know about it. . . ." She then calls on different students to share their descriptions until she's reasonably convinced that they associate the five attributes with the word *mammal*.

In subsequent lessons and units, the term *mammal* arises and Ms. Bohrer sets up cues (e.g., "What does that mean again? Well why do you say a fish isn't a mammal?") to lead students to recall the relationship she taught in this lesson.

LESSONS FOR COMPREHENSION OBJECTIVES

By engaging students in learning activities that lead them to comprehend communications, you obviate one of the more mystifying aspects of subject matter content, namely, negotiating language. Comprehension-level lessons provide students with systematic strategies for understanding *messages* and acquiring meaning from *communication modes* that are conventional to course content.

Comprehension of a Particular Message

Literal and Interpretive Understanding. Lessons for comprehension of particular messages should be concerned with two stages of understanding:

1. *Literal understanding*. Students literally understand a message if they can accurately translate its explicit meaning. For example:

VIGNETTE 3.13

Cynthia examines the following definition from a psychology textbook:

> OPERANT CONDITIONING. A type of learning in which behavior is strengthened if followed by reinforcement, or suppressed if followed by punishment (Myers, 1986, p. 656).

She then displays *literal understanding* of the definition by formulating the following explanation: "Operant conditioning is a way behavior in animals (including people) is either encouraged because it's followed by rewards or discouraged because its followed by punishment."

---

2. *Interpretive understanding*. Students understand a message at an interpretive level if they can infer implicit meaning and explain how aspects of the communication are used to convey the message. For example:

VIGNETTE 3.14

From examining the aforementioned definition of operant conditioning, Cynthia displays *interpretive understanding* of the definition by extending her previous explanation with the following:

> The definition indicates that because of operant conditioning animals will repeat a behavior again and again as long as the behavior is followed by a positive reinforcer. "Behavior is strengthened" indicates a new habit being formed or an old one being sustained. On the other hand, the part about suppression of behavior and punishment suggests that because of operant conditioning new habits can be prevented or old ones broken.

Designing Learning Activities for Literal Understanding. Interpretive understanding depends on literal understanding. Thus, the initial phase of a comprehension lesson should promote literal understanding. To design the learning activities, you will need to analyze the message to be comprehended, identifying the requirements of students regarding:

> *vocabulary*. What general, special, and technical terms and symbols will they need to understand in order to translate the message? Meanings of words, expressions, and symbols are learned through simple knowledge-level lessons. Are there any prerequisite simple knowledge-level objectives that

should be achieved before students are ready for the comprehension-level activities?

concepts. What concepts does the author of the message assume the students have conceptualized prior to receiving the communications? In Vignettes 3.13 and 3.14, Cynthia's understanding of the definition depended on her prior conceptualization of at least two concepts, reinforcement and punishment.

relationships. What relationships does the author of the message assume the students have conceptualized prior to receiving the communications? In Vignettes 3.13 and 3.14, Cynthia's understanding of the definition depended on her prior conceptualization of a fundamental relationship between stimuli and responses.

communication modes. What conventional modes of communications are used to convey the message with which students need to be able to comprehend? Cynthia's explanations in Vignettes 3.13 and 3.14 suggest she understands how to read typically stated definitions. Comprehending a definition requires specialized skills as does comprehending proofs, technical directions, graphs, maps, diagrams, body language, and other types of communication modes.

Once these five prerequisites are achieved, *literal* understanding of a message is effected through a four-stage *direct instructional* lesson:

1. *The message is sent to the students.* For example, the definition of operant conditioning is stated orally and in writing.
2. *The message is rephrased and explained.* For example, "In other words, operant conditioning is a phenomenon by which behaviors are encouraged because they are reinforced or discouraged because they are punished."
3. *Students are questioned about specifics in the message.* For example, "What is meant by a behavior being suppressed?"
4. *Students are provided with feedback on their responses to the questions raised in the third phase.* To the aforementioned question, for example, a student has responded, "That means the animals begin to feel bad." The teacher then provides feedback by saying, "No, the word is *suppression,* not *depression.* Suppressing behavior in this case means that the animal is less likely to display the behavior in the future."

Designing Learning Activities for Interpretive Understanding. Interpretive understanding of a message is achieved with learning activities that utilize more inquiry and open-ended questions and discussions than the direct instruction for literal understanding. Students are stimulated to examine the message, extracting its main idea, data base or facts, assumptions, and conclusions.

A Lesson for Comprehension of a Particular Message. In Vignette 3.15, note how Ms. Loyocono shifts from direct instructional activities during the literal understanding phase to activities in which students generate ideas during the phase for interpretive understanding.

VIGNETTE 3.15

As part of a unit on the U.S. government, Ms. Loyocono would like for her fifth-graders to achieve the following objective:

> Explain in their own words the Preamble of the U.S. Constitution (*Cognitive: comprehension*)

Before designing the lesson for the objective, she carefully reads the Preamble (see Figure 3.12) to identify vocabulary words, concepts, and relationships with which students would need to be familiar before they're ready to learn to comprehend the document.

Figure 3.12. Preamble to the Constitution of the United States (1787)

We the people of the United States, in order to form a more perfect Union, establish justice, insure domestic tranquility, provide for the common defense, promote the general welfare, and secure the blessings of liberty to ourselves and our posterity, do ordain and establish this Constitution for the United States of America.

Happily, she determines that any prerequisite concepts (e.g., justice) and relationships (e.g., those who passed the Constitution were representing the people of the United States and were authorized to speak for those they represented) were already targeted in previous conceptualization lessons. The only terms she thinks need to be added to their vocabulary are *tranquility* and *posterity*. Thus, she plans to conduct a brief direct lesson on the meaning of those two terms before embarking on the comprehension lesson on the Preamble.

She opens the lesson at the end of one class period by directing students to read the Preamble from their textbooks for homework. The following day each thought unit in the document is read and rephrased; then Ms. Loyocono questions students about the meaning of the thought unit and reinforces or corrects answers. Here is a sample exchange:

Ms. Loyocono: We the people of the United States—Who are the authors referring to by "We the people"? Enu-Lai?

Enu-Lai: The people living in the country?

Ms. Loyocono: But it says "*We* the people." You mean that all the people in the United States wrote this document?

Enu-Lai: No, but the guys who wrote this were speaking for everyone in the country.

Ms. Loyocono: Oh, that's right! I should remember that the authors were delegated to act for the people in their own states. . . . With that cleared up, read the next part and stop at the word *justice*, Pat?

Pat: "to form a more perfect . . ."

Within 15 minutes, this literal understanding phase of the lesson is completed and Ms. Loyocono moves into inquiry instruction for interpretive understanding. She engages the students in a session in which her questions stimulate discussions

(continued)

VIGNETTE 3.15 (continued)

about the authors' purposes for the Preamble and why such phrases as "secure the blessings of liberty to ourselves and our posterity" were included.

After the discussion, Ms. Loyocono takes out a box containing 32 slips of paper, each with a different word from the Preamble (e.g., "people," "form," "perfect," "union," "establish," "justice," "insure," and "tranquility"). She quickly goes around the room to each of the 24 students directing them to randomly select three of the slips, copy down the three words, and return the slips to the box. She then makes the following assignment:

> Rewrite the Preamble but without using any of the three words you drew from the box. However, write it so that the meaning of the original document is unchanged. Don't let your version say anything that's not in the actual Preamble nor leave out anything that's in the actual Preamble.

The lesson ends the following day after different students' versions are read and critiqued for how well they retained the original meaning of the Preamble.

Comprehension of a Communications Mode

The language of a content area (e.g., history, physical education, home economics, or mathematics) contains specialized communications with conventions that students need to understand before comprehending messages via those modes. A lesson for a comprehension of a communications mode should include learning activities that (a) use direct teaching methods to inform students about the special conventions of the mode and (b) use inquiry methods for helping students develop strategies for using that mode. For example:

VIGNETTE 3.16

Ms. McGiver has planned her pre-algebra course so that students confront textbook word problems in every unit. However, after the first two units, she realizes that students are experiencing difficulty solving word problems, not necessarily because they don't understand the particular mathematics applicable to the problem, but because they have never developed strategies for solving word problems in general. Thus, she decides to insert a special unit designed to teach general strategies for solving any kind of word problem. Her first objective is to get them to *comprehend* problems as typically presented in textbooks. She states the objective as follows:

> From reading a textbook word problem, students will (a) identify the question posed by the problem, (b) clarify the question in their own words, (c) specify the variable to be solved, and (d) list facts or data provided in the statement of the problem (*Cognitive: comprehension*)

Ms. McGiver begins her lesson by displaying the following word problem with the instructions, "Just read this carefully without trying to solve it:"

VIGNETTE 3.16 (continued)

Tom is on a television quiz show. He scores 5 points by correctly answering
his first quiz show question. He then misses the second question and loses
10 points. What is his score after the two questions?

Ms. McGiver knows that everyone in the class can readily solve that problem.
So, she's not surprised to hear some students blurt, "Aw, that's easy! It's -5."
But rather than accept their solutions she insists they follow her directions:

Ms. McGiver: Now that you've read the problem, I want you to copy down
and answer these questions:

She displays:

1. Solving this problem answers what question?

2. What *variable* does answering the question require you to solve?

3. What information are you given with which to work?

After several minutes:

Ms. McGiver: How did you answer the first question, Stephanie?

Stephanie: What is his score after the two questions?

Ms. McGiver: Did anyone answer that question in a way that's essentially different from Stephanie's? Okay, Michelle?

Michelle: I put -5. Isn't that right?

A number of students interrupt, saying, "That 's what I got; -5!" But Ms.
McGiver only gives them an icy stare then turns back to Michelle.

Ms. McGiver: What is the question you were to answer?

Michelle: What was the score after the two questions?

Ms. McGiver: No, read the first question from your paper.

Michelle: Solving this problem answers what question?

Ms. McGiver: Now, answer *that* question, Warren.

Warren: What is the score after two questions?

Ms. McGiver: If your answer to the first question doesn't essentially agree with
what Stephanie and Warren read, then change it right now so it does. . . .
Okay, how did you answer the second question, Bonita?

Bonita: How many points Bill is behind.

Ms. McGiver: Behind! Why "behind," Bonita?

Bonita: Because he lost more points than he gained.

Ms. McGiver: Angelo?

Angelo: The variable is how many points he has left. You don't know if he's
behind or not until you solve the problem.

(continued)

VIGNETTE 3.16 (continued)

RITA: But 10 is bigger than 5—

MS. MCGIVER: You didn't listen to what Angelo said. Repeat what you said, Angelo.

ANGELO: Just that you've got to know the variable before you solve for it. They're naming the variable after they solve it; so it's no longer a variable.

MS. MCGIVER: Angelo, you're getting into some pretty sophisticated ideas there. Thank you. I think Angelo has hit on the reason we're confused. We need to try this on a problem that you won't solve so easily and then answer these questions before you—quote—'know the solution.' . . . Here's the problem. Answer the same questions for it.

She displays:

An airplane travels at 250 mph for 2 hours in a direction of 138° from Albion, NY. At the end of this time, how far west of Albion is the plane?

Some of the students grumble that the problem is too hard, but Ms. McGiver simply uses a stern look and a gesture to tell them to just answer the three questions. After four minutes:

MS. MCGIVER: Read your answer to the first question, Hartense.

HARTENSE: How far west of Albion is the plane?

MS. MCGIVER: Anybody disagree? . . . Okay, what do you have for the second question, Wil?

WIL: How far west the plane is.

MS. MCGIVER: Far west from where, Joan?

JOAN: From that place in New York.

MS. MCGIVER: What kind of variable is it? . . . Anybody? . . . Okay, Stephanie.

STEPHANIE: What do you mean?

MS. MCGIVER: I mean is it an angle size, distance, weight, or what?

STEPHANIE: It's a distance.

MS. MCGIVER: So what's the variable, Mike?

MIKE: The distance from the town.

MS. MCGIVER: Okay, what did you put for the third question, Zeke?

ZEKE: I made a list: airplane going 250 miles an hour, two hours, at 138°.

MS. MCGIVER: Does anyone have any more to add? Okay, Joe.

JOE: It's by Albion, New York.

MS. MCGIVER: Now, let's go back and answer the questions again for the first problem. . . .

After they go through the first problem again, Ms. McGiver explains that they are to answer those three questions for every word problem they work for this class until she notifies them differently. She plans to continue going over this process for comprehending word problems until they appear to do it automatically.

LESSONS FOR
KNOWLEDGE-OF-A-PROCESS OBJECTIVES

Facilitating Process Skills through Direct Instruction

Gaining proficiency with a process usually requires students to be engaged in learning activities that are more tedious and less interesting than learning activities for other types of objectives (e.g., conceptualization). Sometimes games (e.g., the one integrated into Ms. Pillow's Spanish lesson in Vignette 5.13) can be used to relieve tedium and boredom during the practice stages of lessons for knowledge-of-a-process objectives. In any case, knowledge of a process is effected through *direct instruction* in a *nine-stage* lesson.

Before you are in a position to design learning activities that will take students through the nine stages of the lesson, you must *analyze the process*, *delineating the steps for students to execute*. The first few times you do this, you may be quite surprised to discover that processes involve more steps than you, who are already proficient with them, had imagined. Shoenfeld (1985, p. 61) pointed out, "It is easy to underestimate the complexity of ostensibly simple procedures, especially after one has long since mastered them." For example, Ms. Tankersley delineates a 12-point process for multiplication in Vignette 3.17.

VIGNETTE 3.17

Ms. Tankersley proficiently multiplies two-digit whole numbers by one-digit whole numbers without much conscious effort. Thus, she doesn't consider the algorithm to be very complex until she analyzes the process to identify the steps her third-graders will need to know to achieve the following objective:

Compute the product of any two-digit whole number by any one-digit whole number (*Cognitive: knowledge of a process*)

She identifies 12 steps in the process for them to learn by noting exactly what she remembers as she walks through the following computation:

$$\overset{2}{5}7$$
$$\underline{\times\quad 4}$$
$$228$$

The 12 steps are:

1. Recognize the task is to multiply.
2. Recognize that the multiplicand is a two-digit number, and thus memory of multiplication facts alone will not be adequate.
3. Check to see if numerals are aligned for the algorithm.
4. Remember first to multiply 7 by 4.
5. Remember that $7 \times 4 = 28$.
6. Write the "8" from the "28" as follows:

(continued)

VIGNETTE 3.17 (continued)

$$\begin{array}{r} 5\ 7 \\ \times\ \ 4 \\ \hline 8 \end{array}$$

7. Carry the "2" of the "28":

$$\begin{array}{r} \overset{2}{5}\ 7 \\ \times\ \ 4 \\ \hline 8 \end{array}$$

8. Remember to multiply 5 by 4.
9. Remember that 5 × 4 = 20.
10. Remember to add the carried 2 to the 20.
11. Compute 2 + 20 to be 22.
12. Write "22" to the left of the "8":

$$\begin{array}{r} \overset{2}{5}\ 7 \\ \times\ \ 4 \\ \hline 2\ 2\ 8 \end{array}$$

You may think that enumerating 12 steps for the process Ms. Tankersley plans to teach is "complicating the simple." However, please keep in mind that Ms. Tankersley's students are just being introduced to this process and each step represents a potential hurdle that she may have to help them negotiate.

After examining steps in the process, you need to identify any prerequisite skills or abilities students might need to acquire before being ready to learn the process. Ms. Tankersley, for example, should feel confident that her students have conceptualized the idea of multiplication, are skilled with certain addition algorithms, and can recall multiplication facts before attempting to teach the process in the example.

Once you have the steps in the process clearly delineated in your mind and students have achieved prerequisite objectives, the nine stages of the lesson you conduct are:

1. *Explanation of the purpose of the process.* Processes are based on relationships. If your students have already experienced conceptualization-level lessons on relationships underlying a process, then explaining the purpose of the process is a trivial task. The first stage generally involves nothing more than making an announcement such as, "We've been multiplying numbers like 34 by numbers like 2. Now we're going to learn to do it for numbers like 28 by 7. With these numbers, we're going to have to do some regrouping."

2. *Explanation and practice estimating or anticipating outcomes from the process*. Although process skills are acquired through knowledge-level learning, students need to get into the habit of estimating or anticipating outcomes before executing the process. This (a) tends to add a little interest to the task as students may become interested in checking their prediction skills, (b) provides an informal check on the accuracy of the process, and (c) maintains some connection between the process and its underlying relationships. For example:

VIGNETTE 3.18

Ms. Tankersley directs her third-graders, "I'm about to show you a question on a card. The answer is a number. As soon as you see the question, you are to quickly guess the answer and write it down on the sheet in front of you. I don't expect you to know the exact number, but try to guess one that's close to it. . . . Ready, here it is." The card reads, "What is 36×7?"

She solicits a number of answers ranging from 7 to 8,000. Displaying the card once again, she says, "Now let's take more time to think about an answer. Multiplying 36 by 7 should give us a number that's larger or smaller than 36? . . ." She spends another six minutes reviewing previously learned estimating skills in which they look at 37×7 and pin it down between 30×7 and 40×7.

---

3. *Explanation of a general overview of the process*. In this stage, students are provided with an outline of the process they'll be executing. This is particularly important for complex processes in which students are likely to get so involved in detail that they lose sight of the overall task. For example, before explaining detailed steps of the tennis serve, an instructor demonstrates a serve and tells the class, "There are seven phases of the serve: First, the planning phase; second, positioning; third, the toss; fourth, the back swing; fifth, impact; sixth, follow-through, and seventh, repositioning. Here, I'll serve another one in slow motion and list the phases as I do it. Then we'll break down each stage into steps and . . ."

4. *Step-by-step explanation of the process*. This is the paramount stage of the lesson in which the process is delivered to the student. You begin by explaining the first step of the process to the students, and then have them try it. You then explain how the result of the first step triggers the second, and the second step is explained and tried. Movement to subsequent steps and the steps themselves are each explained and tried in turn.

5. *Trial test execution of the process*. Students are assigned exercises selected to demonstrate any error patterns they may have learned by mistake. The purpose of this stage is to obtain formative feedback on just what aspects of the process students execute correctly and which ones they do not. This includes how they go about (a) estimating or anticipating outcomes, (b) executing each step in the process itself, (c) checking for and correcting errors. Figure 3.13 illustrates sample exercises Ms. Tankersley assigned and her annotations to one student's responses.

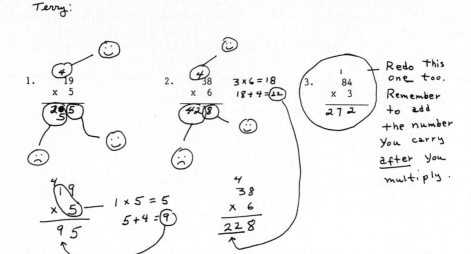

Figure 3.13. Ms. Tankersley Gives Terry Feedback during Knowledge-of-a-Process Lesson.

6. *Error pattern analysis.* Students' responses to the trial test exercises are analyzed to diagnose just how students are executing the process (e.g., as indicated by Ms. Tankersley's annotations in Figure 3.13). Chapter 6 provides explicit suggestions for analyzing students' error patterns.

7. *Correction.* Students are provided with additional explanations as warranted by the error pattern analysis.

8. *Practice.* Students polish their skills and overlearn the process through practice exercises.

9. *Recycle prior phases as warranted by formative feedback.* Students' work continues to be monitored as they use the process in subsequent learning activities for other unit objectives.

A Nine-Stage Lesson for a Knowledge-of-a-Process Objective

Here is an example of a teacher engaging students in learning activities relevant to a knowledge-of-a-process objective:

VIGNETTE 3.19

Ms. Schinzus is conducting a unit on cardiopulmonary resuscitation (CPR) for her high school health science class. She has already completed relevant conceptualization and application lessons as well as ones for a number of CPR subskills (e.g., how to take the carotid pulse and locate the xiphoid process at the bottom of the sternum). Now, she begins a lesson for the following objective:

VIGNETTE 3.19 (continued)

Demonstrate proper techniques for administering CPR (*Cognitive: knowledge of a process*)

For this unit, Ms. Schinzus breaks with the typical pattern and teaches this process skill *after* rather than before the related application-level lesson. She does this because of the potential dangers of students knowing how to perform CPR (i.e., a knowledge-of-a-process skill) before they are able to make sound judgments regarding when it should be administered (i.e., an application-level ability).

Students already know why and when CPR should be administered from the earlier conceptualization and application lessons, so she only needs to briefly review the purposes for the first stage of the knowledge-of-a-process lesson. She then uses several examples of victims in need of CPR to explain results CPR might be expected to produce in various situations.

For the third stage, she demonstrates the administration of CPR on a dummy and outlines the stages of the operation. She says for example, "I've just completed my assessment and have decided to ventilate the victim. . . . Now after that initial ventilation, I'm checking for circulation by taking the carotid pulse. . . . I've decided to continue with the CPR procedure. To do that I must locate the appropriate point to apply pressure while minimizing further trauma to this victim. . . . That's what I'm doing now, locating the xiphoid process so I can protect it and apply pressure just above it. . . . Okay, now I position my hands for compression and begin compression procedures. One and 2 and 3 and 4 and 5 and 1 and . . . and 15. Now, I ventilate by . . ."

Next, Ms. Schinzus explains each step one-at-a-time for each phase of the procedure. She does this by having a student attempt to follow her directions in front of the class. At each step, she points out what is and is not being properly demonstrated. She only has four dummies for 29 students, so she divides the class into four groups directing them to take turns walking through the steps and to critique one another's technique. She monitors the activity carefully, stepping in to reinforce proper procedures and correct improper ones.

Students read a CPR manual for homework. The following day, Ms. Schinzus directs students to respond to several essay questions about CPR. While the rest of the class is occupied with that task, she has students demonstrate the procedure to her on a dummy one at a time. Individually, she coaches them on techniques and corrects errors.

Periodically over the next few weeks, she provides opportunities for students to practice and overlearn the process. This continues although she has since moved on to units relative to other topics.

LESSONS FOR APPLICATION OBJECTIVES

When confronted with a problem, a student who has achieved an application-level objective can determine how, if at all, the content of that objective can be utilized in a solution to the problem. During application-level lessons, students learn to put into practice previously conceptualized concepts and relationships and previously memorized conventions and processes.

Deductive Reasoning

Application-level learning depends on students using *deductive reasoning* (Beyer, 1987, pp. 30–32). *Deductive reasoning* is inferring that a specific or particular problem is subsumed by a more general idea (i.e., concept) *or rule* (i.e., abstract relationship). It is the cognitive process by which people determine whether or not what they know about a concept or abstract relationship is applicable to some unique situation.

The use of *syllogisms* is inherent in deductive reasoning. A syllogism is a scheme for inferring problem solutions in which a conclusion is drawn from a *major premise* and a *minor premise*. The major premise is a general rule or abstraction. The minor premise is a relationship of a specific to the general rule or abstraction. The conclusion is a logical consequence of the combined premises. For example:

> *Major premise:* Citrus fruits are a source of vitamin C.
> *Minor premise:* This lemon is a citrus fruit.
> *Conclusion:* This lemon is a source of vitamin C.

Although not normally expressed formally, people use that same syllogistic, deductive reasoning in real-life problem solving. For example:

VIGNETTE 3.20

Gary is planning an exercise program for himself. It is his understanding that for heart and lung health he should do an aerobic exercise at least every other day. He thinks: "A rhythmic, sustained exercise that elevates heart and respiratory rates continually for at least 20 minutes is aerobic. . . . I plan to weight lift for strength. Can that count for my aerobic exercise? . . . No, because it doesn't really get me breathing hard nor is weight lifting a sustained exercise. . . . I like softball and flag football; I could join teams—that can be quite vigorous. . . . But they're more stop-and-go rather than sustained. . . . Bicycling? If I bike vigorously for a half an hour, then I would sustain elevated heart and respiratory rates. . . . I'll plan on biking at least four times a week."

Facilitating Application-Level Learning

A *deductive learning activity* is one that *stimulates students to reason deductively*. An application-level objective is achieved through a four-stage lesson; the first two stages utilize deductive learning activities. The four stages are:

1. *Initial problem confrontation and analysis.* In the initial activity of this phase of the lesson, you confront students with a pair of problems. The pair is chosen so that the problems are very similar except that the content of the application-level objective applies to the solution of one of the problems but not the other. Suppose, for example, that the following objective is to be achieved:

Given a real-life problem, decide if the solution requires computing the area of a polygonal region, and, if so, determine how to find that area (*Cognitive: application*)

The content of the objective applies to the solution of the first of the following pair of problems, but not the second:

A. The front wall surrounding the chalkboard is quite drab. Students suggest that they make decorative posters on standard sheets of cardboard and use them to completely cover the wall as begun in Figure 3.14. How many posters will be needed to complete the task?

B. There is a nasty looking crack just above the chalkboard on one side wall of the classroom. Students suggest that they make decorative posters and use them to hide the crack as begun in Figure 3.15. How many sheets will be needed to complete the task?

You then engage students in a *deductive questioning/discussion* session in which students describe how they would go about solving each problem and then explain why the objective's content was used in one case, but not the other. For example, see Vignette 3.21.

Figure 3.14. Classroom Wall Partially Covered with Decorative Posters

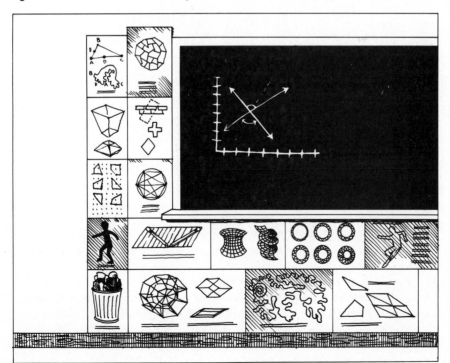

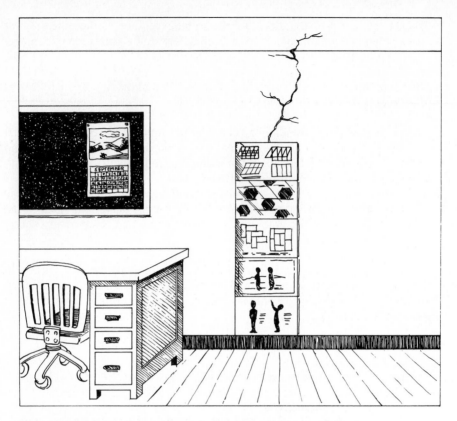

Figure 3.15. Partially Covered Crack in One of the Classroom Walls

---

VIGNETTE 3.21

Mr. Cummings uses the two sample problems (listed as problems A and B earlier) for the aforementioned objective on polygonal area. He engages one student in the following exchange:

MR. CUMMINGS: How would you go about solving problem A?

PATSY: I'd divide the wall around the board into rectangles. And then find out how many sheets would fit into each rectangle.

MR. CUMMINGS: But how would you go about finding out the number of sheets to use?

PATSY: I'd have to just puzzle the sheets in.

MR. CUMMINGS: But how would you know how many puzzle pieces to use?

PATSY: By trying it.

MR. CUMMINGS: But suppose you wanted to find out how many sheets you needed without wasting a bunch of sheets. Is there an easier way?

PATSY: Oh, you mean by computing the area of the wall. Yeah! I could add up

VIGNETTE 3.21 (continued)

the rectangles' areas and divide that by the area of one sheet. Then I'd have it.

Mr. Cummings: Now, what about problem B, how would you solve that one?

Patsy: Just measure the length of the crack and divide that by the width of a sheet and that would give you the number of posters.

Mr. Cummings: Why didn't you compute areas for problem B like you did for problem A?

Patsy: B isn't an area problem.

Mr. Cummings: Why not? How is it different from A? They seem pretty similar to me.

Patsy: With A we had to spread the posters all out. In B the sheets are lined up in just one row.

Adapted with permission from *Teaching Mathematics in Secondary and Middle School: Research-based Approaches* (pp. 110–111), by J. S. Cangelosi, 1992, New York: Macmillan. Copyright © 1992 by Macmillan Publishing Company.

2. *Subsequent problem confrontation and analysis.* Learning activities for the second stage are similar to those of the first except that students analyze solutions to additional pairs of problems. The pairs are selected so that students are exposed to a wide variety of circumstances and varying psychological noise in which to determine if the content is applicable. For the objective on areas of polygonal regions, subsequent problems would include circumstances other than covering a wall with posters. How many pairs of problems to include and how difficult each is should depend on how easily students are distinguishing between problems to which the content applies and those to which it doesn't. If they readily explain why the content works in one case, but not another, then you should engage them in more difficult problems. On the other hand, select easier problems and delay the start of the third phase if they are experiencing serious difficulties.

3. *Rule articulation.* In this stage, students formulate rules for when the content of the objective applies to the solution of a problem. If conceptualization of the content preceded the lesson, then this often involves no more than rephrasing rules discovered during conceptualization lessons. In cases in which students began the application lesson with some conceptual learning gaps relative to the content, this phase may require some inductive learning activities to help them rediscover rules.

4. *Extension into subsequent lessons.* As suggested in Chapter 1, teaching is a complex art; one lesson does not always end before another begins. Achievement of one application-level objective is enhanced during the first two phases of lessons for subsequent application-level objectives. In Vignette 3.21, Mr. Cummings's questions stimulated Patsy to reason deductively about lengths (a topic from a previous unit) for the problem to which area computations did not apply. In a subsequent unit on volume, Mr. Cummings will likely pair a problem that can be solved via a volume relationship with one that can be solved via an area

relationship. Thus, application lessons on one content extend into those for subsequent content.

A Four-Stage Lesson for an Application Objective

Here is an example of an application-level lesson:

VIGNETTE 3.22

Ms. Goldberg's first-grade class is in the latter stages of a unit on subtraction. She has already conducted a conceptualization lesson in which students discovered subtraction facts (e.g., $17 - 8 = 9$), a knowledge-of-a-process lesson for using both addition and counting to find differences between two whole numbers, and a simple knowledge lesson for remembering subtraction facts. Now, she is planning the specifics for tomorrow's lesson for the following objective:

> Distinguish between problems that can and those that cannot be efficiently solved by using subtraction (*Cognitive: application*)

She thinks to herself, "For the initial problem confrontation and analysis, I need to come up with a pair of problems—one with a solution that uses subtraction, another that doesn't. . . ."

Initially, her example and nonexample problems are:

> *Example:* Sally has 15 books on her shelf; she takes away 4 and gives them to Amanda. How many books are left on the shelf?
> *Nonexample:* Dustin has some money and Casey has some money. They agree to add their money together and buy a computer game disk from the toy store. How much money can they spend for a video game disk?

She thinks, "The nonexample uses addition; it would be nice to have another nonexample that uses counting. I just don't want them to develop the misconception that if the solution doesn't require subtraction, then it requires addition. Also, if I start this lesson off with two nonexamples, I might as well have a second example problem too. So, . . .

Further thought leads to two more problems:

> *Nonexample:* Brandon started reading a book from page 1. He just finished page 16. How many pages has he read?
> *Example:* Sybil had 19 stickers in a box before she took away 7 to decorate her door. How many stickers are left in her box?

She thinks: "I'll give them a tasksheet with the numerals 1, 2, 3, and 4 and a blank by each. I'll read them the first problem slowly and ask them to put a plus if they'd add to solve it, a minus if they'd subtract, and an *N* if they'd do neither. Then, we can discuss why they put what they put and move on and do the same for each of the other three problems. . . . Okay, . . . uh-oh! The way I've worded the problems isn't going to work! Look at those 'give-away' words. 'Takes away' in the first subtraction problem and 'took away' in the other one—they'll just call

VIGNETTE 3.22 (continued)

that subtraction not from deductive reasoning based on their comprehension of the problem, but just because of a memorized association between 'takes away' and subtraction. The first nonexample has the word *add*! I've got some modifying to do. . . .

The modified versions are as follows:

Example: Brandon started reading a 20-page book from page 1. He is now on page 16. How many pages must he read to finish the book?

Nonexample: Sally has 15 books on her shelf, she takes away 4 and gives them to Amanda. How many books did Sally give Amanda?

Nonexample: Dustin has some money and Casey has some money. They agree to buy one computer game disk and share it. How much money can they spend for a disk?

Example: Sybil had 19 stickers in a box before she used 7 to decorate her door. How many stickers are still in her box?

She's quite pleased with this new set of problems, especially because one of the nonexamples includes the words "takes away."

Additional problems and deductive questioning activities are developed for the second stage of the lesson. She intends for her questions to stimulate discussions leading into the rule articulation stage. During that stage, students are to conclude that subtraction problems involve questions about how many are left in a set after part of the set has been removed. She's confident of the success of that stage because of her students' prior experiences during the conceptualization lesson on subtraction.

Just as Ms. Goldberg plans to confront students with addition problems during this subtraction unit, she'll confront them with subtraction problems as nonexamples for application lessons in subsequent units (e.g., on measuring length and numeration systems).

LESSONS FOR CREATIVITY OBJECTIVES

Some Thoughts on Creativity

An objective that specifies *creativity* as its learning level requires students to think divergently to originate ideas, hypotheses, or methods. Creativity is the development of new mental patterns. People tend to produce creative ideas in response to dissatisfaction with available methods, ideas, beliefs, and principles for dealing with perplexing situations.

Contrary to the popular belief that aptitude for creative production is found only in rare, exceptional individuals, virtually everyone possesses creative talents (Torrance, 1966). It is rare for talent to be recognized and rewarded. Historically, society and its institutions (e.g., schools and churches) have frowned on and generally discouraged creative thinking (Strom, 1969, pp. 222–236). Divergent reasoning threatens common beliefs and established "truths." Irrational thought and emotionally controlled behaviors are often associated with mental instability. However, Gordon (1961, p. 6) suggested that irrational, emotionally charged thought tends to produce an environment more conductive to creative production than rational, controlled thought. Joyce and Weil (1986, p. 165) stated, "Non-rational interplay leaves room for open-ended thoughts that can lead to a mental state in which new ideas are possible. The basis for decisions, however, is always rational; the irrational state is the best mental state for exploring and expanding ideas, but it is not a decision-making state."

Creativity thrives in an environment in which ideas are valued on their own merit, not on the basis of how they were produced or who produced them (Strom, 1969, pp. 258–267). In such an environment, irrationally produced ideas are evaluated with the same regard as those resulting from a rational process. The attention afforded an idea should not depend on the eminence of its originator.

Gordon's (1961) studies challenge typical views about creativity with four ideas:

1. Creativity is important in everyday circumstances; it should not only be associated with the development of great works.
2. Creativity is utilized in all fields, not just the arts.
3. Creative thoughts can be generated by groups as well as solitary individuals via similar processes. This is contrary to the common view that creativity must be an intensely personal experience.
4. The creative process is not mysterious; it can be described and people taught to use it.

Gordon's fourth point is critical to justifying the inclusion of creativity-level lessons in curricula. However, how to best teach for creativity is still not well understood. One difficulty is resolving the phenomenon that creative thoughts seem to rise unpredictably (Bourne, Dominowski, Loftus, & Healy, 1986, pp. 9–10).

Preserving Creativity

Studies indicate a steady decline in most students' curiosity and creative activities during their school years; Strom (1969) stated:

> Given the great number of children with creative prospect and the fact that it represents a natural evolving process, the first concern among educators ought to be one of preservation. Creativity will develop if allowed to grow, if teachers permit and encourage a course already begun (cf. Gowan et al., 1967). A primary clue comes from the process itself—allowing inquiry, manipulation, questioning, guessing, and the combination of remote thought elements. Generally, however, the preferred cognitive style of learning creatively is discouraged [in typical classrooms]. Studies indicate that discontinuities in creative development occur at several grade levels and that the losses are accompanied by a decline in pupil curiosity and interest in learning. At the same grade levels at which creative loss occurs, increases are noted in the incidence of emotional disturbance and egregious behavior. Among Anglo-American cultures, the greatest slump in creative development seems to coincide with the fourth grade; smaller drops take place at kindergarten and seventh grade. Children at each of these grades perform less well than they did one year earlier and less well than children in the grade below

them on measures of divergent thinking, imagination, and originality. This problem was ignored, since it was judged to be a developmental phenomena instead of man-made or culture-related (Torrance, 1962). Not long ago it was first recognized that in certain cultures the development of creative thinking abilities is continuous. And, even in our own country, under selective teachers who encourage creative boys and girls and reward creative behavior, no slump occurs at grade four. (pp. 259–260)

As a teacher, you can choose not to include creativity-level objectives in your curricula. However, simply managing to preserve students' creativity and allowing it to grow requires some conscious effort on your part.

Fostering Creativity

Consistent with contemporary curriculum reformation movements (e.g., Brandt, 1988; California State Department of Education, 1987; National Council of Teachers of Mathematics, 1989; Resnick & Klopfer, 1989), you may choose, not only to preserve your students' creativity, but also to conduct lessons that help them achieve creativity-level objectives. Just as activities for affective objectives can be efficiently integrated into lessons for cognitive objectives (e.g., Vignette 3.3), so too can activities fostering creativity be interwoven with those for other types of objectives (especially conceptualization). The strategy is to conduct these other lessons so that students feel free to question, make mistakes, and disagree with ideas, even yours. Particularly important is for them to be positively reinforced (Cangelosi, 1988a, pp. 35–37) for depending on themselves and on their own devices for decision making and problem solving.

Although the creative process is not well understood, some promising methods for teaching for creativity have been tried and studied with encouraging results (Bourne, Dominowski, Loftus, & Healy, 1986, p. 9). Strom (1969, p. 261) recommended that students be exposed to examples of creative production (e.g., through historical accounts of inventions and discoveries and through teachers' modeling divergent thinking in "think aloud" sessions). Beyer (1987, pp. 35–37) pointed out the importance of heuristic activities such as brainstorming, open-ended questioning sessions, and discussions in which ideas for consideration are critiqued regarding purpose, structure, advantages, and disadvantages.

One of the more systematic and researched methods for fostering creativity is referred to by its designer, William J. J. Gordon (1961) as *synectics* (Joyce & Weil, 1986, pp. 159–183).

Synectics

Synectics is a means by which *metaphors* and *analogies* are used to lead students into an illogic state for situations where rational logic fails. The intent is for students to free themselves of convergent thinking and to develop empathy with ideas that conflict with their own. Three types of analogies are used in learning activities based on synectics:

1. *Direct analogies.* Students raise and analyze comparisons between the subject matter content and some familiar object or concept. For example:

How is a historical event like a tossed salad?

What's the difference between a noun–verb agreement and frozen yogurt?

Which is rounder, a hexagon or a television show?

2. *Personal analogies*. Students empathize with the content, losing themselves in some imaginary world. For example:

Be the variable number $1/x$ such that $-1 < x < 0$. Describe how do you feel as x moves from near -1 to about $-.5$. Describe how you feel as x moves from $-.5$ nearer and nearer to 0.

You're the English language. You must give up either all of your verbs, all of your nouns, all of your pronouns, or all of your adjectives. You get to choose which kind of words to give up. What kind is it and why?

You live in a world in which all people begin life by recovering from a fatal illness or accident and get younger with each passing year. People who live out their lives move from old age, to middle age, to young adulthood, to adolescence, to childhood, to being babies, to being embryos within their mothers, and finally to vanishing completely. Describe what your society and life is like.

3. *Compressed conflicts*. Compressed conflicts usually involve metaphors containing conflicting ideas. For example:

Draw two parallel lines that intersect one another.

Explain how to study history without any record or memory of the past.

Show how two different things can occupy exactly the same space at the same time.

The metaphors and analogies are intended to stimulate students to reconceptualize old ideas, thus promoting divergent thinking.

A Lesson Designed to Foster Creativity

Synectics are used in the following example:

VIGNETTE 3.23

Mr. Walker routinely integrates lessons for creativity with lessons for other types of objectives. His history students have already experienced comprehension lessons relative to historical accounts of activities of people such as Adolph Hitler, Charles R. Drew, Martin Luther King, Jr., Susan B. Anthony, Abraham Lincoln, and Robert Kennedy. They are aware, for example, that Hitler displayed extreme prejudice against black people and that Drew was a physician-scientist whose work made blood transfusions practical. Drew died in 1950 for lack of a blood transfusion when he was turned away from a "whites-only" hospital in North Carolina.

Mr. Walker plays on their knowledge of such events during a lesson for the following objective:

VIGNETTE 3.23 (continued)

Generate a variety of novel scenarios illustrating nontraditional views explaining why certain historical figures behaved as they did (*Cognitive: creativity*)

He directs the students to begin writing down names of historical figures that they have been studying over the past two weeks. He calls a halt to the activity after three minutes and asks Alena to write the fourth name on her list on the board and Lydia to write her sixth. "Adolph Hitler" and "Charles R. Drew" are displayed.

Mr. Walker directs the class, "Please take out a sheet of paper and number it from negative three to two. Leave about three lines of writing space after each numeral. . . . For number negative three, you've got 45 seconds to answer this question: How would a conversation between Hitler and Drew be like a bolt of lightening? . . . Number negative two: How would the conversation be like boiled spaghetti? . . . Number negative one: If you told Hitler your feelings about Drew and then Drew your feelings about Hitler, why do you suppose someone might accuse you of being unpatriotic? . . . Number zero: How are Hitler and Drew just alike? . . . Number one: Write out a question about the conversation for the class to discuss. . . . Number two: Explain why Drew might admire Hitler. . . . Please put your pens down for now. How did you answer negative three, Redfield?" Redfield: "A bolt of lightening is caused by a build up of opposite electrical charges that neutralize one another. When those two talk, they'd be throwing charges at one another—but they'd never really get anywhere." Mr. Walker: "We'll come back to that answer and others for number negative three, but first read us yours for negative two, Maxine." Maxine: "Their conversation would start off stiff like un-boiled spaghetti. Then after a while things would heat up and cool down and they'd soften up to one another—especially because Hitler was interested in medical research. So, you see . . ."

Additional responses are reported, compared, and discussed. New items are introduced with other pairs of names to stimulate students to make direct analogies, personal analogies, and compressed conflicts.

For homework, students write brief scenarios about varying combinations of historical figures interacting in imaginative ways. The lesson culminates the following day with students sharing their inventive stories and discussing how the events in the stories reflect the thinking of the characters.

LESSONS FOR PSYCHOMOTOR OBJECTIVES

Voluntary Muscle Capability

Students' abilities to perform specific psychomotor skills are limited by their voluntary muscle capabilities. Endurance, strength, flexibility, agility, and speed relative to particular muscle groups may need to be developed before and during skill training. Development of these capabilities is effected through appropriately prescribed exercises. Some students may require medically prescribed physical therapy or treatment to overcome or at least cope with disabilities that interfere with psychomotor learning.

Designing appropriate and safe exercises for achievement of voluntary-muscle-capability objectives requires specialized preparation in physical education that includes work in anatomy, physiology, and kinesiology. Even if you are not a professional physical educator, you need to be aware of voluntary-muscle-capability prerequisites to psychomotor skills you attempt to teach (e.g., writing in legible cursive, following standard lines of printed reading matter with the eyes, or operating a drill press). To help students develop those capabilities defer to physical educators with special expertise in the areas of concern.

Ability to Perform a Specific Skill

Students' abilities to perform a particular psychomotor skill are not only dependent on their voluntary muscle capabilities, they are also dependent on their cognitive knowledge of how to perform the skill. Ordinarily, lessons for psychomotor skills are integrated with those for knowledge of the relevant processes. Learning activities for knowledge of the process are likely to be emphasized early in the lessons while practice leading to enhancement of the psychomotor aspect of the skills dominates the latter segments of the combined lessons. For example:

VIGNETTE 3.24

During recreation units earlier in the school year, Ms. Barr had her seventh-grade physical education class participate in a number of games (e.g., basketball and volleyball) without much prior instruction. Now she has the students engaged in a unit specifically on basketball rules and skills. Two of the 12 objectives for the unit are:

G. Describe the appropriate techniques for shooting a jump shot (*Cognitive: knowledge of a process*)
H. Increase jump shooting accuracy (*Psychomotor: ability to perform a specific skill*)

For Objective G, she conducts a lesson that includes the nine stages listed in the section "Facilitating Process Skills through Direct Instruction." However, Ms. Barr realizes that simply knowing how one should shoot jump shots (i.e., achieving Objective G) does not mean one can shoot jump shots. For students to achieve Objective H, they must be able to perform the process without having to consciously think of each step along the way. A basketball player who thinks about each step— "square myself with the basket, position my shooting hand, keep my shooting elbow in so my arm is vertical to the floor, cradle the ball with my guide hand, bring . . . , follow through with my elbow extended and my wrist flexed"—is not very likely to make many baskets, especially under game conditions. The psychomotor response has to be automatic, fluid, smooth, and quick. Repeatedly performing the steps correctly conditions neural networks and muscular responses to execute the skill without the students consciously thinking about each step one at a time. Thus, she has students "go through the motions," demonstrating each step she explains during the fourth stage of the lesson for Objective G. She wants to maximize opportunities for students to correctly practice the skill.

Corresponding to the fifth, sixth, and seventh stages of the cognitive lesson, Ms. Barr coaches students through attempts to shoot jump shots. Although students may remember correct procedures, they will often fail to perform them because their

VIGNETTE 3.24 (continued)

muscles aren't yet trained to follow those particular directions from their brains. For example, Ms. Barr observes Bill shooting the ball. She asks, "How are you supposed to jump, Bill?" Bill: "Straight up." Ms. Barr: "You jumped sideways that time." Bill: "Gee! I thought I went straight up." To get Bill to consistently jump straight up, Ms. Barr keeps giving him feedback as he practices. Making subtle, seemingly subconscious adjustments during multiple attempts, Bill begins to jump straight up. At that point he needs to practice to sustain that desired conditioned response. Unfortunately, as Bill concentrates on jumping straight up, other steps in the process tend to fall apart. For example, while thinking about jumping straight up, he forgets to keep his elbow tucked in and he makes fewer shots jumping straight up then when he was jumping sideways. Thus, Ms. Barr provides him with verbal encouragement because the natural reinforcement of making more shots won't take effect until he puts all the steps together into one fluid process. That happens only after adequate practice.

Practicing a skill can be quite boring for students. Motivating students to cooperate with you and engage in your lessons the way you designed them is the focus on the next two chapters.

SELF-ASSESSMENT EXERCISES FOR CHAPTER 3

I. Select the one response to each of the following multiple-choice items that either completes the statement so that it is true or accurately answers the question:

A. Ordinarily, the lesson for a conceptualization-of-a-relationship objective should be sequenced in a unit so that _____.
  a. students memorize the relationship before it is conceptualized
  b. students memorize the relationship after it is conceptualized
  c. achievement of the objective culminates the unit
  d. students learn to apply the relationship before it is conceptualized

B. Which one of the following strategies is *least* likely to enhance students' achievement of an appreciation objective?
  a. Students use the objective's content to solve problems that concern them.
  b. The teacher tells students how important understanding the content will be to them.
  c. The teacher demonstrates that use of the content can save time.
  d. Students discover the content for themselves.

C. Student perplexity is a critical ingredient in learning activities for all BUT which one of the following types of objectives?
  a. Creativity
  b. Ability to perform a specific skill
  c. Conceptualization
  d. Application

D. Inquiry instructional activities are appropriate for which one of the following types of objectives?
  a. Voluntary muscle capabilities
  b. Simple knowledge
  c. Knowledge of a process
  d. Application

E. According to this textbook, which type of objective is the most difficult to design lessons for and also the type that virtually all other types of cognitive objectives depend?
   a. Creativity
   b. Application
   c. Knowledge of a process
   d. Conceptualization

F. Lessons for application objectives require _____.
   a. direct instruction
   b. inductive learning activities
   c. deductive learning activities
   d. use of mnemonics

G. Lessons for conceptualization objectives require _____.
   a. direct instruction
   b. inductive learning activities
   c. deductive learning activities
   d. error pattern analysis

H. Lessons for simple-knowledge objectives require _____.
   a. direct instruction
   b. inductive learning activities
   c. deductive learning activities
   d. error pattern analysis

I. Lessons for knowledge-of-a-process objectives require _____.
   a. direct instruction
   b. inductive learning activities
   c. deductive learning activities
   d. use of mnemonics

J. Lessons for ability-to-perform-a-specific-skill objectives require _____.
   a. practice
   b. synectics
   c. use of mnemonics
   d. inquiry instruction

K. Literal and interpretive understanding are associated with what level of learning?
   a. Conceptualization
   b. Application
   c. Comprehension
   d. Creativity

L. Synectics is used in learning activities for what type of objective?
   a. Willingness to try
   b. Comprehension
   c. Application
   d. Creativity

M. Error pattern analysis is used in learning activities for what type of objective?
   a. Simple knowledge
   b. Comprehension
   c. Willingness to try
   d. Knowledge of a process

N. Students are stimulated to formulate generalizations from work with specifics during _____.
   a. inductive learning activities
   b. direct instruction
   c. deductive learning activities
   d. lessons for interpretive understanding

    O. Students utilize syllogisms during _____.
        a. inductive learning activities
        b. direct instruction
        c. deductive learning activities
        d. lessons for interpretive understanding
        Compare your responses to the following: A-b, B-b, C-b, D-d, E-d, F-c, G-b, H-a, I-a, J-a, K-c, L-d, M-d, N-a, O-c.

II. In your response to Exercise III for the self-assessment exercises for Chapter 2, you formulated a set of objectives. In light of your work with Chapter 3, sequence the objectives according to when you would address them in a unit. Also, you may want to modify some and delete or add others. For each of the objectives, design and describe a lesson for helping a group of students achieve that objective. For each objective, make sure that your design is guided by principles for learning activities pertaining to the objective's learning level. Compare your work on this exercise to someone else's.

SUGGESTED READING

Beyer, B. K. (1987). *Practical strategies for the teaching of thinking*. Boston: Allyn & Bacon.

Bourne, L. E., Dominowski, R. L., Loftus, E. F., & Healy, A. F. (1986). *Cognitive processes* (2nd ed.). Englewood Cliffs, NJ: Prentice Hall.

Bruner, J. S. (1960). *The process of education*. New York: Vintage books.

Christoplos, F., & Valletuttie, P. J. (1990). *Developing children's creative thinking through the arts*. Bloomington, IN: Phi Delta Kappa Educational Foundation.

Dillon, R. F., & Sternberg, R. J. (Eds.). (1986). *Cognition and instruction*. San Diego, CA: Academic Press.

Grady, M. P. (1990). *Whole brain education*. Bloomington, IN: Phi Delta Kappa Educational Foundation.

Hunkins, F. P. (1989). *Teaching thinking through effective questioning*. Boston: Christopher-Gordon Publishers.

Jones, B. F., Palincsar, A. S., Ogle, D. S., & Carr, E. G. (Eds.). (1987). *Strategic teaching and learning: Cognitive instruction in the content areas*. Alexandria, VA: Association for Supervision and Curriculum Development.

Joyce, B., & Weil, M. (1986). *Models of teaching* (3rd ed.). Englewood Cliffs, NJ: Prentice Hall.

McDiarmid, G. W., Ball, D. L., & Anderson, C. W. (1987). Why staying one chapter ahead doesn't really work: Subject-specific pedagogy. In M. J. Dunkin (Ed.), *The international encyclopedia of teaching and teacher education* (pp. 193–205). Oxford: Pergamon Press.

Rosenshine, B. (1987). Direct instruction. In M. J. Dunkin (Ed.), *The international encyclopedia of teaching and teacher education* (pp. 257–262). Oxford: Pergamon Press.

Swartz, R. J., & Perkins, D. N. (1990). *Teaching thinking: Issues and approaches* (rev. ed.). Pacific Grove, CA: Midwest Publications.

TAKING WHAT YOU'VE LEARNED TO THE NEXT LEVEL

No matter how well you design lessons with (a) attention-grabbing problems and examples for affective objectives, (b) inductive learning activities for conceptualization objectives, (c) direct instructional activities for simple knowledge objectives, (d) direct and inquiry activities for comprehension objectives, (e) direct instructional and error pattern analysis activities for knowledge-of-a-process objectives, (f) deductive learning activities for application objectives, (g) various heuristic activities, including synectics, for creativity objectives, and (h) direct instructional and exercise activities for psychomotor objectives, your efforts may still fail if you do not solve the most worrisome task faced by teachers, especially beginning teachers (Cangelosi, Struyk, Grimes, & Duke, 1988; Doyle, 1986; Steere, 1988, pp. 5–9; Weber, 1986). That task is to obtain and maintain your students' cooperation so that they willingly engage in your well-designed learning activities. It does little good for you to present a perfectly clear explanation of a process unless your students are following along with you as you intend. Masterfully selected examples and problems raised during questioning/discussion sessions go for naught unless students courteously engage in exchanges and seriously address the issues at hand. Error pattern analysis is useless unless students are motivated to improve their skills. The success of homework and seatwork assignments depends on the effort students are willing to put forth. Formative feedback hardly serves as a guide to you if students either fail to try or cheat on measures of their achievements.

How to elicit students' cooperation and engage them in your direct instructional, inductive, deductive, individualized work, homework and other types of learning activities are the topics of Chapters 4 and 5.

CHAPTER 4

Managing Student Behavior

GOAL OF CHAPTER 4

This chapter suggests ways for you to gain and maintain your students' cooperation. Chapter 4 will help you

1. differentiate between examples and nonexamples of each of the following: (a) allocated time, (b) transition time, (c) on-task behavior, (d) engaged behavior, (e) off-task behavior, (f) disruptive behavior, (g) isolated behavior, (h) behavior pattern, (i) businesslike classroom environment, (j) descriptive communication, (k) judgmental communication, (1) supportive reply, (m) assertive communication, (n) hostile communication, and (o) passive communication (*Cognitive: conceptualization*)
2. explain why the success of teachers' lessons depended on how well they plan and implement ways of teaching students to be on task (*Cognitive: conceptualization*)
3. given a teaching assignment within your area of specialization, describe a plan for managing student behavior in your classroom (*Cognitive: application*)
4. explain fundamental principles for (a) communicating with students in a way that increases the likelihood that they will choose on-task instead of off-task behaviors, (b) establishing a favorable climate for learning, (c) establishing rules of student conduct, (d) establishing classroom procedures, and (e) dealing with off-task behaviors (*Cognitive: conceptualization*)

A WELL-DESIGNED LESSON GONE AWRY

Chapter 3 provided suggestions for designing lessons consistent with research-based principles. However, even when you design a lesson that is appropriate for your objective, learning activities are unlikely to go as planned unless you include measures for gaining and maintaining students' cooperation. Consider the following example:

VIGNETTE 4.1

Mr. Ballam's class of 23 fourth-graders is organized into three reading groups: the "Blues," "Greens," and "Purples." To help his students focus their reading on a purpose, he plans a lesson for the following objective:

> Given a reading assignment or after making a reading selection, explain the purpose for the reading (*Cognitive: comprehension*)

Mr. Ballam's plans to spend 60 minutes on the first day of the lesson as indicated by Figure 4.1.

On the day Figure 4.1's plan is attempted, each group is at its reading area as Mr. Ballam announces to the whole class: "Okay, listen up! Everyone open your readers and the Blues quietly read "Making Things" on page 31, the Greens read "Surprises" on page 44, and the Purples read "People in Our House" on page 37. About 10 students actually follow the directions and begin reading, but the others do not begin. Some misunderstand and think they should be reading as a group. Others failed to catch the page numbers for their reading groups either because they weren't ready to listen when Mr. Ballam began the directions or because they were busy attending to the first part of the directions (i.e., locating and opening their readers) while the titles and page numbers were being listed.

Chris raises his hand from his place among the Greens. Mr. Ballam: "Yes, Chris." Chris: "What are we supposed to be doing?" Mr. Ballam: "What did I tell you to do?" Chris: "I don't know." As students stop what they're doing to listen to the exchange, Mr. Ballam responds, "If you'd of listened in the first place, you'd know you're supposed to be reading page 44 like everyone else." "I thought it was

Figure 4.1. Mr. Ballam's Plan for the First Day (60 minutes) of a Reading Lesson

Unit 3: Reading for a Purpose

Objective A: Given a reading assignment or after making a reading selection, explain the purpose for the reading (*Cognitive: comprehension*)

Agenda for the 60-minute session:
1. Direct the students to silently read short stories from their texts. The Blues will read "Making Things," the Greens "Surprises," and the Purples "People in Our House."
2. Allow 15 minutes for the three groups to complete the silent readings.
3. Combine the three groups for a large-group session.
4. Have members of each group explain what they read to everyone else.
5. Raise questions leading students to bring together ideas from the three readings as a lead-in for me [Mr. Ballam] to suggest that the class plan a project in which students make a surprise for someone with whom they live.
6. Distribute copies of the essays "Things to Make in School" for the Blues to read for homework, "Unusual Gifts" for the Greens to read for homework, and "Planning a Project" for the Purples to read for homework.
7. As time permits, direct students to begin the homework.

VIGNETTE 4.1 (continued)

page 37!'' cries Maureen from the Purples. Mr. Ballam: "It *is* page 37 for your group, but not for the Greens." "*Everyone* else isn't reading either!" Chris protests. Mr. Ballam: "That's because they aren't good listeners either. If you'd . . ."

Eleven minutes later, all the students finally seem to understand the assignment, but while some are just getting under way, others finish. Stacy: "Mr. Ballam, I'm done; what'd you want us to do now?" Mr. Ballam: "Just wait until everyone is done, then we'll have a class discussion." The noise level increases as more students complete the assignment and begin disturbing the late starters, some of whom never seriously undertook the task.

After 16 more minutes of restating the directions and attempting to deal with incidents of off-task behavior, Mr. Ballam announces, "I want everyone to turn their chairs to the front so we can talk about what you just read." Annette shouts, "I'm not finished!" Mr. Ballam: "Well, why not? You should be by now!" Annette: "Because you—" Mr. Ballam: "Oh, never mind. It's not that critical; just listen to the others. . . . Ron! What are you doing with that hat on? You know that we're not allowed to wear hats in the classroom!"

Four minutes later the chairs have been rearranged for the large-group discussion. Mr. Ballam begins, although three students continue to read, "Let's begin with the Purples. Maureen, tell the class what 'People in Our House' was all about." Maureen: "I liked it a lot." Lavelle: "Yeah, you would. You're so freaky!" Mr. Ballam: "She is not freaky; Maureen is an excellent student. You'll be sorry for being rude." Maureen: "As I was trying to say, it was a good story about how people who live together depend on one another." Mr. Ballam: "Excuse me, Maureen, but some people in here aren't listening. . . . Chris and Brenda, why aren't you paying attention?" Chris: "I'm not in the Purples. I thought y'all were discussing the Purples' story." Mr. Ballam: "We are, but we're all supposed to be listening." Chris: "Okay, okay, so I'm a criminal." Most of the students laugh as Mr. Ballam responds, "I didn't say you're a criminal!" Maureen finally finishes explaining what she liked about the selection and a similar report is heard on "Surprises" from one of the Greens. However, the time Mr. Ballam allocated for the reading lessons is exhausted before even one report is heard from the Blues.

Mr. Ballam is frustrated. Only two groups reported and the reports didn't provide summaries of the selections, only expressions of how well the students enjoyed reading them. Consequently, there was no discussion leading to a suggestion for the planned project. In spite of this, Mr. Ballam tells the class as he distributes copies of the essays, "Read these for homework and I'll explain why we're doing all this tomorrow. We're going to have a class project you'll really enjoy—one in which you'll get to make something special for someone." Nancy: "Aw! It's too hard for me to make something really nice." Mr. Ballam: "Oh, it's really easy. You're smart; you won't have any trouble at all."

TEACHERS' MOST PERPLEXING PROBLEM

Why do some teachers orchestrate smoothly operating classrooms where students cooperatively and efficiently go about the business of learning with minimal disruptions (e.g., Mr. Landastoy in Vignette 3.8) whereas others (e.g., Mr. Ballam) ineffectively struggle with student misbehaviors, trying to involve them in planned learning activities? Mr. Ballam violated some very basic behavior management principles.

Whether your teaching experiences are satisfying or marked by constant, frustrating struggles trying to get students to cooperate with you depends largely on how well you apply fundamental, research-based behavior management principles. Overwhelmingly, teachers indicate classroom management and discipline problems cause their greatest difficulties and lead to feelings of inadequacy during their first two years of teaching (Cangelosi, Struyk, Grimes, & Duke, 1988; Evertson, 1989). According to studies conducted over the past 75 years, improper management of student behavior is the leading cause of teacher failure (Bridges, 1986, p. 5).

ALLOCATED AND TRANSITION TIMES

Examine Mr. Ballam's plan displayed in Figure 4.1. Note that four learning activities are planned:

1. Students are to silently read short stories as indicated by agenda items 1 and 2.
2. In a large-group session, students are to explain the three reading selections (items 3 and 4).
3. Mr. Ballam is to conduct a questioning/discussion session in which ideas from the three readings stimulate the class to plan a project to make surprises.
4. Students begin reading essays and complete the assignment for homework.

The time periods in which you plan for your students to be involved in learning activities are referred to as *allocated time*. Thus, Figure 4.1's plan provides for four different *allocated time* periods. The time students spend *between learning activities* is referred to as *transition time*. If Figure 4.1's plan is followed, transition time should occur during the following periods:

1. while students are entering the classroom or shifting from the previous period to the reading period, obtaining the directions for the initial assignment taking out their reading texts, and locating the assigned page
2. as indicated by item 3, when they have just stopped the first learning activity, are receiving directions for the second, and are moving from the reading group arrangement to the large-group arrangement
3. just after item 4's learning activity as they receive directions for and shift to the questioning/discussion session indicated by item 5
4. when Mr. Ballam calls a halt to item 5's activity, makes the assignment for homework and item 7's independent work session, and distributes the essays to read
5. as the reading period ends and the students either exit the classroom or wait for the next period.

STUDENT BEHAVIORS

On-Task Behavior

A student's behavior is *on task* whenever the student is attempting to follow the teacher's directions during either transition or allocated time. The students in the following examples are *on task*:

> As Damian enters the classroom for Russian I class, he sees his teacher point to the assignment on the board. He immediately goes to his desk and begins the assignment.
>
> During a questioning/discussion session, Jacelyn listens to what her teacher and peers are saying, occasionally volunteering her own questions, comments, and responses to other's questions.

Engaged Behavior

A student exhibits *engaged* behavior by being on task during allocated time. In other words, whenever students are attempting to participate in a learning activity as planned by the teacher, the students are engaged in the learning activity. The students in the following examples display engaged behaviors:

> During a questioning/discussion session, Jacelyn listens to what her teacher and peers are saying, occasionally volunteering her own questions, comments, and responses to other's questions.
>
> Corina works on the tasksheet exercises assigned by her teacher.

Off-Task Behavior

A student's behavior is *off task* whenever the student fails to be on task during either transition or allocated time. The students in the following examples are *off task*:

> As Vincent enters the classroom for his Russian I class, he ignores the teacher's directions to begin the assigned exercises; instead, he grabs Mike and begins arguing with him over a disagreement they had earlier.
>
> During a questioning/discussion session about the differences between verbs and nouns, Seritta quietly daydreams about the horse she hopes to have some day.

Disruptive Behavior

A student's behavior is *disruptive* if it is off task in such a way that it interferes with other students being on task. Thus, a student who is being disruptive not only fails to cooperate during transition or allocated time, but also prevents or discourages others from behaving in accordance with the teacher's plans. The students in the following examples are being *disruptive*:

> As Vincent enters the classroom for his Russian I class, he ignores the teacher's directions to begin the assigned exercises; instead, he grabs Mike and begins arguing with him over a disagreement they had earlier.

During a questioning/discussion session about the differences between verbs and nouns, Sybil interrupts others while they are talking and makes jokes that distract others from concentrating on the planned topic.

Figure 4.2 provides examples of student behaviors classified as *on task, engaged, off task,* and *disruptive.*

Isolated Behavior

An incident in which a student exhibits a particular behavior is considered *isolated* if that behavior is not habitual for that student. In the following examples, Dedra's *off-task* behavior during a particular lecture and Len-Taos's *on-task* behavior during a particular exercise are *isolated*:

Ordinarily, Dedra diligently attends to and takes notes during her teacher's presentations. However, today, she is excited about being offered a job and she thinks about the job rather than concentrating on her teacher's explanations about setting up a spreadsheet.

Ordinarily, Len-Taos puts very little effort into his mathematics assignments—completing only mindless one-step exercises and skipping others. However, because an unusual aspect of today's assignment interests him, he assiduously works through every exercise.

Figure 4.2. Examples of Student Behaviors

ON TASK

Engaged in Learning Activities

- Responding to questions during a questioning/discussion session in a manner consistent with the procedures established by the teacher
- Attempting to solve a problem posed in class
- Making suggestions, raising questions, and posing problems as directed by the teacher for group discussion session

On Task during Transition Time

- Listening to the teacher's directions for the next learning activity
- Moving from a small-group to a large-group class arrangement as directed by the teacher
- After completing a test, patiently and quietly waiting for other students to finish theirs

OFF TASK

Disruptive

- Throwing paper across the room while the teacher is explaining an assignment at the chalkboard
- Fighting with another student as the two are about to leave the classroom
- Making a rude remark in response to the teacher's question

Nondisruptive

- Daydreaming during an explanation of an assignment
- Working on an exercise for Spanish class during time allocated for individualized work on a health science exercise
- Discreetly using unauthorized notes to cheat on a test

Behavior Pattern

A student displays a *behavior pattern* by habitually repeating a particular type of behavior. For example:

> Ron almost always diligently attends to his teacher's lectures and carefully takes notes.
>
> Marilyn and Devon frequently talk to one another in social studies class, but the conversations are rarely about social studies.

TEACHING STUDENTS TO BE ON TASK

Learned Behaviors

Socializing with friends, eating, sleeping, partying, watching television, and playing games are the kinds of behaviors that people (e.g., your students) are ordinarily inclined to exhibit. Entering a classroom in an orderly fashion, working on task-sheet exercises, listening to a lecture, engaging in an inductive questioning session, taking tests, raising a hand before speaking, and doing homework are the kinds of behaviors we expect from our students. Such on task behaviors tend to conflict with those that people are naturally inclined to exhibit, thus on task behaviors need to be *taught* to students. On task behaviors (e.g., the six listed in Figure 4.2) are *learned* by students. If you expect your students to choose to cooperate with you and be on task, then you need to *teach* them just how to do that and make sure their efforts are reinforced.

Communicating Expectations

You are responsible for helping your students achieve learning objectives and, thus, engaging them in learning activities. This requires motivating them to be on task themselves and preventing them from disrupting the learning opportunities of their classmates. But because of experiences they may have had with other teachers who were either less conscientious or less able than you in obtaining and maintaining their cooperation, they say initially come to your class not knowing just how serious you are regarding these responsibilities. So, one of your first tasks will be to communicate exactly how you expect them to behave in your classroom. Consider how the teacher in Vignette 4.2 fails to heed that advice.

VIGNETTE 4.2

Mr. Boone is conducting the third day's lesson of an algebra I class. He asks, "Who can tell me what a *variable* is?" Four students raise their hands, but before Mr. Boone calls on one of them, Mike yells out, "A variable is a letter that stands for a number."

(continued)

VIGNETTE 4.2 (continued)

Mr. Boone: Where did you learn that?

Robin: That's what we had in pre-alg——

Mr. Boone: We are supposed to wait our turn to talk.

Robin: "Mike didn't!"

Mr. Boone: Then, Mike was rude. Anyway, this is really important; get it down.

Mr. Boone writes down the following on the overhead projector:

A variable is a quantity, quality, or characteristic that can assume more than one value

Most of the students are unable to read what's on the overhead screen; some don't bother trying. Carney whispers to Mai-Lin, "What's that say?" Mr. Boone sees them and snaps, "Apparently you two don't need to understand this or else you wouldn't be wasting your time talking!" . . .

Near the end of the period, Mr. Boone makes a homework assignment and warns, "I'll be checking to see that it's done first thing tomorrow. If you don't have it, you'll lose points on your grade."

The next day, he has the students place their homework papers on their desks and he quickly walks by each desk, checking the names of those who don't have anything written down for the assignment. No further reference is made to the homework.

Adapted with permission from *Teaching Mathematics in Secondary and Middle School: Research-based Approaches* (p. 126), by J. S. Cangelosi (1992), New York: Macmillan. Copyright © 1992 by Macmillan Publishing Company.

Although Mr. Boone said, "We're supposed to wait our turn to talk," he tolerated Mike's speaking ahead of those who raised their hands waiting their turn to speak. Thus, he unwittingly communicated to the class that he does not take his own dictates very seriously and does not expect them to either. By presenting the "important" definition on the overhead so that it was difficult for most of the class to read, he unwittingly hinted that the subject matter content isn't important enough for him to take the trouble to express it clearly. Mr. Boone also played down the importance of the topic at hand by raising the irrelevant question, "Where did you learn that?" Calling Mike "rude" and being sarcastic with Carney and Mai-Lin encourages antagonistic relationships. Students learn that they are expected to compete with Mr. Boone in a game of "put-downs." The way homework was assigned and checked suggested that the experience of doing the homework is not as important as having something down on paper to avoid a loss of "points."

By contrast, the messages students receive in Vignette 4.3 are the messages their teacher intends for them to receive.

VIGNETTE 4.3

Ms. Strong is conducting the third day's lesson of an algebra I class. She says, "I'm going to ask you a question. You are to take 30 seconds to silently formulate an answer in your mind. Then, if you want to share it with the class, please raise your hand to be recognized. The question is, 'What is a variable?'" Sybil yells, "It's a—" Ms. Strong immediately faces Sybil, interrupting her with a stern look and a nonverbal gesture indicating "Silence!" Thirty seconds later, Ms. Strong calls on John who says, "A variable is a letter that stands for a number." "That's a definition that appears in some books. I'm glad you remembered it. However, you need to understand a different definition for variable for the work we'll be doing in here. Here's our definition," she replies as she displays the following overhead transparency slide:

> A <u>**VARIABLE**</u> is a quantity, quality, or characteristic that can assume more than one value.

Near the end of the period, Ms. Strong makes a homework assignment that's clearly related to the day's lesson about variables. The next day, she begins the period with a short test with which students who diligently worked on the homework assignment have no trouble, but with which other students have difficulty.

Adapted with permission from *Teaching Mathematics in Secondary and Middle School: Research-based Approaches* (p. 126), by J. S. Cangelosi (1992), New York: Macmillan. Copyright © 1992 by Macmillan Publishing Company.

Reinforcing On-Task Behaviors

Once students learn how you expect them to behave, you need to make sure that their cooperative, on-task behaviors are *positively reinforced*. A *positive reinforcer* is a stimulus occurring after a behavior that increases the probability of that behavior being repeated in the future. In Vignette 4.3, Ms. Strong positively reinforced students doing homework by following up the assignment with a short test that was rewarding only for those who had done the homework. She also avoided positively reinforcing Sybil's speaking-out-of-turn behavior by not allowing her to have the floor.

Consistent positive reinforcement of isolated behaviors results in the formation of behavior patterns; furthermore, students will extinguish a behavior that proves unrewarding (Cangelosi, 1988a, pp. 33–37, 218–220). Thus, it is critical for you to make sure that your students' on-task behaviors, not their off-task behaviors, are positively reinforced.

Planning for Students to Be On Task

Students' understanding of your expectations, positive reinforcement of on-task behaviors, and discouragement of off-task behaviors are such critical factors to your teaching success that you cannot afford to allow them to be functions of chance. You need to deliberately design strategies for teaching students to be on task as an integral part of your plans to help them achieve learning goals. Such plans should include methods for (a) establishing a favorable climate for learning, (b) communicating effectively, (c) establishing rules of conduct, (d) establishing classroom procedures, (e) conducting engaging learning activities, and (f) dealing with off-task behaviors. These topics are addressed in the remainder of this chapter and in Chapter 5.

ESTABLISHING A FAVORABLE CLIMATE FOR LEARNING

Priority on the Business of Learning

Your students are in the *business of learning*; you are in the *business of teaching* (i.e., helping them learn). Vignette 4.1 illustrates a case in which a teacher, Mr. Ballam, struggles unsuccessfully to get students engaged in learning activities. His students did not appear to consider learning very serious business. As is true in many classrooms (Jones, 1979), a major portion of the time students spent in Mr. Ballam's class is wasted with matters unrelated to the business of learning (e.g., inefficient transitions, and off-task verbal exchanges). Whether your teaching experiences are dominated by exhausting, frustrating struggles with off-task student behaviors or by satisfying efforts engaging students in smoothly run learning activities, depends largely on whether your students consider your classroom a place for "killing time" or a place for conducting the business of learning.

Students come to realize that learning is serious business in your classroom, not from you telling them so, but from the attitude you display from the first day you walk in the room. First of all, *you* must sincerely believe that the lessons you plan for your students are vital to their achievement of worthwhile learning goals. Then you demonstrate that belief by (a) getting the class off to a businesslike start, (b) being prepared and organized, (c) modeling professional, purposeful behavior, (d) orchestrating efficient transitions, and (e) maintaining a comfortable, nonthreatening environment.

A Businesslike Beginning

Students arrive in your class on the first school day with some preconceived notions on what to expect and what is expected of them. Even the vast majority of beginning kindergarten students anticipate being required to follow teachers' directions and know that antisocial behaviors (e.g., fighting) are unacceptable. Experience has taught older students that screaming, talking out of turn, leaving a classroom without permission, and blatant rudeness are among the behaviors teachers don't appreciate. But experience has also taught them that teachers vary considerably when it comes to dedication to their work, what they tolerate, expectations, awareness of what students are doing, assertiveness, decisiveness, predictability, respect for students, and respect for themselves. In their initial encounters with you they will not yet know (a) how seriously you take your responsibility for helping them learn, (b) which specific student behaviors you expect, which you demand, which you tolerate, which you appreciate, which you detect, which you ignore, which you reward, and which you punish, and (c) how predictably you react to their behaviors. Thus, your students are initially filled with uncertainties about you. During this period of uncertainty, they will be observing your reactions, assessing your attitudes, assessing their place in the social order of the class, assessing their relationship with you, and determining how they will behave in your classroom. Students tend to be more attentive to your words, actions, and reactions, during this "feeling out" period of uncertainty; consequently it is an opportune time for you to communicate some definitive messages that establish the classroom climate and set the standards of behavior for the rest of the course. Thus, it is critical that you begin each course in a very businesslike fashion tending to the work at hand: learning and teaching.

Being businesslike does not require being somber, stiff, or formal. The business of learning and teaching is best conducted in a friendly, relaxed atmosphere where hearty laughter is appreciated. Being businesslike *does* require that learning activities, whether enjoyable or tedious, be considered important and that matters unrelated to achievement of learning goals be dispatched efficiently.

To effect a businesslike beginning to your course, immediately involve students in a learning activity with the following features:

> *Directions for the activity are simple and unlikely to confuse anyone.* This allows your students to get to the business of learning without experiencing bewilderment over "What are we supposed to be doing?" This initial experience teaches students to expect to understand your directions and enhances the chances that they will attend to them in the future. If students are confused by your initial directions, they may not be as willing to try to understand subsequent directions. Later, after they have developed a pattern of attending to your directions, you can begin introducing more complicated procedures to be followed.
>
> *The activity involves them in a task that is novel for them, but one in which they are likely to succeed and experience satisfaction.* Leaving them with the impression that they successfully learned something should serve to positively reinforce engaged behaviors.
>
> *All students are concurrently engaged in the same activity.* Later in the school year, it will be advantageous to have students working on differentiated learning activities. But in the early stages of a course, having all students working on the same task allows you to keep directions simple, monitor the class as a whole, and compare how different students approach the common task. Besides, until you become better acquainted with students, you hardly have a basis for deciding how to individualize.
>
> *The activity is structured so that you are free to monitor student conduct and immediately stem any displays of off-task behaviors.* Jacob Kounin (1977) demonstrated that students are more likely to cooperate with a teacher they believe is "on top of things" and in control of classroom activities. He coined the term *withitness* to refer to a teacher's awareness of what

students are doing. You are in a better position to be *with-it* during activities in which you are free to move about the classroom and position yourself near students than at times when your movements are restricted (e.g., when stationed at a chalkboard, standing behind a lectern, or sitting at your desk). Surely you want to be especially with-it during the early stages of a course.

Following are two examples of ideally designed beginnings to a course or school year.

VIGNETTE 4.4

It is the opening day of a new term at Blackhawk Trail High School. The bell ending second period rings and the bell to indicate the beginning of third period will ring in five minutes. Mr. Stockton, in preparation for the arrival of this third-period earth science class, turns on a video player showing a tape on a prominently displayed monitor with the audio volume control turned up rather loudly. As required by school policy, Mr. Stockton stations himself just outside the classroom door between second and third period. As students enter the room, they hear Mr. Stockton's voice coming from the video monitor, "Please have a seat in the desk displaying a card with your name. If no desk has a card with your name, please sit in one of the desks with a blank card. There you will find a marking pen for you to print and display your first name. Once seated in your desk, please take out one sheet of paper and a pen or pencil. You will need them when third period begins. I would appreciate you clearing your desk top of everything except your name card, pencil or pen, and paper. This message will be repeated until the beginning of third period. After the bell, the directions for today's first lesson will appear on the screen." The message, which is printed on the screen while it can be heard in Mr. Stockton's voice, is repeated continually until five seconds after the third-period bell. Mr. Stockton has moved into the room. He moves among the students, gently tapping one inattentive student on the shoulder and pointing toward the monitor. Several times he gestures to the monitor in response to students trying to talk to him.

The message on the video changes. Mr. Stockton's image appears on the screen with this message: "I am about to perform an experiment. It will take six and a half minutes. During that time, please carefully watch what happens. When the experiment is completed, you will be asked to describe in writing just what you observed. Remember those two words, *describe* and *observe*. We will find them to be very important during this course in earth science. . . ."

As the experiment appears on the screen, Mr. Stockton watches the students. When the videotape is over, the students are directed to spend seven minutes writing a paragraph describing what they saw. Mr. Stockton circulates around the room reading over students' shoulders as they write. At the end of the seven minutes, he calls on several students to read their paragraphs. A class discussion ensues in which a distinction is made between describing observations and making judgments.

Mr. Stockton judges the lesson a success because all students seem to realize that they had made observations and successfully described them. Mr. Stockton distributes copies of the course syllabus and goes over it item by item. Frequent references to observing and recording experiments, such as the one everyone had just commonly shared, are made as the goals of the earth science course are discussed.

VIGNETTE 4.4 (continued)

Textbooks are distributed and some administrative tasks are taken care of before the period ends. Mr. Stockton indicates that classroom rules and organizational procedures will be discussed at the next meeting.

By the way, while the students were viewing the videotape, Mr. Stockton checked the role and posted the attendance report outside the classroom door for school office personnel to pick up.

Adapted with permission from *Classroom Management Strategies: Gaining and Maintaining Students' Cooperation* (pp. 58–59), by J. S. Cangelosi (1988), White Plains, NY: Longman.

VIGNETTE 4.5

Ms. Phegley spent the first two days of the school year just helping her first-graders to get accustomed to their new surroundings. She spent the majority of the time getting to know these six-year-olds and teaching them how to follow rules of conduct and some basic routines (e.g., procedures for using the drinking fountain and getting to and from the cafeteria).

On the third day, as the students are seated at their places, Ms. Phegley announces, "Everyone put your hands on your head like this." She puts both her hands atop her head and the students follow along. Ms. Phegley: "Now keep your hands up there until you see me take mine off of my head." Smiling brightly, she surveys their faces with deliberation. Ms. Phegley: "Taped under your table is an envelope containing your very own word." Roger and Ethan begin to reach under their tables. Ms. Phegley: "My hands are still on top of my head. . . . Thank you for waiting. Now, look around the room. What do you see on the wall just above the boards?" "Posters!" "Cards!" "Words!" are some of the replies. Ms. Phegley: "Yes, I agree! There are posters and cards hanging all around the room with words on them. How many are there?" "Too many!" "One, 2, 3, 4,—10, there are 10!" "No, more than 10!" Ms. Phegley (interrupting): "I'll tell you how many there are. There are as many words on the wall as there are of you. There's one for each of you. One of those words belongs to Louise, and one belongs to Granville, and one belongs to Marva—" "And one belongs to me!" shouts Mickey. "Which one is mine?" asks Gwynn. "Oh! I know," says Claudia, "the envelopes under our tables will tells us!" Ms. Phegley: "That's right; they will. When I take my hands off of my head, that is the signal for you to take the envelope from under your desk and— Tamara, look where my hands are—When I take my hands off my head, that is the signal for you to take the envelope from under your desk and find out which word on the wall it matches. Once you've found your word, you are to go quietly stand under it. I'll tell you what we'll do next after all of you are quietly standing under your own word. Do you want to ask me anything before I take my hands from my head? . . ."

The learning activity continues and eventually culminates with students comparing similarities and differences in their words. Ms. Phegley chose this activity for the first week of school, not only because it helps the students develop some reading readiness skills, but because it gets them used to following her directions and is one with which they could all achieve success. Some students were quicker than others

(continued)

Preparation and Organization

Both Mr. Stockton and Ms. Phegley left their students with the impression that directions are to be strictly followed and learning activities are important business to be taken seriously. It took more *preparation* time for Mr. Stockton to demonstrate the science experiment via video presentation than it would have had he conducted the experiment "live." However, this extra effort in preparation made it much easier for Mr. Stockton to start the first class session smoothly and have students engaged in a learning activity while he was free to manage the setting. The video presentation also lent Mr. Stockton's learning activity a professional touch that told students, "This is serious business. I'm serious enough to make the extra effort to thoroughly organize and prepare. The same is expected of you." Preparing name cards for students was a simple matter, but it contributed to the success of Mr. Stockton's initial meeting with students. Name tags designating seating arrangements provide students with a hint of order in the classroom. Even though Mr. Stockton has approximately 150 students per term at Blackhawk Trail High, because of the name tags, he can call each student by name on the very first day of school. Students whose attention is drifting are more likely to be cued back on task when hearing their name than something like "the guy in the yellow shirt."

By distributing a clearly organized course syllabus, Mr. Stockton suggested to students that the coursework is purposeful, well-organized, and will be conducted in a businesslike manner. An example of a course syllabus is displayed in Figure 8.2.

Ms. Phegley's preparation for placing materials into her first-graders' hands was a bit more elaborate than Mr. Stockton's. Instead of simply distributing word cards to her students in class, she placed them in envelopes before class started and taped them under table tops where they would be out of the students' sights. What advantages did she gain by going to this extra trouble? Gains reaped by the extra time Ms. Phegley spent in preparation included the following: (a) The first-graders were able to discover "their very own" words at the same time without waiting for them to be handed out one at a time. (b) By being taped under the table tops, the word cards were kept out of sight and thus did not become distracting toys before Ms. Phegley was ready for the students to work with them; (c) having an unknown word located in an unusual place added an air of mystery that helped hold students' attention while Ms. Phegley related the directions for the learning activity; (d) having the words already distributed before class left Ms. Phegley more freedom during class to supervise and orchestrate the activities.

Generally speaking, the more work you put into your preparation before class, the less work it will take you to maintain a smoothly operating class. The benefits of exceptional preparation for highly organized learning activities increase over time for at least two reasons: (a) Materials prepared for one class (e.g., Mr. Stockton's videotape and Ms. Phegley's posters for displaying words) can be reused with or refined for subsequent classes. (b) The businesslike attitude a well-prepared, highly organized teacher models for students has a lasting effect that will help establish on-task and engaged student behavior patterns.

Before the start of a school year, spend some time alone in your classroom visualizing exactly what you want to be going on there throughout the upcoming school session. Picture yourself conducting different learning activities and managing transition times. What traffic patterns for student movement do you want followed? How will you control the sounds in your classroom? For example, do you want only one person speaking at a time during large-group sessions and several speaking in hushed tones during small-group activities? What procedures do you want students to follow for such matters as sharpening pencils, using computers, going to the rest room, using the drinking fountain, and obtaining and returning supplies? How do you plan to make time for completing your work that does not involve interacting with students? Anticipate problems that might arise (e.g., students refusing to follow directions or supplies that don't arrive on time) and simulate alternative ways of responding to those problems.

Here is a list of questions one teacher made in preparation for the opening of school (Cangelosi, 1988a):

I. *Classroom Organization and Ongoing Routines*
   1. What different types of learning activities (e.g., video presentations, large-group demonstrations, small-group buzz sessions, and independent project work) do I expect to conduct this term?
   2. How should the room be organized (e.g., placement of furniture, screens, and displays) to accommodate the different types of learning activities and the corresponding transition times?
   3. What rules of conduct will be needed to maximize engagement during the different types of learning activities and to maximize on-task behaviors during transition times?
   4. What rules of conduct will be needed to discourage disruptions to other classes or persons located in or near the school?
   5. What rules of conduct are needed to provide a safe, secure environment in which students and other persons need not fear embarrassment or harassment?
   6. How will rules be determined (e.g., strictly by me, by me with input from the students, democratically, or some combination of these)?
   7. When will rules be determined (e.g., from the very beginning, as needs arise, or both)?
   8. How will rules be taught to students?
   9. How will rules be enforced?
   10. What other parts of the building (e.g., detention room or other classrooms) can be utilized for separating students from the rest of the class?
   11. Whom, among building personnel, can I depend on to help handle short-range discipline problems and whom for long-range problems?
   12. How do I want to utilize the help of parents?
   13. What ongoing routine tasks (e.g., reporting daily attendance) will I be expected to carry out for the school administration?
   14. What events on the school calendar will need to be considered as I schedule the class' learning activities?

    15. What possible emergencies (e.g., fire or student suffering physical trauma) might be anticipated and, considering school policies, how should I handle them?

II. *One-Time-Only Tasks*

    1. How will I communicate the general school policies to my students?

    2. What special administrative tasks will I be required to complete (e.g., identifying number of students on reduced payment lunch program and checking health records)?

    3. What supplies (e.g., textbooks) will have to be distributed?

    4. Are supplies available and ready for distribution in adequate quantities?

    5. How will I distribute and account for supplies?

    6. Are display cards with students' names ready?

    7. How should I handle students who appear on the first day, but are not on my roll?

    8. What procedures will be used to initially direct students into the classroom and to assigned places?

    9. For whom on the student roster might special provisions or assistance be needed for certain types of activities (e.g., students with hearing losses and students confined to wheelchairs)?

III. *Reminders for the First Week's Learning Activities*

    1. Do lesson plans for the first week call primarily for learning activities that (a) have uncomplicated, simple-to-follow directions, (b) are challenging but with which all students will experience success, (c) have built-in positive reinforcers for engagement, and (d) simultaneously involve all students?

    2. Do the first week's lesson plans allow me to spend adequate time observing students, getting to know them, identifying needs, and collecting information that will help me make curricula decisions and design future learning activities?

    3. Do plans allow me to be free during the first week to closely monitor student activities and be in a particularly advantageous position to discourage off-task behaviors before off-task patterns emerge, and positively reinforce on-task behaviors so that on-task patterns do emerge? (pp. 55–57)

Modeling Businesslike, Purposeful Behavior

You teach your students the importance of learning what you intend to teach them and being on task in your classroom more by the attitudes you consistently demonstrate than by telling them, "It's important to learn this," and "You should pay attention." Your classroom behavior serves as a model for students to imitate. Which of the teachers in the next two examples demonstrates to her class that she affords the business of learning and teaching highest priority? Which one allows herself to be easily distracted from that business?

VIGNETTE 4.6

Just as the fourth-period bell rings signaling the beginning of English class, one of Ms. Griffith's students, Barney, begins telling her about a movie he saw last night.

VIGNETTE 4.6 (continued)

Not wanting to seem disinterested, Ms. Griffith continues to talk with Barney, delaying the start of the lesson by seven minutes.

Later during the period, while explaining to the class the differences between primary and secondary reading sources, Ms. Griffith notices Ellen staring off into space, seemingly oblivious to the explanation. Without moving from her position in front of the room, Ms. Griffith stops her presentation to the class and says to Ellen, "Earth to Ellen, earth to Ellen—come in Ellen, return to this planet for your English lesson!" Ellen glares back at Ms. Griffith who retorts, "Don't glare at me, young lady! You're the one in outer space instead of where you should be!" Embarrassed in front of her friends, Ellen half-smiles and appears to pay attention. Ms. Griffith says, "That's better; now, keep paying attention." But Ellen isn't thinking about the primary and secondary reading sources about which Ms. Griffith is talking. As she pretends to attend to the lesson, Ellen's mind is focused on her embarrassment. She feels Ms. Griffith insulted her. Furthermore, some of the other students who were engaged in the learning activity prior to the incident, are no longer concentrating on the lesson.

A few more minutes into the explanation, Ms. Griffith notices Mr. Tang, the principal, beckoning her to the door. She abruptly stops the lesson with, "Just a minute class. I have some business to take care of with Mr. Tang." In a few minutes, the class gets noisy and Ms. Griffith turns from her conversation in the doorway to yell, "Quiet in here! I can't hear what Mr. Tang is saying; it's important!" Eight minutes later, Ms. Griffith is ready to reengage the students in the lesson, but it takes a while for most of them to shift their thoughts back to the content.

VIGNETTE 4.7

Just as the fourth-period bell rings signaling the beginning of English class, one of Ms. Del Rio's students, Bonita, begins telling her about a movie she saw last night. Not wanting to seem disinterested, but recognizing that the lesson should begin, Ms. Del Rio says, "I really want to hear about that movie, but I'm afraid it's time to start class. Please tell me about it when we have the time."

Later during the period, while explaining to the class the differences between primary and secondary reading sources, Ms. Del Rio notices Abdul staring off into space, seemingly oblivious to the explanation. Without missing a word in her presentation to the class, Ms. Del Rio moves by Abdul and gently pats him on the shoulder. Abdul "wakes up" from his daydream and appears to be attending to the explanation, which continues without interruption as she moves about the room.

A few minutes later, Ms. Del Rio notices Ms. Lignagarious, the principal, beckoning her to the door. Rather than stop in midexplanation, she acknowledges Ms. Lignagarious with a hand signal indicating "just a moment, I can't stop now." In 2 minutes, with Ms. Lignagarious still waiting in the doorway, Ms. Del Rio reaches a stopping point and tells the class, "Keep that last thought in mind, 'Secondary reading sources may not contain critical details contained in primary sources,' while I quickly find out what Ms. Lignagarious needs." At the door, Ms. Lignagarious attempts to engage Ms. Del Rio in a conversation about a meeting to be held that night. However, Ms. Del Rio responds with, "I can't stop my lesson right now. Please come back in 25 minutes, I'll have them doing independent work then." After

(continued)

VIGNETTE 4.7 (continued)

that 22-second interruption, she returns to the explanation by asking, "Now, what was the last thought I asked you to keep in mind? . . . Okay, Gaston." Gaston: "You said that secondary . . ."

Efficient Transitions

Unlike Ms. Griffith, Ms. Del Rio indicated to her students that time allocated for learning is too precious to be wasted. By efficiently using the transition times between learning activities you not only save allocated time; you also communicate to your students the importance of getting down to business. The efficiency of your transitions is at least partially dependent on how you manage to take care of administrative chores, direct students into learning activities, distribute learning materials, and prepare illustrations and audiovisual aids.

Taking Care of Administrative Chores. Administrative chores (e.g., checking the roll, collecting lunch money, and completing accident reports) are a necessary aspect of your responsibilities as a teacher. However, it it not necessary to spend over a third of your class time, as many teachers do, with such noninstructional matters (Cangelosi, 1988a, p. 19; Jones, 1979). As Mr. Stockton demonstrated in Vignette 4.4, you can check attendance, homework, and other things while students are busy working on an assignment or test. A seating chart and prepared forms with students' names and grids for checking off such things as whether or not an assignment has been completed facilitate record keeping and other routine matters with minimal infringement on class time.

Directing Students into Learning Activities. The directions for a learning activity are delivered during the preceding transition period. That transition period is efficient only if those directions are delivered concisely and clearly enough for students to be properly engaged in the learning activity with only minimal delays. Suggestions for giving directions are provided in Chapter 5. For now, keep in mind how Mr. Stockton and Ms. Phegley, in Vignettes 4.4 and 4.5, managed to communicate very specific directions to students while remaining free to closely monitor student behavior during the transition period.

Distributing Learning Materials. Having materials laid out for students ahead of time helps streamline transition periods. Ms. Phegley, for example, had taped envelopes under students' desks before they arrived. Materials in students' hands before they are needed can be a distraction. Ms. Phegley's method allowed her to distribute materials ahead of time in a way that heightens students' curiosity without being a distraction.

Preparing Illustrations and Audiovisual Aids. Contrast the efficiency of the transition in the next example to that of the transition in the example that follows it.

VIGNETTE 4.8

Ms. Steele announces to her social studies class, ''There are seven major features of the 'Bill of Rights' with which I want you to be familiar. Please jot each down in your notebooks as I put it on the chalkboard. Then we'll discuss the features in some detail.'' With her back to the class, Ms. Steele lists the first feature on the board. The students try and copy from the board as she writes, but they must *wait* for her to finish writing and move out of their lines of vision. Ms. Steele turns around ready to discuss the first feature, but the students are still copying. Some finish the five lines of text sooner than others. Ms. Steele begins her explanation of the feature after most look up from their notebooks, leaving only a few still writing.

With the discussion on the first feature completed, Ms. Steele turns her back again to the class, and repeats the process for the second through the seventh features. By the time she gets to the fourth feature, the chalkboard area that could be readily viewed by the students is exhausted, so she erases the first several features to make room. Erasing is, of course, time consuming and it prevents her from using the display relative to those earlier features later in the discussion. During the periods when Ms. Steele was writing on the board, some students amused themselves by daydreaming or whispering among themselves. Some of those students had difficulty getting reengaged in the discussion each time Ms. Steele faced the class to explain and discuss another one of the seven features.

Adapted with permission from *Classroom Management Strategies: Gaining and Maintaining Students' Cooperation* (pp. 70–71), by J. S. Cangelosi (1988), White Plains, NY: Longman.

VIGNETTE 4.9

Mr. Piowaty announces to his social studies class, ''There are seven major features of the 'Bill of Rights' with which I want you to be familiar. Please jot each down in your notebooks as I display it on the overhead screen. Then we'll discuss the features in some detail.'' Mr. Piowaty observes the students readying their notebooks and then flips on the overhead projector. The first feature is displayed; he watches as the students make their copies. During the ensuing explanation and discussion on the feature, Mr. Piowaty makes notes on the overhead transparency and highlights phrases in the description of the first feature. He does this without ever turning his attention from the class.

The class is cued that it is time to attend to the second feature when Mr. Piowaty replaces the first transparency with one describing the second feature. The process is repeated for the remainder of the features without Mr. Piowaty ever having to turn away from the class or the students having to wait for either the description of the feature to be written out or for their lines of sight to be cleared. Throughout the learning activity, Mr. Piowaty was able to control what the students could view on the screen. Descriptions of features not being discussed were not displayed. However, Mr. Piowaty was able to bring back into view previously discussed features if he wanted to draw comparisons or raise other points about them.

Adapted with permission from *Classroom Management Strategies: Gaining and Maintaining Students' Cooperation* (pp. 71–72), by J. S. Cangelosi (1988), White Plains, NY: Longman.

Whenever feasible, consider preparing visual and even audio presentations before they are needed in class. This initially infringes on your out-of-class time, but remember that these materials will still be available for use in subsequent classes. Thus, the net savings in time works in your favor. Mr. Piowaty did not take students' time writing on the chalkboard with his back to the class, thus he minimized transition time and facilitated keeping students on task. Overhead projectors, videocassette recorders, and microcomputers (especially with word-processing, desktop publishing, and graphic capabilities), display computers, and video disk players are only a few of the widely available cost-effective devices that make it easier for you to conduct high-quality professional demonstrations that streamline transitions and enhance the businesslike atmosphere of your classroom.

A Comfortable, Nonthreatening Environment

Schools are frightening places for many students (McLaren, 1989). Many school environments are contaminated by an atmosphere in which students fear that the immediate risks of becoming enthusiastic about learning outweigh the long-range benefits. Why does such an atmosphere exist? The following contributing factors have been suggested (Cangelosi, 1988a, p. 76):

The threat of physical violence in schools may be so great in the minds of some students that they are more concerned about surviving each school day without being seriously injured than they are about academic concerns.

Some students may fear that their efforts to achieve learning goals will be ridiculed by peers who do not value academic achievement.

Some students believe that if they put an effort into learning activities and still fail to achieve learning goals, they will either be labeled ''stupid'' or fail to live up to a previously acquired label of ''smart.''

Because they feel that a teacher has challenged or embarrassed them in front of their peers, some students consider engaging in learning activities tantamount to collaborating with a resented authority figure.

The existence of any or all of the aforementioned factors does not excuse misbehavior or disengagement in learning activities. However, to establish a climate in your classroom that is favorable to learning, you must see to it that fear and discomfort are overcome by students' learning that your classroom is a safe haven for intellectual pursuits. You teach your students that attitude by the manner in which you communicate with them and establish and consistently enforce sensible rules of conduct.

COMMUNICATING EFFECTIVELY

Proximity and Body Language

Put yourself in the place of a student sitting in Mr. Bertoux's class. As pictured in Figure 4.3, he's telling you and your classmates something.

Now, visualize yourself in Mr. Tramonte's class. As pictured in Figure 4.4

Figure 4.3. Mr. Bertoux Speaking to You

Figure 4.4. Mr. Tramonte Speaking to You

he's telling you and your classmates something. To which of the two teachers do you think you might have listened more carefully?

Research suggests that students are more likely to listen to a teacher who is facing them, making eye contact, and nearby than one in the posture illustrated by Mr. Bertoux in Figure 4.3 (Cangelosi, 1988a, pp. 89–91; Jones, 1979). Mr. Bertoux's body language suggests that he doesn't take what he's saying seriously enough to face his listeners. Mr. Tramonte's body language clearly tells students, "I'm talking to you and I expect you to be listening to this important message!" Your posture, body position, location in the room, use of eye contact, gestures, and facial expressions provide students with an indication of the degree to which you are in control, care for them, and expect to be taken seriously.

Get in the habit of facing and making eye contact with students to whom you are speaking. When addressing the entire class, move your eyes about the room, making eye contact with one student after another. Managing to focus your eyes on individual students regularly during the course of classroom activities, occasionally making positive expressions and gestures (e.g., smile, wink, or thumb up) when you've caught their eye, helps establish an atmosphere of mutual respect. When addressing only one or two students at a time, body positioning can be used to clearly indicate to whom your message is intended. Which teacher in the following two examples displays the more effective use of body language?

VIGNETTE 4.10

Ms. White's students are working individually on an assignment at their desks; she moves about the room responding to questions and providing one-to-one help. While reviewing an exercise with Ellis, she hears Joyce and David talking to one another from the other side of the room. Without turning from Ellis, she yells, "Knock it off, you two!" Others in the class stop their work to find out to whom she's speaking.

VIGNETTE 4.11

Ms. Lundstrom's students are working individually on an assignment at their desks; she moves about the room responding to questions and providing one-to-one help. While reviewing an exercise with Davalon, she hears Norton and Eva talking to one another from the other side of the room. She softly tells Davalon, "Excuse me I'll be back within 35 seconds." Ms. Lundstrom pivots and faces Norton and Eva, calmly walks directly toward them, and squats down so they are on the same eye level. With her shoulders parallel to Norton's, she looks him in the eyes and in a firm, but hushed voice says, "I would like for you two to work on these exercises without further talk." She immediately turns directly to Eva, achieves eye contact, and repeats the message. Standing up, she pivots and returns to Davalon.

Ms. Lundstrom's mannerisms made it clear that what she had to say was meant only for Norton and Eva. Other students didn't need to stop their work to find out that her message didn't apply to them. It is to your advantage to speak so the entire class can hear you *only* when you expect all students to focus their attention on your words. Having experiences stopping their work to listen to you only to find out you are speaking to someone else conditions students to "turn you off."

Descriptive versus Judgmental Communications

Students feel less threatened, less defensive, and more willing to engage in learning activities when working with teachers who consistently use *descriptive* language than when working with teachers who use judgmental language (Van Horn, 1982). *Descriptive language* verbally portrays a situation, behavior, achievement, or feeling. *Judgmental language* verbally summarizes an evaluation of a person, achievement, or behavior with a characterization or label (Cangelosi, 1988a, p. 83). Judgmental language that focuses on personalities is especially detrimental to a climate of cooperation in the classroom (Ginott, 1972). Mr. Pierce uses *descriptive* language in the following examples:

> Four-year-old Linka shows a picture he just painted to Mr. Pierce who exclaims, "The yellows and bright blues in your picture make me think of a clear, sunny day!"
> Dalphia and Jan begin talking to one another as Donald is addressing the class explaining his perceptions on an issue. Mr. Pierce says, "Excuse me, Donald." Turning to Dalphia and Jan, he says, "Your talking is preventing me from concentrating on what Donald is explaining to us."
> Mr. Pierce returns Ted's test paper with the following comment written by one of the items: "You completed the steps of the algorithm without a single error. However, your answer doesn't take into account that the denominator cannot be zero."

Judgmental language is used by Ms. Tobias in these next three examples:

> Four-year-old Leo shows a picture he just painted to Ms. Tobias who exclaims, "You're a great artist; that's a gorgeous picture!"
> Katherine and Mark begin talking to one another as Tom is addressing the class explaining his perceptions of an issue. Ms. Tobias says, "Excuse me, Tom, but there are a couple of rude people in here!"
> Ms. Tobias returns Juanita's test paper with the following comment written by one of the items: "You're too mechanical; be more of a thinker."

The extra thought required in using descriptive instead of judgmental language will be well worth the benefits in terms of student attitudes and classroom climate. You should consistently make descriptive instead of judgmental comments to your students for the following reasons:

> *Descriptive language is far richer in information than is judgmental language.*
> Students gain specific information about their work, behavior, or situation

from your descriptive comments. Judgmental comments only provide broad labels (e.g., "good" and "bad") that students would be better off determining for themselves in light of specific information. Once your students learn that your comments tend to be filled with helpful information, they are likely to be more attentive to your words.

Descriptive language focuses on the business at hand, not on personalities. Communicating about work to be performed, rather than judgments about those performing the work, enhances the businesslike atmosphere of the classroom. Comments such as "You're rude!" or "You're smart!" detract from the business of engaging in learning activities.

Unlike judgmental language, descriptive language avoids the labeling of students and the dangerous practice of confounding academic achievement with self-worth. The delicate and complex relationship among students' self-concepts, desires to be loved and accepted, and experiences with successes and failures is a topic for extensive study (Cangelosi, 1988a, pp. 23–41, 83–110; Dreikurs, 1968; Ginott, 1965, 1972; Harris, 1969). It is a common mistake to think that students will be motivated to cooperate and study diligently because their teachers praise them for appropriate behaviors and academic achievements and withhold praise or criticize them for misbehaving and failing to achieve. To the contrary, such tactics are more likely to backfire than to motivate desirable behaviors and efforts. For example, Ms. Tobias's reference to Katherine and Mark as "rude people" may lead them to believe she no longer respects them and their only course is to try and live down to their reputations as "rude people." Overhearing a teacher label one student as "smart" because that student correctly answered a question can trigger this in the mind of another student: "I didn't know the answer, so I must be dumb!" The praise may also have an adverse effect on students who are called smart. They may feel pressure to live up to the label. In time, the students might protect the reputation as "smart" simply by avoiding tasks at which they could fail.

Supportive versus Nonsupportive Replies

The teacher in Vignette 4.12 tries to encourage a student to confidently pursue a task, but reaps the opposite effect:

VIGNETTE 4.12

Mr. Williams's students individually work on an exercise translating sentences from Spanish to English. As he passes Janelle's desk, she says, "I can't figure these out; they're too hard for me!" He responds, "Janelle, these should be easy for a smart girl like you! Here, I'll show you how simple they are. . ."

What impact do you think Mr. Williams's well-intentioned response had on Janelle's attitude about translating sentences and working with him? She said the exercises are "hard;" he said they should be "easy for a smart girl." Besides denying her feelings, Mr. Williams has indicated that if she thinks the exercises are hard, she's not smart. Janelle is less inclined to work with Mr. Williams because in her mind, he doesn't listen to what she says (he contradicted her statement) and he thinks she's stupid. His response to Janelle's expression of frustration failed to demonstrate that he understood that she was experiencing difficulty, thus Mr. Williams's reply was *nonsupportive*. A reply to an expression of feelings (usually frustration) is considered *supportive* if the response clearly indicates that the feelings have been recognized and not judged to be right or wrong. Here is an example of a teacher making a supportive reply:

VIGNETTE 4.13

Mr. Cottle's students individually work on an exercise translating sentences from Spanish to English. As he passes Tina's desk, she says, "I can't figure these out; they're too hard for me!" He responds, "You're having difficulty picking out the Spanish verbs; that can be a real struggle. . . . Let's look at this one. . . ."

Mr. Cottle demonstrated that he heard and understood what Tina said. Once he let her know that he recognizes her frustration and she doesn't have to feel uncomfortable about it, Tina is ready to work with him on the Spanish. He listened to her and now she is prepared to listen to him.

Assertive versus Hostile or Passive Communications

Studies examining traits of teachers whose students display high levels of on-task behaviors suggest that your students are more likely to cooperate with you and be on task if you consistently communicate with them in an *assertive* manner rather than in either a *hostile* or *passive* manner (Canter & Canter, 1976).

Your communications are *assertive* when you send exactly the message that you want to send being neither intimidating nor intimidated. For example:

VIGNETTE 4.14

Nettie begs her teacher, Ms. Triche, "Please give us more time to finish that paper. It's not fair for us to have to have it by Friday!" Mary Frances: "Could we wait 'til Monday to turn it in?" Others in the class chime in with comments such as, "Oh, please Ms. Triche, be nice just this once!" Nettie: "We've got a game Thursday night and I know you want to support the team!" Nau: "You wouldn't want us to miss the game, would you?"

Ms. Triche is tempted to "be nice," "show support for the team," and enjoy the students' cheers she'd receive by giving into their wishes. However, she also realizes the consequences of delaying the assignment. Some students will fall behind

(continued)

---

in their work. If she doesn't get the papers until Monday she won't be able to examine and annotate them over the weekend, disrupting her schedule. Furthermore, she knows that by adjusting their own schedules, the students could complete the work on time without missing the game.

Ms. Triche announces to the class, "I understand that you are worried about making it to this important game and still finishing your work on time. You have cause for concern. Because changing the due date will mess up our schedule and because I need the weekend to go over your work and provide you with feedback, the work is still due on Friday." "That's not fair!" cries Porter. Ms. Triche: "Yes, I know it seems unfair to you. Now, let's turn our books to page 177. . . ."

A less assertive teacher in Ms. Triche's situation may have feared jeopardizing a friendly relationship with the students by not agreeing to their request. Actually, her assertive communications enhances her relationship with students because students learn that she takes their work very seriously and her plans for them are well thought out and not changed whimsically. Furthermore, had she altered her plans, thus inconveniencing herself and causing the class to fall behind, she may have disappointed herself for failing to do what she thought best. Such disappointments often lead to feelings of resentment directed toward the students (Wolpe & Lazarus, 1966).

Rather than being assertive, your communications are *hostile* when they are intimidating or include personal innuendoes and insults. Ms. Triche would have displayed *hostile* communications if she had responded to the students' request as follows:

> "You people are always trying to get out of work! Do you think your game is more important than schoolwork? Schoolwork will take you a lot farther in life than games. Besides, if you weren't so lazy, you'd have this paper finished in plenty of time for your game!"

Hostile communications encourage antagonistic feelings that detract from an atmosphere conducive to cooperation and learning. *Passive* communications erode the teacher's ability to control classroom activities. Your communications are passive when you fail to convey the message you want because you are intimidated or fearful of the reactions of the recipients of your message. Ms. Triche's communications would have been passive if she had responded to the students' request as follows:

> "Well, we really need to have these papers done by Friday. I really should be going over them this weekend. I wish you wouldn't ask me to do this because I . . . But, okay, just this once—because this is an important game."

Being Responsible for One's Own Conduct

People who frequently communicate passively tend to feel that others control their lives for them. However, except for the relatively unusual cases where one person physically accosts another, one person cannot *make* another do something.

Once students realize this and realize you hold them responsible for their own conduct, they are disarmed of excuses for misbehavior. Eavesdrop on this otherwise private conversation between two teachers:

VIGNETTE 4.15

Mr. Suarez: Didn't you have Carolyn Smith in pre-algebra last year?

Ms. Michelli: Yes. How's she getting along in algebra I?

Mr. Suarez: Awful! Today, I asked her why she didn't have her homework and she told me she had better blinking things to do than my blinking homework.

Ms. Michelli: Except I bet she didn't say "blinking." Her vocabulary is more to the point.

Mr. Suarez: Exactly, she used the "f-word" out loud in front of the whole class.

Ms. Michelli: What did you do?

Mr. Suarez: I was really dumfounded; I didn't know what to do. So, I bought myself some time, by telling her to meet me after school today.

Ms. Michelli: If she shows up, what do you plan to do?

Mr. Suarez: I had planned to take firm measures to prevent her from pulling this kind of thing again. But then, Bill who has her for biology told me she's an abused child and we need to give her every break. After he told me the kinds of things she's suffered, I understand why she's so uncooperative. How do you think I should handle it?

Ms. Michelli: First of all, knowing about her unfortunate situation helps us understand why she misbehaves. But you don't do her a favor by excusing misbehavior. Sure, she has it rougher than the rest of us, but she's still capable of conducting herself in a civil, cooperative way in your classroom. Our job is to hold her to the same standards of classroom conduct we expect of everybody else. We're aware of her background, so it's easier for us to respond to her misbehaviors constructively, rather than angrily.

Mr. Suarez: So, I should stick with my plan for being firm with her.

Ms. Michelli: Let's hear it, and you also need to come up with a strategy if she fails to show up this afternoon.

Mr. Suarez: Well, first, in no uncertain terms I plan to tell her that . . ."

Adapted with permission from *Teaching Mathematics in Secondary and Middle Schools: Research-based Approaches* (p. 139), by J. S. Cangelosi (1992), New York: Macmillan. Copyright © 1992 by Macmillan Publishing Company.

To lead students to understand that they are in control of their own conduct, consistently use language that is free of suggestions that one person can determine how another chooses to behave. Purge utterances such as the following from your communications with students: "You made me lose control." "You hurt his feelings!" "Watch out or you'll get her into trouble." "Does he make you mad?" "If she can do the experiment, so can you."

Replace such nonsense with remarks like these: "It's difficult for me to control myself when you do that." "He felt bad after you said that!" "Be careful not to influence her to do something she'll regret.'' ''Do you get mad when he does that?'' ''We know the experiment is possible; she did it.''

Remind students that they are in control of and responsible for their own conduct whenever they say things such as, ''Well, Sue made me do it!'' or ''Why blame me? I wasn't the only one!''

Communicating with Parents

A Cooperative Partnership. Ideally, you, each student, and the student's parents form a cooperative team working together for the benefit of the student. Unfortunately, all parents are not able and willing to contribute to such a team. But whenever you do elicit parents' cooperation in support of your work with their children, you reap a significant advantage in managing student behavior and, thus, helping students achieve learning goals. Most, though not all, parents are in a position to (a) encourage their children to cooperate with you and engage in schoolwork, (b) provide time and space for their children to do homework and monitor their attention to homework assignments, (c) motivate their children to attend school regularly, and work with you in addressing discipline problems their children might present in your classroom.

The key to gaining parents' cooperation is establishing and maintaining an active, two-way channel of communications. Such a channel for each student needs to be opened before either problems arise that call for immediate parental help (e.g., serious disruptive behavior patterns) or summative evaluations of student achievement (especially those involving low or failing grades) must be reported. You open communication channels before crises arise by keeping parents apprised as to what learning goals their children should be striving to achieve and how you are attempting to help them reach those goals. Parents need to be informed as to how they can help in the process. Basically, you have two vehicles for keeping parents informed, *conferences* and *written communiques*.

Teacher/Parent Conferences. Conferences between parents and teachers are more common in elementary schools than they are for secondary schools. Each elementary teacher is involved with fewer students, with greater responsibilities for each, than is the typical secondary school teacher. It is quite common for elementary schools to periodically devote entire school days for conferences between teachers and parents. Although this practice is not as common in secondary schools, secondary teachers also need to find time for conferences with parents. Following are suggestions for you to consider whenever you meet one of your student's parents for a scheduled conference (Cangelosi, 1988a)

1. Prepare an agenda for the conference that specifies the purpose of the meeting (e.g., to increase the rate at which the student completes homework assignments), a sequence of topics to be discussed, and a beginning and ending time for the conference.
2. Except for special situations, invite the student to attend and participate in the conference. (Healthier, more open attitudes are more likely to emerge when the student, as well as the guardian and you, is involved.)
3. Schedule the meeting in a small conference room or other setting where distractions (e.g., a telephone) are minimal and there is little chance for outsiders to overhear the conversation.

4. Provide a copy of the agenda to each person in attendance. During the meeting, direct attention to the topic at hand by referring to the appropriate agenda item and by using other visuals (e.g., report card or test).

5. Throughout the conference, concentrate remarks on descriptions of events, behaviors, and circumstances. Focus on needs, goals, and plans for accomplishing goals. Completely avoid characterizations and personality judgments.

6. During the conference be an active listener so that you facilitate two-way communications between you and those at the meeting and, thus, increase the likelihood that you get your planned message across and learn from the others at the meeting, gaining ideas for working more effectively with the student. (p. 104)

Written Communiques. Besides conferences with parents, which out of necessity are infrequent, some teachers send home weekly or monthly newsletters designed to apprise parents of what their children's classes are doing. Figure 4.5 provides an example.

Figure 4.5. Example of Teacher's Newsletter for Parents (*Source*: From *Classroom Management Strategies: Gaining and Maintaining Student Cooperation* [p. 105] by James S. Cangelosi, 1988, White Plains, NY: Longman. Reprinted by permission.)

PARENTS' NEWSLETTER FOR AMERICAN HISTORY II, THIRD PERIOD

From Jake Bertolli, Teacher

Vol. 1, Number 24, Week of March 16–20

Looking Back

Our last letter mentioned that we had begun a unit on the latter 19th-century industrialism in the United States. I think a majority of the class were a bit bored with the material dealing with some of the major personalities (e.g., Carnegie and Rockefeller) that influenced industrialization in that era. However, I was quite pleased with the enthusiasm nearly everyone showed for the lessons on worker-management issues of that time. The problems that lead to the enactment of child labor laws seemed particularly intriguing to a number of the students. Based on my statistical analysis of the results, the test the class took last Friday seemed to provide a pretty accurate indictor of what most students achieved during the week. The class average on the test was 37.3; that was slightly higher than I had anticipated.

This Week

This week we will be discussing the rise of trusts in this country and move into the presidency of Woodrow Wilson (elected in 1912). The relationship between the economic climate in the United States and the fighting of World War I will be a major focus of the class. One of the goals of the lesson is to help your daughter or son to understand how one event (e.g., a corporation in the United States decides to expand) influences another event (e.g., strategic plans for a battle in Europe).

Homework assignments will include: (a) Read pp. 588–661 from the textbook for Thursday's class; (b) watch the show from 8:30 too 9:30 P.M. on channel 7, Tuesday night, and be prepared to discuss its content at Wednesday's class; (c) complete a worksheet, to be distributed Thursday, and attach it to the test to be given on Friday; (d) prepare for Friday's test.

Looking Forward

Next week, we will compare what we learned about the rise of industries and corporations near the turn of the century to today's world economic situation. In subsequent weeks, we'll return our attention to the 1920s and examine some causes of war and ways to achieve peace.

By taking the time to write such form letters, you foster the goodwill and understanding of students' parents. Their understanding of what you are trying to accomplish with their children will serve you well when you need to call on them to help you deal with behavior problems.

Professional Confidences

Violations of Trust. What, if anything, bothers you about the behavior of the teachers in the next three examples? (Adapted with permission from *Classroom Management Strategies: Gaining and Maintaining Students' Cooperation* [p. 106], by James S. Cangelosi [1988], White Plains, NY: Longman.)

VIGNETTE 4.16

Two teachers, Mr. Bates and Ms. Saddler, are talking in the 45th Street Sixth-Grade Center faculty room. Mr. Bates: "How's it going?" Ms. Saddler: "There must be a full moon! The kids are a bit nutsy today. Just hope you never have Arla Neville. She can't follow what's going on, so she entertains herself by bugging me. Why do I have to have all the retards?"

VIGNETTE 4.17

Bill Kresie, a high school coach and social science teacher, meets one of his friends, Vickie Dobson, in the grocery store. Mr. Kresie: "Hi, Vickie." Ms. Dobson: "Well, hello, Bill. It's nice to see you. What've you been up to?" Mr. Kresie' "Same ole' stuff. How about you?" Ms. Dobson: "Well, you know my daughter, Christine—" Mr. Kresie: "Yes, lovely girl. How's she doing?" Ms. Dobson: "She just broke up with Ronald Boher and has taken up with Don Palmer." Mr. Kresie: "Really! Good move on her part. Ronald's a real loser. He went out for football, you know, and showed no guts at all. I had Don in American history. Bright, bright kid!"

VIGNETTE 4.18

In a parent–teacher conference with Gary Mastoroni's father, Ms. Mauger tells him, "You know Gary is doing quite well. I wish all my students were like Gary. If I could get Elmo Thompson to cooperate like Gary, I'd jump for joy!"

Trust between a teacher and a student is an important ingredient in establishing a classroom climate that is conducive to cooperation, on-task behaviors, and engagement in learning activities. Teachers violate that trust when they gossip about students or share information obtained through their role as teachers with people who need not be privy to that information. Ms. Saddler, in the first of the three aforementioned examples, was frustrated and obviously needed to talk about her difficult day. Her behavior was understandable, but was it professional? Was it excusable? Her baneful use of the label "retards" displayed Ms. Saddler's disregard for at least some accepted professional standards. If all the teachers at 45th Street Sixth-Grade Center understand that the faculty room is a place for teachers to vent some of their frustrations and what is said does not leave the faculty room, then Ms. Saddler's comments may never get back to students. Once students acquire the idea that teachers gossip about them, they are far less likely to feel comfortable in trusting those teachers. In the two latter examples, Mr. Kresie and Ms. Mauger can hardly hope that their comments about students will not be spread by the "outsiders" to whom they spoke.

Privileged Information. Surely, there are times when you, as a teacher, should communicate information and express your judgments about students' achievement levels and behaviors to others. Who should be privileged to those communications? Typically, the following are considered to have a right and need to know (Cangelosi, 1988a):

1. For most cases, *students* need to be kept apprised of their own status regarding achievement of learning goals and evaluations of classroom conduct.
2. The student's *parents* often need to be aware of their child's level of achievement and behaviors for two reasons: (a) Parents who understand just what their children are and are not accomplishing in school are in an advantageous position to serve as partners to teachers to help their children cooperate and achieve. (b) Parents are legally responsible for their children's welfare. They do, after all, delegate and entrust some of their responsibilities to teachers. They should know how the school is impacting their children.
3. *Professional personnel (e.g., a guidance counselor or another of the student's teachers) who have instructional responsibilities for that student* sometimes need to know about the student's achievement and behaviors so that they are in a better position to help that student.
4. *Professional personnel (e.g., the principal, subject area supervisor, or curriculum director) whose judgments impact the curricula and conduct of the school* sometimes need to be aware of an individual student's achievements or behaviors so that they will be in an advantageous position to make school-level decisions.
5. A school often acts as an agency that qualifies students for occupations, as students at other institutions, or for other privileges (e.g., scholarships); consequently it may sometimes be necessary for a *representative of an institution to which a student has applied* to have knowledge of evaluations of that student's achievements and behaviors. However, school personnel should seriously consider following a policy that they release information on students' achievements or behaviors to such representatives only with students' and their guardians' authorization (p. 107).

ESTABLISHING RULES OF CONDUCT AND CLASSROOM PROCEDURES

Necessary Rules of Conduct

In virtually all schools, there is a published set of *school rules* for student conduct (e.g., "Fighting is prohibited on school property."). Furthermore, teachers typically have their own set of rules for how students are to conduct themselves in the classroom. The *classroom rules of conduct* you establish should provide students with general guidelines for their behavior while under your supervision. The purposes of those rules (Cangelosi, 1990a) are to:

1. Secure the safety and comfort of the learning environment
2. Maximize on-task behaviors and minimize off-task behaviors
3. Prevent the activities of the class from disturbing other classes and others outside of the class
4. Maintain acceptable standards of decorum among students, school personnel, and visitors to the school campus (p. 29)

A few well-understood, broadly stated rules that clearly serve the four aforementioned purposes are preferable to a great number of specific, difficult-to-remember rules (Emmer, Evertson, Sanford, Clements, & Worsham, 1989, pp. 21–23). For example, rules similar to those listed in Figure 4.6 may be all you need, providing you make sure your students clearly understand them and that they are consistently enforced.

Having such rules prominently displayed in the classroom reminds students of how you expect them to behave and helps you efficiently respond to students' disruptive behaviors. For example:

VIGNETTE 4.19

Ms. Ayers has the rules listed in Figure 4.6 displayed on the front classroom wall. As she explains some fundamental keyboarding techniques, she notices Synda lightly jabbing Jim's arm with the point of her pencil. Jim jerks away and barks, "Stop it!" With the class' attention already disrupted, Ms. Ayers stops speaking to the class, walks directly to Synda, looks her in the eye, and says, "Please meet with me right after class today, so we can schedule a time to discuss ways to prevent you from violating the first rule again." Ms. Ayers continues the explanation.

Figure 4.6. The Rules of Conduct Ms. Ayers Displays in Her Classroom

CLASSROOM RULES OF CONDUCT

Rule 1:
 Respect your own rights and those of others. (Note: All students in this class have the right to go about the business of learning free from fear of being harmed, intimidated, or embarrassed. Ms. Ayers has the right to go about the business of helping students learn in the manner in which she is professionally prepared to do without interference from others.)
Rule 2:
 Follow directions and procedures as indicated by Ms. Ayers.
Rule 3:
 Adhere to school rules.

Although rules (e.g., Ms. Ayer's) are necessary because they serve the afore-mentioned four purposes, having *unnecessary* rules can be disruptive and detract from a businesslike atmosphere. For example:

VIGNETTE 4.20

Mr. Leggio grew up with the idea that it is rude for men to wear hats indoors. Without much thought, he instituted a "no-hat-wearing" rule for the male students in his classroom. His efforts to enforce the rule have caused a number of disruptions to learning activities. On most days, Mr. Leggio stands by the doorway at the beginning of each period to check on students for such things as chewing gum and boys wearing hats. Often, this delays the start of learning activities.

Today, while Mr. Leggio is writing on the chalkboard, Mark slips on a baseball hat. Ten minutes later, Mr. Leggio notices it, stops the lesson and snaps, "I'll take that hat young man!" Mark: "Why?" Mr. Leggio: "You know you're not supposed to wear a hat in here!" Mark: "Why?" Mr. Leggio: "Because it's not polite." Mark: "Who does it hurt?" Mr. Leggio: "Me. I can't teach you when you're wearing a hat!" The class laughs and Mr. Leggio begins to feel uncomfortable. Feeling a need to assert his authority, he yells, "Either you give me the hat right now, or you're out of this class for good!" Mark grins and slowly swaggers up to the front of the room and gives up his hat. Mark turns away from Mr. Leggio, making a face mocking Mr. Leggio as he slowly returns to his desk. The class laughs, but Mr. Leggio is not sure why as he continues the lesson.

Adapted with permission from *Teaching Mathematics in Secondary and Middle School: Research-based Approaches* (p. 144), by J. S. Cangelosi (1992), New York: Macmillan. Copyright © 1992 by Macmillan Publishing Company.

Mr. Leggio cannot justify his no-hat-wearing rule on the basis of the first three of the four purposes for having classroom rules of conduct (i.e., securing the safety and comfort of the learning environment; maximizing on task behaviors and minimizing off task behaviors; or preventing the activities of the class from disturbing other classes and others outside of the class). He may argue that the rule helps maintain acceptable standards of decorum among students, school personnel, and visitors to the school campus. However, he should be careful that any rule based on that fourth purpose clearly helps maintain an atmosphere of politeness and cooperation, not just imposes his personal tastes on students.

The unpleasant consequences of having *unnecessary* rules of conduct include: (a) Teachers become responsible for enforcing rules that are difficult to defend. (b) When students find some rules to be unimportant, they generalize that others may be unimportant also. (c) Students who are penalized for resisting unnecessary rules are likely to become disenchanted with school and distracted from the business of learning.

Procedures for Smoothly Operating Classrooms

Whereas rules of conduct define general standards for behavior, *classroom procedures* are the specific operational routines for students to follow. How smoothly classroom operations proceed is typically dependent on how well procedures have been established for movement about the room, use of supplies, transitions between learning activities, large-group sessions, small-group sessions, individualized work, and administrative functions. As indicated on pages 135–136, you need to determine such procedures when you organize your classroom and courses for an upcoming school term. During the course of a term, however, situations may arise that lead you to either modify previous procedures or develop new ones. For example:

VIGNETTE 4.21

Mr. Romano has 14 hand-held battery-operated calculators available in his classroom for use by his 34 fifth-graders. Students generally have free access to the calculators, which are kept in a box on the work table in the back of the room. A fresh supply of batteries is maintained from the class treasury.

    Several months into the school year, Mr. Romano notices that some calculators have been left on after being used and some students have failed to return them promptly to the box. Some students complain that they have trouble obtaining a working calculator when needed. To address the problems, Mr. Romano institutes and teaches the following procedures to the class:

> The batteries will be removed from the calculators and those batteries will be held in storage. Two fresh batteries will be distributed to each student from those already in storage and from additional ones purchased from the treasury. Each calculator will be marked with an identification numeral and kept in the supply box without batteries. Students may check out a calculator by writing their name, time, date, and the calculator's numeral on a checkout–checkin sheet attached to the supply box. To use the calculator, students insert a pair of their own batteries, which are to be removed and retained by students when they return the calculator. Students are required to maintain their own supply of batteries just as they do pencils and paper. Batteries will be available for sale at a profit to the class treasury.

Teaching Rules and Procedures to Students

Formulating necessary rules and routine procedures will lead to a smoothly operating classroom only if students comprehend the rules and procedures, understand just how to follow them, are positively reinforced for following them, and suffer consequences for violating them. Thus, you need to apply sound pedagogical principles to deliberately teach students about rules and procedures just as you do to teach them about academic content. The time you spend explaining and demonstrating rules and routine procedures will result in time saved because students will spend more time on task and transitions will be more efficient. Here is an example of a rule of conduct being taught to primary students:

VIGNETTE 4.22

Experience has taught Ms. Jackson, a second-grade teacher, that students need to be assertive in protecting their own rights and protecting themselves from abuse. During the first week of the school year, Ms. Jackson introduces the first of her four classroom rules of conduct printed boldly on a bright yellow poster: "RESPECT YOUR OWN RIGHTS."

She announces to the class, "Clifton and Rosario will perform a skit to help us better understand rule 1. Imagine that they're out in the school yard waiting for the first bell to ring. Clifton will be playing the part of Joe, who is a fourth-grader. Rosario will be Bob, a second-grader. Okay, men, you're on."

Holding his lunch box, "Bob" walks near "Joe." Joe grabs Bob by the shoulder and says, "Hey! Where you going, buddy?" Bob: "Just to my classroom." Joe lets go of Bob and asks, "You wanna be my friend, don't 'ya?" Bob: "Sure." Joe: "I want to be your friend too. What'd 'ya got in the box?" Bob: "My lunch." Joe: "Let me look at it—might be something in there for me." Bob: "Naw, I don't want to be late for class; the bell is about to ring." Joe: "I thought you were gonna be my friend?" Ms. Jacksons interrupt the role playing and says, "Thank you. Let's stop the skit long enough to discuss what we've seen. I want each of you to think of what Bob can do so that he won't break rule 1." A discussion ensues in which suggestions are made as to what Bob should do to protect himself from being either talked into something he really doesn't want to do or from being bullied in case Joe threatens him.

Later, Clifton and Rosario act out several different endings to the skit.

DEALING WITH OFF-TASK BEHAVIORS

A Systematic Approach

By establishing a favorable classroom climate, communicating effectively, establishing necessary rules and procedures, and conducting engaging learning activities (the topic of Chapter 5), you avoid many of the off-task behaviors that are so pervasive in most of today's classrooms. However, with a group of 30 or so students, you will still have to deal with some isolated off-task behaviors and off-task behavior patterns. The key to dealing effectively with off-task behaviors—including those that are disruptive, rude, or even antisocial—is to calmly utilize systematic teaching strategies for getting students to supplant off-task behaviors with on-task behaviors. It is quite natural for teachers to *feel* like retaliating against and displaying their power over students who are infringing on the rights of those about them. But such knee-jerk responses are virtually always counterproductive (Cangelosi, 1988a, pp. 183–214). Rather than allowing emotions to cloud her thinking, the teacher in the following example systematically and thoughtfully deals with a serious disruptive behavior pattern:

VIGNETTE 4.23

Al, one of Ms. Reid's fourth-graders, is engaged in a small-group learning activity with four other students playing "geography bingo." The game leader calls out, "The largest continent." Paul exclaims, "Bingo! It's Asia and I've got it right here for bingo!" Al stands up and yells at Paul, "You stupid asshole! I had that one too! I could've got bingo!" With those words, Al shoves Paul down and upsets the other students' game cards. Ms. Reid arrives on the scene, firmly grabs Al by the arm, and briskly walks him to a point just outside the classroom door. Looking directly into Al's face, she calmly says, "Wait here while I check to see if Paul is hurt." Without giving Al a chance to speak, she unhesitatingly turns and walks back to where the incident occurred as other students gather around Paul who, though still lying on the floor, is beginning to communicate his plans for retaliation. Ms. Reid interrupts Paul, saying, "I'm sorry that Al pushed you down, but I'm happy that you are not hurt." Helping Paul to his feet, Ms. Reid continues speaking without giving anyone else a chance to complain about Al nor giving Paul a chance to make further threats. Ms. Reid: "Blaine and Carol, I would appreciate you helping each other pick up this mess and getting the bingo game started again. Let's go with just four players this time. Everyone else, please return to your work. Thank you for cooperating." Ms. Reid quickly returns to Al standing in the doorway and says, "Right now, I don't have time to work with you on your misbehavior during geography bingo. Now, I have a class to teach and it's time for you to work on geography. We'll just have to wait until tomorrow morning to discuss this matter. When your bus arrives tomorrow morning, you come immediately to the classroom and meet me at my desk. Will you remember, or should I phone your house tonight to remind you?" Al: "I'll remember." Ms. Reid: "Fine! Now, you still have 13 minutes to work on geography. Go get your geography book and bring it to me at my desk." At her desk, Ms. Reid directs Al to complete a geography exercise at a work table located away from the rest of the class. The exercise is a drill on the same geography skills that the bingo game was designed to develop.

At the end of the school day, when Ms. Reid experiences her first solitary moments after the students have been dismissed, she thinks to herself: "I bought myself some time to figure out what to do about Al's outbursts. That was a real chance I took grabbing him. With his temper, he might've turned on me. This is the third or fourth time something like this has happened while Al was involved in a group activity. What makes him so aggressive?—Well, that's not what I have to worry about right now. My job is to prevent this from happening again. I'll exclude him from any small-group activity for the time being. Today, I hope he didn't think the geography book exercise was a punishment. I don't want to teach him to hate geography. But, he's got to understand that antisocial behavior isn't tolerated in my classroom! What do I do? I could just explain my dilemma to him and ask him to think of a solution. That tactic worked really well with Grayson. But Grayson is a different chemistry than Al. Al's not ready for that yet. He's too defensive; he'd be telling me how it wasn't his fault and all. . . . Okay, here's what I'll do:

1. I don't want to give him a chance to argue and be defensive when we meet tomorrow, so I will not even try to explain the reasons for the way I'm dealing with the problem. I'll simply tell him what we're going to do and not defend the plan.
2. I will assign him to work by himself away from others in the class when he would normally be involved in some small-group activity. His independent

---

VIGNETTE 4.23 (continued)

assignment will be over content similar to the small-group activity in which others will be engaged.

3. I'll watch for indicators that he is modifying his antisocial behavior pattern and is becoming more willing to cooperate in group activities.

4. Gradually I'll work him back into noncompetitive group activities as I see encouraging indications that there will be no more trouble. It'll probably quite a while before he's ready for competitive activities.

"Okay, how shall I present this plan to him tomorrow? What will I do if he doesn't show up tomorrow? I'd better prepare for that possibility. . . . "

Adapted with permission from *Classroom Management Strategies: Gaining and Maintaining Students' Cooperation* (pp. 186–187), by J. S. Cangelosi (1988), White Plains, NY: Longman.

Note how Ms. Reid viewed the problem of eliminating the undesirable behavior pattern as she would view a problem of how to help a student achieve a learning objective. By applying teaching techniques to the job of teaching students to choose cooperative on-task behaviors instead of uncooperative off-task behaviors, she is able to focus her time, energy, and thought on the real issues at hand. In the example, she did not try to moralize to Al about the evils of fighting. She realized that such preaching would fall on deaf ears. Teachers who do not systematically focus on the behavior to be altered tend to compound difficulties by dwelling on irrelevant issues. In Vignette 4.1, Mr. Ballam dwells on irrelevant issues with quips such as, "If you'd of listened in the first place," "They aren't good listeners either!", and "She is not freaky."

Do not interpret your students' off-task behaviors as a personal attack on you. It's annoying to have your plans disrupted, your efforts ignored, and authority questioned by students. But they do it out of ignorance, boredom, frustration, or for other reasons that do not threaten your personal worth. Keeping this in mind helps you to maintain your wits well enough to take decisive, effective action that terminates the misbehavior and reduces the probability of it recurring in the future.

Twelve Suggestions for Confronting Off-Task Student Behaviors

Suggestion 1: Deal with Off-Task Behavior as You Would with Any Other Student Need. Suppose you are trying to teach your students about something (e.g., properties of matter) other than how to read. However, your lesson plan depends on the students' comprehending what they read from a textbook. One of your students appears to lack the reading skill to comprehend the necessary information from the reading assignment. Visualize yourself dealing with this all-too-familiar situation. Are you angry with this child for not knowing how to read as well as you would like? My guess is that rather than reacting in anger to the lack of reading proficiency, you would take steps either to help the student improve the reading skills or to work around the difficulty (e.g., by finding a means to communicate the information that didn't depend on reading skill).

Now suppose that you are trying to teach your students something (e.g., properties of matter) other than how to behave. However, your lesson plan depends on the students' cooperatively engaging in the learning activity you have designed for them. One of your students talks when it is time to listen and refuses to follow your directions for attempting an assignment. Visualize yourself dealing with this all-too-familiar situation. Are you angry with this child for not cooperating with you?

Most of us are more likely to react in anger to students' lack of cooperative, on-task behaviors than to their lack of some prerequisite academic skill. But being on-task is also prerequisite to learning and also needs to be taught to students just like a prerequisite academic skill. Students learn to supplant off-task behaviors with requisite on-task behaviors when we respond to their displays of off-task behaviors with sound, systematic pedagogical techniques, not when we respond out of anger.

Suggestion 2: Deal Decisively with an Off-Task Behavior or Don't Deal with It at All.
What are students learning about the need to follow Ms. Rockwell's directives from their experiences in this example?

VIGNETTE 4.24

Some of Ms. Rockwell's students are busy taking a test while others are supposedly working with computers in the back of the room. Ms. Rockwell is doing paperwork at her desk as she becomes concerned that conversations among those at the computer stations are interfering with the thoughts of the test-takers. She yells from her desk, "No talking in the back!" The students stop talking momentarily, but within a minute the conversations are again loud. "Didn't I say no talking?" Ms. Rockwell yells. This time, the noise level hardly drops at all. Five minutes later, Ms. Rockwell tries, "Hey, you back there, I've already told you to stop talking! This is your last warning." In another four minutes, she tries again, "How many times do I have to say—no talking?" The talking continues.

Adapted with permission from *Teaching Mathematics in Secondary and Middle Schools: Research-based Approaches* (p. 148), by J. S. Cangelosi (1992), New York: Macmillan. Copyright © 1992 by Macmillan Publishing Company.

Ms. Rockwell's test-takers should have been afforded the opportunity to work in undisturbed silence. Thus, the disruptive talking should have been dealt with—not ignored. However, *ignoring* the talking would have been preferable to Ms. Rockwell's indecisive approach. She actually reminded her students that she told them "no talking" while allowing the talking to continue. She might as well have said, "See, you don't have to worry about what I tell you. There are no consequences." She should not give commands she doesn't plan to enforce (e.g., by walking to the back of the room, turning off the computers, having the students wait in another location—e.g., office, gym, outside, or a colleague's classroom—until after the test, and having them make up the computer work after school).

Suggestion 3: Control the Time and Place for Dealing with Disruptions. In Vignette 4.23, Ms. Reid focuses her immediate efforts on getting the class reengaged in the learning activities after Al's outburst. She waited until she found time to develop a plan for dealing with him in a setting that she could readily control. Had she attempted to teach Al to change his disruptive behavior pattern at the scene of the incident right after it occurred, she would have had to contend with the following: (a) She would be burdened with supervising the rest of the students and, thus, could not focus her full attention on working out a solution to the problem with Al; (b) Al would have an audience of peers whose perceptions are more important to him than anything Ms. Reid might be trying to tell him at the moment; (c) she would have had little time to think through a plan; and (d) neither she nor Al would have had time to cool down from the incident.

Don't feel obliged to demonstrate your authority by dealing with a student who has been disruptive in front of the class. Usually, it is more efficient to first get everyone back on task and then work on preventing future occurrences at a time and place away from other students. It will be easier to work with the disrupter when that student is not on stage in front of peers. There's no need to be concerned that other students will think that the disruption went unpunished; word will get back that you handled the situation decisively (Cangelosi, 1990a, p. 53).

Suggestion 4: Leave Students Face-saving Ways to Terminate Misbehaviors. You are asking for trouble by ever doing anything that leads students to feel embarrassed in front of their peers. If you expect dignified behaviors from your students, you need to avoid situations where students feel their dignity is compromised. Thus, your strategies for dealing with off-task behaviors, even annoying rude ones, should consider how to leave students face-saving ways of choosing on-task behaviors. This is often difficult to do. When students behave rudely, it is tempting to respond with clever comebacks or put-downs. Not only does this practice destroy a healthy climate; it can also backfire as it did in this example:

VIGNETTE 4.25

Mr. Sceroler is urging his eighth-grade class to get their homework in on time as he says, "There's nothing I can do if you don't have the work for me to see." Ronald from the back of the room, in a barely audible tone, quips to the student next to him, "He could always go jack off!" Having overheard the comment, Mr. Sceroler yells at Ronald, "What was that you said?" Ronald begins to grin and look around at his classmates. "You were trying to show off for us and now you can't say anything! What did you say?" Ronald whispers with his head down, "Nothing." Mr. Sceroler, seeing Ronald back down, begins to feel confident as he continues, "What was that? Speak up. What did you say?" Now facing Mr. Sceroler, Ronald says in a loud voice, "I said I didn't say nothin'!" Mr. Sceroler retorts, "You can't even

(continued)

VIGNETTE 4.25 (continued)

use decent English. Of course you didn't say anything. You aren't capable of saying anything, are you?'' Some class members laugh. Enjoying the audience, Mr. Sceroler smiles. Ronald, very concerned with what his classmates are thinking, suddenly stands up and shouts at Mr. Sceroler, "I said you could always go jack off, but then I forgot, you don't have a dick!''

Adapted with permission from *Classroom Management Strategies: Gaining and Maintaining Students' Cooperation* (pp. 196–197), by J. S. Cangelosi (1988), White Plains, NY: Longman.

By trying to outwit Ronald instead of providing him with a face-saving way of getting back on task, Mr. Sceroler extended what would have been a self-terminating incident into a most unfortunate confrontation with unhappy consequences for all concerned. After hearing Ronald's initial remark, what was Mr. Sceroler's purpose in asking, "What was that you said?" Ronald tried to end the incident by not replying, but Mr. Sceroler's persistence left Ronald with only two options: either lying or repeating what would surely be interpreted as an obscenity. Had the teacher in this example behaved professionally as a secure adult instead of trying to demonstrate superiority over an adolescent, he would have either ignored the remark or politely directed Ronald to meet with him at a more convenient time.

Suggestions 5: Terminate Disruptions without Playing the "Detective Game." In Vignette 4.25, Mr. Sceroler knew that Ronald was the one who made the rude comment. However, many times, teachers are unable to detect the source of disruptions. Here is such an example:

VIGNETTE 4.26

Mr. Cambell's lectures, class discussions, and individual help sessions are habitually interrupted by a few students who covertly hoot, "Ooohh-ooooh-ooooh." Initially, he reacted to the disruptive noise by asking, "Okay, who's the owl in here?" His frequent attempts to identify the culprits have been fruitless. Students are getting bolder with the hooting and more clever at concealing the sources. Apparently, more students are joining in on the game.

Frustrated, Mr. Cambell seeks the advice of another teacher, Ms. Les. She suggests that the students don't really intend to make his life so miserable, which is what he's allowing to happen, but they are simply enjoying a game of cat and mouse that he's unwittingly playing with them. She says he can terminate the game by no longer trying to catch the culprits. She advises him to devise a plan for getting the culprits to stop their discourteous disruptions without having to identify them. She tells him:

   "Stop worrying about identifying the hooters. Confront the class with the fact that you do not appreciate the rudeness. Explain that you are responsible for

VIGNETTE 4.26 (continued)

teaching them, but you cannot do so effectively when they are making that noise. Ask them to respect your rights and one another's rights to go about the business of teaching and learning.

"Follow up that little speech with some action. Anytime you've got a lesson going in which you're lecturing, conducting a discussion, or explaining something and you hear that noise, immediately initiate an alternative learning activity that doesn't require you to speak to students—one that is less pleasant and allows you to closely monitor their every move."

Taking Ms. Les's advice, Mr. Cambell explains his feelings to the class and there is no hooting for several days. Then, while explaining how to find the standard deviation of a distribution, once again he hears the dreaded "Ooohh-ooooh-ooooh." Abruptly, he stops the explanation and silently and calmly displays a transparency on the overhead with the following message: "Open your books to page 157. Study the material on standard deviation, work the examples and exercises on pages 157–171. Most of what we planned to talk about in class today is covered on those pages. Do not forget we have a test Thursday. It covers the unit objectives on means, variances, and standard deviations. Good luck."

Mr. Cambell watches them reluctantly work through the text material without his help. Some students start to ask him questions, but a stern look and signal for silence puts an end to that.

Adapted with permission from *Teaching Mathematics in Secondary and Middle School: Research-based Approaches* (pp. 149–150), by J. S. Cangelosi (1993), New York: Macmillan. Copyright © 1992 by Macmillan Publishing Company.

Suggestion 6: Utilize the Help of Colleagues, Parents, and Supervisors: Don't Be Fooled by the "Myth of the Good Teacher." In Vignette 4.26, Mr. Cambell sought the counsel of a trusted colleague. But, unfortunately, some teachers are deluded by what Canter and Canter (1976, pp. 6–7) referred to as the "myth of the good teacher." According to the myth, really "good" teachers handle all their own discipline problems without outside help; seeking help is considered a sign of weakness. In reality, consulting with colleagues is a mark of professional behavior (Bang-Jensen, 1986; Cangelosi, 1990a, p. 56; Raney & Robbins, 1989). Furthermore, your supervisors are legally and ethically responsible for supporting your instructional efforts (Cangelosi, 1991; Stanley & Popham, 1988; Stiggins & Duke, 1988), and parents typically have greater influence over their children than do teachers (Canter & Canter, 1976).

Suggestion 7: Have Alternative Lesson Plans Available for Times When Students Do Not Cooperate as You Planned. Expect your students to cooperatively engage in learning activities. Your confident expectations increase the chances that they will. Do not abort a well-designed learning activity as soon as it does not go as smoothly as you planned. However, by being prepared in the event that some students refuse to cooperate, you protect yourself from operating under the stress of having no alternative if the activity should be aborted. Vignettes 4.23 and 4.26 demonstrate the advantage of having alternate and less-enjoyable activities ready for times when students' off-task behaviors render the original plan unworkable. Ideally, the alternative activities target the same objectives as the original activities.

Suggestion 8: Concern Yourself with Decreasing Incidences of Nondisruptive Off-Task Behavior as You Must with Decreasing Disruptive Off-Task Behaviors. Nondisruptive off-task behaviors (e.g., mind-wandering, daydreaming, failing to attempt assignments, being under the influence of drugs during learning activities, and sleeping in class) are easier to disregard than disruptive behaviors that infringe on the rights of the whole class. However, you should be concerned with all forms of student off-task behaviors because when students are off task, they are failing to benefit from your planned lessons and are, thus, diminishing their chances of achieving learning goals. Your responsibility for helping them achieve learning goals includes helping them supplant off-task with on-task behaviors. Furthermore, nondisruptive students who are off task tend to fall behind in a lesson. Once students miss one part of a lesson, they are likely to not learn from a subsequent part even though they may reengage in the learning activities. Those unable to follow a lesson are likely candidates for boredom and disruptive behaviors.

Suggestion 9: Allow Students to Recognize for Themselves the Natural Consequences of Failing to Attempt Assignments. When students fail to attempt assignments, some teachers punish them or artificially manipulate their grades. But if your assignments are really necessary for students to succeed, then punishment or grade manipulation may be unnecessary. The teacher in Vignette 4.27 comes to realize just that:

VIGNETTE 4.27

Ms. Chung, a junior high teacher, uses a procedure in which each student's grade is determined by the number of points accumulated during a semester. Her students have two means of accumulating points: (a) Half of the total possible points are based on their test scores; (b) the other half are awarded for homework that, when turned in on time, is scored according to the number of correct responses.

Ms. Chung discovers that a number of students receive high marks on their homework, but low marks on their test papers. Under her system, such students are able to pass the course. After analyzing the matter she realizes that these students are either copying their homework from others or having others do it for them. Thus, she decides to change her grading procedures. She will annotate students' homework to provide them with feedback, but she will not grade their homework so that it influences their semester reports. Ms. Chung begins to make a concerted effort to assign homework and design tests so that completing homework will clearly be an effective way to prepare for tests.

To begin conditioning her students to the new system, she assigns homework one day, and then administers a test the next that covers the same objectives as the homework.

Adapted with permission from *Cooperation in the Classroom: Students and Teachers Together,* Second Edition, pp. 59–60, by J. S. Cangelosi, copyright 1990, National Education Association.

Suggestion 10: Never Use Corporal Punishment. Thee may be times when you need to physically restrain students fro the purpose of preventing them from injuring themselves or others (including you). But do not confuse necessary physical constraint with the administration of corporal punishment. Corporal punishment is physical pain intentionally inflicted on students for the purpose of making them sorry for something they did. For you or any other teacher to inflict such a form of punishment is far more harmful than helpful (Curwin & Mendler, 1980; Rose, 1984; Welsh, 1985). Although numerous prominent professional organizations (e.g., the National Education Association, American Federation of Teachers, and American Psychological Association) have issued statements adamantly opposing its use in school and its use has been banned in some states (e.g., New Jersey), corporal punishment continues to be widely, but inconsistently, practiced in schools (Jones & Jones, 1990, pp. 296–299; National Education Association, 1972; Van Dyke, 1984; Wood, 1982). The arguments against the use of corporal punishment and in favor of more effective and less destructive discipline practices are compelling (see, for example, Azrin, Hake, & Hutchinson, 1965; Azrin, Hutchinson, & Sallery, 1964; Bandura, 1965; Bongiovanni, 1979; Cangelosi, 1988a, pp. 207–208; Delgado, 1963; Hyman & Wise, 1979; Kohut & Range, 1979; Rust & Kinnard, 1983; Strike & Soltis, 1986; Sulzer-Azaroff & Mayer, 1979; Ulrich & Azrin, 1962; Welsh, 1985).

Suggestion 11: Maintain Your Options: Avoid "Playing Your Last Card." Understand the extent and limits of your authority. Never threaten a student with anything unless you know you can follow through. For example, if you tell a student, "Either start working now or you're out of this class for good!" what are you going to do if the student refuses? You have extended your authority as far as it reaches, exhausting your options. Obtain the help of supervisors well *before* you run out of ways of dealing with problems.

Suggestion 12: Know Yourself and Your Students. Continually examine your motives for your work with students. Be receptive to differences among your students. What works with one may be a disaster with another. New ideas should be tried out cautiously—first with individuals you know best and then extended to others as they prove promising. The better you understand yourself and your students, the more likely you will be able to gain students' cooperation and respond sensitively, flexibly, decisively, and effectively to discipline problems whenever they do occur.

CONDUCTING ENGAGING LEARNING ACTIVITIES

"School is so dumb!" "Class is boring!" "This stuff is so dry!" "Why should I care about this stuff? I'm never going to use it!" "I don't have time to do this homework!" "It's so boring just sitting here listening to her jabber away about verbs and nouns!" "None of this has anything to do with me!" Embedded in those familiar cries are the more common reasons why students get off task during learning activities. To keep students on task, you must not only establish a favorable classroom climate, communicate effectively, establish necessary rules and procedures, and effectively deal with off-task behaviors, you must also plan and conduct learning activities that hold students' attention. Chapter 5 provides suggestions for doing just that.

SELF-ASSESSMENT EXERCISES FOR CHAPTER 4

I. Select the one response to each of the following multiple-choice items that either completes the statement so that it is true or accurately answers the question:

A. Time for students to achieve learning objectives increases as _____.
   a. more time is spent on knowledge-level activities instead of intellectual-level activities
   b. more time is spent on intellectual-level activities instead of knowledge-level activities
   c. allocated time decreases
   d. transition time decreases

B. Which one of the following statements is true?
   a. Students who are on task are engaged in learning activities.
   b. Students who are off task are being disruptive.
   c. Engaged behaviors are never off task.

C. Students develop on-task behavior patterns because _____.
   a. isolated on-task behaviors were positively reinforced
   b. isolated off-task behaviors were positively reinforced
   c. of inherent instincts about right and wrong

D. Students develop off-task behavior patterns because _____.
   a. isolated on-task behaviors were positively reinforced
   b. isolated off-task behaviors were positively reinforced
   c. of inherent instincts about right and wrong

E. A classroom with a businesslike atmosphere is characterized by _____.
   a. democratic decision making
   b. authoritarian decision making
   c. a highly formalized structure
   d. purposeful activity

F. Which one of the following contributes to a businesslike classroom atmosphere?
   a. use of descriptive language
   b. use of judgmental language
   c. maximizing transition time
   d. consistent use of corporal punishment for unbusinesslike student behaviors.

G. Students tend to be most receptive to signals about your expectations of them _____.
   a. right after examinations
   b. during the first few days of a course
   c. during the last few days of a course

H. A supportive reply to a student tends to communicate _____.
   a. assertiveness
   b. passiveness
   c. acceptance of feelings
   d. value judgments

I. By "withitness," Kounin (1977) referred to how _____.
   a. well teachers maintain students on task and engaged in learning activities
   b. aware teachers are of what's going on in the classroom
   c. well teachers display enthusiasm for learning
   d. assertively teachers conduct themselves with students

I. **A.** Compare your responses to the following: A-d, B-c, C-a, D-b, E-d, F-a, G-b, H-c, I-b.

II. This chapter provided suggestions for managing student behavior (e.g., positively reinforce on-task behaviors, organize and prepare for efficient transitions, focus on the business of learning, and use descriptive instead of judgmental language). In Vignette 4.1, Mr. Ballam failed to heed a number of those suggestions. Reread that vignette and identify behaviors Mr. Ballam exhibited that were inconsistent with the suggestions. Indicate what he might have done differently to improve his classroom climate and to encourage students to be on task. Compare your work on this exercise to someone else's.

III. Apparently Mr. Stockton and Ms. Phegley spent an extraordinary amount of time preparing for the class session described in Vignettes 4.4 and 4.5. In what ways were their preparations for class more elaborate than what you expect from most teachers? How do you think those efforts will pay practical dividends for them throughout the remainder of the school year? Compare your response on this exercise to that of someone else.

IV. You have just been assigned a classroom and received your teaching schedule for the upcoming school year at a school familiar to you. Consider how you might answer the questions appearing on pages 135–136 for (a) "classroom organization and on-going routines," (b) "one-time-only tasks," and (c) "reminders for the first week's learning activities."

V. You have just directed your students to independently work on a tasksheet you've devised. Although you were quite clear that they were to silently complete the work by themselves, you notice Hartense and Blythe talking together. You walk over to them and realize their discussion is relevant to the tasksheet. State an example of a *descriptive* comment you could make to them. State an example of a *judgmental* comment you could make to them. What are the relative advantages and disadvantages of making the first instead of the second comment? Compare your work on this exercise to someone else's.

VI. After you've assigned students to write an original essay, Adonis exclaims to you, "I could never come up with anything original!" State an example of a *supportive* comment you could make to Adonis. State an example of a *nonsupportive* comment you could make. What are the relative advantages and disadvantages of making the first instead of the second comment? Compare your work on this exercise to someone else's.

VII. After you've assigned a group of exercises for students to complete, Zeke exclaims to you, "We've already got too much work to do! Do we really have to do *all* of these?" State an example of an *assertive* comment you could make to Zeke. State an example of a *passive* comment you could make. State an example of a *hostile* comment you could make. What are the relative advantages and disadvantages of making the first instead of either the second or third comment? Compare your work on this exercise to someone else's.

VIII. What principle suggested in this chapter does Ms. Jones violate by making the following comment to a student? "You made John hit you when you pushed him!" What principle does Mr. McFarland violate by telling a school custodian, "I'm glad this day is over; that Jensen kid is impossible to teach!"

Did you note that Ms. Jones failed to convey that the students are responsible for and in control of their own behaviors? Do you think Mr. McFarland violated a professional trust by sharing privileged information about a student?

IX. Observe a class in an elementary, middle, junior high, or high school. Distinguish the transition times from the allocated times during the class. For each transition period and each allocated period note one student who is on task and another who is off task. Describe the behaviors that led you to believe they were on task and off task respectively. If you were in the teacher's place, what might you do to positively reinforce the on-task behavior? What might you do to discourage recurrences of the off-task behavior?

X. In your response to Exercise II of the self-assessment exercises for Chapter 3, you described lessons for a sequence of objectives for a teaching unit. Now, formulate and describe a plan for obtaining and maintaining students on task during that unit. Include your plans for efficient transitions, alternative learning activities if needed, notes to yourself on communicating with students, and contingency plans for dealing with potential situations to which students are off task. Compare your work on this exercise to someone else's.

SUGGESTED READING

Cangelosi, J. S. (1988). *Classroom management strategies: Gaining and maintaining students' cooperation.* New York: Longman.

Cangelosi, J. S. (1990). *Cooperation in the classroom: Students and teachers together* (2nd ed.). Washington, DC: National Education Association.

Canter, L., & Canter, M. (1976). *Assertive discipline: A take-charge approach for today's educator.* Seal Beach, CA: Canter and Canter Associates.

Evertson, C. M. (1989). Classroom organization and management. In M. C. Reynolds (Ed.), *Knowledge base for the beginning teacher* (pp. 59–70). Oxford: Pergamon Press.

Ginott, H. G. (1972). *Teacher and child.* New York: Avon Books.

Jones, L. T. (1991). *Strategies for involving parents in their children's education.* Bloomington, IN: Phi Delta Kappa Educational Foundation.

Tauber, R. T. (1990). *Classroom management from A to Z.* Fort Worth, TX: Holt, Rinehart & Winston.

TAKING WHAT YOU'VE LEARNED TO THE NEXT LEVEL

Keeping in mind the research-based principles for designing lessons suggested in Chapter 3 and those for gaining and maintaining students' cooperation, turn your attention to Chapter 5's concern: How to conduct learning activities in ways that grab and hold students' attention.

CHAPTER 5

Engaging Students in Learning Activities

GOAL OF CHAPTER 5

This chapter explains how to conduct learning activities in ways that encourage student engagement. Chapter 5 will help you

1. explain effective ways of providing directions, initiating student engagement, maintaining engagement, utilizing formative feedback to regulate pace and determine modifications, and achieving closure for each of the following types of learning activities: (a) Large-group interactive lecture sessions, (b) large-group intellectual-level questioning/discussion sessions, (c) large-group recitation sessions, (d) cooperative task-group sessions, and (e) independent work sessions (*Cognitive: conceptualization*)
2. explain how to incorporate meaningful homework assignments into lessons and to teach students to engage in those assignments (*Cognitive: conceptualization*)
3. select and integrate types of learning activities (e.g., questioning/discussion or independent work) for each teaching unit that are appropriate for your students, you, the learning objectives, and the available resources (*Cognitive: application*)

INTEGRATING DIFFERENT TYPES OF LEARNING ACTIVITIES INTO LESSONS

Direct instructional strategies are needed to help students achieve knowledge-level and psychomotor objectives whereas inquiry instructional strategies lead students to achieve affective and intellectual-level objectives. As indicated in Chapter 3, the stages of research-based lessons (e.g., the seven stages for a conceptualization lesson listed on page 77) require lessons that integrate various combinations of different types of learning activities including large-group interactive lecture sessions, large-group intellectual-level questioning/discussion sessions, large-group recitation sessions, cooperative task-group sessions, independent work sessions, and homework assignments. Determining when to use combinations of these types of learning activities and how to keep students engaged in them are the concerns of this chapter.

ENGAGING STUDENTS IN LARGE-GROUP INTERACTIVE LECTURE SESSIONS

Appropriate Uses of Large-Group Interactive Lecture Sessions

Large-Group Sessions. You should plan to use large-group sessions whenever you want all students in the class to be concentrating on a common center of activity (e.g., a speaker, demonstration, or illustration). Such sessions provide an efficient means for class members to share a common experience that they draw on in subsequent learning activities. For example: (a) Students individually pattern their own outlines for essays they plan to write on how the outline for another essay was developed in a large-group discussion session. (b) While responding to a student's request for individual help answering questions from a textbook exercise, a teacher refers to notes the student took during a large-group lecture session.

Lectures. A lecture is a monologue. To be engaged in a lecture-type learning activity, students must attentively listen to the lecturer. Taking notes and attempting to follow a prescribed thought pattern may also be a required aspect of engagement. This type of engagement, requiring students to be cognitively active while physically inactive, is not easily maintained for extended time periods for students of any age and virtually impossible to sustain with younger students. Lectures that continue uninterrupted for more than 10 minutes without being integrated with other types of learning activities are ill-advised (Cangelosi, 1988a, p. 144). Quina (1989) stated:

> In recent years the lecture has been disregarded and maligned by some educators. Much empirical research has been amassed to show shortcomings of the lecture as an instructional vehicle. Some common arguments are that students have too short an attention span to focus on a lecture for more than 10–15 minutes at a time. Without correct feedback it is easy to misunderstand what has been said. NLP (Neurolinguistic Programming) operators say that only 7 percent of what we receive as a message is carried by the words one uses in a speech. The speaker's tonality carries 38 percent of the message and his body posture carries 55 percent of the message (Robbins, 1987). Most teachers are not specifically trained in oratorical skills. There is the conjoint problem of teachers tending to focus on subject matter, forgetting *how* they are communicating, and lapsing into a monotone delivery—the deadliest form of a lecture. There is, moreover, the tendency of the lecturing high school teacher to imitate the lecture format, the style of delivery, and the technical vocabulary of the college professor. (pp. 140–141)

This is *not* to say that you should exclude lectures from your teaching. Lectures provide a valuable means by which you can present information, provide explanations, demonstrate processes, stimulate inductive reasoning, and stimulate deductive reasoning. However, to maintain students engaged in lectures, you need to do more than just talk. You must organize and design lectures so that you employ attention-focusing techniques (e.g., illustrations, advanced organizers, and body language) and continuously integrate activities into lectures that stimulate interactions between you and the students.

Interactions. Unless you continue to evoke student responses during a lecture, you will be unable to detect just what message they are receiving. Consequently you may dwell on points they already understand, fail to elaborate as needed, and fail to correct misunderstandings. Furthermore, students need feedback on whether or not what they are understanding is what they are supposed to be understanding. Left as passive receptors of your words, they will not remain engaged for very long, even though they may be quite adept at appearing to listen—following you with their eyes, nodding on occasion, and even smiling at humorous sidetracks. Mind wandering will be rampant unless you frequently solicit student reactions and input.

Interactive Lecture Sessions. To take advantage of lectures as a mode of instruction without ''losing'' students in the process, plan for nontraditional *interactive lecture sessions* in which your oral discourses are inextricably meshed with activities that evoke interactions between you and your students. How to utilize and engage students in that type of learning activity is the question addressed in the remainder of this section.

Direct Instructional Methods in Interactive Lecture Sessions. Direct instructional methods appropriate for knowledge-level objectives and literal understanding relative to comprehension-level objectives can readily be incorporated into interactive lecture sessions. Use monologues to present and explicate information, but mix them with interactive techniques that will focus attention, keep students alert, provide you with formative feedback, add variety to the presentation when points need to be repeated, provide students with feedback on their understanding, and positively reinforce their efforts. Here is an example:

VIGNETTE 5.1

Mr. Santiago is in the midst of a large-group interactive lecture session designed to help his students achieve the following objective:

State Newton's first law of motion (*Cognitive: simple knowledge*)

He states the relationship specified by the objective, displays it on the overhead projector and says, ''Read this aloud for us, Val.'' Val reads, ''Objects at rest stay at rest and objects in motion stay in motion in a straight line at a constant speed, unless a force acts on them to move or change their motion.'' Mr. Santiago: ''Now, as Val just pointed out to us, the first law of motion covers two situations. Let's

(continued)

VIGNETTE 5.1 (continued)

look at the two situations separately. What's the first situation, Amy?" Amy: "An object at rest." Mr. Santiago: "And the second, Paul?" Paul: "An object in motion." Mr. Santiago: "What does the law say about an object at rest, Carmel?" Carmel: "It stays at rest." Mr. Santiago: "Unless what? Read this part of the law my pointer is on now, Carmel." Carmel: "It says, unless a force . . ."

Note that the questions Mr. Santiago used in this direct instructional lesson are not the open-ended, "develop-a-hypothesis" type of questions used in lessons for intellectual cognitive objectives (e.g., those raised by Mr. Landastoy in the inductive lesson in Vignette 3.8). Students' responses during an interactive lecture session using direct instruction are elicited with questions or directives such as "Repeat what I just said," "Read this for me," and "What did we do first?"

Inquiry Instructional Methods in Interactive Lecture Sessions. For intellectual-level objectives, you can use the large-group interactive lecture mode to stimulate students to reason in various ways. If for instance, your target is a conceptualization objective, examples and nonexamples of the concept or principle can be explained and illustrated in a monologue and then questions and discussions used to lead students through an inductive process.

Common Misuses of Large-Group
Interactive Lecture Sessions

To my query about what he had learned from a psychology course, a high school student once replied "I learned all kinds of stuff about why people act the way they do. I think of people differently now. When they don't act right, I'm more understanding instead of always getting mad." "Your teacher must have done a great job with your class," I commented. "Not really, she made us figure all this stuff out on our own. We learned a lot, but she didn't do much teaching—mostly gave us things to do, asked us a lot of questions, and let us know how we were doing."

My high school friend seems to have a view that most people don't develop until they've been in college for a few years, the view being that to "teach," one must lecture. Therein lies the basis for the most common misuse of interactive lecture sessions: *There is too much lecture and not enough interaction.* Unlike my high school friend's psychology teacher, some teachers bring from their college experiences the mistaken idea that teaching is spewing forth words of wisdom. The consequences of the overuse of lectures is students being told things they need to figure out for themselves in order to learn at an intellectual level. There is then an overemphasis on knowledge-level learning.

By contrast, interactive lecture sessions are also misused when the interactive aspects degenerate into unstructured "bull sessions." Some teachers, especially those who do not consistently use assertive communications, have difficulty controlling class discussions so that exchanges focus on intended topics. How to manage meaningful discussion sessions is addressed in subsequent sections of this chapter.

Two Contrasting Examples

The teacher in the first of the following two examples (Vignettes 5.2 and 5.3) needs to learn how to conduct a large-group interactive lecture session from the teacher in the second of the examples.

VIGNETTE 5.2

Mr. Johnson's 26 students are sitting at their desks. Nine students have paper and pencil poised to take notes while others are involved with their own thoughts. He begins, "Today, class, we're going to study about a measure of central tendency called the 'arithmetic mean.' Some of you may have already heard of it." He turns to the chalkboard and writes, continuing to speak, "The arithmetic mean of N number equals the sum of the numbers divided by N." Keeping his side to the class so he can write on the board and glance at the class, he says, "For example, to compute the mean of these numbers: 15, 15, 20, 0, 13, 12, 25, 40, 10, and 20—we would first add the numbers to find the sum. Right?" He looks at the class but doesn't notice whether students appear to respond to his question, turns back and adds the numbers on the board. . . . "So the sum is 170. Now, because we have 10 numbers, N in the formula is 10 and we divide 170 by N or 10. And what does that give us? It gives us 17.0. So, the arithmetic mean of these numbers is 17.0. Is that clear?"

Mr. Johnson stares at the class momentarily; he notices Armond nodding and softly saying, "Yes." With a smile, Mr. Johnson quickly says "Good! Okay, everybody, the arithmetic mean is a very important and useful statistic. Suppose, for example, I wanted to compare this group of numbers—" From his notes he copies the following numbers on the board: 18, 35, 30, 7, 20, and then continues, "to these over here." He points to the previous set of data. Mr. Johnson: "What could we do? . . . Ramon." Ramon: "Compute that arithmetic thing you told us about." Mr. Johnson: 'That's right! We could compute the arithmetic mean. . . . 18 plus 35 plus 30 plus 7 plus 20 is . . . 110, and 110 divided by N which in this case is 5, okay?— which is 22.0. Okay? Now, that means this second data set has a higher average than the first—even though the first had more numbers. Any questions? . . . Good! . . . Oh, okay, Angela." Angela: "Why do you write 17.0 instead of just 17? Isn't it the same thing?" Mr. Johnson: "Good question. Hmmm, can anybody help Angela out? . . . Well, you see in statistics the number of decimal places indicates something about the accuracy of the computations, and, for that matter, the data gathering device. So that one decimal point indicates that the statistics are more accurate than if we had just put 17 and 22 and not as accurate as if we had put, say 17.00000 or 22.00000. . . . Got it? That was a good question. Do you understand, now?" Angela, "I guess so." Mr. Johnson: "Good! Now, if there're no more questions, there's some time left to get a head start on your homework. . . ."

Adapted with permission from *Classroom Management Strategies: Gaining and Maintaining Student's Cooperation* (pp. 144–147), by J. S. Cangelosi (1988), White Plains, NY: Longman.

VIGNETTE 5.3

Ms. Erickson's 27 students are quietly sitting at their desks, each poised with paper and pen or pencil. She has previously taught them how to take notes during large-group interactive lecture sessions and then after the session organize the notes and transfer them into their required notebooks.

Why Is Ms. Erickson Looking at Students' Feet?

After distributing the form appearing in Figure 5.1, she faces the class from a position near the overhead projector and says, "I'm standing here looking at you people and I just can't get one question out of mind." Very deliberately she walks in front of the fourth row of students and quickly, but obviously looks at their feet. Then she moves in front of the first row and repeats the odd behavior with those students. "I just don't know!" she says shaking her head as she returns to her position by the overhead.

She switches on the overhead displaying the first line of Figure 5.1, and says, "In the first blank on your form, please write: Do the people sitting in the fourth row have bigger feet than those in the first row?" She moves closer to the students, obviously monitoring how well her directions are followed. Back by the overhead as they complete the chore, she says, "Now, I've got to figure a way to gather data that will help me answer that question." Grabbing her head with a hand and closing her eyes, she appears to be in deep thought for a few seconds and then suddenly exclaims, "I've got it! We'll use shoe sizes as a measure. That'll be a lot easier than using a ruler on smelly feet!" Some students laugh, and one begins to speak while

VIGNETTE 5.3 (continued)

Question to be answered: _____

_____

Data for row 4: _____

Data for row 1: _____

Treatment of row 4's data:

Treatment of row 1's data:

Treatment to compare the two sets of data:

Results: _____

_____

Conclusions: _____

_____

Figure 5.1. Form Ms. Erickson Uses During an Interactive Lecture Session

two others raise their hands. But Ms. Erickson quickly says, "Not now, please, we need to collect some data." She flips an overlay off of the second line of the transparency, exposing "Data for Row 4."

Ms. Erickson: "Those of you in the fourth and first rows, quickly jot down your shoe size on your paper. If you don't know it, either guess or read it off your shoe if you can do it quickly. . . . Starting with Jasmine in the back and moving up to Lester in the front, those of you in the fourth row call out your shoe sizes one at a time so we can write them down in this blank at our places." As the students volunteer the sizes, she fills in the blank on the transparency as follows: 6, 10.5, 8, 5.5, 6, 9. Exposing the next line, "Data for Row 1," on the transparency, she asks, "What do you suppose we're going to do now, Pauline?" Pauline: "Do the same for row 1." Ms. Erickson: "Okay, you heard her; row 1, give it to us from the back so we can fill in this blank." The numbers 8.5, 8, 7, 5.5, 6.5, 6.5, 9, and 8 are recorded and displayed on the overhead.

Ms. Erickson: "Now, I've got to figure out what to do with these numbers to help me answer the question." Several students raise their hands, but she responds, "Thank you for offering to help, but I want to see what I come up with." Pointing to the appropriate numbers on the transparency, she seems to think aloud saying, "It's easy enough to compare one number to another. Jasmine's 6 from row 4 is greater than Rolando's 8.5 from row 1. But I don't want to just compare one individual's number to another. I want to compare this whole bunch of numbers [circling

(continued)

VIGNETTE 5.3 (continued)

row 4's set of numbers with an overhead pen] to this bunch [circling row 1's]. . . .
I guess we could add all of row 4's numbers together and all of row 1's together and
compare the two sums—the one with the greater sum would have the larger group
of feet.''

A couple of students try to interrupt with, ''But that won't wor—'' but Ms.
Erickson motions them to stop speaking and asks, ''What's the sum from row 4,
Lau-chou?'' Lau-chou: ''. . . 45.'' Ms. Erickson: ''Thank you. And what's the sum
for row one, Stace?'' Stace: ''59.'' ''Thank you. So now row one has the bigger
feet because 59 is greater than 45,'' Ms. Erickson says as she writes ''59 > 45.''
Ms. Erickson: ''I'll pause to hear what some of you with your hands up have to say.
Evangeline?'' Evangeline: ''That's not right; it doesn't work.'' Ms. Erickson: ''You
mean 59 isn't greater than 45, Evangeline?'' Evangeline: ''59 is greater than 45, but
there's more feet in row 1.'' Ms. Erickson: ''All the people on row one have only
two feet just like the ones on row 4. I carefully counted. [students laugh] Now that
we've taken care of that concern, how about other comments or questions—Brook?''
Brook: ''You know what Evangeline meant! She meant there's more people on row
1. So what you did isn't right.'' Ms. Erickson: ''Alright, let me see if I now understand
Evangeline's point. She said we don't want our indicator of how big the feet are to
be affected by how many feet, just the size of the feet. . . . So, I've got to figure
out a way to compare the sizes of these two groups of numbers, when one has more
numbers. I'm open for suggestions. Kip?''

Kip: ''You could drop the two extra numbers from row 1; then they'd both have
6.'' Ms. Erickson: ''That seems like a reasonable approach. I like that, but first let's
hear another idea—maybe one where we can use all the data. Myra?'' Myra: ''Why
not do an average?'' Ms. Erickson: ''What do you mean?'' Myra: ''You know, divide
row 4's total by 6 and row 1's by 8.'' Ms. Erickson: ''How will that dividing help?—
seems like just an unnecessary step, Tom.'' Tom: ''It evens up the two groups.''
Ms. Erickson: ''Oh, I see what you people have been trying to tell me! Dividing row
4's sum of 45 by 6 counts each number 1/6. And dividing row 4's sum of 59 by 8
counts each number 1/8. And that's fair because 6 one-sixths is whole, just like 8
one-eighth is whole. How am I doing, Jasmine?'' Jasmine: ''A lot better than you
were.''

Flipping over another overlay, she displays the next two lines of Figure 5.1 and
says, ''Let's write: The sum of row 4's numbers is 45 and 45 divided by 6 is what,
Lester?'' Lester: ''7.5.'' Ms. Erickson: ''Thanks. And on the next line we write, 59
divided by 8 is what, Sandy?'' Sandy: ''7.375.'' Ms. Erickson: ''Because 7.5 is
greater than 7.375, I guess we should say that row 4's feet are larger than row 1's
feet. That is, of course, if you're willing to trust this particular statistic—which is
known as the MEB. Any questions? . . . Yes, Evangeline.'' Evangeline: ''Why, 'the
MEB'?'' Ms. Erickson: ''Because I just named it that after its three inventors, Myra,
Evangeline, and Brook. They're the ones who came up with the idea of dividing the
sum.'' The class breaks into laughter.

Ms. Erickson shifts to direct instruction to help students remember the formula,
practice using it, and remember its more conventional name, *arithmetic mean*, during
the remainder of the session.

Providing Directions

There are some behaviors you expect your students to exhibit during *every* large-group interactive lecture section. As soon as Ms. Erickson's students recognized they were about to begin such a session, they immediately got ready to take notes and focused on her. This is a routine *procedure* she taught them to follow in the very beginning of the course. However, there are also expected behaviors that vary from one large-group interactive lecture session to another. These may involve how to take notes on a form you developed just for one session or how to follow a particular thought pattern (e.g., inductive reasoning for one session and absorbing information for another). For such behaviors not covered by routine procedures, you need to provide students with specific, explicit *directions*.

Providing students with directions is quite unlike conducting inquiry lessons; with directions, there should be no guesswork for students. Very direct, exacting messages are sent. In Vignettes 4.4 and 4.5, Mr. Stockton and Ms. Phegley exemplified the art of giving precise directions that get learning activities off to a smooth start.

Initiating Student Engagement

Ready to Listen. In Vignette 5.2, Mr. Johnson began talking to his class of 26 students although only 9 were ready to listen and take notes. He should take a lesson from Ms. Erickson and develop the attitude "I don't speak until you're ready to listen!" Remember, if your students aren't ready to listen on cue, you can always shift to an alternate learning activity (as did Mr. Campbell in Vignette 4.26). The rule is not to begin the interactive lecture session until all students appear attentive with necessary materials (e.g., paper and pencil) ready and potential sources of distractions (e.g., a book that won't be used during the session) put away.

Establishing Set. The second rule for initiating engagement is to *establish set*. Establishing set is focusing attention on and setting up the students for the task at hand. Ms. Erickson established set in three ways. First, she distributed the form appearing in Figure 5.1. This helped structure the situation and provided a focal point to which she could direct students' attention throughout the session. The form gave students an idea of what they would be doing. Second, her curious behavior, deliberately staring at feet, encouraged students to take notice and wonder, "What's she going to do next?" Third, her deliberate movements established *cues* she would take advantage of for the remainder of the session. For example, after distributing the form, she walked directly to a point near the overhead projector and faced the class. From that position she spoke to the students. Silently, she walked directly to a point in front of the fourth row, then to a point in front of the first row, and then back to the position near the overhead where she once again spoke to the class. When she wanted students to look at an illustration, she switched on the overhead projector. When she wanted them to stop looking at it, she turned the overhead off or controlled what they could see with transparency overlays. These movements conveyed cues to students associating her location and movements with what they should be doing throughout the session (e.g., listen attentively when she's by the overhead).

Communicating to students the purpose of the session also helps establish set. Ms. Erickson's session was part of a conceptualization-level lesson and she was stimulating inductive reasoning; thus she did not explicitly state the purpose in the first stage of the activity. She did, however, indicate that she had a question they would be addressing (i.e., "Do the people sitting in the fourth row have bigger feet than those in the first row?"). For a session in which direct instructional methods are appropriate (e.g., for a knowledge-of-a-process objective), establishing sets should include an explicit statement of what the session is intended to accomplish.

Maintaining Engagement in Large-Group Interactive Lecture Sessions

Once you have initiated student engagement for a large-group interactive lecture session, that engagement needs to be sustained. Here are suggestions for doing so:

> *Refer students to an outline of the presentation, session agenda, note-taking form, or other form at climactic or transitional points during the session.* Ms. Erickson used the form in Figure 5.1 to focus students' attention and structure the activity. Consider taking that idea a step farther by having an outline of the presentation (e.g., Figure 5.2), a session agenda (e.g., Figure 5.3, p. 178), or a note-taking form (e.g., Figure 5.4, p. 179) in the hands of students or displayed on an overhead transparency that you can use to direct attention and provide a context for ideas, topics, and subtopics. Having such advanced organizers in students' hands facilitates their note taking and helps you monitor their engagement (e.g., by sampling what they write on Figure 5.4's form). By using transitional remarks (e.g., "Moving on to item four . . .") in conjunction with an outline or agenda, you help students "maintain their bearings" during sessions.
>
> *Make use of illustrations.* Not only to pictures, graphs, diagrams, flow charts, tables, and printed words highlight and supplement oral speech, students are more likely to attend to and comprehend what they see than to what they hear. Of course, illustrations need to be intelligible and clearly visible to all students. Plan to exhibit illustrations so you need not be confined to one location and unable to monitor the class.
>
> *Speak directly to students, moving your eyes about the room, making eye contact with one student after another.* Reread the section beginning in Chapter 4 entitled "Proximity and Body Language."
>
> *Develop a pattern of nonverbal cues for indicating expected student behaviors.* Ms. Erickson grabbed her head and closed her eyes to indicate that she should be allowed to think without interruption. Later she used a hand motion to let students know it was not yet time for them to raise questions. Note that when she was ready for students to speak, she made it clear by saying, "I'll pause to hear what some of you with your hands up have to say." The likelihood of your students responding to your cues increases after they learn the routine your sessions follow. Ms. Erickson's students, for example, were willing to hold their questions and comments because they knew from previous sessions that she would provide a time for them.

Unit: Preventing Drug Abuse
Session Topics: (a) Legal and Illegal Drugs
                (b) Dangers of Drug Abuse
Date: 10/18

Presentation Outline

I. Objectives
   A. Distinguish between legal and illegal drugs
   B. Explain some reasons why some people began taking drugs
   C. Compare physical and psychological drug dependence
II. The nature of drugs
   A. Definition
   B. Some relevant terms:
      1. drug abuse
      2. synthetic drug
      3. legal drug
      4. over-the-counter drug
      5. prescription drug
      6. overdose
      7. illegal drug
III. Causes of drug abuse
   A. Relieving pain
      1. Physical
      2. Emotional
   B. Euphoria
   C. Other
IV. Effects of drug abuse
   A. Chief effect
   B. Side effect
   C. Tolerance
V. Stages of drug abuse
   A. Experimental
   B. Occasional use
   C. Regular use
   D. Addiction
VI. Dependence and addiction
VII. Withdrawal
VIII. Complications
IX. Summary
X. Tomorrow's session
XI. Assignment

Figure 5.2. Example of Presentation Outline Distributed to Students for an Interactive Lecture Session

Move about the room purposefully, neither pacing aimlessly nor confining yourself to one location. Quina (1989) suggested dividing the room into quadrants:

Beginning teachers sometimes unconsciously pace the floor, moving from one side of the room to another. The observing students' heads move as though they are watching a tennis match. To avoid this, think where you want to be standing as you develop parts of your lecture. You can divide the room into quadrants and intentionally move into each quadrant at different stages of your lecture. For example, after introducing the question "Why do we need to communicate?" the teacher may move to the left side of the room, give some information on com-

Meeting Agenda for 10/1
Geography, Fourth Period

1. Hello (0.50–0.75 minutes)
2. Formative quiz and roll (15–16 minutes)
3. Review quiz items and discuss some subset of the following questions as needed according to the quiz review:
   A. What is demography?
   B. What types of problems concern demographers?
   C. How is life expectancy computed?
   D. What are some of the fundamental factors influencing the distribution of the world's population?
   (10–20 minutes)
4. Lecture presentation on further applications of demographic studies—particularly those utilizing birthrates and death rates.
   (10–15 minutes)
5. Homework assignment (2–4 minutes)
6. Head start on homework (7–21 minutes)
7. Prepare for dismissal (1–1.75 minutes)
8. Be kind to yourself (1310 minutes)

Figure 5.3. Example of a Class Meeting Agenda Distributed to Students

municating in pantomime, provide a quick pantomime, then move to the right side of the room to discuss ways we designate things, illustrate by pointing to objects, and then ask a related question, "How is pointing and acting things out like using words?" The teacher may then walk to the back of the room and ask even more pointed questions: "What would happen if we did not have words? What would it be like if words were not available right now?" The shift in position in the room corresponds to the development of the lecture, providing a spatial metaphor for organization. As the teacher walks back to the front of the room to sum up, the very return to the front of the room, to the beginning point, suggests a completion, a completed square, circle, or other shape. These movements are intentional. They can be planned in advance or they can be used spontaneously. Either way, they are intentional—not random pacing. (pp. 141–142).

Consider the advantages of videotaping lecture presentations ahead of time and playing them for students in class. Videotaped lectures can be previewed, edited, and corrected before being presented. Lecturers on videotape do not "forget" nor become distracted. During a videotaped lecture presentation, you are free to monitor student behaviors, stopping, starting, and replaying the tape as formative feedback warrants. The tapes can be saved and presented in subsequent sessions and with other classes.

Use humor and other attention-grabbing devices without allowing them to distract from the business at hand. You are a teacher, not an entertainer. Don't feel obliged to entertain students. However, by *strategically* injecting humor or dramatics into the sessions, you relieve boredom and increase engagement. *Strategic* is the operable word here. Do not allow student laughter to flatter you into the trap of valuing the entertainment aspects of your sessions more than the educational outcomes. Also be cautious of anyone's being offended by your humor or dramatics and of students' being the butt of jokes.

Topic: Developing the Quadratic Formula
Date: 3/9

Main Ideas	Marginal Notes
The need for a general method:	
Completing the square method:	
The need for an easier method:	
Completion of the square example:	
Generalizing completing the square method:	
Reforming expressions to obtain the formula:	
Examples of equations solved with the formula: #1	
#2	
#3	

Summary:

What to do next:

Figure 5.4. Example of a Note-taking Form a Teacher Distributed to Students for Use During a Lecture Presentation

Interject students' names into lectures and relate content to areas that interest them. The most important concern to most students is themselves. Hearing their names stimulates students' attention. For example: "I'll bet Trina agrees that life would be quite different without gravity. Gretchen might have a little more trouble holding onto that pen."

When students need to be following a thought pattern, let them hear you think aloud. To be engaged in lectures, students need to *actively* listen, trying to follow prescribed thought patterns. You facilitate this level of engagement by verbally walking students through cognitive processes leading to conclusions.

Except for relatively brief quotes, avoid reading to the class. Rather than read a lecture to students, have them read it for themselves. For a brief quote you want read during a lecture presentation, consider calling on a student to read it aloud. This increases student involvement, adds variety, and distinguishes between messages that originate with you and those from other sources.

Speak on the students' level (both structurally and relative to vocabulary); make sure vocabulary and notations that are requisite for comprehension of the lecture have been previously taught. Oftentimes, students become disengaged during a lecture because the teacher uses an unfamiliar word, expression, or symbol. The teacher continues, assuming the students understand. But rather than listening, students are trying to figure out what they didn't previously comprehend. Remember they can't return to a previous passage in a lecture to look up what's missed as they can with printed material. Once one point is missed, they are likely to miss subsequent ones.

Strategically vary your voice volume, inflection, pitch, and rhythm according to the message you want to send; avoid monotone. Even when the message itself is important and exciting, a monotone speech is a recipe for boredom. Punctuate your sentences with voice variations.

Follow key statements and questions with strategic pauses. If you raise a question, students should be expected to at least formulate an answer in their minds before it is answered for them. Pauses indicate points to be pondered.

Routinely take time to breathe deeply. This helps you stay alert and control your voice. It also has a calming effect if you happen to be nervous.

Pace your speech so that the sessions move briskly but so that students still have time to absorb your messages and take notes. This point, of course, varies considerably according to the type of lesson you're teaching. A lecture for an inquiry learning activity would ordinarily proceed at a slower pace than one using direct instruction. Quina (1989, p. 143) suggested that between 110 and 130 words per minute is optimal.

Using Formative Feedback

Complex decisions you make as you orchestrate learning activities include determining (a) when to move from one phase of a session to the next; (b) how to regulate the pace of the activities; (c) whether to repeat, skip over, or change messages; (d) whether to extend or abbreviate an activity; and (e) how, if at all, the plan for the session should be modified. These decisions should be based on formative feedback relative to how well students are cooperating and learning. Unless you obviously talk to the back wall the whole session, you can't help but acquire formative feedback while conducting large-group interactive lecture sessions. Are students staying on task? If they aren't understanding what is being said, they're not likely to remain attentive. If they already know what is being said, they're not likely to remain attentive. Thus, level of attentiveness, unless it's coerced, is an indicator of how the session is proceeding. There are also the overt displays of understanding or misunderstanding associated with facial expressions, comments, and body language.

But acquisition of accurate formative feedback is too critical to the success of the lesson to be left to chance indications you may be fortunate enough to detect. Formative feedback should be systematically sought by integrating specific tasks for students to perform and pointed questions for them to answer throughout the session. Questions such as, "Are there any questions?" "Does everybody understand?" and "Okay?" do little to inform you about how well students are following the session or understanding the lesson. To provide formative feedback, questions and directives must be more to the point. For example: "We don't know the speed of the object, but we do know something about its acceleration. . . . What do we know, Alma?" "Repeat Alma's answer for us, Loo-Lau." "Quickly work this example on your note outlines, while I zip around peeking over shoulders."

Not only does the success of a learning activity depend on how well you utilize formative feedback while you're conducting it, but your abilities to conduct activities, such as large-group interactive lecture sessions, improve with experience *if* you use formative feedback to learn what does and doesn't work. Chapter 6 deals with evaluating student achievement; it includes ideas for collecting accurate formative data.

Achieving Closure

Students' engagement in interactive lecture sessions is positively reinforced by climactic moments in which it is clear that they have learned something of value. Thus, it is important that they are not left "hanging" for too long. Plan for moments throughout the session in which ideas come together and students recognize progress toward an objective. Timing is critical. Save enough time for summarizing the main points and for students to practice with or apply the concepts, specifics, relationships, or processes dealt with during the session. Once they realize that your interactive lectures are structured so that ideas raised during a session are brought together as a coherent whole at the end of the session, they will tend to "hang with you" and tolerate perplexity during subsequent sessions.

ENGAGING STUDENTS IN LARGE-GROUP INTELLECTUAL-LEVEL QUESTIONING/DISCUSSION SESSIONS

Intellectual-Level Questions

Compare the type of question Ms. Neilson asks to those of Mr. Mustophose in Vignettes 5.4 (p. 182) and 5.5 (p. 183).

In Vignette 5.4, Ms. Neilson's questions taxed her students' memories. Her questions helped them to remember how to spell certain words. Such questions provide Ms. Neilson with formative feedback on what they remember and provides students with both corrective feedback and a repetitive drill to help them

---

VIGNETTE 5.4

MS. NEILSON: How do you spell the word *road* as it used in the sentence "Let's walk down the *road*," Tyler?

TYLER: R-O-D-E

MS. NEILSON: Tyler has just spelled the word *rode* when it's used in sentences like "I rode my horse in the parade." But now I'd like you to remember how to spell another word that has the exact same sound—the one that reminds us of a street or a path like in the sentence, "The road is rough and bumpy." Tyler, you either take another shot at that word or call on someone else to try.

TYLER: Biff

BIFF: R-O-A-D

MS. NEILSON: That is correct. The next word is *running*, as in the sentence, "I'm *running* down the road with my dog." Hasheen?

HASHEEN: R-U-N-N-I-N-G

MS. NEILSON: Is that the correct spelling for *running*, Tawny?

TAWNEY: I don't know.

MS. NEILSON: "Tawny only: Uncover your word list and tell us if Hasheen's spelling is correct.

TAWNY: . . . Yes, it is.

MS. NEILSON: Good! Now, how do you spell . . .

---

remember. Such questions are *knowledge-level*. Mr. Mustophose's questions, on the other hand, were more open-ended and designed to guide student's thought patterns leading to discovery. Unlike, Ms. Neilson's questions, Mr. Mustophose's questions could have more than one correct answer. Mr. Mustophose's questions taxed students intellectual cognitive abilities (i.e., either conceptualization, comprehension, application, or creativity). Such questions are *intellectual-level*.

Appropriate Uses of Intellectual-Level Questioning/Discussion Sessions

Intellectual-level question/discussion sessions in which a teacher raises intellectual-level questions for students to answer, analyze, and discuss are necessary components of lessons for intellectual-level objectives. In Vignette 3.8, Mr. Landastoy's lesson for a *conceptualization* objective on *opinions and facts* included a large-group intellectual-level questioning/discussion session to stimulate inductive reasoning. Questions were raised about the examples and nonexamples listed in Figure 3.4 and 3.5; differences and similarities were discussed. In Vignette 3.15, Ms. Loyocono's lesson for a *comprehension* objective relative to the U.S. Constitution included a large-group intellectual-level questioning/discussion session to involve the students in interpreting aspects of the Preamble and analyzing its logical underpinnings. In Vignette 3.21, Mr. Cummings's lesson for an *application* objective on *polygonal area*, included a large-group intellectual-level questioning/discussion session to stimulate deductive reasoning. Questions were ad-

VIGNETTE 5.5

MR. MUSTOPHOSE: Class, I have a map of a country that tells us something about its geography but nothing else. We don't know anything about where people live in this country or what they do for a living. Our task is to make some educated guesses about where the people are located—like where they may have established cities and towns and what they might do for a living.

He displays Figure 5.5 on the overhead screen, allowing one minute for students to silently view the map.

Figure 5.5. Mr. Mustophose's Overhead Transparency Display

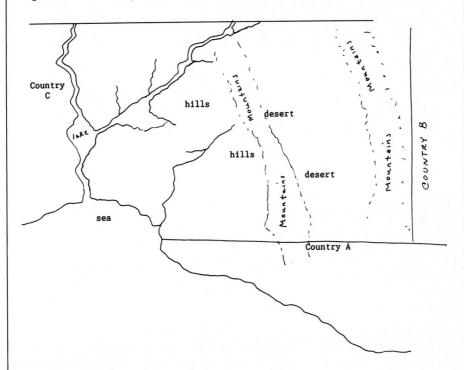

MR. MUSTOPHOSE: Describe what you see, Sandra.

SANDRA: A map of a country. It's next to two—no, three other countries and there's a sea at the bottom. There's mountains on the right and desert, some more mountains—and like a real big river on the left.

MR. MUSTOPHOSE: Repeat Sandra's description using north, south, east, west in place of up, down, left, right, Anthony.

ANTHONY: Next to three countries, mountains toward the east, then a desert, more mountains, and a sea to the south, and rivers on the west side.

MR. MUSTOPHOSE: Where do you think most of the people in this country live, Julian?

(continued)

VIGNETTE 5.5 (continued)

JULIAN: In cities and towns.

MR. MUSTOPHOSE: Where do you think Julian's cities and towns are located, Franco?

FRANCO: All over

MR. MUSTOPHOSE: Where would the most populated—the one with the most people be located, Franco?

FRANCO: In the east.

MR. MUSTOPHOSE: Why?

FRANCO: That's where New York is and that's the biggest city in the United States.

MR. MUSTOPHOSE: Okay, Jeannie.

JEANNIE: But Los Angeles is in the west and that's a big city too.

MR. MUSTOPHOSE: In the United States are there more larger cities in the east or in the west, Mary?

MARY: East.

MR. MUSTOPHOSE: Why do you suppose that's true, Dan?

DAN: Because Columbus discovered America in the east and that's just where people first came.

MR. MUSTOPHOSE: Andy?

ANDY: The reason is 'cause people live where there's more water and stuff—not where there's deserts and stuff.

MR. MUSTOPHOSE: Where's most of the water located in this country? . . . Julian.

JULIAN: The south and west.

MR. MUSTOPHOSE: Where do you think the biggest city will be, Asad?

ASAD: Somewhere near the sea, where there's also rivers.

MR. MUSTOPHOSE: Yes, Mary

MARY: Maybe not, because maybe where they're mountains the city is safest from other countries that might . . .

---

dressed leading to a solution of a problem about decorating the classroom. In Vignette 3.23, Mr. Walker's lesson for a *creativity* objective on *views of historical figures* included a large-group intellectual-level questioning/discussion session to stimulate divergent thinking. Raising open-ended questions and sharing analyses of responses are inherent in the synectics Mr. Walker applied.

Common Misuses of Intellectual-Level Questioning/Discussion Sessions

In response to the overemphasis on knowledge-level skills and underemphasis on intellectual-level learning in most classrooms today (Goodlad, 1984, pp. 197–245; Swartz & Perkins, 1990, pp. xvi, 8–90), arguments favoring an emphasis on inquiry and discovery instruction leading to intellectual-level learning are widely circulated (e.g., Hunkins, 1989; Jones, Palincsar, Ogle, & Carr, 1987; Resnick and Klopfer, 1989). This push has unfortunately nurtured the mistaken belief among some teachers that discovery or inquiry lessons are always superior to direct instruction. Of course, some knowledge-level objectives should be included among the objectives for most teaching units. Direct instruction, not inquiry instruction, is appropriate for knowledge-level objectives. But those well-intentioned teachers who have been "oversold" on the virtues of inquiry instruction inappropriately attempt to get their students to discover content that is not discoverable. They then inappropriately conduct intellectual-level questioning/discussion sessions for what should be knowledge-level objectives. For example:

VIGNETTE 5.6

Mr. Butterfield wants his students to discover why "%" is used to denote percent. Displaying the symbol he initiates a questioning session:

MR. BUTTERFIELD: Why do you suppose the percent sign looks like this, Valerie?

VALERIE: I don't know. . . . Is it that the slash is sort of like a fraction sign?

MR. BUTTERFIELD: That's a good thought! Any other ideas, Roosevelt?

ROOSEVELT: What Valerie said makes sense.

MR. BUTTERFIELD: Can you add something?

ROOSEVELT: . . . It could be the two little circles stand for the two zeros in 100.

MR. BUTTERFIELD: That could be. Okay, let's move on to our next topic for the day.. . . .

There is no logically discoverable reason why the percent symbol looks as it does. The symbol is simply a convention whose usage evolved over several centuries (Amundson, 1969). Historical accounts of such conventions can be found in literature. Sharing such accounts with students serves as a nmemonic for remembering the symbol and its meaning. However, trying to get students to discover the evolution of a convention via intellectual-level questioning/discussion sessions is not only an inefficient use of class time, it's impossible.

For knowledge-level objectives, knowledge-level questioning sessions are appropriate, but not intellectual-level questioning/discussion sessions. There are times when you should raise open-ended questions during direct instructional lessons for knowledge-level objectives. But ordinarily such questions are rhetorical. For example, Mr. Butterfield might have initiated his lesson in knowledge of the percent symbol with a question, "Why do we use this symbol for percent?" But instead of having students try to discover the answer, he should have just paused a moment and then used direct instructional methods to relate the historical account (either in a brief lecture or reading assignment).

Avoiding Mr. Butterfield's type of misuse is a matter of attending to the learning level of your objective. Another type of misuse is more difficult to overcome because it stems from the fact that conducting effective large-group intellectual-level questioning/discussion sessions is a sophisticated art, requiring in-depth understanding of pedagogical principles, students, and subject-matter content. It is quite a challenge to determine (a) when to raise what questions with whom, (b) how to respond to students' answers, comments, and questions, and (c) whether a discussion should be abbreviated, extended, or redirected. Besides your academic preparation, experience will help you avoid the following causes of unsuccessful intellectual-level questioning/discussion sessions:

> *The teacher fails to comprehend what students are saying and consequently responds inappropriately to their answers, comments, and questions.* For example:

VIGNETTE 5.7

Ms. Checketts's fifth-graders are in the midst of a health science unit designed to discourage students from abusing drugs. Her objectives include the following:

Explain the five "benefits of being drug-free" as enumerated on pp. 167–168 of the textbook (Meeks & Heit, 1990) (*Cognitive: comprehension*)

She is now conducting an intellectual-level questioning/discussion session for that objective.

Ms. Checketts: Read the second one for us, Megan.

Megan: You will think clearly. People who use harmful drugs cannot think clearly. They cannot perform well at work or school. They cannot make responsible decisions and solve problems. People say "no" to drugs because drugs change a person's ability to think and make wise decisions.

Ms. Checketts: Do you agree with that, Varnell?

Varnell: Well, not really. I don't take drugs but I don't always think clearly. Also, I know people who do take drugs but they still solve problems in school and stuff.

Ms. Checketts was expecting Varnell to agree with the statement. When he said, "Well, not really," she began thinking of ways to counter his point of view. Consequently she failed to carefully listen and comprehend his point, which demonstrated a sophisticated-level of comprehension of the statement. Thus, she responds, "You really should say 'no' to drugs because they really do interfere with your problem-solving abilities and your relationships."

Varnell did not intend to speak against saying "no" to drugs, but Ms. Checketts's response suggested to the class that he did.

> *The teacher fails to play upon students' responses to further probe questions.* Even though Ms. Checketts thought Varnell's statement countered the point she wanted to make with the class, she could have followed through with analytical questions about what he said that would have stimulated further thinking and helped her make the point—which should be about

the effects of drug abuse, not whether or not the book's statement is literally true. For example, "Do you think Varnell is disagreeing with the *intent* of the author's statement or the way the statement is *worded*?" After calling on another student for that answer, she could turn to Varnell and ask, "Is that what you meant?"

Some teachers, not wanting to appear unaccepting of students' answers, routinely respond with vague praise to virtually anything students say, and then proceed with the session as if the students said nothing. For example:

VIGNETTE 5.8

MR. RAY-SOAR: What are some of the things we know about Asia, Mark?

MARK: Asia is the most crowded part of the world.

MR. RAY-SOAR: Good! What else, Emily?

EMILY: I think Asia has had more wars and stuff that's hard on people than anywhere else.

MR. RAY-SOAR: Super! Carl?

CARL: Everybody in Asia is poor.

MR. RAY-SOAR: That's a good try. What do you want to add, Leitka?

LEITKA: A lot of the stuff we buy here is made in Taiwan, Japan, Korea, China, places like that.

MR. RAY-SOAR: That's for sure. Okay, now Europe is another important area for . . .

Out of frustration with students' answers, the teacher aborts the session in favor of direct instruction, "telling" them what they should have discovered for themselves. When students' responses to questions don't move the class's thinking along planned lines and students appear restless, it is tempting to change strategies in midsession. However, the difficulty may not stem from students's inability to grasp ideas as much as from the teacher's failure to (a) adequately structure the session with the aid of outlines, forms, and other advanced organizers for focusing attention (e.g., Figures 5.2, 5.3, and 5.4); (b) use appropriate probes that stimulate students to examine their own responses in ways that lead them back on track; and (c) utilize formative feedback for pacing and modifying activities (e.g., deciding whether to reduce or increase psychological noise of examples).

When students' responses and comments deviate from the planned thought pattern, you need to refocus them with less open-ended questions, as Ms. Moore does in Vignette 5.9.

VIGNETTE 5.9

While helping her students learn to read graphs, Ms. Moore displays Figure 5.6 with an overhead projector and says, "Mr. Dotted's class took the same history test as Mr. Broken-Line's class. Here are the graphs of the two classes' scores; this dotted graph is from Mr. Dotted's class. . . . And this broken-line graph is from Mr. Broken-Line's class. . . . The question I have for you is which class scored better over-all? . . . Rasheeda."

Figure 5.6. Which Class Scored Better Overall?

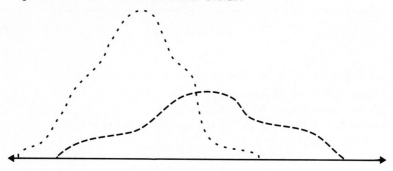

RASHEEDA: Mr. Dotted's class did better.

Ms. MOORE: Why?

RASHEEDA: Because the graph is higher.

Ms. MOORE: Which of the two classes has the greater or higher average score?

RASHEEDA: The dotted one's higher.

Ms. MOORE: I'm going to run my pointer over this line representing the possible scores from lower to higher. Rasheeda, stop me when I get to the average of the dotted class. . . .

Ms. Moore runs the pointer along the line as shown in Figure 5.7. When the pointer is under the peak of the dotted curve, Rasheeda exclaims, "Stop," and Ms.

Figure 5.7. Ms. Moore Moves Her Transparency Pen along the Horizontal Axis

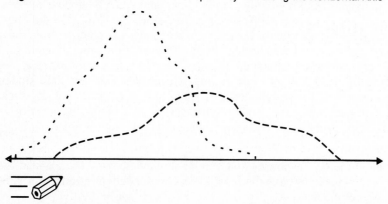

VIGNETTE 5.9 (continued)

Moore marks the spot. The activity is repeated with the broken-line curve and Rasheeda stops Ms. Moore when the pointer is under the peak of the broken-line graph. With Figure 5.8 now displayed on the screen, the class is ready to formulate the generalization Ms. Moore had in mind when she began the session.

Figure 5.8. Now Which Class Scored Better Overall?

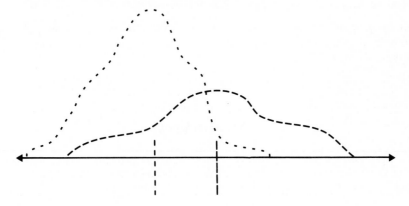

Ms. Moore: Which of the two classes has the higher average?

Rasheeda: The broken-line one.

Ms. Moore: Does anyone want to venture a rule for determining overall performance from reading a graph? . . . Marion.

Marion: The better scores are more to the right than the lower ones. So, . . .

Another strategy is to "jump" on a student's comment or answer that has any semblance of directing thinking in the desired direction and rewording it just enough to assure that what needs to be said is said.

For example, when Rasheeda answered, "The dotted one's higher," Ms. Moore might have twisted what she actually heard slightly and said, "I hear Rasheeda saying that the *graph* of the dotted curve has a higher peak. But does that necessarily mean individuals in the group have higher scores?"

The teacher fails to sufficiently structure the session or be assertive enough to maintain the focus on the business at hand; thus the activity degenerates into a "bull session." Critics of inquiry instructional activities point out how often open-ended questions and class discussions drift from the intended topic, wasting time that teachers should be using to "cover" the material with direct approaches. The solution is not to abandon necessary intellectual-level questioning/discussion sessions, but for you to structure activities with advanced organizers and to utilize assertive communications.

Classroom management strategies for engaging all, not only several, students in formulating answers to questions are not applied. Affording every student opportunities to respond to questions and participate in discussions seems possible to some only in small group sessions. Examples in the next section illustrate how you can achieve full student participation in large, whole-class sessions.

Initiating and Maintaining Student Engagement in Large-Group Intellectual-Level Questioning/Discussion Sessions

Teachers typically conduct large group intellectual-level questioning/discussion sessions so that students answer questions aloud almost as soon as the first one volunteers as in Vignette 5.10.

VIGNETTE 5.10

Ms. Bernstein uses large-group inductive questioning strategies to stimulate her 23 second-graders to reflect on their experiences playing a game in the school yard the previous day. It is all part of a lesson for the following objective:

> Distinguish between examples and nonexamples of circles and explain the defining attributes of a circle (*Cognitive: conceptualization*)

> **Ms. Bernstein:** I'd like for someone to tell us about the racing game we played with the soccer ball yesterday. Okay, Simon.
> **Simon:** Two of us raced at a time to see who could get the ball first.
> **Ms. Bernstein:** Draw a picture showing how we *first* lined up and where the ball was.

Simon draws the picture shown in Figure 5.9.

> **Ms. Bernstein:** Now, draw a picture showing how we lined up *after* changing the rules.

Figure 5.9. First Picture Simon Drew on the Board

Simon draws the picture shown in Figure 5.10.

VIGNETTE 5.10 (continued)

Figure 5.10. Second Picture Simon
Drew on the Board

Ms. Bernstein: Why did we change the game?

Stephanie: Because it wasn't fair before; some people were closer to the ball than others.

Ms. Bernstein: Why was the second way fairer?

Aaron: Because everybody was just as close.

Ms. Bernstein: What shape did you make after we fixed the game?

Stephanie: A circle.

Ms. Bernstein: Why was that better than being on a straight line?

Aaron: Because we went around the ball so that I wasn't closer or far-rer away than Bobby or anybody.

Ms. Bernstein: So, what is a circle then?

Aaron: A circle kind of goes even all around so that . . .

Ms. Bernstein's questioning/discussion session probably helped Stephanie, Aaron, and maybe Simon achieve the objective. But what about the other 20 students in the class? For students to be engaged in activities in which intellectual-level questions are raised, they must do more than passively listen to their classmates' responses. They don't necessarily have to be recognized and state their answers for the group, but they do need to formulate and articulate their own answers.

Ms. Bernstein allowed Stephanie to answer aloud immediately after the initial question was raised, so most students did not have time to formulate their own answers. They quit thinking about their own answers to listen to Stephanie's. Only the outspoken, quick-to-respond students engaged in the learning activity as they should. Ms. Bernstein did not allow enough time to elapse between when questions were asked and when they were answered aloud for the class. The overall average time teachers wait for students to respond to in-class questions is less than two seconds (Arnold, Atwood, & Rogers, 1974). After experiencing a few sessions like Ms. Bernstein's in which they are asked questions that they don't have the opportunity to answer, most students learn to not even attempt to formulate their own responses. Some will politely listen to the responses of the few, others entertain themselves with off-task thoughts, and others, if allowed, entertain themselves with disruptive behaviors (Cangelosi, 1988a, p. 155). How, then, can you conduct intellectual-level questioning/discussion sessions so that all students formulate answers to each questions? Here are two possibilities:

Preface questions with directions for all students to answer each question in their minds without answering aloud or volunteering answers until you ask them to do so. Here's an example of a teacher applying that option to Ms. Bernstein's situation:

VIGNETTE 5.11

After Ms. Rackley has a student describe the game using illustrations similar to Figures 5.9 and 5.10, she says to the class, "I am going to ask you a question, but I don't want anyone to answer aloud until I call on you. Just answer the question in your mind. . . . Why did we change the game?" Two students eagerly raise their hands and say, "Oh, Ms. Rackley!" She is tempted to call on them to positively reinforce their enthusiasm, but she resists, instead cuing them to follow directions with a gesture and stern look. She waits, watching students' faces. Convinced after 40 seconds that all have thought about the question and most have an answer ready, she asks, "Janelle, do you have an answer?" Janelle nods.

MS. RACKLEY: Good! How about you, Doris?

DORIS: Yes.

MS. RACKLEY: Fine! Are you ready, Lurma?

LURMA: Not yet.

MS. RACKLEY: Just think aloud for us. Let's hear your thoughts about why we thought it was fairer to be lined up like this . . . rather than like this . . .—the way we were when we started.

LURMA: I'm not sure how it matters; the fast ones win anyway. But being around the ball makes it even—so it's all who's fast. That's not fair either.

MS. RACKLEY: Thank you for that important observation. Now, I'd like some volunteers to share their answers with us. Okay, Crenshaw?

CRENSHAW: The second time was like a circle, and a circle is even all around. So, . . .

You might direct students to write answers to questions on forms you supply or on their own paper as you circulate about the room, quietly reading samples of their responses. Mr. Landastoy applied such as strategy in Vignette 3.8.

You might also consider having students formulate and discuss answers in small cooperative task-groups and then making group reports of their findings and conclusions to the large group. Engaging students in these types of sessions is addressed in a subsequent section of this chapter. Here are some additional ideas to keep in mind as you go about designing and conducting large-group intellectual-level questioning/discussion sessions:

> Apply the same principles for providing directions (e.g., be direct and exacting) and initiating student engagement (e.g., establish set) as you would for large-group interactive lecture sessions.
>
> Formative feedback is inherent in questioning sessions; use it to regulate activities.
>
> As with interactive lecture sessions, climatic moments in which students recognize that they've learned something and final closure are critical to the success of intellectual-level questioning/discussion sessions.

Responding to Students' Questions

If during these sessions students feel they've been asked a lot of questions but haven't received many answers, they feel unfulfilled and thus closure is not achieved. Keep in mind that you not only raise questions for students' responses, but you also need to respond to students' questions. Your strategies for addressing their intellectual-level questions should differ from those for their knowledge-level questions.

Student-initiated Intellectual-Level Questions. Imagine yourself conducting a large-group session as part of an application-level lesson on genetics. A student, Nancy, asks you, "Suppose there's some inherited defect in which, if parents had it there's a 25 percent chance that a kid they have will also have the defect. What if they have two kids, what's the chances that one or both will have the defect? Is it 50 percent or does it stay 25 percent?"

Such a question is answerable via a cognitive process, namely deductive reasoning, that involves more than just recalling a response. Being in the midst of an application-level lesson dealing with genetics, you want to respond in a way that will advance the cause of the lesson. You have at least four options:

> *Answer the question directly.* This would be the easiest and quickest thing to do. Give the answer, and because it's an intellectual-level question, explain the rationale for it. For example, you might respond, "Actually, Nancy, I think the probability would be somewhere between 25 percent and 50 percent. Think of the probability of neither of the two children inheriting the defect. The chances of the first not having it is 75 percent; the chances of the second not having is also 75 percent. It's a compound probability of two independent events, so you multiply .75 by .75. And that would be . . . about .56 according my calculator. So, if there's a 56 percent chance of neither having it, there must be a 44 percent chance that one or both will get it. . . . Get it?"
>
> *Use a think-aloud strategy.* Rather than directly explain the answer, you may spend more time demonstrating what goes through one's mind when for-

mulating a solution. For Nancy's question, you would be modeling the application-level behavior you want the students to learn by giving the following response: "Gracious, Nancy, that's a challenging question. Let's see, how would I go about solving that one? . . . You've got two kids, the first or older one, and then the second. The probability of the first having the defect is 25 percent, did you say? . . . Okay. And is the probability of the second one having it affected by whether or not the first one has it? . . . No. So, no matter what, the probability for the second is also 25 per-cent. . . . So, the first thing that comes to mind is to add the two and I get the 50 percent that you got, Nancy. . . . Let me see, is that right? . . . It couldn't be because if the parents had, say, five children, that would be .25 five times and that would be a probability of 1.25 or 125 percent—that's impossible. The probability has got to be less than 1. . . . Oh, let's try it case by case. What's the probability of the first having it and the second not having it? . . . Chances are .25 for the first and then .75 for the second not to have it. That's what? . . . The multiplication rule applies so .25 times .75 is . . . about .19. That takes care of one case. . . . Now, what about the first not having it, but the second one does—that's another .19. . . . What's left? . . . Both of them having it. That's .25 times .25, which is . . . about .06. . . . That's all the possibilities, so add them up because they're mutually exclusive events and we get. . . 44 percent. Does that seem right? . . . Oh! I shouldn't have spent all that time, I just thought of an easier way. . . . Couldn't we have just looked at the complement?—and then we'd only have one case to figure! . . . The probability of neither child having the defect would be simply .75 squared and that's . . . about .56. . . . So, our answer should be 100 percent minus 56 percent or 44 percent—same thing as before, but I found it with less work."

Probe back to the student. Even more time consuming, but probably more beneficial for the student, is to respond with a sequence of your own questions that stimulate the students to engage in the type of reasoning demonstrated by the "think-aloud" example. For example:

You: What makes you think it might be 50 percent?
NANCY: There's 25 percent chance the first one has it, right?
You: Right.
NANCY: And 25 percent for the second one. So, that's another 25 percent chance—giving you a total of 50 percent.
You: Then what would the probability be of having at least one child with the defect if the family had five children?
NANCY: Five times .25.
You: Which is?
NANCY: . . . ahh, 1.25. . . . That's not possible!
You: Why don't you try a case-by-case strategy?
NANCY: Like what?
You: Here, come up to the board and . . .

You would continue along these lines, leading Nancy through the thought process.

Probe and redirect the question to other students. To involve more students in the activity, respond with leading questions, but direct them to other students as well as Nancy. For example:

You: Which do you think it right, 50 or 25 percent, Wil?

Wil: It's got to be more than 25 percent because that's the probability if they had only one child.

You: So does that make it 50 percent, Rheen?

Rheen: That's all that's left.

You: Okay, class, assuming Rheen is correct, compute the probability of at least one child having the defect if the family has five instead of only two children. Quickly, now, everyone. . . . Okay, what did you get, Nancy?

Nancy: I got 1.25, but that can't be because . . .

Student-initiated Knowledge-Level Questions. Imagine yourself conducting a large-group session as part of a lesson on genetics when a student, Juan, asks you, "What does *congenital* mean?" Such a question is answerable by recalling a response, in this case, a definition. Your options, of which there are at least five, are simpler to implement than those for intellectual-level questions:

> *Answer the question directly.* For example, you say, "Congenital means existing from birth, but not necessarily genetic. For example if a fetus' brain fails to develop properly because the mother smoked, then the baby—if it lives—would suffer from a *congenital* defect."
>
> *Use a "how-might-we-find-that-out" strategy.* For example:

You: We really need to know what that means. Where should we go to look that up?

Juan: It's probably in the book, but I don't know where.

You: Why don't you try the index? That should give us some page numbers.

> *Refer the student to a source to be used right away.* Say, for example, "Quickly, get the dictionary off the shelf there, look up the definition and read it to the class."
>
> *Refer the student to a source to be used later on.* You might respond, "You can find the definition in your textbook or you may use my dictionary. Please look it up in one or the other and share it first thing in class tomorrow."
>
> *Redirect the question to another student.* For example:

You: Who remembers the definition of *congenital*? . . . Okay, Vincent.

Vincent: You said it's a condition a baby is born with.

ENGAGING STUDENTS IN LARGE-GROUP RECITATION SESSIONS

Knowledge-Level Questions

To the eyes of an untrained classroom observer, large-group recitation sessions may hardly be distinguishable from large-group intellectual-level questioning/discussion sessions. In both types of sessions the teacher raises questions for students to answer. However, the level of questions and the level of student learning differ dramatically. Recitation sessions are dominated by knowledge-level questions requiring students to *remember* answers or how to find answers, *not* use reasoning to formulate answers. Ms. Neilson, in Vignette 5.4, conducted an exemplary large-group recitation session. Her questions (e.g., "How do you spell the word *road*?") were *knowledge level.*

Appropriate Uses of Large-Group Recitation Sessions

Recitation sessions in which a teacher raises knowledge-level questions provide students with reviews of what they need to remember, experiences hearing correct answers they need to retain in memory, and feedback on the accuracy of what they remember. Furthermore, the teacher gains formative feedback on what students do and don't know. Such sessions play an important role in knowledge-level lessons.

Common Misuses of Large-Group Recitation Sessions

As with other types of learning activities, recitations are not always used as they should; the more common misuses include the following:

> *A teacher attempts to help students achieve an intellectual-level objective via a recitation instead of an intellectual-level questioning/discussion session.* Ordinarily this is a consequence of either teachers not knowing how to ask intellectual-level questions or becoming so frustrated with students' responses to intellectual-level questions that they shift to knowledge-level questions.
>
> *A teacher uses a large-group recitation session to test what students know, using the results to make summative evaluations affecting students' grades.* As indicated in Chapter 6, there are far more accurate and efficient ways of collecting data on student achievement for grading purposes than holding a large-group recitation. Some teachers and many students think of in-class questioning sessions as times for "putting students on the spot" and "proving how smart" (and, thus, dumb) they are. Such an attitude detracts from the value of any large-group questioning session, either intellectual-level or knowledge-level, as a learning activity. Testing for summative evaluation purposes needs to be clearly distinguished from learning activities.
>
> *A teacher attempts to use students' anticipation of such a session to motivate them to memorize what they need to know or else be embarrassed in front of their peers.* The threat of being embarrassed in the classroom tends to discourage rather than encourage student engagement and effort (Cangelosi, 1988a, pp. 76–79).
>
> *A large-group recitation session is used to provide students with practice on a particular skill that could be more efficiently practiced in another type of learning activity arrangement (e.g., an independent work session)* For example:

VIGNETTE 5.12

To help his students remember rules they've studied for subject-predicate agreement, Mr. Simpson conducts a large-group recitation session, part of which proceeds as follows:

MR. SIMPSON: Should I say "They *is* going to the store," or "They *are* going to the store," Michelle?

MICHELLE: Are.

MR. SIMPSON: Why is Michelle correct, John?

JOHN: Because "they" is more than one so you must use the plural verb.

MR. SIMPSON: That's right. Now, in which of these two sentences do we have proper subject-verb agreement: "Cheryl and Roxanne *go* to the same school," or "Cheryl and Roxanne *goes* to the same school." Mike?

MIKE: Go.

MR. SIMPSON: What rule did you . . .

Although there's nothing particularly wrong with Mr. Simpson's recitation session, there may well be times when this type of activity would more efficiently provide practice for students if it were designed as an independent work session. With the independent work session, each student could respond to all Mr. Simpson's questions on an exercise sheet. He could provide some individual help during the session and then "check" answers in a large-group setting afterward.

Initiating and Maintaining Student Engagement in Recitation Sessions

Here are some ideas to keep in mind when designing and conducting large-group recitation sessions:

> *Games can be used to excite student interest.* The term recitation is associated with boredom in the minds of most people. Yet, television quiz shows and board games such as "Trivial Pursuit" enjoy immense popularity although they are forms of recitations (i.e., knowledge-level questions are addressed). Thus, you might consider tailoring some of your recitation sessions along the lines of some of the popular quiz games. For example:

VIGNETTE 5.13

Periodically, Ms. Pillow has her Spanish class play a game with the following rules:

1. One student is selected as the *game conductor*, another as *game scorekeeper*.
2. The rest of the class is divided into two teams, X and Y.

(continued)

VIGNETTE 5.13 (continued)

3. Six members of each team are selected to serve as that team's *panel*.
4. Panels X and Y sit at separate tables in front of the room.
5. The game conductor randomly draws the name of a nonpanelist member of one of the teams. That student then selects one of the following categories for the first question to the opposing team: (a) vocabulary words: English to Spanish; (b) vocabulary words: Spanish to English; (c) common Spanish expressions: Spanish to English; (d) grammatical rules; (e) structural rules; and (f) potpourri.
6. The game conductor randomly draws a question card from the selected category and asks the question to the panel (X if the student selecting the category is from Y, and vice versa).
7. The panel members have 15 seconds to confer and answer the question. If they answer their team is awarded two points. If they fail, then the panel members call on a nonpanelist from their team for the answer. If the team member correctly answers the question, the team gets one point. If that member doesn't, then the conductor asks the same question to the other panel, and that team goes through the same process. If no correct answer is forthcoming, then the conductor announces the correct answer and no points are awarded.
8. A second nonpanelist is randomly chosen to select a category and steps 6 and 7 are repeated. However, a new category has to be selected; no previously selected category can be chosen until all categories have been used once. Each time a panel calls on one of its nonpanelist team members to answer a question, they must select a student who has not been called on earlier in the game.
9. The game continues along these lines (repeating the cycle established in steps 6–8) until a prespecified number of questions have been asked.

Most recitation sessions should probably be integrated with other types of learning activities. This idea is in contrast to the previous one in which an elaborate game is set up for a recitation. Such games, though usually quite engaging for most students, are time consuming and can hardly be used every day. As you conduct various types of learning activities, even those targeting intellectual-level objectives, it's wise to insert knowledge-level questions relative to content that is relevant at the time. For example:

VIGNETTE 5.14

As Mr. al-Sabah is conducting an inductive lesson on genetics, a student remarks, "You can't prevent a sickness that you were born with." The term *congenital* had been introduced the day before, so Mr. al-Sabah responds, "What do we call such a condition?"

When raising a question, you are more likely to get the whole class to listen to the question if you don't use the name of the student you call on until after the question is articulated. For example:

VIGNETTE 5.15

Ms. Hall asks, "Donna, why should people floss their teeth everyday?" When Justin heard Donna's name he knew he wouldn't be called on, so he didn't think about the answer. Later Ms. Hall asks, "What can happen if you let plaque stay on your teeth? . . . Okay, Margaret," This time, Justin paid attention to the question longer and even took time to think of an answer before Ms. Hall called on Margaret.

Calling on students in a sequence they can't predict tends to enhance their attention to questions. This idea works for the same reason as does withholding the student's name until after a question is asked. To achieve an unpredictable sequence, all students must feel they have an equal opportunity to be called on for each question. This means that over the course of several sessions, students have been called on about an equal number of times. Furthermore, students who have just responded are still candidates for the next question.

Although the length of wait time between when you ask a knowledge-level question and when a student addresses it aloud needs not be as long as for intellectual-level questions, students still need time to recall a response before they're interrupted by someone telling them the answer.

Although large-group recitation sessions are poor sources of data for summative evaluations of student achievement, they inherently provide formative feedback that should be used in regulating the session.

ENGAGING STUDENTS IN COOPERATIVE TASK-GROUP SESSIONS

Appropriate Uses of Cooperative Task-Group Sessions

For some learning activities, it may be more efficient for you to organize your class into several subgroups rather than a single large group. Intra-class grouping arrangements in which students in each group work on a common task provide greater opportunities than whole class activities for students to interact with one another, tasks to be tailored to special interests or needs, and a wide variety of tasks to be addressed during class.

Cooperative learning activities in which students learn from one another have proven to be quite successful (Foyle & Lyman, 1989; Joyce & Weil, 1986, pp. 215–305; Voorhies, 1989). Students can engage in cooperative learning activities in large-group settings, but small task-group sessions are particularly well-suited for students teaching one another.

Peer Instruction Groups. In a peer instruction group, one student teaches others, either presenting a brief lesson, tutoring, or providing help with a particular exercise. Traditionally, this type of activity involves a student who is advanced, relative to achievement of a particular objective, working with students who need special help in achieving that objective. For example:

VIGNETTE 5.16

Mr. Santiago notes the following from the results of a unit test on laws of motion he administered to his 28 sixth-graders:
Regarding test items 3, 4, 7, and 16, all of which are relevant to students' conceptualization of speed or acceleration:

Amanda responded correctly to all four, whereas none of the following students got more than one of those items: Oral, Nedra, Malinda, Armond, and Paul.

Regarding test items, 5, 6, 10, 11, 13, and 14 all of which are relevant to students' comprehension of Newton's laws of motion:

Casey responded correctly to all six items, whereas none of the following students got more than two of those items: Oral, Malinda, Paul, Teri, Kathy, and Scott.

Mr. Santiago thinks that (a) Amanda's and Casey's insights into the content would be enhanced by experiences teaching their peers; (b) the other eight aforementioned students will not succeed in the next unit until they better achieve certain objectives from this unit; and (c) Oral, Malinda, and Paul need to conceptualize speed and acceleration before they can comprehend the laws of motion. Thus, he decides to conduct a session in which the class is subdivided into three groups:

Group 1, in which Amanda explains speed and acceleration and how she worked test items 3, 4, 7, and 16 to Oral, Nedra, Malinda, Armond, and Paul.
Group 2, in which Casey explains laws of motion and how he worked test items 5, 6, 10, 11, 13, and 14 to Teri, Kathy, and Scott.
Group 3, in which the other 18 students work independently on an assignment.

But peer instruction does not have to involve mentor students who display more advanced achievement levels than their peers. Consider the idea demonstrated by Vignette 5.17:

VIGNETTE 5.17

Ms. Tohmatsu integrates historical topics into most of the units for her psychology class of 25 students. As part of a unit on learning theories, she subdivides the students into groups of 5 students and assigns historical topics as follows:

Group A

Topic: Connectionism theory
Students: Akiko, Malinda, Bryce, Amy, Chuck

Group B

Topic: Faculty psychology
Students: Pete, Joseph, Tom, Mary, Dominica

Group C

Topic: Franz Gall and Johann Spurzheim
Students: Nancy, Don, Jan, Hiro, Darnell

Group D

Topic: The origins of teaching machines
Students: Sylvia, Herman, Wren, George A., George T.

Group E

Topic: Gestalt theory
Students: James, Keiko, John, Tab, Nelson

She then conducts an hour-long small task-group session in which each of these five groups study and discuss its topic using references from Ms. Tohmatsu's resource library. For homework, students prepare a 15-minute lesson on their group's topic to be presented to 4 students from the other groups. Over the next two days, Ms. Tohmatsu conducts additional small-task group sessions in which the 5 students from each group concurrently present their 15-minute lessons to groups of 4 students from other groups. For example:

Akiko presents her lesson on origins of connectionism theory to Pete, Nancy, Sylvia, and James. Pete presents his on faculty psychology to Akiko, Nancy, Sylvia, and James. Nancy presents hers on Franz Gall and Johann Spurzheim to Akiko, Pete, Sylvia, and James. Sylvia presents hers on the origins of teaching machines to Akiko, Pete, Nancy, and James. And James presents his on Gestalt theory to Akiko, Pete, Nancy, and Sylvia. The other four groups for the rounds of lessons are:

- Malinda, Joseph, Don, Herman, Keiko
- Bryce, Tom, Jan, Wren, John
- Amy, Mary, Hiro, George A., Tab
- Chuck, Dominica, Darnell, George T., Nelson

Practice Groups. Large-group recitation sessions do not always provide the most efficient ways for students to review, drill, and receive feedback for knowledge-level objectives. With small-group arrangements, several students can be concurrently reciting. For example, students work in groups of three. One student reads questions from a pack of card. Feedback is provided after each response. The role of questioner rotates. Another possibility is for students to play memory games (e.g., one patterned after the board game "Trivial Pursuit") in groups of five.

Interest or Achievement-Level Groups. Intra-class groups may be organized around interests (as in Vignette 5.18), achievement levels (as in Vignette 5.19), or combinations of interest and achievement (as in Vignette 5.20):

VIGNETTE 5.18

Ms. Hamowitz sometimes groups her students according to their varied areas of interest. Throughout a unit on addition of fractions, she uses four different interest groups: (a) sports, (b) pets, (c) cooking, and (d) music. For the unit's conceptualization lesson, each of the four groups works within its interest area during the *task confrontation* and *task work* stages (as explained on page 77). Reports from the four groups are then used in subsequent lesson stages in large-group sessions.

The four subgroup arrangement is further utilized in other lessons, such as one for an application-level objective. In general, the small interest group sessions are used for students to confront tasks in their respective areas of interests, followed by large-group sessions in which the arithmetic commonly used by all four groups is discussed and analyzed.

VIGNETTE 5.19

To help her deal with the wide range of student achievement levels in her third-grade class, Ms. Mills conducts virtually her entire science course with the 29 students partitioned into the following three groups: (a) the "green" group, which consists of 7 students who average about 3.5 weeks per teaching unit; (b) the "blue" group, which consists of 14 students who average about 2.5 weeks per teaching unit; and (c) the "gray" group, which consists of 8 students who average about 1.0 week per teaching unit.

For all practical purposes, she conducts three courses in one. She is able to manage such a configuration by rotating large-group, small-group, and individualized sessions among the greens, blues, and grays.

VIGNETTE 5.20

Mr. Fleming uses informal observations, surveys, and formal tests to preassess his English students' achievement levels and interests. The results influence the various grouping patterns he uses for cooperative learning activities.

   During one lesson designed to improve students' writing abilities, students are to work in pairs, gathering information on a topic, and then presenting a written report to the class as a whole. From his prior observations and assessments, Mr. Fleming believes Blanca possesses advanced writing skills, but little interest in skateboarding. Brandon, on the other hand, displays little interest or talent for writing but seems obsessed with skateboarding. Mr. Fleming decides to pair Blanca and Brandon together for the writing assignment and require them to report on the topic of skateboarding. He hopes that the arrangement will allow the strengths of one student to complement those of the other. Brandon will learn about writing from Blanca while Blanca will depend on Brandon's knowledge and interest in skateboarding to complete the report. The assignment challenges Blanca's writing skill because she will have to write about an unfamiliar subject. Brandon may increase his interest in writing because he will be depended on to provide the expertise on the writing topic.

Problem-solving Groups. Cooperative task-group sessions can facilitate students' concurrently working on a variety of problems that are subsequently used in large-group activities. Vignette 5.21 (pp. 204–209) is an example of such a session being used within an application-level lesson.

Common Misuses of Small Task-Group Sessions

Research studies examining how students spend their time in classrooms indicate that students tend to have poor engagement levels in small-group learning activities unless the teacher is actively involved in the session (Fisher, Berliner, Filby, Marliave, Cahen, & Dishaw, 1980). But a teacher cannot be in the middle of several groups at once and oftentimes subgroups fail to address their tasks due to a lack of guidance. For example, see Vignette 5.22 (pp. 209–210).

VIGNETTE 5.21

Mr. Breland has his 23 pre-algebra students working in four groups, A, B, C, and D, in the arrangement illustrated by Figure 5.11. as part of a lesson for the following objective:

> When confronted with a real-life problem, determine whether or not computing a ratio will facilitate a solution of the problem (*Cognitive: application*)

Figure 5.11. Mr. Breland's Class Arrangement for a Small Co-operative-Group Problem-Solving Session

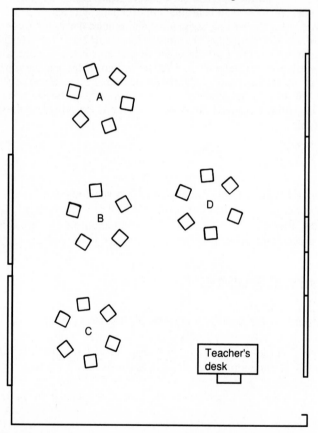

As directed by Mr. Breland, each group has 18 minutes to answer the questions listed on its tasksheet and prepare a 6-minute oral report of its work to the class as a whole. The four tasksheets are depicted in Figure 5.12.

Figure 5.12. Four Tasksheets for Groups A, B, C, and D in Mr. Breland's Pre-Algebra Class

Group A

DIRECTIONS: Answer the following questions based on the box score from Tuesday's Flyers-Tigers basketball game. Prepare a 5-minute oral report to the class that explains what problem-solving strategies you used to answer the questions.

VIGNETTE 5.21 (continued)

Flyers 79, Tigers 75

Flyers	min.	fgm-fga	ftm-fta	reb	ass	pf	tp
Champagne	23	4–7	2–2	8	1	4	10
Noto	28	9–19	6–8	4	2	2	26
Kora	21	3–4	4–9	11	3	4	10
Guillory, K.	15	2–7	2–3	2	0	0	8
Demouy	32	4–6	0–0	3	10	3	8
Guillory, T.	11	0–3	0–0	0	2	1	0
Miller	20	7–13	1–1	1	1	0	15
Knight	5	0–0	0–0	0	0	2	0
Losavio	5	1–3	0–0	0	0	0	2
Totals	**160**	**30–62**	**15–23**	**29**	**19**	**16**	**79**

Tigers	min.	fgm-fga	ftm-fta	reb	ass	pf	tp
Cassano	32	11–19	0–0	4	3	4	22
Silva	30	2–9	5–8	7	0	4	9
Burke	14	0–6	1–2	2	1	2	1
Parino	32	12–27	5–5	9	7	3	29
Price	22	4–5	0–0	4	7	5	8
Weimer	19	3–6	0–4	6	2	1	6
Bowman	11	0–4	0–1	1	1	0	0
Totals	**160**	**32–76**	**11–20**	**33**	**21**	**19**	**75**

1. By how much did the Flyers win?

2. Which team made the most three-point field goals?

3. Who made more field goals, Noto or Parino?

4. Who was the more accurate field goal shooter out of Noto and Parino?

5. Who scored more points for the amount of time they played in the game out of Noto and Parino?

6. Because the Tigers made more field goals than the Flyers, how did the Flyers manage to score four more points than the Tigers?

7. If Kora had played the whole game and rebounded at the same rate he did for the time he was in the game, what would his rebound total have been?

8. For which of the previous seven questions did you compute ratios to help you determine your answers?

(continued)

VIGNETTE 5.21 (continued)

Group B

DIRECTIONS: Answer the following questions based on the labels from the two soup cans. Prepare a five-minute oral report to the class that explains what problem-solving strategies you used to answer the questions.

CHICKEN WITH LETTERS

Size: 10.6 oz. (298 gr.)   *Price:* 58¢

Nutritional Information

Serving size (condensed) .... 4 oz.
Serving size (prepared) .... 8 oz.
Per serving:
   Calories 60
   Protein (grams) 3
   Simple sugars (grams) 1
   Complex carbohydrates (grams) 6
   Fat (grams) 2
   Cholesterol (mg) 10
   Sodium (mg) 870

Percentage of U.S. Recommended Daily Requirement:

Protein 4		Riboflavin 2
Vitamin A 8		Niacin 4
Vitamin C ....*		Calcium ....*
Thiamine 2		Iron 2

* Contains less than 2% of the US RDA of this nutrient.

NOODLES AND CHICKEN

Size: 10.6 oz. (298 gr.)   *Price:* 61¢

Nutritional Information

Serving size (condensed) .... 4 oz.
Serving size (prepared) .... 8 oz.
Per serving:
   Calories 80
   Protein (grams) 3
   Simple sugars (grams) 1
   Complex carbohydrates (grams) 8
   Fat (grams) 3
   Cholesterol (mg) 15
   Sodium (mg) 960

Percentage of U.S. Recommended Daily Requirement:

Protein 4		Riboflavin 2
Vitamin A 25		Niacin 6
Vitamin C .... *		Calcium ....*
Thiamine 4		Iron 4

* Contains less than 2% of the US RDA of this nutrient.

VIGNETTE 5.21 (continued)

1. Which soup do you get more grams for the money?

2. Which soup has more vitamins?

3. Which soup has more cholesterol?

4. Which soup has more vitamins per calorie?

5. Which soup is the best buy considering only the amount of iron it provides?

6. What appears to be more expensive calories or complex carbohydrates?

7. How many grams of sodium is contained in the entire can of Noodles and Chicken?

8. For which of the previous seven questions did you compute ratios to help you determine your answers?

Group C

DIRECTIONS: Answer the following questions based on the list of songs from audiotape albums. Prepare a five-minute oral report to the class that explains what problem-solving strategies you used to answer the questions.

RABID DOG IN CONCERT

Price: $9.98

Side One	*Side Two*
Every Rose Ain't a Flower (2:55)	Feelin' Too Much Pain (3:06)
Three Woman Dog (4:20)	Too Fine To Be Mine (2:30)
After the Pigs Come Home (3:01)	Too Young (3:11)
Smilin' 'stead of Cryin' (4:44)	Lucy the Lucky One (2:05)
My Kind of Party (3:15)	It Lasts Forever (8:09)
Allison (2:02)	

THE SENSATIONAL SCREAMERS ONE MORE TIME

Price: $8.79

Side One	*Side Two*
Who Likes to Kill Animals? (5:17)	Reasons to Live (3:11)
Help Is on the Way (2:10)	Not Much More to Say (5:12)
Casey the Drum-Man (2:14)	Not too Much Longer (2:09)
Momma Said It's Okay (3:29)	No-Mo-Dough (2:45)
Comfort (4:04)	Not Much Help (3:00)
One More Time (3:35)	Mindy, Mindy (1:55)

(continued)

VIGNETTE 5.21 (continued)

1. Which of the two tapes has more songs?

2. Which of the two tapes has more songs for the money?

3. Which of the two tapes has the more minutes of music?

4. Which of the two tapes has the more minutes of music for the money?

5. Which of the two tapes do you like better?

6. On the average, how long does one side of these two tapes play?

7. What's the difference between the longest and shortest songs on the two tapes?

8. For which of the previous seven questions did you compute ratios to help you determine your answers?

Group D

DIRECTIONS: Answer the following questions based on the data given about crime in our city during the years 1990 and 1991. Prepare a five-minute oral report to the class that explains what problem-solving strategies you used to answer the questions.

	1990	*1991*
Population	320,000	323,000
Murders	34	37
Rapes	99	112
Robberies	704	691
Aggravated assaults	1,001	1,120
Burglaries	3,092	3,212
Thefts by larceny	7,344	7,360
Motor vehicles thefts	1,611	1,786

1. Did crime increase or decrease from 1990 to 1991?

2. Which type of crime is the most common?

3. Relative to the size of the population, did the rate of murders go up or down from 1990 to 1991?

VIGNETTE 5.21 (continued)

4. Relative to the size of the population, did the rate of burglaries go up or down from 1990 to 1991?

5. The rate relative to population of what type of crime increased the least?

6. The rate relative to population of what type of crime increased the most?

7. What's the difference between the longest and shortest songs on the two tapes?

8. For which of the previous seven questions did you compute ratios to help you determine your answers?

As the groups complete their tasks, Mr. Breland circulates about the room monitoring each one, cuing students on task as the need arises. After the session, a designated member of each group reports its findings. Mr. Breland then conducts a large-group intellectual questioning/discussion session for the *rule articulation phase* (see p. 109) of the application-level lesson. Prompted by Mr. Breland's deductive questions, students examine and compare the four group reports to articulate the rules for applying ratios to real-life problems.

Adapted with permission from *Teaching Mathematics in Secondary and Middle School: Research-based Approaches* (pp. 182–186), by J. S. Cangelosi (1992), New York: Macmillan. Copyright © 1992 by Macmillan Publishing Company.

VIGNETTE 5.22

Ms. Clay has her pre-algebra students organized into four subgroups similar to the arrangement in Figure 5.11. She directs them, "I want each group to discuss when we use ratios to solve real-life problems. . . . Okay, go ahead and get started." After six minutes discussing what they're supposed to be doing, the students in one group no longer bother with ratios and socialize with one another. Ms. Clay hardly notices that they're off task as she's busy explaining to another group what she meant for

(continued)

VIGNETTE 5.22 (continued)

them to be doing. A third group becomes quite noisy, and Ms. Clay raises her voice from her position with the second group and announces, "Better keep it down in here. You won't learn how to apply ratios unless you get on the stick and get your discussion going." In the fourth group, Magdalina dominates the first five minutes telling the others about ratios. She stimulates Ann's interest and the two of them engage in a conversation in which Magdalina reviews what Ms. Clay explained in a previous session about computing ratios. The other three members of the group are doing other things unrelated to the topic.

After managing to get the second group on track, Ms. Clay moves to the noisy third group, saying, "You people aren't following directions; you're supposed to be discussing problems that use ratios. . . ." She then tells the group what she had hoped they'd discover for themselves.

After spending nine minutes with the second group, Ms. Clay calls a halt to the activity and announces, "Okay, class let's rearrange our desks back. . . . Now, that you understand when to apply ratios, I want to move on to . . ."

Ms. Clay failed to initiate student engagement because her directions did not spell out the tasks each subgroup was to address and just how to go about completing the task. Without an advanced organizer (e.g., similar to Mr. Breland's in Figure 5.12) for focusing students' attention, it was difficult for her to efficiently provide guidance to one group while still monitoring the others. Furthermore, her students are less likely to diligently engage in her next small task-group session because they failed to achieve closure in this one and Ms. Clay did not follow up on the work they did in the subgroups. Unlike Mr. Breland, she did not take what the subgroups did and use it in a subsequent activity.

Ms. Clay also illustrated another common misuse of cooperative task-group sessions by stepping in and doing the second group's work for it. Some teachers get so frustrated with subgroups failing to maintain their focus that they break into lectures when they should simply ask a leading question or two and let the students do their own work. Otherwise, a large-group session would be more efficient.

Whereas the failure of Ms. Clay's session was due at least in part to a lack of structure, sometimes intra-class grouping is misused because of inflexible structure. Recall Vignette 5.19 in which Ms. Mills's class is subdivided into three achievement levels—the "green," "blue," and "gray" groups. Although this type of organization can compensate for some differences in student learning rates, it should carry a warning label:

Subdividing a class into achievement-level groups does not result in "homogeneous" subgroups. Thus, it is important to remember that any one subgroup varies considerably on each of a multitude of student variables (Cangelosi, 1974).

Care must be taken that students do not get "locked" into an achievement-level group and become labeled "bright," "average," or "dull" (California State Department of Education, 1987, pp. 55–70; Ginott, 1972).

Initiating and Maintaining Student Engagement in Small Task-Group Sessions

Here are some suggestions for designing and conducting small task-group sessions:

Clearly define not only tasks for each subgroup, but also the individual responsibilities of each member of the subgroup. All members of a subgroup are jointly responsible for completing the shared task and each member is given an individual assignment. For example, in a five-member group, Pam serves as chair, Ben reminds others to stick to the topic and stay on task, Marty takes notes, Charles reads directions aloud, and Dan distributes, monitors the use of, and collects materials.

All subgroup members are accountable for completing the joint task as they are accountable for their individual assignment. As Ms. Hudson monitors a cooperative task-group activity, she notices Charles misusing an instructional manipulative. She tells Dan, "You're responsible for these materials. Shouldn't Charles put that down?" Later, when the task is complete, Ms. Hudson makes sure that she directs her evaluative comments to each subgroup as a whole rather than singling out the efforts of individuals.

Utilize efficient and routine procedures for making transitions into and out of small-group activities. To avoid the time-wasting chaos following a teacher's direction such as, "Let's move our desks so that we have four groups of five or six each," establish procedures whereby students efficiently move from one classroom arrangement to another. See Vignette 5.23.

Prepare an advanced organizer for such sessions. Tasksheets, such as the ones in Figure 5.12, direct students' focus and provide them with an overall picture of what they are expected to accomplish in their groups.

Specify directions and the task before attempting to engage students. It's far more efficient to make directions clear to everyone before students have turned their attention to their individual subgroups. Avoid having to interrupt small-group work to clarify directions that the whole class should hear.

Monitor groups' activities, providing guidance as needed without usurping subgroups' responsibilities for the designated task. You should move from one group to another, cuing students on task without actually becoming a member of any one group. See Vignette 5.24.

VIGNETTE 5.23

The variety of learning activities Ms. Morrison uses in teaching her 28 second-graders frequently necessitates the students' changing from one grouping arrangement to another. To facilitate the transitions she has several posters clustered together on one wall of the classroom. When she is ready for her students to stop one activity and begin another, she strikes a small gong located near the cluster of posters. Her students have learned that this is the cue for them to stop whatever they are doing and silently pay attention to Ms. Morrison. Once she has their attention, she uses the posters to give directions for making the transition into the next session.

Figure 5.13. Ms. Morrison's Poster for Signaling Whether or Not Talking is Allowed

Ms. Morrison, for example, points to a part of the poster shown in Figure 5.13 to indicate whether or not talking is allowed. Pointing to one of the numerals on Figure 5.14's poster indicates the sizes of the groups they are to form. If she points

VIGNETTE 5.23 (continued)

to "1," they work individually, "2" indicates they work in pairs, "6" they form subgroups of six persons each, and "whole class" indicates a large-group activity.

Figure 5.14. Ms. Morrison's Poster for Signaling How to Group for a Learning Activity

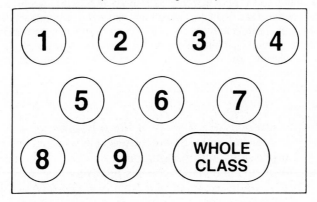

Adapted with permission from *Classroom Management Strategies: Gaining and Maintaining Students' Cooperation* (p. 69), by J. S. Cangelosi (1988), White Plains, NY: Longman.

VIGNETTE 5.24

Mr. Breland stops and sits in with Group C as they struggle with Question 4 from Figure 5.12. One student tells him, "I like the Sensational Screamers better. Doesn't that make a difference?" Mr. Breland turns to the group, "What does '*more* minutes of music' mean?" Noticing the discussion is on track, he moves over to Group B, continuing to keep an eye on all the groups.

Model active listening techniques. Students do not automatically know how to listen to one another without you showing them. From classes they take with teachers other than you, they may have acquired this misperception that anything of "academic importance" (i.e., will be on the test) is said by teachers, not peers. Thus, you should demonstrate that you intently listen to them and make use of what they say. For example:

VIGNETTE 5.25

Mr. Breland stops and sits in with Group B as they struggle with Question 6 from Figure 5.12. As Emily is commenting, John attempts to engage Mr. Breland with his own private question, "Mr. Breland, this doesn't make—" But Mr. Breland uses a frown and hand motion to cue John to be quiet, then says to the group, "Excuse me, Emily, would you repeat that last part about adding the two prices? I missed what you said about that." Emily repeats and finishes her comment. Mr. Breland says, "Thank you. That should shed some light on John's concern. John raise your concern with the group." John: "To me, the question ought to be . . ." Later in the large-group session, Mr. Breland plays off of different comments students made in their subgroups.

Use formative feedback to regulate activities. Engaged behaviors during cooperative task-group sessions are observable as students should be involved in discussions and working on a specified task. Thus, formative feedback for regulating the activities is relatively easy to obtain.

Plan for closure points, especially for lengthy sessions. As with other types of sessions, students need to experience climactic moments to positively reinforce engagement. Having a sequence of questions on Figure 5.12's tasksheets rather than just one overall question to answer helped Mr. Breland achieve this goal.

Follow up on subgroup work by utilizing it in subsequent learning activities. In Vignette 5.22, Ms. Clay's students' work was left "hanging," not seeming to make any impact on whatever else went on in class. In Vignette 5.21, students put the outcomes of their efforts to productive use.

ENGAGING STUDENTS IN INDEPENDENT WORK SESSIONS

Appropriate Uses of Independent Work Sessions

A major share of scholarly activity is solitary; inducting concepts, discovering relationships, executing processes, and solving problems are behaviors for which people often need quiet "think" time. The most common way allocated time was spent in pre-20th-century classrooms in the United States was in independent work sessions. Students sat at their desks working on exercises (Cubberley, 1962, pp. 288–370). Today, students can often be observed working independently in front of computers. Such sessions are appropriately used in a variety of ways:

> *As an integral part of an inquiry lesson, students work independently on tasks that were previously defined during a large-group interactive lecture or questioning/discussion session. The work from the independent session is subsequently used in follow-up activities.* In Vignette 3.8, Mr. Landastoy used an independent work session for students to complete the tasksheet

shown in Figure 3.5. The results of students' independent work was then used in a follow-up large-group inductive questioning session.

As an integral part of direct instruction, students independently practice what has just been explained to them in a large-group activity. The teacher provides individual guidance during the independent work session. Students receive feedback on what they practiced either in a subsequent large-group session or by the teacher collecting and then annotating their work. For example:

VIGNETTE 5.26

After explaining how to use latitudinal and longitudinal coordinates to locate points on maps, Mr. Davis-Fodor directs his geography students to complete a related exercise as he circulates about the room monitoring work and providing help as needed. He uses his observations of their work as formative feedback to regulate the remainder of the lesson.

Students use part of a class period to begin a homework assignment in an independent work session. This practice allows them to start the assignment while the teacher is still available to provide guidance.

Independent work sessions are essential to most teaching units. However, they need to be integrated with other types of learning activities, monitored, and guided. Rosenshine (1987) stated:

Studies have shown that when students are working alone during seatwork they are less engaged than when they are being given instruction by the teacher. Therefore, the question of how to manage students during seatwork, in order to maintain their engagement, becomes of primary interest.

One consistent finding has been the importance of a teacher (or another adult) monitoring the students during seatwork. Fisher et al. (1980) found that the amount of substantive teacher interaction with students during seatwork was positively related to achievement and that when students have contacts with the teacher during seatwork their engagement rate increases by about 10 percent. Thus it seems important that teachers not only monitor seatwork, but that they also provide academic feedback and explanation to students during their independent practice. However, the research suggests that these contacts should be relatively short, averaging 30 seconds or less. Longer contacts would appear to pose two difficulties: the need for a long contact suggests that the initial explanation was not complete and the more time a teacher spends with one student, the less time there is to monitor and help other students.

Another finding of Fisher et al. was the teachers who had more questions and answers during group work had more engagement during seatwork. That is, another way to increase engagement during seatwork was to have more teacher-led practice during group work so that students could be more successful during seatwork.

A third finding (Fisher et al. 1980) was that when teachers had to give a good deal of explanation during seatwork, then student error rates were higher. Having to give a good deal of explanation during seatwork suggests that the initial explanation was not sufficient or that there was not sufficient practice and correction before seatwork.

Another effective procedure for increasing engagement during seatwork was to break the instruction into smaller segments and have two or three segments of instruction and seatwork during a single period. (p. 261)

Common Misuses of Independent Work Sessions

The more common misuses stem from teachers failing to attend to the suggestions implied by Rosenshine's report. The consequences of imprecise directions, inadequate preparation for the task, and inefficiently administered teacher-help include the massive time-wasting Jones (1979) identified in his classroom observations of independent work sessions. Jones reported teachers perceived spending an average between 1 and 2 minutes per conference with individual students during the sessions. His observations indicate the actual average to be about 4 minutes for a single conference. Even in a class with as few as 15 students, devoting more than 45 seconds to any one conference is inefficient. For example:

VIGNETTE 5.27

Ms. McGuire's 31 students are individually working at their desks on a long-division exercise. Maud and 12 other students have their hands up beckoning her help. She goes to Maud who says, "I don't know how to do these." Ms McGuire: "What is it you don't know how to do?" Maud: "I don't understand enough to know what I don't know!" Ms. McGuire: "Let's look at this second one here. How many times do you think this seven goes into nine?" Maud: "Is that what we're supposed to do first?" Ms. McGuire: "Yes." Maud: "So what did you ask me?" Ms. McGuire: "How many times does seven go into nine?" Maud: "Is it one?" Ms. McGuire: "That's right. Now, write the one right here. . . ." Maud: "Is that right?" Ms. McGuire: "Yes." Maud: "What do I do next?" Ms. McGuire: "Because it didn't divide it evenly, you need to. . ."

In the meantime, other students are waiting feeling they cannot continue the exercise until Ms. McGuire gets to them. But she doesn't get to most who request help. While waiting, students find ways to entertain themselves.

Initiating and Maintaining Student Engagement in Independent Work Sessions

Here are some ideas to consider when designing and conducting independent work sessions:

By providing explicit directions, clearly defining the task beforehand, you avoid many of the nagging questions about what to do. The idea is to devote the time you spend conferring with individual students guiding them on *how* to complete the task, not reiterating directions in response to questions such as, "What are we supposed to be doing?"

Having artifacts (e.g., notes, a sample exercise, and a list of steps in an algorithm) from the preceding group learning activity still visible to students (e.g., on the chalkboard or in their notebooks) during an independent work session provides a reference that facilitates the efficiency with which students receive help. For example:

VIGNETTE 5.28

Ms. Connors has just conducted a large-group interactive lecture session that included an explanation of a long-division algorithm, a demonstration of the process with an example, and the class "walking through" an example with her guidance. Leaving the two completed examples and the step-by-step outline of the algorithm on the chalkboard, Ms. Connors directs the students into an independent work session in which they are to practice the algorithm on a tasksheet.

In a few minutes, Gary's and Lawanda's hands are up. Silently acknowledging Lawanda with a wink and hand gesture, Ms. Connors moves to Gary's desk; Gary says, "I don't know where to start." Ms. Connors, seeing that Gary has nothing written on his sheet, says, "Read the first two steps from the board and then look at what we did first for the example on the right. I'll be back within 30 seconds." She moves directly to Lawanda's desk who says, "Is this right?" Detecting that she's begun the first exercise by estimating too small a number for the partial quotient, she responds, "It's not wrong, but you can make it easier on yourself by estimating that number a little closer. Try the next larger number." She walks back to Gary as Lawanda blurts out, "Oh, yeah! The four—" Realizing she's being disruptive, Lawanda grabs her mouth, muffling the rest of the sentence.

Back at Gary's desk, Ms. Connors sees that he is now started, and softly tells him, "Just keep following the steps on the board and checking how that example is worked—one step at a time. I'll check with you every few minutes. By this time five others have their hands up. By referring to the outline and examples and raising pointed questions, Ms. Connors has all five students back on track within a minute. She continues moving about the room, responding to students' requests for help and volunteering guidance as she sees fit from observing their work. At no time does she spend more than 20 seconds at a time with any one student.

You can provide efficient individual guidance and help to students, but only if you organize for it prior to the session and communicate assertively during the session. Both Ms. Connors in Vignette 5.28 and Mr. Bench in Vignette 5.29 illustrate this point.

Cooperative learning activities can be incorporated into independent work sessions to increase opportunities for students to receive help. For example:

VIGNETTE 5.29

At the beginning of the school year, Mr. Bench fashions from a towel rack the "flag-raising" device pictured in Figure 5.15. He then produced enough such devices to install them on the corners of the students' desks in his fifth-grade classroom. Each is supplied with a yellow, red, and green flag that can be raised one at a time.

Figure 5.15. Mr. Bench Installed "Flag Raisers" on Students' Desks.

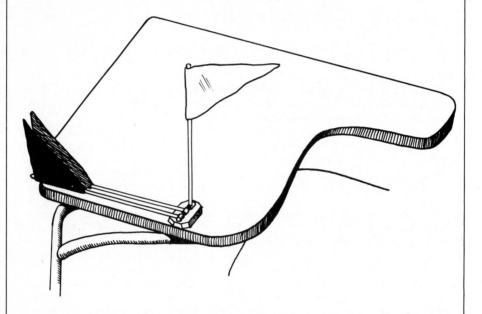

He then established a procedure for independent work sessions by which students display (a) a yellow flag as long as they are progressing with the work and do not feel a need for help, (b) a red flag to indicate a request for help, and (c) a green flag to indicate that they've finished the work and are willing to help others.

As Mr. Bench monitors a session, he responds to a red flag by either helping the student himself or by signaling to a student with a green-flag display to provide the help. The system has four distinct advantages over more conventional hand-raising procedures: (a) Cooperative learning among students is encouraged; (b) when waiting for help, students can continue doing some work without having to be burdened with holding up a hand; (c) students who finish the task before others have something to do that will not only help their peers, but will be a learning experience for them also; and (d) the systematic air of the procedure enhances the businesslike environment of the classroom.

VIGNETTE 5.29 (continued)

Mr. Bench's Flag-raising Routine

To avoid having students who finish early idly waiting for others to complete a task, you can sequence independent work sessions so they are followed by individual activities with flexible beginning and ending times. Students do not work at the same pace. Unless the task can be completed by all in less than 10 minutes, you need to manage independent work sessions to accommodate students' finishing at varying times. One solution is to schedule a subsequent activity that "early finishers" can start (e.g., begin the homework assignment), but be sure to plan an activity that can be conveniently interrupted when you are ready to halt the independent work session (e.g., when almost all students have completed the task). Here is an example:

VIGNETTE 5.30

Ms. Jung includes a long-range assignment that requires students to use microcomputers. The assignment is made at the beginning of the unit, but isn't due until the day of the summative unit test. Her classroom is equipped with 11 microcomputers, but she has no fewer than 24 students in any one of her classes.

For independent work sessions she has established a routine in which students who finish the task before the session is completed are to work on their unit-long computer assignment. Those who may have already completed the computer assignment have the option of either beginning their homework assignment or utilizing the computers in other ways (e.g., playing games).

As with other types of learning activities, students need feedback to correct errors, reinforce correct responses, and positively reinforce engagement. Formative feedback is facilitated during independent work sessions because each students' efforts are reflected by a product (e.g., written responses to exercises).

ENGAGING STUDENTS IN MEANINGFUL HOMEWORK

Cooper (1989a, p. 7) defined homework as "tasks assigned to students by school teachers that are meant to be carried out during non-school hours." "This definition excludes (a) in-school guided study, (b) home study courses, and (c) extracurricular activities. It does include assignments given by first-period teachers that students complete while ignoring a second-period lecture!" (Cooper, 1989b, p. 86).

Appropriate Uses of Homework

Homework provides students with opportunities for solitary work at their own pace. The crowded social setting of a classroom is not particularly conducive to the concentrated, undisturbed thinking that's essential for achievement of intellectual-level objectives. Furthermore, school schedules often do not permit adequate classroom time to be allocated for practice exercises that are essential for achievement of knowledge-level objectives. Posamentier and Stepelman (1990, p. 48) suggested that for many students classroom instruction serves as a forum for exposure to new material, whereas the genuine learning experiences occur while they are engaged in homework. Learning activities via homework assignments complement classroom activities as preparations for classroom activities, extensions of classroom activities, and follow-ups to classroom activities.

As Preparations for Classroom Activities. One way you help students associate subject matter content with their own real worlds is to engage them in learning activities utilizing objects, ideas, data, and structures from students' outside-of-school environments. Rather than always working with textbook and in-school materials, at least occasionally assign homework by which students collect materials or information for use in classroom activities. See Vignette 5.31.

VIGNETTE 5.31

Mr. Greene directs his students near the end of a class period, "As part of your homework assignment, locate three circles defined by objects in or near your home. Anything that determines a circle will be fine—the base of a light, a bicycle wheel, a dinner plate, the top of your little brother's head. After locating each of your three circles, measure its diameter and circumference. Write the measurements down and bring in the three pairs of numbers to class tomorrow."

Figure 5.16. The Form Mr. Greene Used on an Overhead Transparency to Record Data Students Collected for Homework

Person	Object	Circumerence C	Diameter D	C/D

The next day, Mr. Greene displays Figure 5.16 with the overhead projector and directs students, one at a time, to call out circumference/diameter pairs. Students contribute one of their pairs as Mr. Greene completes the form (Figure 5.17).

Figure 5.17. Mr. Greene Records One Pair of Measurements from Each Student.

Person	Object	Circumerence C	Diameter D	C/D
Barbara	ring	6.8 cm	2.2 cm	3.09
Andrea	barrel bottom	32"	10"	3.20
Jerry	jar	19"	6"	3.17
Oral	base of light fixture	78.74 cm	25 cm	3.15
Glenn	wheel	81.5"	26"	3.13
Karel	top of head	7.75"	2.94"	2.94

Mr. Greene then conducts an inductive questioning/discussion session leading students to discover the ratio of the circumference of any circle to its diameter is a constant that is slightly greater than three (i.e., the number π).

Adapted with permission from *Teaching Mathematics in Secondary and Middle Schools: Research-based Approaches* (p. 191), by J. S. Cangelosi (1992), New York: Macmillan. Copyright © 1992 by Macmillan Publishing Company.

You may sometimes initiate a lesson with a homework assignment that exposes students to a problem or task that stimulates them to direct their thoughts toward a topic you plan to introduce during the next classroom session. See Vignette 5.32.

VIGNETTE 5.32

The day before she plans to introduce the formula for computing the area of a rectangle (i.e., area = length × width) to her fourth-graders, Ms. Charog assigns the Figure 5.18's tasksheet for homework.

Figure 5.18. The Tasksheet Ms. Charog Assigned for Homework

WHICH OF THE TWO LARGE RECTANGLES IS LARGER? <u>A</u> or <u>B</u? _____

<u>A</u>

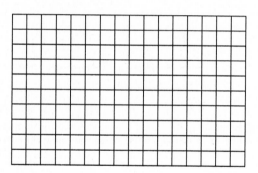

<u>B</u>

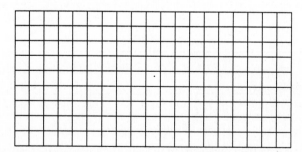

The next day, most students agree that rectangle B is larger than A. Some complain about how boring it was to count that many squares. Ms. Charog jumps on the students' expressed need for some shortcuts and embarks on her planned inductive lesson to discover the relationship, *area = length × width*.

Some skills or knowledge needed for participation in an upcoming classroom activity may be efficiently acquired during a homework assignment. For example:

VIGNETTE 5.33

Mr. Konz distributes a list of words he plans to use during a large-group interactive lecture session the next day. For homework, he directs the students to look up and memorize the definitions for those words.

VIGNETTE 5.34

For homework, Ms. Musso assigns some background reading on some famous poets. The next day, she draws on students' knowledge of those poets during a lesson on how to write different types of poems.

Traditionally, students depend on time allocated for homework to study for in-class tests. Assignments to study for tests need to be specific; students do not naturally know how or what to study without specific instruction from you. Students can be assigned "take home" tests for purposes of formative feedback that you utilize to regulate classroom activities. For example:

VIGNETTE 5.35

Unsure of just how ambitious objectives should be for an upcoming unit on nutrition, for homework, Ms. Bergman assigns a test over tentative objectives for the upcoming unit. The next day she has students explain how they approached different test items in a "think aloud" session. She uses the feedback from this activity to determine what the next unit's objectives should be.

As Extensions of Classroom Activities. Independent work sessions have the disadvantage that students complete assigned tasks at different times. Often, there is inadequate allocated class time to allow all students to complete independent work. Also, practice exercises to polish knowledge-of-a-process skills may be too time consuming to schedule during the school day. Homework assignments relieve at least some of the pressure of trying to squeeze necessary work into class periods.

As Follow-Ups to Classroom Activities. For some objectives, students need time alone, analyzing content at their own pace. For example:

VIGNETTE 5.36

Mr. Santiago designs a lesson for helping students achieve the following objective:

> Given a real-life problem, determine whether or not any combinations of New-ton's first three laws of motion apply to the solution of that problem and, if so, formulate a solution to the problem using that combination (*Cognitive: application*)

He believes that students will learn to apply the laws of motion only with ex-perience trying it out *on their own* with numerous problems. Many students, he's noted, lack the confidence to depend on their own thinking; they would rather be told a solution than to devise one. Consequently, he wants them to experience their initial success applying the laws of motion by themselves, not in a social setting.

Thus, he structures the lesson so that he spends nearly an entire class period in a large-group interactive lecture session explaining how to do a homework as-signment. He begins by saying, "Your homework assignment for tonight will be to solve three problems that I will distribute on a tasksheet at the end of today's period. When you solve these problems, I want you to follow a procedure I'm about to explain to you." He then spends the next 45 minutes explaining the problem-solving procedure. The day's classroom activities presented the procedure to the students, but the homework is the activity leading them to learn to apply it.

A more common type of homework assignment that, like Ms. Santiago's, is a follow-up to classroom activities is homework that is used to provide formative feedback on what was learned in class. A lesson is presented in class and students are assigned exercises that serve as a formative test over the day's objectives. The results are used to reinforce what was learned and identify areas in need of remediation.

Common Misuses of Homework

The benefits of homework are widely debated in educational literature (Coulter, 1987). Arguments against assigning homework focus, not on whether or not home-work can be an effective learning activity, but on how it is routinely misused by some teachers. Misuses include the following:

> *Teachers mindlessly assigning homework out of tradition and habit with little attention to purpose or selection of exercises.* "Do the odd-numbered ex-ercises for section 7–4 in the textbook," is echoed in classrooms day after day with only the section designation varying (Farrell & Farmer, 1988, pp. 5–6; Jesunathadas, 1990). Such assignments typically degenerate into un-necessarily repetitious drudgery that colors students' perceptions of schoolwork.
>
> *Homework assignments that are disconnected to classroom activities.* In such cases, students' only motivation for doing homework is to receive points toward grades or to avoid their teachers' wrath. What they learn and how well they do on tests appears unrelated to whether or not they complete

homework assignments. Homework is perceived as "in addition" to learning as it is assigned as neither a preparation for, extension of, nor follow-. up to classroom activities.

Homework either (a) being assigned as a punishment for misbehavior or failure to achieve or (b) not being assigned as a reward for cooperative behavior or achievement. "For every minute this noise continues, they'll be five extra pages added on to your homework assignment!" "Because you've work so hard today, you can enjoy your evening—No homework! [cheers] . . . But be ready to get back to work tomorrow!" For years, such utterances have managed to perpetuate the idea that learning activities are unpleasant, unrewarding. Although the threat of homework or anticipation of "getting out of" homework may sometimes discourage misbehaviors, it also devalues homework as a learning activity (Cangelosi, 1988a, pp. 36–41).

Initiating and Maintaining Engagement in Homework Activities

Figure 5.19 lists recommendations for homework policies that Cooper (1989a) deduced from a synthesis of a decade of research studies.

Engagement in a homework assignment usually requires students to understand directions for the assignment, schedule time outside of class for the work, resist distractions in a relatively unsupervised setting, and complete the work by a specified deadline. Every day for the first few weeks of a course, assign clearly defined, specific tasks for homework. Spend class time during that early stage of the course to teach students to schedule time for homework and efficient ways of completing it. Follow up on every assignment. Until you make a concerted effort to teach them, your students are unlikely to (a) know how to schedule time for homework, especially considering that they have assignments from other courses besides yours; (b) discriminate whether content relative to an assignment should be memorized, figured out by themselves, or found out from an outside source; (c) know how to study; and (d) know how you expect results of their homework to be reported.

Besides actually conducting a lesson in "how to do homework," you should keep initial assignments relatively simple and highly structured. Directions should be explicit and feedback descriptive. Your extra efforts along these lines during the first few weeks of a course will pay dividends in time saved and assignments completed once students learn your routine and expectations. Students will develop a *behavior pattern* of engaging in homework if their efforts are positively reinforced.

Positively reinforce engagement in homework and punish failure to attempt homework by designing units so that success in classroom activities, especially tests, depends on homework efforts. Students can be motivated to faithfully engage in homework without you resorting to awarding "points toward grades" for turning in assignments. Recall the system Ms. Chung initiated in Vignette 4.27. Beginning class periods with a short test that includes items similar to exercises from the previous homework assignment teaches students the importance of doing homework far better than preaching to them about the importance of homework

For Districts

Homework is a cost-effective instructional technique. It can have positive effects on achievement and character development and can serve as a vital link between the school and family.

Homework should have different purposes at different grades. For younger students, it should foster positive attitudes, habits, and character traits. For older students, it should facilitate knowledge acquisition in specific topics.

Homework should be required at all grade levels, but a mixture of mandatory and voluntary homework is most beneficial.

The frequency and duration of mandatory assignments should be:

1. Grades 1 to 3—one to three assignments a week, each lasting no more than 15 minutes
2. Grades 4 to 6—two to four assignments a week, each lasting 15 to 45 minutes
3. Grades 7 to 9—three to five assignments a week, each lasting 45 to 75 minutes
4. Grades 10 to 12—four to five assignments a week, each lasting 75 to 120 minutes

For Schools

The frequency and duration of homework assignments should be further specified to reflect local school and community circumstances.

In schools where different subjects are taught by different teachers, teachers should know:

1. What days of the week are available to them for assignments
2. How much daily homework time should be spent on their subject

Administrators should:

1. Communicate the district and school homework policies to parents
2. Monitor the implementation of the policy
3. Coordinate the scheduling of homework among different subjects, if needed

Teachers should state clearly:

1. How the assignment is related to the topic under study
2. The purpose of the assignment
3. How the assignment might best be carried out
4. What the student needs to do to demonstrate that the assignment has been completed

For Teachers

All students in a class will be responsible for the same assignments, with only rare exceptions.

Homework will include mandatory assignments. Failure to turn in mandatory assignments will necessitate remedial activities.

Homework will also include voluntary assignments meant to meet the needs of individual students or groups of students.

All homework assignments will *not* be formally evaluated. They will be used to locate problems in student progress and to individualize instruction.

Topics will appear in assignments before and after they are covered in class, not just on the day they are discussed.

Homework will not be used to teach complex skills. It will generally focus on simple skills and material or on the integration of skills already possessed by the student.

Parents will rarely be asked to play a formal instructional role in homework. Instead, they should be asked to create a home environment that facilitates student self-study.

Figure 5.19. A Recommended Homework Policy (Reprinted with permission from *Homework* [pp. 190–191] by Harris Cooper, 1989, White Plains, NY: Longman. Copyright © 1989.)

or threatening to lower grades if they don't do it. Here's an example of a teacher demonstrating a businesslike attitude to motivate students to do homework:

VIGNETTE 5.37

On Monday, Mr. Davis gives a homework assignment in which each student is to select a topic from a given list and to write a one-page essay on that topic. On Tuesday, he collects the work from 23 of the 28 students in the class. That night, he annotates each essay providing editorial comments and constructive feedback. Wednesday, the essays are returned. While the rest of the students are modifying their essays based on his feedback in an independent work session, he calls aside the five students, Davalon, Donna, Linda, Martin, and Pruitt, who did not complete the homework and says, "I'm sorry you didn't give me an opportunity to provide you with feedback on the essays that were assigned for homework." Pruitt: "I would've done it but—" Mr. Davis interrupts, saying, "It doesn't make any difference why you didn't do it. I've just got to figure out when you can get this done so I can get my critiques back to you before you leave school today. You need that from me before you're able to go on to our next lesson." Linda: "I forgot—" Mr. Davis: "Please let me think how to help you. . . . I've got it! Here's what we'll do. I'll meet you in here as soon as final announcements are completed this afternoon. As soon as you've finished your first drafts of the essays, I'll provide you with feedback on them."

Keep in mind that unless you're working in a self-contained classroom situation, your students have other assignments besides yours. Fewer well-chosen exercises tend to be more productive than a lengthy assignment that is more time consuming for you and the students. Long-range assignments that students are expected to take days to complete should be broken out in a sequence of shorter assignments with due dates for progress points toward completion. Consistently heeding this suggestion in the early stages of a course encourages students to get into a routine of doing homework. Otherwise, they tend to be overwhelmed by lengthy assignments or delay starting long-range assignments until just before they are due.

To elicit parents' cooperation in encouraging and supervising homework, utilize ideas from Chapter 4's section, "Communicating with Parents." What you gain from taking this suggestion varies considerably depending on students' home situations. Some students do not even live with responsible guardians. But whenever you do elicit parental support, students' engagement in homework activities tends to increase remarkably.

SELF-ASSESSMENT EXERCISES FOR CHAPTER 5

I. Analyze the cognitive process a person would use to answer the following questions; classify each question as either *knowledge-level* or *intellectual-level*:
  A. According to DiBacco, Mason, and Appy (1991, p. 66), what percentage of the American colonists belonged to a church just prior to the "Great Awakening"?

    B. What is a mammal?

    C. Would it be better to measure this distance in kilometers or meters?

    D. Does Newton's second law of motion apply in this case?

    E. Have you ever used a computer before today?

    F. Why do you suppose it took so long for native Americans to be given the right to vote in the United States?

    G. What's the product of 679.5 and 43.09?

    H. When you were asked which two of these three groups were alike, why did you choose the two on the right?

    I. Who was Maria Gaetana Agnesi?

        Compare your responses to these: Knowledge-level: A, B, E, G, and I. Intellectual-level: C, D, F, and H.

II. Design a *cooperative learning* activity in which students learn from one another for one of the objectives from Figures 2.2–2.8. Compare your work on this exercise to someone else's.

III. Compare Ms. Rackley's method of engaging students in intellectual questioning sessions in Vignette 5.11 to that of Mr. Landastoy in Vignette 3.8. Which of the two methods do you expect to use more? Explain why. Exchange your work on this exercise with someone and discuss similarities and differences between the two.

IV. Observe the activities in an elementary, middle, junior high, or high school classroom for at least an hour. For each allocated time period, classify the type of learning activity as either a(n) (a) *large-group interactive lecture*, (b) *large-group recitation*, (c) *large-group intellectual-level questioning/discussion*, or (d) *independent work* session. Select one of the sessions and design an alternate type of learning activity. Explain the relative advantages and disadvantages of the two approaches for the given circumstances. Compare your work on this exercise to someone else's.

V. Devise a game for students to play in small groups that would help them achieve a knowledge-level objective within your teaching specialty area. Now, modify the game so that it can be used in a large-group session. Exchange your game designs with those of a colleague who also completed this exercise.

VI. In the section of this chapter entitled "Responding to Student Questions," four ways of responding to student-initiated intellectual-level questions and five ways of responding to their knowledge-level questions are listed. Discuss with a colleague the relative advantages and disadvantages of those different response styles.

VII. Retrieve the work you did in responding to Exercise II of the self-assessment exercises for Chapter 3 and Exercise X of the self-assessments exercises for Chapter 4. Classify the different learning activities identified by your lesson designs as (a) *large-group interactive lecture*, (b) *large-group recitation*, (c) *large-group intellectual-level questioning/discussion*, and (d) *independent work* sessions. In light of thoughts you've had since you last worked on these lesson designs, would you now modify the designs? Explain why or why not.

SUGGESTED READING

Cooper, H. (1989a). *Homework*. White Plains, NY: Longman.

Cooper, H. (1989b). Synthesis of research on homework. *Educational Leadership, 47*, 85–91.

Hilke, E. V. (1990). *Cooperative learning* Bloomington, IN: Phi Delta Kappa Educational Foundation.

Hunkins, F. P. (1989). *Teaching thinking through effective questioning*. Boston: Christopher-Gordon Publishers.

Kayfetz, J. L., & Stice, R. L. (1987). *Academically speaking*. Belmont, CA: Wadsworth.

Ruetten, M. K. (1986). *Comprehending academic lectures*. New York: Macmillan.

Slavin, R. E. (1988). Cooperative learning and student achievement. *Educational Leadership, 46*, 31–33.

Slavin, R. E. (1991). Synthesis of research on cooperative learning. *Educational Leadership, 48*, 71–82.

Voorhies, R. (1989). Cooperative learning: What is it? *Social Studies Review, 28*, 7–10.

TAKING WHAT YOU'VE LEARNED TO THE NEXT LEVEL

Having examined how to define learning goals (chap. 2), design lessons for achieving those goals (chap. 3), and manage student behaviors and maintain engagement during those lessons (chaps. 4–5), it is time to turn your attention to the business of how to assess student achievement. Assessments of student achievement of *specific objectives* are needed for obtaining formative feedback during the course of a teaching unit. Assessments of student achievement of *learning goals* are needed for summative evaluations used to determine students' grades.

CHAPTER **6**

Assessing Student Achievement

GOAL OF CHAPTER 6

This chapter introduces fundamental measurement and evaluation principles and explains how to develop and use measurement items for assessing student achievement of your learning objectives and tests for assessing how well they achieve your learning goals. Chapter 6 will help you

1. distinguish between the measurements and evaluations you make and clarify the role each plays in assessing student achievement (*Cognitive: conceptualization*)
2. explain why a measurement's validity depends on its relevance and reliability (*Cognitive: conceptualization*)
3. explain why the value of a measurement depends on its validity and usability (*Cognitive: conceptualization*)
4. describe the common uses of three types of measurements of student achievement: teacher-produced tests, commercially produced tests, and standardized tests (*Cognitive: simple knowledge*)
5. be aware of the need to use systematic procedures to design and construct valid measurements of student achievement tests and to use available references for implementing such procedures (*Affective: appreciation*)
6. design items relevant to any objective you include in a teaching unit, whether the objective's learning level is simple knowledge, knowledge of a process, comprehension, conceptualization, application, creativity, affective, or psychomotor (*Cognitive: application*)

DIFFICULT DECISIONS

Formative Evaluations

Consider the complex questions you face as you plan and conduct teaching units; for example:

Who in the class has conceptualized the concepts of *speed* and *acceleration*? Is the class ready to move on to my knowledge-level and application-level lessons on those concepts or should I extend this conceptualization lesson?

Are these students following my explanation for measuring acceleration? Should I go back and review the steps, push on, or stop and have them practice the steps up to this point?

Unless these students have achieved the goal of this unit on laws of motion, they're not ready to start the one on energy. Who is ready to move on and who isn't?

By answering such questions, you make *formative evaluations* that are necessary for designing and regulating lessons. However, your empirical senses (i.e., sight, hearing, touch, smell, and taste) are incapable of directly observing what is in students' minds to determine the degree with which they achieved or are achieving learning objectives. Thus, you must set up situations that evoke students to make observable responses that provide you with indirect evidence of their learning. Doing this so that the evidence, though indirect, reflects students' actual achievement of learning objectives is no trivial task. It requires you to apply a sophisticated understanding of your learning goals (including the content and the learning levels specified by the objectives), how your students think, and fundamental principles and techniques for assessing student achievement.

Summative Evaluations

There are also complex questions for you to answer at the conclusions of teaching units; for example:

What grade for this unit should I assign Rachael?

Mark's father wants a report on his progress in reading. What should I tell him?

Did Charog achieve this goal well enough to receive at least a C?

You make *summative* evaluations of how well students achieved learning goals so that you can determine individual grades and periodically report on students' achievements to the students themselves, their parents, and to authorized professionals (e.g., your school's principal). As a teacher, you make far more formative than summative evaluations as your instructional behaviors are continually being influenced by formative feedback. However, because students and parents tend to be so grade conscious, you are likely to find them keenly interested in your periodic summative evaluations but barely aware of your ongoing formative evaluations. In any case, you are responsible for both types of evaluations, and summative, like formative, requires access to data that reflect how well your students have achieved learning goals and objectives.

COMMON MALPRACTICE

Observations and tests provide the data bases for teachers' evaluations of student achievement. Unfortunately, studies examining the validities of tests commonly used in schools (both commercially prepared and teacher-prepared) and the evaluation methods of many teachers suggest that testing malpractice and inaccurate evaluations are widespread (Stiggins, Conklin, & Bridgeford, 1986). Too often, faith is placed in poorly designed tests that tax students' test-taking skills but don't reflect actual achievement of the teachers' learning goals (Cangelosi, 1990b, p. 3). Of particular concern are incongruencies between learning levels specified by objectives and the actual learning levels measured by the tests. It is quite common for teachers to include intellectual-level and affective learning objectives for their units, but then to only test their students for achievement at the knowledge level. The consequence of this practice is pointed out by Stiggins (1988):

> Teacher-developed paper-and-pencil tests and many tests and quizzes provided by textbook publishers are currently dominated by questions that ask students to recall facts and information. Although instructional objectives and even instructional activities may seek to develop thinking skills, classroom assessments often fail to match these aspirations. Students who use tests to try to understand the teachers' expectations can see the priority placed on memorizing, and they respond accordingly. Thus poor quality assessments that fail to tap and reward higher-order thinking skills will inhibit the development of those skills. (p. 365)

RESEARCH-BASED PRACTICE

Although testing is widely malpracticed, you *can*, as do many teachers, manage to collect valid data and accurately evaluate students' achievements of your learning objectives—no matter what the learning levels. To do this, you must apply research-based measurement and evaluation principles and techniques for assessing student achievement. This chapter provides a basic introduction to fundamental research-based principles and techniques for measuring students' achievement and suggestions on how to develop test items for the learning levels listed in Figure 2.9. Other references provide more comprehensive treatises of these principles and techniques for developing and selecting valid tests (e.g., Cangelosi, 1982, 1990b; Ebel & Frisbie, 1986; Gronlund & Linn, 1990; Hopkins, Stanley, & Hopkins, 1990; Kubiszyn & Borich, 1987; Linn, 1989; Popham, 1990; Tuckman, 1988).

MEASUREMENTS

A *measurement* is the process by which data are gathered through empirical observations. Teachers measure by seeing what students do, reading what they write, and hearing what they say. What you remember or record from those observations provides the data for your formative and summative evaluations of students' achievements. Typically, teachers depend on tests for the data they use in evaluations. *Tests* are planned measurements by which teachers attempt to create opportunities for students to display their achievements relative to specified learning goals.

Tests are composed of *items*. Each item of a test confronts students with a task and provides a means for observing and quantifying their responses to the task. Examine the sample of four test items displayed in Figure 6.1. Note that

ITEM

Task presented to students:
(Oral directions and response in a one-to-one format) The teacher places a world globe (nations distinguished by colors and printed names) in front of the first-grade student and spins it around (randomly). Then the teacher tells the student, "Point to Cuba."

Scoring key:
(3 points possible) +1 if the student first turns to the Western hemisphere. +1 if the student points in the vicinity of the Gulf of Mexico, Bahamas, and Caribbean Sea. +1 if the student points to Cuba.

ITEM

Task presented to students:
MULTIPLE-CHOICE: Circle the letter in front of the response that correctly answers the question:
  While playing basketball, Nancy turns her right ankle inward. There is pain and swelling. Immediate first aid should include which one of the following?
  A. Encourage Nancy to walk and keep the ankle "loose"
  B. Have Nancy sit with her foot down in a bucket so that the swollen area is submerged in ice
  C. Elevate the foot and apply an ice pack to the swollen area
  D. Massage the swollen area, applying a deep-heat rubbing compound

Scoring key: +1 for circling "C" only; 0 otherwise

ITEM

Task presented to students:
(The student is seated at a desk with a flat top and supplied with kindergarten writing paper and a pencil and shown a card with a capital *O.* The teacher says, "This is a capital *O.*" The picture is removed and the teacher says, "Make a capital *O* on your paper.")

Scoring key:
Check one blank in each category:
  A. Positioning of paper:
        left of 11 o'clock _____ 11–12 o'clock _____
        12 o'clock _____ 12–1 o'clock _____
        right of 1 o'clock _____ position unstable _____
  B. Hand used:
        left _____ right _____ both _____
  C. Wrist position:
        straight _____ hooked _____ unstable _____
  D. Method of grasping pencil:
        standard and satisfactory _____
        not standard, but satisfactory _____
        Describe: _____

        _____

  E. Direction of printing:
        clockwise _____ counterclockwise _____
        both or other _____
        Explain: _____

        _____

  F. Continuity of the printing:
        nonstop motion _____ pauses _____
        other _____ Explain: _____

        _____

(continued)

Figure 6.1. Sample of Four Test Items Relevant to a Variety of Learning Objectives

ITEM

Task presented to students:
Pretend that you have a friend in the fifth grade who writes you this note:

"In math class we were told how to find the area of a rectangle. I know how to use this formula: Area = length × width.

But, I don't understand *why* multiplying the length and width gives me the area. Our teacher didn't explain that to us. Since you're in the sixth grade, would you please explain to me why $A = l \times w$?"

Use about one sheet of paper to write your fifth grade friend a note that explains *why* the area of a rectangle equals its length times its width. Include one or two pictures to help you with the explanation. But, fill most of the page with sentences.

Scoring key:
(8 points possible) Points distributed as follows:

+1 if the overall explanation accurately distinguishes area from other geometrical properties

+1 if the goal of determining the number of unit squares inside the bounds of the rectangle is established

+1 if the number of units in the length is related to the number of unit squares in the area

+1 if the number of unit squares in the width is related to the number of unit squares in the area

+1 if the idea of multiplication as repeated addition (e.g., as a way of counting by widths or lengths) is used

+1 if the explanation uses at least one appropriate paradigm

+2 according to the following rating scale:

2 if at least ⅔ of a page is filled and there are no mathematical errors in the explanation

1 if at least ⅔ of a page is filled and there is one and only one mathematical error and it doesn't involve a misconception about area

0 if less than ⅔ of a page is filled, if there is an indication of a misconception about area, or if there is more than one mathematical error

Figure 6.1. (Continued)

what is labeled as "task presented to students" is the aspect of the item that confront students on a test. The item's "scoring key" provides the rules the teacher uses to observe and quantify students' responses to the item. The students' *test score* is the sum of the scores they receive on the items that comprise the test.

EVALUATIONS

An *evaluation*, whether formative or summative, is a *value judgment*. You cannot solve for a qualitative variable like how well one of your students achieved a learning goal without making a value judgment (i.e., evaluation). Such evaluations are necessarily dependent on measurement results (e.g., students' test scores). However, do not make the mistake of equating measurement results or test scores with student achievement. An assessment of a student's achievement of a unit's learning goal involves two distinct steps:

1. measurement results are obtained relative to a *quantitative* variable (e.g., the score the student obtained on the unit test)

2. an evaluation is made relative to a *qualitative* variable (i.e., the student's achievement of the learning goal) in light of the measurement results

Measurement results only provide evidence of, not a definitive reflection of, student achievement. How well the results or scores reflect actual achievement depends on the *validity* of the measurement. Thus, how much one of your evaluations is influenced by test scores should be a function of the test's *validity*.

MEASUREMENT VALIDITY

A measurement is valid to the same degree that it is both *relevant* and *reliable*.

Relevance to Student Achievement of Stated Learning Goal

A measurement is *relevant* to the same degree that its test items pertain to the content and the learning levels specified by the objectives that define the learning goal. A test item pertains to the content and learning level specified by an objective if students must operate at the specified learning level with the specified content in order to successfully respond to the item. How well do the three test items designed by the teacher in Vignette 6.1 pertain to her objective?

VIGNETTE 6.1

To help her evaluate her seventh-graders' achievement of the learning goal for a unit on surface areas, Ms. Curry is designing a test. The unit has nine objectives. The ninth objective is:

> When confronted with a real-life problem, determine whether or not computing the area of a surface will help solve the problem (*Cognitive: application*)

She constructs three items intended to be relevant to that ninth objective:

1. *Task presented to the students:*
   (multiple-choice) Computing a surface area will help you solve one of these three problems. Which one is it?
   A. We have a large bookcase we want to bring into our classroom. Our problem is to determine if the bookcase can fit through the doorway.
   B. As part of a project to fix up our classroom, we want to put stripping all along the crack where the walls meet the floor. Our problem is to figure how much stripping to buy.
   C. As part of a project to fix up our classroom, we want to put carpet down on the floor. Our problem is to figure how much carpet to buy.

(continued)

VIGNETTE 6.1 (continued)

Scoring key: +1 for "C" only; 0 otherwise

2. *Task presented to the students:*
    (multiple-choice) What is the surface area of one side of this sheet of paper you are now reading? (Use your ruler to help you make your choice.)
    A. 93.5 square inches
    B. 93.5 inches
    C. 20.5 square inches
    D. 20.5 inches
    F. 41 square inches
    G. 41 inches

Scoring key: +1 for "A" only; 0 otherwise

3. *Task presented to the students:*
    (multiple-choice) As part of our project for fixing up the classroom, we need to buy some paint for the walls. The paint we want comes in two different size cans. A 5-liter can costs $16.85 and a 2-liter can costs $6.55. Which one of the following would help us decide which can is the best buy?
    A. Compare 5 × $16.85 to 2 × $6.55
    B. $16.85 ÷ 5 to $6.55 ÷ 2
    C. Compare $16.85 − $6.55 to 2/5

Scoring key: +1 for "B" only; 0 otherwise

Adapted with permission from *Designing Tests for Evaluating Student Achievement* (p. 28), by J. S. Cangelosi (1990), White Plains, NY: Longman.

How well do Ms. Curry's items match the stated objective? The first one appears relevant because it requires students to *apply* (the objective's learning level) their understanding of *surface areas* (the objective's content). Of course students might select "C" for item 1 just by guessing, but to increase one's chances from one third based on random guessing, one must reason deductively about surface area.

Item 2 does not seem to match the objective very well. The correct response of "A" can be selected simply by remembering how to compute a surface area without having to decide *when* surface area should be computed. Thus, whereas item 2 appears to pertain to the *content* of the objective, namely *surface area*, its learning level is *knowledge-of-a-process* instead of *application*. Item 2 fails to be relevant to the objective because it pertains to the wrong learning level.

Item 3 requires students to operate at the application level as specified by the objective. However, the item fails to match the objective because its content is not surface area.

Measurement Reliability

For a test to produce valid results, it must not only be relevant to the intended learning goal, it must also be *reliable*. A measurement is reliable to the same degree that it can be depended on to yield consistent, noncontradictory results. To be reliable a test must have both *internal consistency* and *scorer consistency*.

Internal Consistency. Suppose a student tells you, "I hate school; it's so boring!" You respond, "You must really hate getting up in the morning to go to school." The student: "Oh, I hate it alright, but I don't mind going everyday because there's so much to learn—and I really like seeing my friends. Most of my teachers are okay too!" Does this student like school or not? The student's comments are contradictory. Thus, the results of the informal measurement based on what you heard the student say lack *internal consistency*.

Consider the internal consistency of partial test results Ms. Curry obtained in Vignette 6.2:

VIGNETTE 6.2

Ms. Curry administers a 22-item test to help her evaluate students' achievement of the learning goal for a unit on surface area. Two of the test's items, 7 and 19, are intended to measure the sixth of the Unit's nine objectives. The sixth objective is:

> Given the dimensions of a right triangle, compute its areas (*knowledge of a process*)

Items 7 and 19 are as follows:

7. *Task presented to the students:*
   What is the area bounded by a right triangle with dimensions 5 cm, 4 cm, and 3 cm? (Display your computations and place your answer in the blank.)

   Answer: _____

   Scoring key: 4 points maximum score distributed as follows:
   +1 if $A = (\frac{1}{2})bh$ is used
   +1 if 4 and 3 are used in a computation, but not 5
   +1 if 6 (irrespective of the units) is given as the area
   +1 if the answer is expressed in square centimeters (cm^2)

19. *Task presented to the students:*
    What is the area of the interior of triangle ABC if angle B measures 90°, AB = 6 cm, BC = 8 cm, and AC = 10 cm? (Display your computations and place your answer in the blank.)

    Answer: _____

    Scoring key: 4 points maximum score distributed as follows:
    +1 if $A = (\frac{1}{2})bh$ is used
    +1 if 6 and 8 are used in a computation, but not 10
    +1 if 24 (irrespective of the units) is given as the area
    +1 if the answer is expressed in square centimeters (cm^2)

(continued)

VIGNETTE 6.2 (continued)

Curious about how well her students achieved the sixth objective, Ms. Curry notes five students' performances on items 7 and 19:

Student	*Points on Item* 7	*Points on Item* 19
Roxanne	4	4
Luanne	1	0
Izar	0	4
Mel	3	2
Jan	4	1

Relative to the sixth objective, the data suggest that Roxanne has a high level of achievement, Luanne's is low, and Mel's may be somewhere in between. However, Ms. Curry is perplexed by the performances of Izar and Jan on these two items. Does Izar know how to compute areas of right triangles? Item 7 suggests not, whereas item 19 indicates yes.

Adapted with permission from *Designing Tests for Evaluating Student Achievement* (p. 30), by J. S. Cangelosi (1990), White Plains, NY: Longman.

At least for Izar and Jan relative to the sixth objective, Ms. Curry's test yielded contradictory results. If the test results are dominated by such inconsistencies, the test lacks *internal consistency* and is, therefore, unreliable. On the other hand, if the results do not contain a significant proportion of contradictions and are more in line with what Ms. Curry obtained for Roxanne, Luanne, and Mel, the test is internally consistent (Cangelosi, 1990b, pp. 29–31).

For a test to produce internally consistent results, it must be designed so that the tasks presented by items are clearly and unambiguously specified for students. For students to respond consistently to items, they must clearly understand the task required by each each item. Directions need to be unambiguously communicated. Here are three examples of students confronted with vaguely defined tasks:

VIGNETTE 6.3

During a social studies test, Leo reads, "Who discovered America?" He thinks, "Columbus sailed to the New World in 1492. But there were native Americans there long before then. I wonder how I'm supposed to answer this? Maybe I should answer 'the Vikings' who sailed before Columbus. Or should it be John Cabot who got to what's now the United States because Columbus only got to the Caribbean?"

VIGNETTE 6.4

On a language arts test, Ebony reads the following:

Directions: Circle the correct form of the verb for the sentence:
   My friend and brother [is, are] coming.

She thinks, "If 'my friend' is 'my brother' then the answer is 'is.' If they are supposed to be two different people then 'are' is the answer."

VIGNETTE 6.5

Ms. Lord includes the following essay item on a physiology test: "Discuss the passage of blood through the human heart." One of her students, Monique, reads the item and thinks, "It takes two to have a discussion! With whom am I supposed to discuss this? What does she want me to write? How about, 'It's a good thing blood passes through the heart or else I'd be dead.' This is not time to be funny; you're running out of time. Okay, I'll give her a paragraph on how important it is for blood to pass through the heart."

When Ms. Lord returns the test papers to the class, she comments about that item, "Three of you wrote way too much. Georgina filled up four pages and didn't have enough time to finish the rest of the test. But most of you didn't write enough—not even explaining why blood moves through the heart." The following discussion ensues:

BART: You only gave me one point out of 10 and I did what you said—wrote *why* blood moves through the heart!

MS. LORD: Read your answer.

BART: So that oxygen-rich blood replaces oxygen-poor blood—that is why blood passes through the heart.

TRACI: You were supposed to write more than that!

BART: I explained why blood passes through the heart like Ms. Lord said!

MS. LORD: That's not what I meant. You should have written more and described *how* blood passes through the heart.

MONIQUE: But it says "discuss"—not "describe how or why." I'll bet everybody in the class "discussed the passage of blood through the human heart"!

MS. LORD: But some did so in a nice one-page essay; others just wrote a sentence.

MONIQUE: How were we to know what to do? Entire books are written describing blood passing through the heart. You didn't want us to write a book!

Ms. Lord now realizes that the item's task was not clearly defined. After class she thinks about how to reword the item for the next time she tests for the objective. She decides on the following:

(continued)

VIGNETTE 6.5 (continued)

With the aid of a diagram, explain the mechanics of how venous blood, while in the heart, is transported through the human heart and to the lungs. Make sure you indicate the direction and locations of the venous blood while in the heart. Note how the action of the heart maintains the flow. Use between one and two pages for your entire response, including the diagram.

The refined version of Ms. Lord's item is wordier than the original, but the task is clearer to the students. Similarly, the teachers in Vignettes 6.3 and 6.4 need to reword their items.

To be internally consistent, a test must also include an adequate number of items. A test with a large number of items provides a greater opportunity for consistent student response patterns to emerge than a test with only a few items. The more items on a test, the less affected are the test's results by fortuitous factors. Suppose, for example, that one of a test's objectives is measured by only two true/false items. By random guess, a student has 25 percent chance of scoring 0, 50 percent of scoring 1, and 25 percent chance of scoring 2. Results of the two items are unlikely to consistently discriminate between students who have and have not achieved the objective. However, if there were 10 such true/false items, then random guessing is less of a factor with 0.1 percent chance of scoring 0, 1.0 percent of scoring 1, 4.4 percent of scoring 2, 11.7 percent of scoring 3, 20.5 percent of scoring 4, 24.6 percent of scoring 5, 20.5 percent of scoring 6, 11.7 percent of scoring 7, 4.4 percent of scoring 8, 1.0 percent of scoring 9, and 0.1 percent of scoring 10.

Tests need to be administered under controlled conditions. A scientific experiment is the application of systematic procedures for the purpose of uncovering evidence that helps answer a specified question. An achievement test is a type of scientific experiment in which the question to be answered is how well students have achieved a particular learning goal. The experimental conditions need to be controlled to minimize distractions to students and assure directions are followed. Internal consistency is threatened anytime students' thoughts during testing are interrupted or student cheating is allowed. References are available suggesting how to prevent student cheating without threatening the businesslike, cooperative environment of your classroom (e.g., Cangelosi, 1982, pp. 237–238; 1988a, pp. 259–265; 1990b, pp. 63–69).

Scorer Consistency. A test has *scorer consistency* to the same degree that:

> the teacher (or whoever scores the test) faithfully follows the item's scoring keys so that the test results are not influenced by when the test is scored
> two different teachers, both familiar with the test's content, agree on the score warranted by each item response so that the test's results are not influenced by who scores the test

A test's scorer consistency will be poor if the test is dominated by items that do not have clearly specified scoring keys. Multiple-choice items have very clearly defined scoring keys, thus, consistently scoring them poses no difficulty. Essay, performance observation, interview, and many other types of items require an element of judgment on the part of scorers. To build scorer consistency into such items, scoring keys must specifically indicate just how points are to be distributed or responses recorded. Formulating scoring keys is a major aspect of item design. To score the refined version of her essay item in Vignette 6.5, Ms. Lord might formulate a scoring key such as the following:

Scoring key:
(8 points possible) Points distributed as follows:
+1 for each of the following the student indicates in the essay: (a) venous blood enters through the superior and inferior venae cavae; (b) venous blood gathers in the right atrium; (c) proper role of the valves in the right side of the heart; (d) venous blood gathers in the right ventricle; (e) venous blood exiting the heart through the pulmonary arteries; (f) the heart's pumping motion; (g) how the heart's pumping motion causes the venous blood to flow.
+1 if the essay does not indicate venous blood anywhere that it does not actually reside.

As you design an item for a given objective, keep in mind that the scoring key needs to be formulated along with the task to be presented to students. Some teachers make the mistake of deciding how to score test items after the test is administered. Such an unsystematic approach to test design is a major cause of widespread testing malpractice.

MEASUREMENT USABILITY

No matter how valid a test might be for measuring student achievement, it is of no value to you if it is too time consuming to administer or score, costly to purchase, or threatens the well-being of your students. It must be practical for your needs. Whenever designing or selecting a test to help you assess student achievement, you need to consider the measurement's *usability* as well as its *validity*. A test is usable to the degree that it is inexpensive, brief, easy to administer and score, and does not interfere with other activities.

Figure 6.2 depicts the variables you should take into consideration whenever selecting or designing a test.

Figure 6.2. Test Quality Variables

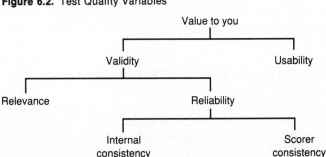

TYPES OF TESTS

Commercially Produced Tests

Achievement tests can be purchased from commercial publishers. Ordinarily, each set of student textbooks is accompanied by a package of materials for the teacher that includes tests—usually a test per chapter. Most such tests emphasize knowledge-level learning. They are hardly relevant to intellectual-level objectives, thus it's rarely advisable to use them for unit tests. However, tests that accompany textbooks provide a source of individual items for knowledge-level learning that you may well incorporate into tests you design yourself. Pools of individual items are available from some commercial outlets. Advertisements for such products are sent to practicing teachers, appear in professional education journals, and are displayed at annual meetings of professional teaching societies.

Unlike tests that are packaged as part of textbook series, some commercially produced tests are administered on a school-wide basis once or twice a year. These are the "big event" tests that some people naively think of as true measures of students' intellectual achievements. Although capable of providing some evidence of an average achievement level of a group of students regarding some broad general areas, commercially produced tests do not yield data relative to the specific achievement of individual students (Cangelosi, 1990b, p. 26).

Standardized Tests

The more familiar, big event, commercially produced tests (e.g., *Stanford Achievement Tests, Metropolitan Achievement Tests, Iowa Test of Basic Skills*, and *California Achievement Tests*) and *standardized*. A standardized test is one that has been field-tested for the purpose of assessing its reliability and establishing normative standards to be used in interpreting scores. Unfortunately, misuses and overuses of standardized tests are quite common, especially in school districts where evaluations of teaching success are untenably linked to students' scores on these tests (Archibald & Newman, 1988; Cangelosi, 1982, pp. 343–349; 1991, pp. 104–105; Houts, 1977; McClaren, 1989, p. 13; Popham, 1988, pp. 129–149). However, numerous sources on how to appropriately use standardized tests are available (e.g., Cangelosi, 1990b, pp. 178–195; Hills, 1986; Hopkins, Stanley, & Hopkins, 1990, pp. 389–481).

Teacher-produced Tests

Standardized achievement tests, like other commercially produced achievement tests almost always emphasize knowledge-level learning. Thus it's imperative for you to design and construct most of your tests yourself. *Teacher-produced* tests provide the most common data for formative and summative evaluations.

DEVELOPING TEACHER-PRODUCED TESTS

You need to apply research-based systematic procedures to design and construct usable tests that provide valid indicators of how well students achieve your particular learning goals. You must begin with clearly defined learning goals as explained herein in Chapter 2. Then the test is planned using a test blueprint to specify:

1. how many points you want to devote to each objective—with more items and points for objectives you judge more important to goal achievement and fewer items and points for less important objectives
2. time you schedule for students to take the test
3. time you schedule for you to score the test
4. types of items to be included on the test (e.g., 20 multiple-choice, 1 essay, and 2 performance observation items)
5. how easy, moderate, and hard items (as defined herein the next section) should be distributed
6. outline of how the test should be structured—indicating placement of directions and items

Detailed suggestions for developing a test blueprint can be found in texts devoted to the art of constructing teacher-made tests (e.g., see Cangelosi, 1990b, pp. 41–78). The most taxing aspect of test construction, however, is not devising the blueprint, but developing a pool of relevant items for each objective on which you want to assess students' achievement. The remainder of this chapter (adapted from Cangelosi, 1990b, pp. 53–177) is intended to help you do just that.

ITEM POOLS

An *item pool* is a collection of test items that are all designed to be relevant to the same learning objective. Developing an item pool from scratch is a time consuming, creative process. However, once you have at least the beginning of pools and incorporate them into an item pool file, you are able to synthesize valid tests much easier than teachers who don't utilize item pools.

The Advantages of Item Pools

There are five reasons to utilize item pools:

Building item pools focuses your attention on one objective at a time, stimulating you to expand your ideas on how student achievement of each objective can be demonstrated.

Each item in a pool is designed to focus on the content and learning level specified by the objective. Thus, a test synthesized from items drawn from item pools is more likely to be relevant than one with items designed as the test is being put together.

Having access to an item pool for each objective before items are actually selected for a test makes it easier to construct the test according to the relative importance of objectives.

Being able to associate each item with a particular objective provides a means for assessing which *specific objectives* were achieved, not just general goal achievement. This facilitates access to *diagnostic* information needed for formative evaluations.

It is much easier and efficient to create and refine tests once a system for maintaining and expanding item pools is in place.

Desirable Characteristics of Item Pools

To take full advantage of having item pools, build them so that each pool contains a variety of types of items (e.g., essay, performance observation, multiple-choice, and interview). Suggestions for designing different types of items and avoiding some of the common pitfalls of those items can be found in numerous measurement and evaluation textbooks (e.g., Cangelosi, 1982, pp. 11–156; Cangelosi, 1990b, pp. 79–133; Ebel & Frisbie, 1986, pp. 126–201; Gronlund & Linn, 1990, pp. 142–210; Hopkins, Stanley, & Hopkins, 1990, pp. 193–266; Kubiszyn & Borich, 1987; 68–114; Tuckman, 1988, pp. 51–124).

Each pool should include easy, moderate, and difficult items. An item is *easy* if at least 75 percent of the students for whom it is intended respond to it correctly. A test needs a number of easy items to measure relatively low levels of achievement. Such items provide information about what students with less than average achievement of the goal have learned. An item is *moderately difficult* if between 25 percent and 75 percent of the students respond to it correctly. Moderate items are valuable for measuring the achievement levels of the majority of students for whom the test is designed. An item is *hard* if no more than 25 percent of the students respond to it correctly. A test needs a number of *hard* items to measure relatively advanced levels of achievement. Unless a test has some hard items to challenge students with advanced goal attainment, the extent of those students' achievement levels is not detected.

Compare the three items in the following example:

VIGNETTE 6.6

Objective 9 of Ms. Curry's sixth-grade math unit on surface area reads:

When confronted with a real-life problem, determine whether or not computing the area of a surface will help solve the problem (*Cognitive: application*)

Three of the items Ms. Curry has constructed for that objective are:

1. *Task presented to the students:*
   (multiple-choice) Carpet is to be bought for the rectangular-shaped floor of a room. The room is 8 feet high, 12 feet wide, and 15 feet long. Which of the following computations would be the most helpful in deciding how much carpet to buy?
   A. $12' + 8' + 15'$
   B. $2 \times (12' + 15')$
   C. $12' \times 8' \times 15'$
   D. $12' \times 15'$

VIGNETTE 6.6 (continued)

Scoring key: +1 for "D" only; 0 otherwise

2. *Task presented to the students:*
   (multiple-choice) Suppose we want to build book shelves across one wall of our classroom. The shelves are to be 18 inches apart. Which one of the following numbers would be most helpful in figuring how many shelves we can fit on the wall?
   A. The area of the wall.
   B. The width of the wall.
   C. The height of the wall.
   D. The perimeter of the wall.

Scoring key: +1 for "C" only; 0 otherwise

3. *Task presented to the students:*
   (multiple-choice) The 13 steps of a staircase are to be painted. Each step is 36″ wide, 12″ deep, and 7″ high. Which of the following computations would be most helpful in determining how much paint will be needed?
   A. $[(12'' \times 13) \times (7'' \times 13)]/2$
   B. $36'' \times [13 \times (12'' \times 7'')]$
   C. $(13 \times 7'') \times (36'' + 12'')$
   D. $13 \times [(36'' \times 7'') + (36'' \times 12'')]$

Scoring key: +1 for "D" only; 0 otherwise

Which of the three items do you think will be easiest for Ms. Curry's students? Which one will be the hardest? She needs items like the first to help her detect the lower bound of her students' achievement of the objective. The third item should help her detect the upper bound.

Typical teacher-produced tests are dominated by easy items with the average score about 80 to 85 percent of the maximum. For purposes of formative feedback, your tests will produce more detailed feedback on student achievement than typical teacher-produced tests if you include easy, moderate, and hard items and design the test so that the average score is about 50 percent of the maximum (Cangelosi, 1982, pp. 309–339; Hoffmann, 1975). Of course, if you apply this suggestion to tests you use to make summative evaluations for determining students' grades, then you should not use traditional percentage grading (e.g., in which 70 percent is required for passing and 93 percent for an A). Alternative methods for converting scores to grades that can tolerate unconventionally difficult tests are explained in many measurement and evaluation textbooks (e.g., see Cangelosi, 1990b, pp. 197–213).

Organize the item pool system so that you can efficiently retrieve existing items, construct tests, create new items, and modify existing items. Figure 6.3. depicts a typical scheme for organizing item pool files.

Course
  Learning Goal
    Objective
      Difficulty Level
        Type of Item

Figure 6.3. Organizational Scheme for Filing Test Items

Computerized Item Pools

A decade ago, teachers organized and managed item pools on index cards in file boxes. Today, microcomputers allow you to organize and manage item pools so efficiently that you can concentrate your energies on the creative aspect of the process—designing the items. Computer programs developed especially for setting up and utilizing item pools are readily available from both commercial and noncommercial sources. Computer software catalogues, computer retail stores, computer magazines, professional journals for teachers, and school district resource and media centers have information on how to obtain the software for such programs. Of course, you don't have to have special software to maintain and manage item pools efficiently with a computer. Many teachers use standard word-processing programs, storing each pool in a document file. Others prefer to write their own programs.

These programs free you from the time-consuming clerical aspects of expanding pools, modifying items, retrieving items in accordance with test blueprints, synthesizing tests, and printing tests—leaving you time and energy for intellectual tasks. The teacher in Vignette 6.7 is using a commercially produced program to add a new item she's just designed to one of her item pools:

VIGNETTE 6.7

Ms. Bell accesses her item pool program and engages the computer in the following exchange:

> COMPUTER: What function do you want?
>   1—review table of contents
>   2—review existing pool
>   3—modify existing pool
>   4—begin new pool
>   ?—help
>
> MS. BELL: "3"
>
> COMPUTER: What pool? Enter code for course/learning goal. If you need a list of the codes, enter "LIST" instead.
>
> MS. BELL: EARTH7/10
>
> COMPUTER: What subfunction do you want?
>   1—review table of contents for EARTH7/10
>   2—add new item

VIGNETTE 6.7 (continued)

    3—modify existing item
    4—delete item
    5—modify existing EARTH7/10 parameters
    ?—help

Ms. Bell: "2"

Computer: What objective? Enter code. If you need a listing of the objectives and codes, enter "LIST" instead.

Ms. Bell: "4"

Computer: What is the difficulty level of the item (e, m, or h)?

Ms. Bell: "m"

Computer: What type of item?

1—multiple choice	2—matching	3—completion
4—true/false	5—essay	6—brief essay
7—display work	8—performance observation	
9—other	?—help	

Ms. Bell: "7"

Computer: Enter the task to be presented.

Ms. Bell: The temperature of a sample of still, dry air is 18°C at the earth's surface. What will be the temperature at an altitude of 975 meters? Please clearly display your work.
    Display of work:

    Answer in degrees Celsius: _____

Computer: Enter the scoring key.

Ms. Bell: 4 points possible distributed as follows:
    +1 for an indication that the student uses the normal lapse rate of 1°C per 150 m
    +1 if the ratio 975 m/150 m is used somewhere in the response
    +1 if the decrease in temperature (6.5°C) is subtracted from 18°C
    +1 if −20°C is given as the final solution

Computer: Do you have any notes to add about this item?

Ms. Bell: *n*

Computer: Your new item has been stored in the EARTH7/10 pool. Do you want to add another item to this pool?

Ms. Bell: *n*

ITEMS RELEVANT TO ACHIEVEMENT OF SIMPLE KNOWLEDGE OBJECTIVES

Stimulus-Response

Please reread the section entitled "Simple Knowledge" beginning on page 54. Note that students achieve a simple-knowledge objective by *remembering* the desired response (e.g., *Area = length × width*) to a particular stimulus (e.g., "formula for the area of a rectangle"). Thus, a simple-knowledge item presents students with the task of exhibiting that, upon exposure to the stimulus, they remember the formula, image, sound, word, symbol, name, date, definition, principle, location, or other content the objective specifies. When designing an item for a simple-knowledge objective, maintain the same stimulus–response relationship that's defined by the objective. For example, design an item that is relevant to the following objective taken from a middle school science curriculum guide:

> So that students will be able to read scientific material, they will recall the meanings of the following terms: *hypothesis*, *empirical observation*, and *experiment* (*Cognitive: simple knowledge*)

Compare your item to the following one, included in the curriculum guide as a sample test item for the stated objective:

> A generalization that appears to be true from direct observation is a(n)
> _____.

"Hypothesis" is the correct response according to the answer key.

The objective is concerned with students being able to know word meanings as they read about science. Thus, it is important for the students to *respond* with a definition on seeing the word *hypothesis*, not respond with *hypothesis* upon seeing a definition. The curriculum guide's sample item reverses the objective's stimulus with its response. The objective's stimulus–response relationship remains intact with the following item:

Task presented to the students:
  What does *hypothesis* mean? _____

_____

  Scoring key:
  (4 points possible) +1 for each of the following that's indicated about a hypothesis: (a) a generalization, (b) unproven, and (c) based on direct observation or experience; +1 if nothing false in included.

Some might favor the curriculum guide's sample item over this latter item because the original item depends less on students' writing skills and is easier to score. However, thinking of a particular word in response to a definition is a different cognitive task than that implied by the objective. To illustrate this difference, answer the following question:

What word means *having an abundance of riches*?

Even though you'll remember the definition of this word when you read it, you may not think of the word on reading its definition. The word is *affluent*, but you may have answered the question with *wealthy*, *opulent*, *rich*, or some other synonym. How many times have you been unable to remember someone's name, although you readily remember who that person is on hearing the name?

Avoiding Responses beyond Simple Knowledge

Students' responses to simple-knowledge items should only depend on how well they remember information. Items are not relevant to simple-knowledge objectives whenever students use reasoning or higher-order cognitive processes to determine responses. But, because an item is designed to measure simple-knowledge behavior does not guarantee that students will respond at the simple-knowledge level. For example:

VIGNETTE 6.8

To measure her first-graders' recall of addition facts, Ms. Blair administers a five-minute test consisting of 12 items similar to the following:

    $7 + 4 =$ _____.

    When Casey confronts this item, he uses his fingers to count to himself, "Eight, 9, 10, 11." He scores 12 out of 12 on the test.

    Casey used knowledge-of-a-process cognitive behavior to respond to Ms. Blair's test items. If Ms. Blair is determined for this to be a simple-knowledge test, she should redesign it so that students do not have time to work through a process. The number of items could be increased and administration time reduced or she could use flash cards and require rapid responses.

    In the following example, a student responds to what was supposed to be a simple knowledge-level item with reasoning because of ambiguous wording:

VIGNETTE 6.9

In a health unit on nutrition, Mr. Brewer emphasizes that the consumption of tea interferes with the body's ability to use iron. To measure if his students remember this fact, he includes the following true/false item on the unit test:

Task presented to the students:

    T F   Drinking tea provides iron for the body.

    Scoring key: +1 for "F" only; 0 otherwise

    Maxine remembers that tea interferes with the body's usage of iron as she reads the statement. However, she moves beyond the simple-knowledge level as she thinks, "Tea is not the way to get iron into the body. But, the statement says, 'drinking tea provides iron.' Tea is mixed with water and most water contains traces of iron. So actually, drinking tea does provide iron. The answer is 'T'."

Mr. Brewer might argue that if Maxine had paid attention in class she would know what he meant by that true/false statement and she would have put "F." However, a simple-knowledge item doesn't and shouldn't contain a warning label for students "not to reason on this one." The problem is best avoided by wording items so that there is little or no room for misinterpretations.

ITEMS RELEVANT TO ACHIEVEMENT OF KNOWLEDGE-OF-A-PROCESS OBJECTIVES

Stimulus-Response-Response- . . . -Response

Please reread the section entitled "Knowledge of a Process" beginning on page 54. Students achieve a knowledge-of-a-process objective by remembering how to carry out a procedure or use a method. Thus, a knowledge-of-a-process item presents students with the task of exhibiting that they know the first, second, third, and so forth steps in the process specified by the objective. A knowledge-of-a-process objective is concerned with students remembering a *sequence* of responses, not only a single response; consequently each student response in the sequence serves as a stimulus to the next response. Thus, the accuracy of subsequent steps in the process is dependent on the accuracy of previous steps in the process. The design of a knowledge-of-a-process item should differ considerably from the design of a simple-knowledge item because of this phenomenon.

Emphasis on the Process, Not the Outcome

Develop your own scoring key for the test shown in Figure 6.4, and then score Shannon's paper as it appears there.

Now that you've completed that task, consider what actually happened in Shannon's case:

VIGNETTE 6.10

Mr. Hancock administered a test to Shannon and his other third-graders to measure their achievement of the following objective:

Compute the product of any two-digit whole number by a one-digit whole number. (*Cognitive: knowledge of a process*)

Shannon's completed test appears in Figure 6.4. Figure 6.5 shows the same paper after Mr. Hancock scored it and returned it to Shannon.

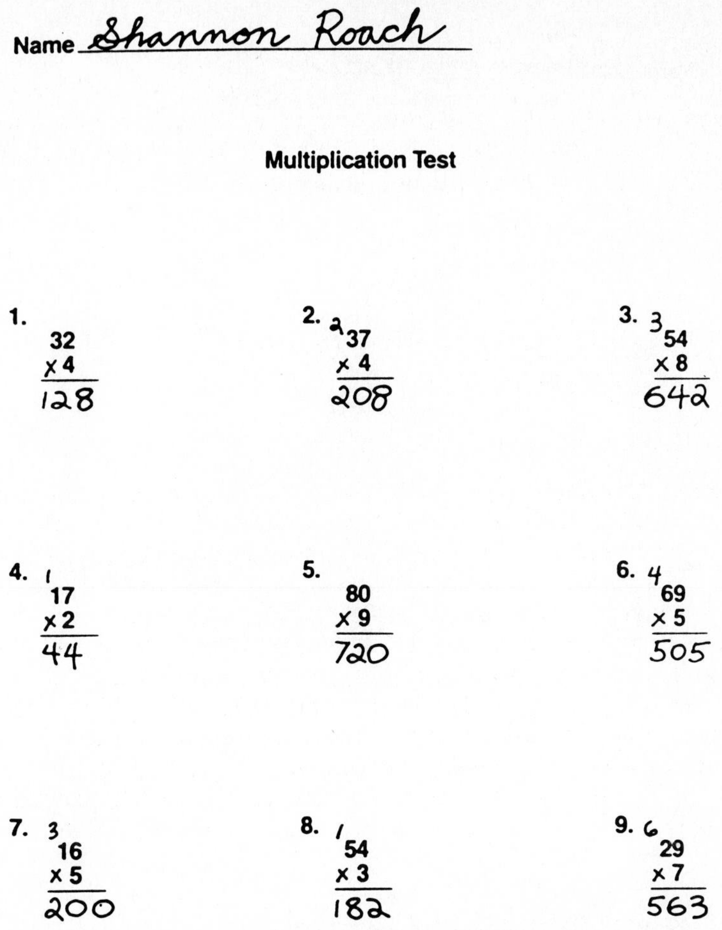

Name *Shannon Roach*

Multiplication Test

1.
```
  32
 × 4
 128
```

2.
```
 ² 37
  × 4
  208
```

3.
```
 ³ 54
  × 8
  642
```

4.
```
 ¹ 17
  × 2
  44
```

5.
```
  80
 × 9
 720
```

6.
```
 ⁴ 69
  × 5
  505
```

7.
```
 ³ 16
  × 5
  200
```

8.
```
 ¹ 54
  × 3
  182
```

9.
```
 ⁶ 29
  × 7
  563
```

Figure 6.4. Shannon's Test Paper (*Source:* From *Designing Tests for Evaluating Student Achievement* [p. 140] by J. S. Cangelosi, 1990, White Plains, NY: Longman. Reprinted by permission.)

What do you think Mr. Hancock learned from the test about Shannon's achievement of the objective? What do you think Shannon learned from seeing the returned paper? Apparently, Mr. Hancock scored the items with a key similar to this one for item 2:

Task presented to the students:

```
   37
 ×  4
```

Scoring key: +11 percent for "148"; 0 otherwise.

However, does the objective imply that Shannon should know that 148 is the product of 37 and 4? No, the objective implies that Shannon should know a process for finding the product of 37 and 4. The objective is concerned not with students' knowing answers, but with knowing how to find answers. For Shannon to obtain

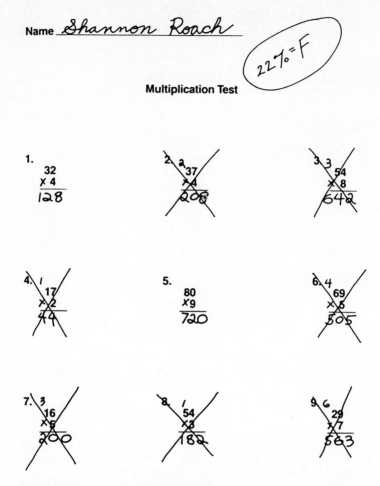

Figure 6.5. Shannon's Test Paper with Mr. Hancock's Marks (*Source:* From *Designing Tests for Evaluating Student Achievement* [p. 141] by J. S. Cangelosi, 1990, White Plains, NY: Longman. Reprinted by permission.)

"148," the correct response to item 2 on Mr. Hancock's test, she would have to execute steps similar to the following:

1. recognizes that the task is to multiply
2. recognizes that the multiplicand is a two-digit number, and thus memory of multiplication facts alone will not be adequate
3. checks to see if the numerals are aligned for the algorithm
4. remembers to first multiply 7 by 4
5. remembers that $7 \times 4 = 28$
6. writes "8" as follows:

$$\begin{array}{r} 37 \\ \times\ 4 \\ \hline 8 \end{array}$$

7. Carries the "2":

$$
\begin{array}{r}
2 \\
37 \\
\times4 \\
\hline
8
\end{array}
$$

8. remembers to multiply 3 by 4
9. remembers that $3 \times 4 = 12$
10. remembers to add the carried 2 to the 12
11. computes $2 + 12 = 14$
12. writes the "14" to the left of the "8":

$$
\begin{array}{r}
2 \\
37 \\
\times4 \\
\hline
148
\end{array}
$$

Once again, examine Shannon's answers in Figure 6.4. How many of the 12 steps just listed did she seem to remember when she took the test? A careful examination of her answers suggests that she actually remembered almost all of the steps, but she consistently executed step 10 prior to step 8. Imagine that instead of Mr. Hancock, Shannon's third-grade teacher is Ms. Tankersley. Shannon's experiences would have been quite different:

VIGNETTE 6.11

Ms. Tankersley administers a four-item test to her third-graders to help assess how well they've achieved the following objective:

Compute the product of any two-digit whole number by a one-digit whole number (*Cognitive: knowledge of a process*)

The following is the second item on the test:

Task presented to the students:

$$
\begin{array}{r}
37 \\
\times4 \\
\hline
\end{array}
$$

Scoring key:
(7 points possible) +1 for each of the following that's detectable from the response: (a) multiplied 7 and 4, (b) placed the one's digit of the partial product (should be "8") as the unit's place in the answer, (c) carried the ten's digit (should be "2"), (d) multiplied 4 and 3, (e) added the carried digit to that partial product (should be $2 + 12$), (f) put the result in its proper place (should be "14"), and (g) answered "148."

The day following the test, Ms. Tankersley returns the scored papers. Shannon's paper, as it was returned to her, appears as Figure 6.6

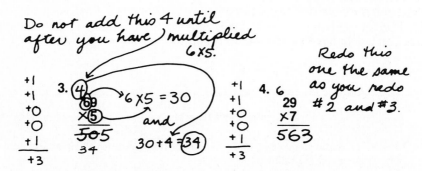

Figure 6.6. Shannon's Test Paper with Ms. Tankersley's Marks (*Source:* From *Designing Tests for Evaluating Student Achievement* [p. 143] by J. S. Cangelosi, 1990, White Plains, NY: Longman. Reprinted by permission.)

The results of Ms. Tankersley's version of Shannon's test indicate exactly what Shannon needs to learn to correct her errors.

Knowledge, Affective, and Psychomotor Components of the Process

Students' abilities to carry out a process (e.g., forming manuscript letters, diagramming a sentence, computing with a mathematical formula, performing cardiopulmonary resuscitation, bench-pressing a barbell, reciting the alphabet, and typing a letter) often depend not only on their knowledge of the process, but also on some affective and psychomotor behaviors. To teach students to perform such a process, you must be concerned with the cognitive knowledge, affective, and psychomotor aspects of the process. Consider the following example:

VIGNETTE 6.12

To measure five-year-old Alex's achievement of the following objective, Ms. Bailey administers the item in Figure 6.7:

> Follow the steps described in the Groves–Haimowitz handwriting manual to write an uppercase *A*. (*Cognitive: knowledge of a process*)

Alex's response to the item appears in Figure 6.8.

Task presented to the students:
  The student is given a pencil and lined paper and told to make a capital letter *A*.

  Scoring key: Using a 5-point check sheet, watch student proceed.

  _____ If a legible *A* is made
  _____ Used exactly 3 strokes
  _____ Strokes were made in proper sequence:

  _____ Each stroke was made in the designated directions:

  _____ Letter properly spaced between lines:

Figure 6.7. Item Ms. Bailey Used with Alex (*Source:* From *Designing Tests for Evaluating Student Achievement* [p. 144] by J. S. Cangelosi, 1990, White Plains, NY: Longman. Reprinted by permission.)

Figure 6.8. Alex's Response to Item from Figure 6.7 (*Source:* From *Designing Tests for Evaluating Student Achievement* [p. 144] by J. S. Cangelosi, 1990, White Plains, NY: Longman. Reprinted by permission.)

Does Alex's response suggest that he's achieved the knowledge-of-a-process objective? The configuration in Figure 6.8 isn't a very accurate representation of an *A*. However, it is possible that Alex *knows* the steps in the process, but lacks the psychomotor skill to put that knowledge into effect. It is also possible that Alex *can* write better *A*'s, but is unwilling to put forth the effort (i.e., he's failed to achieve a requisite affective objective). For purposes of making a formative evaluation that will help her decide how to teach Alex, Ms. Bailey should measure the psychomotor and affective objectives separately from the knowledge-of-a-process objective.

ITEMS RELEVANT TO ACHIEVEMENT OF COMPREHENSION OBJECTIVES

Deriving Meanings from Expressions

Please reread the section entitled "Comprehension" beginning on page 55. Note the two types of comprehension-level objectives. The content of some objectives specifies a particular expressed message (e.g., the First Amendment to the Constitution, quadratic formula, or classroom rules of conduct) for students to translate or interpret. An item relevant to this type of objective presents students with the task of exhibiting the meaning they've derived from the expression specified by the objective. The content of a second type of comprehension objective specifies a particular communication mode (e.g., reading a compound sentence, listening to a debate, or reading signed English) from which students can make meaningful translations or interpretations. An item relevant to this type of objective presents students with the task of exhibiting the meaning from a message expressed in the mode specified by the objective.

Item Response Mode

The principal concern of comprehension objectives is for students to derive meaning from given expressions. In other words, these objectives focus on students' receptions of expressions, not their formulations of expressions. How they exhibit what they understand from expressions is normally not specified by the objective. However, comprehension-of-a-communication item must be designed to provide students with a means of exhibiting that understanding. Consider the following objective and item designed to measure it:

Objective:
  Explain the general provisions in the Bill of Rights (*Cognitive: comprehension*)
Item:
  Task presented to the students:
    Write a paragraph explaining the parts of the Bill of Rights that have anything to do with allowing people to communicate with one another. Use your own words. Don't quote directly from the Bill of Rights.

  Scoring key:
    Note: Score only if the response is limited to one paragraph with no quotes

as directed; otherwise have the students redo the item. (8 points possible) +1 for each of the following "freedoms" whose relevance to communications among people is brought out: (a) religion, (b) speech, (c) press, and (d) assembly; +1 for relevant protections that are brought out from each of the following amendments: (a) 5th, (b) 9th, and (c) 10th; +1 for including nothing false.

This item appears quite relevant to the objective, *providing* that students possess the requisite writing skills. Items should use only response modes (i.e., how the item requires students to express themselves) with which students are competent. For students who lack the necessary writing skills for this essay item, an oral-discourse item or a *group* of multiple-choice items may serve as a suitable substitute.

Novelty

Comprehension is an intellectual learning level, thus it involves reasoning and judgment that takes the learner beyond what is simply remembered. Unlike knowledge-level items, comprehension items present students with tasks that are not identical to tasks they've previously encountered. There should be some aspect of the task presented by the item that is novel to the students. An item relevant to an objective *specifying a particular message* should require students to translate or interpret the expressed message in some way that they've never before encountered. For example:

Objective:
Explain the general provisions in the Bill of Rights (*Cognitive: comprehension*)
Item:
Task presented to the students
(multiple-choice) The First Amendment to the Constitution states, "Congress shall make no law . . . abridging the freedom of speech." This means that the federal government _____.
A. declares that people have the right to express their ideas
B. may not take away people's right to express their ideas
C. must provide a way for its citizens to express their ideas
D. may not bridge gaps between speeches and other forms of free expression

Scoring key: +1 for "B" only; 0 otherwise.

This item measures the comprehension objective providing students select "B" only because of their understanding of the First Amendment, not because they remember having read or heard the exact words of the alternative. To be relevant to the stated objective, the items should provide students with their *initial* exposure to that interpretation expressed in those words.

An item relevant to an objective *specifying a particular communication mode* should require students to translate or interpret an expression that they've not previously encountered. Of course, the expression must use the familiar communication mode specified by the objective. For example:

Objective:

From watching a hearing-impaired person expressing two or more thought units in American Signed English, translate the thoughts into conventional spoken English (*Cognitive: comprehension*)

Item:

Task presented to the students:

(Written directions are accompanied by a videotaped presentation.) When the number for this item appears on the TV monitor, translate the sign language of the person on the screen. After the signing is completed, select the best interpretation from the following and circle the letter of your choice:

A. Stated that only one job is still available
B. Asked if he should continue to seek a job
C. Stated that a few jobs are still available
D. Stated that a particular job is still available
E. Asked if any jobs are still available

Scoring key: +1 for "D" only, 0 otherwise.

For this item to be relevant to the stated objective, it should provide students with their first experience trying to translate exactly what is expressed on the screen. Note that the item does not have students select a direct word-for-word translation. Comprehension involves determining meanings of whole expressions, not simply decoding single symbols, words, or other units of expressions.

ITEMS RELEVANT TO ACHIEVEMENT OF CONCEPTUALIZATION OBJECTIVES

Concepts and Relationships

Please reread the section entitled "Conceptualization" beginning on page 56. Note that the content of a conceptualization objective is either a concept or a relationship.

Grouping Examples

Reread the section entitled "Concept Attributes and Psychological Noise" beginning on page 77. An item relevant to a conceptualization objective that specifies a *concept* for content presents students with the task of discriminating between examples and nonexamples of the concept. For example:

VIGNETTE 6.13

Mr. Boudreaux is adding to his item pool for the following objective:

Group examples of animals according to whether or not they are mammals (*Cognitive: conceptualization*)

VIGNETTE 6.13 (continued)

He thinks, "If I gave them the task of discriminating among familiar animals—like identifying the mammal from a group containing a cat, snake, frog, bird, and fish—they're likely to select the cat just because they *remember* cats are mammals and the others aren't. I need to see if they discriminate based on the attributes of mammals. . . . I know! I'll create some hypothetical animals—ones with mammal attributes and some lacking mammal attributes. For easier items, I'll make the examples clearly stand out from the nonexamples—not many differences in psychological noise, that'll make the attributes stand out on the mammals. For harder items, the distinctions won't be as obvious—more noise—sort of like a duckbill platypus. . . ."

As an easy item, he enters the item shown in Figure 6.9 into his computerized item pool file. Figure 6.10 displays a harder item for the same objective.

Task presented to the students:

Circle the picture of the mammal:

Scoring Key:

+1 for circling the third one only; otherwise +0

Figure 6.9. Easy Item Mr. Budreaux Enters into His Item Pool File

Task presented to the students:

Circle the picture of the mammal:

Scoring Key:

+1 for circling the first one only; otherwise +0

Figure 6.10. Difficult Item Mr. Boudreaux Enters into His Item Pool File

Mr. Boudreaux manipulated the psychological noise in his examples and non-examples to control the difficulty level of conceptualization items. With fewer variables (e.g., having or not having horns) to distract students, Mr. Boudreaux's students will find similarities and differences between the example and the no-nexamples easier to detect in Figure 6.9's item than for Figure 6.10's item. To measure more advanced achievement levels of a conceptualization objective, items are designed using examples with high levels of psychological noise. Lower levels of achievement of conceptualization objectives are measured with items requiring students to discriminate among examples with little interference from psychological noise. Here is an example of an objective and an item relevant to it for a high school or college psychology class:

Objective:
Distinguishes between examples of Pavlov's classical conditioning and other influences on behavior patterns (*Cognitive: conceptualization*)

Item:
Task presented to the students:
(multiple-answer multiple-choice) Circle the letter in front of each of the following that tells of a situation in which a subject is displaying a response to *classical conditioning* (none, one, or more than one letter may be circled):
A. A cat salivates whenever it tastes food.
B. A man hears the sound of a bell from a radio program and recalls the day of his wedding.
C. A man coughs involuntarily when he sees the image of a cigarette in a movie.
D. A dog sits up and begs whenever it is hungry and sees a person holding a bowl.
E. A dog was mistreated by a woman who would often say, "Bad dog!" and hit him. Now the dog flinches every time he hears someone speak.
F. Every time a pupil talked out of turn in a classroom, the teacher required the pupil to stand and face into a corner of the room for an hour. The pupil no longer talks out of turn in that classroom.

Scoring key:
(6 points possible) + 1 for each one of the following circled: "C" and "E"; + 1 for each of the others *not* circled

Notice the role played by psychological noise in the item. Classical conditioning, as you may remember from your study of psychology, is associated with Ivan Pavlov's experiments with dogs being conditioned to salivate to the sound of a bell (Myers, 1986). But with respect to the concept of classical conditioning, dogs, bells, and salivation are psychological noise, not attributes. Nonexamples of classical conditioning are selected as alternatives for the item that include this psychological noise to distract students who remember facts about classical conditioning, but do not truly conceptualize it.

Explaining Why

An item relevant to a conceptualization objective that specifies a relationship for content presents students with the task of explaining why the relationship exists.

Here, for example, is an objective from a sixth-grade math unit and an item designed to measure it:

Objective:
  Explain why the area of a rectangle equals the product of its length and width (*Cognitive: conceptualization*)
Item:
  Task presented to the students:
    Illustrate with one or more pictures why $A = l \times w$ where A = the area of a rectangle, l = its length, and w = its width. Write one paragraph that helps your pictures illustrate why the formula works.

  Scoring key:
    (7 points possible) Points distributed as follows:
      +1 for drawing a rectangle
      +1 for highlighting the units for the length along one edge
      +1 for highlighting the units for the width along an adjacent edge
      +1 for representing the area as the number of unit squares in the rectangle's interior
      +1 for alluding to how adding l to itself w times or w to itself l times yields the same results as counting the unit squares in the rectangle's interior
      +1 for not including anything false
      +1 for not including anything irrelevant

Of course, the item would not be relevant to conceptualization level achievement if students simply reproduced an explanation from memory. Conceptualization items, like all intellectual-level items, confront students with tasks that cannot be accomplished without reasoning beyond what is remembered.

ITEMS RELEVANT TO ACHIEVEMENT OF APPLICATION OBJECTIVES

Deciding How to Solve Problems

Please reread the sections entitled "Application," and "Deductive Reasoning" beginning on pages 57 and 106, respectively. An application item confronts students with a problem and presents them with the task of deducing whether or not a particular concept, relationship, or process is useful in solving that problem. Here is an example of an objective and an item designed to measure it:

Objective:
  From observing the symptoms of a person in distress and from considering the availability and accessibility of other means of help, determine whether or not cardiopulmonary resuscitation (CPR) should be initiated. (*Cognitive: application*)
Item:
  Task presented to the students:
  On a hot summer day, you see a middle-aged jogger grab his chest, stagger for several meters, and fall to the sidewalk. You find him motionless, pupils dilated,

pulse rapid, and skin very dry. Assume that no one else is available to help and you have no immediate means of transporting the victim. In a one-half page essay (a) indicate if and when you should use CPR on this man, and (b) explain the reasons for your decision.

Scoring key:
　(4 points possible) Score 0 if immediate use of CPR is suggested. Otherwise, distribute 4 points as follows:
　　+1 if CPR is NOT suggested for initial aid
　　+1 if rapid pulse is given as a reason for withholding CPR
　　+1 for any other tenable reason for withholding CPR (e.g., victim is displaying signs of heat stroke)
　　+1 for an implicit or explicit indication that symptoms that warrant the use of CPR (e.g., lack of respiration) would be considered

Avoiding "Give-Away" Words

Read Vignette 3.22 in which Ms. Goldberg recognized that she had to avoid "give-away" words so as to tax her students' application-level achievement rather than simply getting them to remember word associations.

Mixing Concepts, Relationships, or Processes

Measuring achievement of an application objective necessitates confronting students with two types of problems: (a) Those with solutions that utilize the relationship specified by the objective, and (b) problems that do not. See, for instance, item 1 in Vignette 6.1. If only problems that use the objective's content are included, students do not have to decide whether or not it is appropriate for the situation. Ability to decide when and when not to use concepts, relationships, or processes is the essence of application-level achievement.

ITEMS RELEVANT TO ACHIEVEMENT OF CREATIVITY OBJECTIVES

Reread two sections, "Creativity" beginning on page 57 and "Some Thoughts on Creativity" beginning on page 111. Unless you devise very unusual curricula for students, relatively few of your objectives specify *creativity* for the learning level. Lessons fostering creativity tend to be integrated with other lessons and extend beyond the confines of a single teaching unit. You may, for example, include short learning activities based on *synectics* within most teaching units, but may only detect an increase in students' creative behaviors over the course of several units. Consequently, assessing achievement at the creativity level may be more of a long-range endeavor than assessing achievement of other types of cognitive objectives.

　Items for creativity objectives consist primarily of:

1. presenting students with tasks relative to the specified content that can be accomplished via divergent thinking
2. scoring students' responses in ways that reflect divergent, rather than convergent, thinking

Note that the scoring keys for simple knowledge, knowledge-of-a-process, comprehension, conceptualization, and application objectives tend to reward convergent thinking (i.e., responses that match previously conceived responses). Following are two examples of creativity objectives, each accompanied by an item designed to be relevant to it (adapted with permission from *Teaching Mathematics in Secondary and Middle School: Research-based Approaches* (pp. 230–231), by J. S. Cangelosi (1992), New York: Macmillan):

Objective:
   Categorize words in unconventional ways and formulate a rule for each category (*Cognitive: creativity*)
Item:
   Task presented to the students:
      (Oral explanation) The students are shown the following five words: *crutch, clutch, find, seek, orphan*. Using language familiar to them, the teacher directs them to make five different subsets from those five words so that each subset contains exactly three of the words. No two subsets should be exactly the same (i.e., contain the same three words). For each of the five subsets, write a rule that explains why those three words are grouped together. Write the rule without actually using any of the original five words. Students are to respond in writing using the following form:
      First Group of Words: _____
      First Rule: _____
      _____
      _____

      Second Group of Words: _____
      Second Rule: _____
      _____
      _____

      Third Group of Words: _____
      Third Rule: _____
      _____
      _____

      Fourth Group of Words: _____
      Fourth Rule: _____
      _____
      _____

      Fifth Group of Words: _____
      Fifth Rule: _____
      _____
      _____

Scoring key: 5-point maximum with +1 for each subset/rule pair that fits the criterion established in the directions

Objective:
  Formulate and prove theorems about subsets of whole numbers (*Cognitive: creativity*)
Item:
  Task presented to the students:
  The number of dots in each of the following arrays is called a *triangular number*:

```
                                                                    •
                                                         •         ••
                                               •        ••        •••
                                      •       ••       •••       ••••
                             •       ••      •••      ••••      •••••
                    •       ••      •••     ••••     •••••     ••••••
           •       ••      •••     ••••    •••••    ••••••    •••••••
  •       ••      •••     ••••    •••••   ••••••   •••••••   ••••••••
• ••     •••     ••••    •••••   ••••••  •••••••  •••••••• •••••••••, etc.
```

  The set of triangular numbers is infinite. Take at least 15 minutes "playing around" examining triangular numbers. Then, make three different statements you think are true about all triangular numbers. These statements should be hypotheses that are not immediately apparent (e.g., "All triangular numbers are positive integers") from just glancing at the numbers. Try to prove one of your statements. Display your work on the proof or proof attempt.

  First statement: _____
  _____
  _____
  Second statement: _____
  _____
  _____
  Third statement: _____
  _____
  _____

  Proof or work toward a proof:

Scoring key:
  The rules are based on comparing responses to those of others. First of all, any blatantly obvious statement (e.g., "No triangular number is imaginary") is eliminated. Then each of the remaining statements is compared to a list of statements compiled from other students who have responded to this item. Comparison statements are sequenced from the most fre-

quently occurring to the least frequently occurring. The statement from this student is then ranked in the sequence and scored the number of points equal to its rank. Thus, if there are 50 comparison statements, 20 of which have been made more than once, then if the statement is equivalent to one of those first 20, it receives a score from 1 to 20 inclusive. If the statement is equivalent to one of the previously unique 30 comparison statements, it receives a score of 21. If the statement is not equivalent to any of the 50 statements, it receives a score of 36 (i.e., a three-way tie for 21st place). If the display of the work on the proof demonstrates a discernible line of thought, the statement score is multiplied by 4. If the statement is actually proven, that score is then doubled.

ITEMS RELEVANT TO ACHIEVEMENT OF VOLUNTARY-MUSCLE-CAPABILITY OBJECTIVES

Endurance, Strength, Flexibility, Agility, and Speed

Please reread the sections entitled "The Nature of Psychomotor Behavior" and "Voluntary Muscle Capability" beginning on pages 59 and 60, respectively.

Typically, voluntary muscle capability can be measured more precisely than other types of learning levels. A voluntary-muscle-capability item presents students with a task that requires them to use the type of capability (i.e., endurance, strength, flexibility, agility, or speed) with the muscle groups specified by the objective.

Measuring Endurance. If the objective's capability is endurance, items should provide a means for observing either the (a) number of continuous repetitions a muscle group can execute a particular work task or (b) amount of time for which the muscle group sustains work. Here, for example, is an objective and an item designed to measure it:

Objective:
  Increase endurance of the abdominal muscles (*Psychomotor: voluntary muscle capability*)
Item:
  Task presented to the students:
    The student is directed to perform as many nonstop bent-leg sit-ups using the technique learned in class.

  Scoring key:
    The number of sit-ups completed before stopping is counted.

Measuring Strength. If the objective's capability is strength, items should provide a means for observing the amount of weight moved a particular distance by the muscle group. Here, for example, is an objective and an item designed to measure it:

Objective:

Increase the strength of the quadricep muscles. (*Psychomotor: voluntary muscle capability*)

Item:

Task presented to the students:

After appropriate warm-up, the student is directed to execute a left leg extension lift on a leg-lift bench. The weight attempted is determined as follows:

The weight is set markedly below the student's maximum for the lift. The lift is attempted with gradually increasing weight (e.g., in 2 kg increments) until the student is unable to perform the lift. Adequate recuperation occurs between attempts.

The item may be administered over several days.

Scoring key: The maximum weight the student lifts is recorded.

Measuring Flexibility. If the objective's capability is flexibility, items should provide a means for observing the angle to which a muscle group extends or flexes a joint. Here, for example, is an objective and an item designed to measure it:

Objective:

Increase flexibility of the lower back muscles (*Psychomotor: voluntary muscle capability*)

Item:

Task presented to the students:

After appropriate warm-up exercises, the student is directed to (a) sit on the floor with knees extended 180 degrees and hands clasped beneath lower thighs and (b) to bring head as far down between knees as possible and hold it there until directions to relax.

Scoring key: The inside angle at the waist is measured and recorded.

Measuring Agility. If the objective's capability is agility, items should provide a means for observing the amount of time it takes muscle groups to respond to a particular stimulus in a prescribed manner. Here, for example, is an objective and an item designed to measure it:

Objective:

Increases eye-to-hand reaction (*Psychomotor: voluntary muscle capability*)

Item:

Task presented to the students:

The student sits at panel consisting of (a) three push-buttons (from left to right, one green, one blue, and one red) and (b) a display of three light bulbs (from left to right, one red, one green, and one blue). The student is directed to immediately push the button that matches the color of the light that flashes. The lights flash one at a time in a randomly determined sequence. A light comes on as soon as any button has been pushed by the student.

Scoring key:

The total number of correct buttons pushed in a one-minute span is recorded.

Measuring Speed. If the objective's capability is speed, items should provide a means for observing the time it takes muscle groups to perform a specified amount of work. Here, for example, is an objective and an item designed to measure it:

Objective:
  Increase speed at which hamstrings flex and quadriceps extend the knees
Item:
  Task presented to the students:
    Students lie face down, flat on a wrestling mat. They are then directed to rapidly execute the following movement as many times as possible in a 30-second span:
      While only moving the lower part of the left leg, bring the left heel into contact with the buttocks and then return to the original position.

  Scoring key:
    Record the number of movements completed in the 30-second span.

Isolating the Muscle Group

Designing items relevant to voluntary-muscle-capability objectives requires at least a rudimentary, working knowledge of anatomy and kinesiology. You, for example, are hardly in a position to design an item for measuring the strength of the muscles of the upper back unless you understand what movements the upper back muscles effect. A sophisticated understanding of anatomy and kinesiology is needed to design items that truly isolate the muscle groups specified by the objective. Measures of chest muscle strength, for example, will be influenced by upper arm strength. Item designers, thus, need to understand how to minimize the role of the upper arms in items relevant to chest strength. Similar problems exist for cognitive and affective measures. It takes a sophisticated understanding of both learning levels and content, for example, to minimize the role of knowledge-level behaviors when designing application items.

Depending on Knowledge of a Process

Items relevant to a voluntary-muscle-capability objective require students to attempt some sort of work that involves a process (e.g., executing a leg lift or pushing buttons in response to a colored light). Students' performances on these items will be influenced by how well they know the steps in the process (i.e., a cognitive skill). For example:

VIGNETTE 6.14

To test students' chest strength, Mr. Ascione records the maximum weight that each bench presses. Using excellent technique, bringing the bar up evenly in a concentrated thrust, Devon benches 160 pounds for his record. Barely managing to balance the bar without dropping it, Richard obtains a record of 110 pounds. However, after some knowledge-of-a-process instruction on technique and several days of practice, Richard's record improves to 185. Devon never benches more than 165.

The processes students are required to use for voluntary-muscle-capability items should be taught and practiced before the items are administered for purposes of making summative or formative evaluations.

Fluctuating Physical Conditions

Students' performances on voluntary-muscle-capability items are influenced by variable physical conditions (e.g., fatigue, warm-up, and food in the stomach). To avoid such fluctuating factors from contaminating measurement reliability, care should be taken so that repeated administrations of the items occur under comparable conditions (e.g., when students have had similar amounts of rest and warm-up).

Equipment and Environment

The type and condition of equipment used in voluntary-muscle-capability items can influence students' performances. Even room temperature and time of day can have a major impact. Thus, comparable equipment and testing conditions should be similar for all administrations of the same item.

Repeatable Measurements

Unlike many cognitive and affective items, the same students can be administered voluntary-muscle-capability items repeatedly without contaminating measurement validity. Test security is no concern for psychomotor tests as it is for most cognitive and affective tests. Students' performance on a psychomotor item cannot be enhanced by their prior knowledge of the item.

Caution

The design and administration of a voluntary-muscle-capability item should include safeguards against injuries and accidents. For example, unless the bent-leg sit-ups are properly executed, a danger of back injuries exists to students taking the abdominal-muscle-endurance item in the section "Measuring Endurance." Again, a knowledge of anatomy and kinesiology, as well as an understanding of the safe operation of equipment, is critical.

ITEMS RELEVANT TO ACHIEVEMENT OF ABILITY-TO-PERFORM-A-SPECIFIC-SKILL OBJECTIVES

Execution

Please reread the sections entitled "Ability to Perform a Specific Skill" and "Knowledge, Affective, and Psychomotor Components of the Process" beginning on pages 60 and 254, respectively. The item shown in Figure 6.7 is designed for a knowledge-of-a-process objective. To diagnose why a student performed poorly on that item, as did Alex according to Figure 6.8, it is necessary to measure the following objective:

Manipulate a pencil well enough to follow the steps for printing an uppercase
A (*Psychomotor: ability to perform a specific skill*)

Here is one example of an item designed to be relevant to that objective:

Task presented to the students:
The student is given three pencils, one that marks red, another that marks blue,
and one that marks green. As the student observes, the teacher puts two colored
dots on lined paper as illustrated here and directs the student to draw a straight
red line from the blue dot to the red dot:

· (blue)

(red) .

If the student succeeds in drawing the line segment straight, touching, but not
starting or finishing significantly away from either dot, then the item continues;
otherwise, the item is terminated. The teacher then puts a green dot as follows
and directs the student to draw a straight blue line from the blue dot to the
green dot:

· (blue)

(red) .

· (green)

If this is successful, the student is told to draw a straight green line from the
middle of the red line to the *middle* of the blue line. The teacher points to those
spots and says "middle," but immediately removes the finger before the student
begins.

Scoring key:
Check the following as satisfactorily completed:

_____ red line _____ blue line _____ green line

For any unsatisfactory lines, comment and illustrate why.

Focus on Steps in the Process

Ability-to-perform-a-specific-skill objectives are concerned with how well students can execute the steps in a process much like knowledge-of-a-process objectives are concerned with how well they can remember the steps in a process.
Thus, the same principles for focusing knowledge-of-a-process items on the steps
in processes instead of final outcomes are applicable to the design of ability-to-
perform-a-specific-skill objectives. Ability-to-perform-a-specific-skill items are
usually performance observations. Using videotape is particularly useful in the

measurement of ability-to-perform-a-specific skill. Here is an example of an objective and an item designed to measure it:

Objective:
  Properly execute a back dive from a three-meter spring board (*Psychomotor: ability to perform a specific skill*)
Item:
  Task presented to the students:
    The student is directed to perform a back dive from a three-meter springboard. The dive is videotaped.

  Scoring key:
    The observer views the videotape repeatedly to complete the following ranking scale:
      A. Rank the parts of the dive first, second, and third from strongest to weakest:
         _____takeoff _____ turn _____ entry
      B. Rank the parts of the *takeoff* from strongest to weakest:
         _____body position _____ height _____ angle
      C. Rank the parts of the *turn* from stronger to weaker:
         _____body position _____ timing for entering the turn
      D. Rank the parts of the *entry* from strongest to weakest:
         _____timing for stopping turn _____ body position _____ angle

Similarities to Voluntary-Muscle-Capability Items

As with voluntary-muscle-capability items, the following should be kept in mind when designing ability-to-perform-a-specific-skill items: (a) Students' performances on the items are influenced by their achievement of knowledge-of-a-process and willingness-to-act objectives; (b) performances will be influenced by fluctuating physical conditions, type and condition of equipment, and environmental factors; and (c) items are repeatable without fear of contamination to validity.

For an ability-to-perform-a-specific-skill objective, students attempt the same tasks presented by relevant items that they practice for lessons designed to help them achieve the objective.

ITEMS RELEVANT TO ACHIEVEMENT OF APPRECIATION OBJECTIVES

Preferences, Opinions, Desires, and Values

Please reread the section entitled "Appreciation" beginning on page 61. When you teach to a cognitive or psychomotor objective, you are attempting to help students to *be able* to do something. When you teach to an appreciation objective, you are attempting to influence their *preferences for, opinions about*, or *desires for* something. The "something," of course, is specified by the objective's content.

Is Appreciation Measurable?

An item is relevant to achievement of a cognitive or psychomotor objective when students who have achieved the objective can perform the task presented by the item with a higher success rate than those who have not achieved the objective. On the other hand, appreciation objectives are not concerned with students being able to do anything. Achievement of an appreciation objective is the acquisition of a particular attitude. You cannot distinguish students who have achieved an appreciation objective from those that haven't based on what they *can* do, so how is it possible for an item to present a task that's relevant to an appreciation objective? To help yourself answer that question, consider the following objective:

Want to maintain a healthy diet (*Affective: appreciation*)

List the names of four or five people you believe have achieved this objective to a high degree. Make a second list of people who you believe have much lower levels of achievement with respect to this objective. Keep in mind that because the objective specifies "appreciation," not "willingness-to-try," your group of achievers may include persons who don't actually attempt to follow a healthy diet, only wish they would. Some achievers may be at the willingness-to-try level and, thus, try to follow a healthy diet, but don't know how.

For the people in your group of high achievers, list one or two observations you made that influenced you to judge that they want to follow a healthy diet. For the people in your group of low achievers, list one or two observations you made that influenced you to judge that they do not highly value following a healthy diet. Your two lists may be somewhat similar to the following:

Observations Indicating High Achievement:

SANDRA: Frequently mentioned that she ought to diet. Once, before eating junk food, said, "I really shouldn't eat this."

KAY: Often inquired about what she should eat to maintain good health. Read magazine articles on nutrition.

EDDIE: Frequently mentioned that he has to start watching what he eats. Asked, "I haven't had much energy lately; I wonder if it's my diet?"

OTIS: Told someone who was eating junk food, "That stuff'll kill you!" Once said, "People ought to drink more water."

Observations Indicating Low Achievement:

PHIL: Once said, "I don't worry about cholesterol. When you die, you die!" Said, "Eating is for pleasure. If God didn't want us to eat sugar and fat, then he wouldn't have given them to us."

MARION: Never reads or talks about nutrition.

JIM: Said, "Listening to the health nuts makes me think if it tastes good, it's bad, and if it tastes bad, it's good! I don't care what they say, I eat the way I want."

MAVIS: "You don't need to worry about what you eat as long as you exercise."

You are able to identify a list of observable behaviors associated with objective achievement, and one associated with a lack of achievement, thus it is possible for you to design items relevant to the objective. The trick is to confront students with situations in which they have a choice of behaving either like a person who has achieved the objective or like one who has not.

Presenting Choices

The items should present students with tasks to which they choose either a response that's associated with appreciation behavior or a response that's associated with a lack of appreciation. For example:

Task presented to the students:
Do you think people should avoid some foods (even if they taste good) and eat others (even if they taste bad)? Check one:

_____ Yes   _____ No

Scoring key: +1 for "Yes" only; 0 otherwise

Task presented to the students:
Sugar-Fizz is a new candy that is being sold in grocery stores. Here are some facts about Sugar-Fizz:
   1. It is not poisonous.
   2. It is not known to cause any fatal diseases.
   3. It has no nutritional value.
   4. There is some evidence that it sometimes lowers the body's resistance to some infections.
Johnny is 14 years old, has no health problem, has never tasted Sugar-Fizz, and has heard it tastes delicious. What should Johnny do? Check only one answer:
_____ A. Eat it whenever he wants, but stop if he gets sick.
_____ B. Try it, but not often.
_____ C. Never even try Sugar-Fizz.
_____ D. Eat it whenever he desires it.

Scoring key:
   (3 points possible) +3 for either "B" or "C" only; +1 for "A" only; 0 for "D."

The Direct Approach

The first of the two items just listed is quite direct. To test if students appreciate something, just ask them. The direct approach is best for situations where students are confident that they risk nothing by answering honestly. Fortunately, you may only want to measure your students' achievement of affective objectives for purposes of formative, not summative, evaluations. Unfortunately, many students have been conditioned to think that teachers only evaluate to grade them. Consequently, you will need to make a concerted effort to teach them when it's "safe" to provide you with honest answers to affective items.

The Indirect Approach

In Vignette 6.15, the teacher uses an indirect approach to measuring achievement of an appreciation objective:

VIGNETTE 6.15

Objective I of Ms. Parino's second-grade citizenship unit is:

Want classmates to succeed in their efforts to learn (*Affective: appreciation*)

Ms. Parino considers using the direct approach and using an item that simply asks, "Do you want your classmates to learn how to do the math we cover in class?" However, she feels such an item won't work for two reasons: (a) The question is ambiguous and would be interpreted differently by different students; (b) Students would try to say what they think she wants them to say.

Consequently, she uses an indirect approach to item design and enters the following into the item pool for Objective I:

Task presented to the students:
(The student is supplied with an audiotape player containing a cassette on which the directions for the item is recorded.) The student is instructed to circle either "Yes" or "No" by each letter on the following answer sheet according to the directions on the cassette:

A. Yes   No
B. Yes   No
C. Yes   No
D. Yes   No
E. Yes   No
F. Yes   No
G. Yes   No

Following is the script on the cassette:
"Things can happen that make us feel happy and sad at the same time. But some things make us only happy or only sad. I'm going to ask you to pretend something and ask you some questions about why you feel happy or sad about what you pretended. [pause] Pretend you are playing third base during a gym class softball game. The other team is batting and their batter strikes out. Does seeing the batter strike out make you feel happy because it will not help your team win? Answer by circling 'Yes' or 'No' next to 'A' on your answer sheet. [pause] Does seeing the batter strike out make you feel sad because it will not help their team win? Circle 'Yes' or 'No' next to 'B.' [pause] Does seeing the batter strike out make you happy because the pitcher for your team did well? Circle 'Yes' or 'No' next to 'C.' [pause] Does seeing the batter strike out make you feel happy because it will make the other team feel sad? Circle 'Yes' or 'No' next to 'D.' [pause] Does seeing the batter strike out make you feel sad because the batter will feel sad? Circle 'Yes' or 'No' next to 'E.' [pause] Does seeing the batter strike out make you feel sad because the game will soon be over? Circle 'Yes' or 'No' next to 'F.' [pause] Does seeing the batter strike out make you feel happy because the batter will feel sad? Circle 'Yes' or 'No' next to 'G.' [pause]"

(continued)

VIGNETTE 6.15 (continued)

Scoring key:
(2 points possible) If the student circled "Yes" for "A" and "No" for "B," then continue scoring the item. Otherwise, do not score the item as it appears the student did not understand the directions. Score +1 for each of the following that is marked "Yes" only: "C" and "E." Score −1 for each of the following that is marked "Yes" only: "D" and "G."

Ms. Parino realizes that this item alone cannot provide much of an indication of students' standings with respect to the objective. However, she thinks that if she draws on a wide variety of situations (e.g., softball, language arts, and the science project) to design and administer several similar items, patterns might emerge from students' responses that indicate progress toward the objective.

ITEMS RELEVANT TO ACHIEVEMENT OF WILLINGNESS-TO-TRY OBJECTIVES

Choosing Behaviors

Please reread the section entitled "Willingness-to-Try" beginning on page 61. Students achieve a willingness-to-try objective by choosing to behave in accordance with a value specified by the objective's content. Although they may lack certain cognitive or psychomotor skills to actually effect the behavior, students achieve the willingness-to-try objective by *attempting tasks*. Here's an example:

VIGNETTE 6.16

Chris' teacher includes the following objective for his class:

Attempt to follow a healthy diet (*Affective: willingness to try*)

Chris is convinced of the value of a good diet and eats according to what he thinks is good for him. However, having yet to achieve some of the cognitive objectives of his teacher's health unit, Chris mistakenly believes that because fat is stored energy, he will gain energy by eating a lot of animal fats. In his enthusiasm for maintaining a healthy diet, Chris makes a concerted effort to consume large quantities of animal fats.

Chris achieved the objective listed in the example because he *acted* on his beliefs about nutritious diets.

Is Willingness to Try Measurable?

Willingness-to-try objectives require students to take some sort of observable action, not only to embrace unseen values, thus they are usually easier to measure than appreciation objectives. Willingness-to-try items are designed similarly to appreciation items. For example:

VIGNETTE 6.17

Mr. Clemente is embarking on a new school year as a junior high social studies teacher. He plans to use a number of learning activities in which students work with partners on projects. One of his long-range goals is for students to increase their interest in reading about social studies topics, so he wants to plan some of the projects so that the more enthusiastic readers are teamed with students who dislike reading. He hopes some of the enthusiastic students' interest in reading will "rub off" on the others. To implement his plan, he needs to assess his students' interest in reading so he'll know whom to team together. Mr. Clemente is not concerned with identifying the more skilled readers, but rather those that enjoy and advocate reading. Thus, he wants to devise items relevant to the following objective:

> Choose to read and express the merits of reading to others (*Affective: willingness to act*)

To begin devising items, he thinks about persons (not necessarily students) whom he considers avid readers and reading advocates. He also thinks of some he believes dislike reading. Asking himself what he's observed about these people to classify them as he did, he develops the following lists of observable behaviors characterizing the two groups:

Observations Indicating High Achievement
1. speak about literary works they've read, are reading, or plan to read
2. when confronted with problems, refer to reading material as solution sources
3. frequent libraries, book stores, and magazine stands
4. recommend reading selections to their friends
5. often seen reading

Observations Indicating Low Achievement
1. complain about the length of readings assigned in school
2. when confronted with problems, seek solution sources that do not require reading
3. when given the option of going to the library or to some other comparable place, do not go to the library
4. while spending time in a waiting room (e.g., in a physician's office) do not pick up available reading materials.

Mr. Clemente builds several items from these lists.

Observing Behaviors

Items can place students in a situation where they have the choice of either behaving like they are willing to try regarding the objective's content or like they are unwilling. Mr. Clemente, for example, developed the following item for the objective listed in Vignette 6.17:

Task presented to the students:
   (Students are directed to wait outside the guidance counselor's office where a variety of books and magazines are prominently displayed)

Scoring key:
An unobtrusive observer in the waiting room uses a watch and makes notes to record the number of minutes students spent:
A. waiting for the counselor
B. looking at, thumbing through, or holding magazines or books, but not actually reading
C. appearing to be reading
Score for the item =

$$2\left(\frac{\text{number of minutes for ``C''}}{\text{number of minutes for ``A''}}\right) + \left(\frac{\text{number of minutes for ``B''}}{\text{number of minutes for ``A''}}\right)$$

The difficulty of this item can be manipulated by varying the interest levels of the reading matter available in the guidance counselor's waiting area. For an easy item, sports, music, video, and teenage magazines would be available. For a hard item, only low-interest reading material would be available.

Inferring Behaviors

Willingness-to-try items (e.g., the previous one) that depend on direct observation of behaviors often lack usability. Thus, items must often be designed that can be incorporated into a usable questionnaire for students to complete. Instead of directly observing the behaviors specified by the objectives, students are asked how they would behave or have behaved in some relevant situations. For example, here is a multiple-choice item relevant to the objective given in vignette 6.17:

Task presented to the students:
Suppose that you find out that next week you will be meeting a visitor from Mexico. You would like to know more about life in Mexico before visiting with this person. Which one of the following would you *most* likely do?
Circle one and only one:
A. Watch the travel channel on television in hopes that you'd see a program about Mexico.
B. Read about Mexico in an atlas.
C. Look up Mexico in an encyclopedia.
D. Phone a travel agent and ask about life in Mexico.
E. Go to the library and ask the reference librarian about Mexico.
F. Wait for the visitor from Mexico to arrive and ask the visitor.
G. Go to the library and look up some references in the card catalog.

Scoring key:
+1 for any one of the following: "B," "C," or "G"; 0 otherwise

Items (e.g., the previous one) for willingness-to-try objectives that do not depend on direct observations are of little value unless they are used along with other similar items that present a variety of situations. As with appreciation items with an indirect approach, a number of items are needed to identify patterns that indicate students' attitudes.

The difficulty of these items can be manipulated by varying the attractiveness of the alternatives. Students, for example, are more likely to select a reading activity over watching a movie if it's a movie they consider boring rather than exciting.

SELF-ASSESSMENT EXERCISES FOR CHAPTER 6

I. Examine each of the following teacher activities and categorize it as either a (a) *formative evaluation*, (b) *summative evaluation*, or (c) *measurement*:
   A. During an independent work session, Ms. Staller sees Robin use a calculator.
   B. Ms. Staller decides to allocate 10 minutes of class time in an intellectual-level questioning/discussion session.
   C. Ms. Staller compiles Illona's score on a test by adding her item scores.
   D. Ms. Staller assigns a letter grade to Illona's test score.
   E. While conducting an inductive lesson, Ms. Staller decides against using a particular example she had planned to include.
   F. Ms. Staller becomes disappointed in Lee's progress to this point in language arts. Compare your answers to these: "B" and "E" are examples of formative evaluations, "D" and "F" summative evaluations, and "A" and "C" measurements.

II. Select the one response to each of the following multiple-choice items that either completes the statement so that it is true or accurately answers the question:
   A. Anytime teachers evaluate student achievement, they _____.
      a. make value judgments
      b. use valid measurements
      d. base results on unit test results
      d. determine better ways of teaching
   B. According to the quote in the section "Common Malpractice," Stiggins (1988) suggested that _____.
      a. all tests emphasize knowledge-level achievement
      b. the cognitive levels at which students are tested tend to limit the cognitive levels at which they learn
      c. commercially produced tests are superior to teacher-produced tests
      d. valid and usable measures of student achievement are virtually impossible to design
   C. Which one of the following is *not* a measurement?
      a. seeing what a student writes on the board
      b. administering a unit test
      c. seeing that Jennifer is unable to complete one of the tasks in an exercise
      d. hearing Jennifer say, "I can't do these."
      e. seeing that Jennifer does not have the correct response to an exercise written on her paper
   D. Which one of the following is a *necessary* condition for measurement relevance?
      a. usability
      b. validity
      c. pertinence to the stated learning levels
      d. internal consistency
   E. Which one of the following is a *sufficient* condition for measurement relevance?
      a. usability
      b. validity
      c. pertinence to the stated learning levels
      d. internal consistency

F. Which one of the following is a *necessary* condition for measurement reliability?
    a. pertinence to the intended content
    b. relevance
    c. usability
    d. scorer consistency

G. Which one of the following is a *sufficient* condition for measurement reliability?
    a. internal and scorer consistency
    b. internal or scorer consistency
    c. usability and relevance
    d. usability or relevance

H. Which one of the following is a *sufficient* condition for a measurement to be a valuable data-gathering tool?
    a. relevance, reliability, and validity
    b. relevance, reliability, and usability
    c. usability, internal consistency, and pertinence to the intended content

I. Which one of the following modifications to an item is most likely to increase the item's scorer consistency?
    a. provide greater latitude for the scorer to use professional judgment
    b. change the format from multiple-choice to essay
    c. make the rules in the scoring key more specific
    d. raise the learning level to which the item is relevant from knowledge to intellectual

J. If a test has been *standardized*, then _____.
    a. it is valid, but may not be usable because of its cost
    b. its reliability has been assessed
    c. it is reliable
    d. it can only be depended on to measure knowledge-level achievement

K. Which one of the following measurement variables depends on the stated purpose of the measurement?
    a. internal consistency
    b. scorer consistency
    c. relevance
    d. usability

L. Which one of the following measurement variables depends on the time it takes to administer a test?
    a. internal consistency
    b. scorer consistency
    c. relevance
    d. usability

M. The value of having *hard* items on a test is to measure the achievement of ____.
    a. less advanced students
    b. more advanced students
    c. intellectual-level objectives
    d. knowledge-level objectives
    e. affective objectives

N. The value of having *easy* items on a test is to measure the achievement of ____.
    a. less advanced students
    b. more advanced students
    c. intellectual-level objectives
    d. knowledge-level objectives
    e. affective objectives

O. It takes an effort to organize and computerize item pools, but once an item pool file is established _____.

    a. test validity is assured

    b. item design requires less creativity on the part of teacher

    c. all test items are selected randomly, thus, decreasing item bias

    d. test construction is less time consuming for the teacher

P. Generally speaking, designing items for affective objectives is easiest for which one of the following situations?

    a. Students realize their achievement of the objectives is to be assessed for formative feedback only—not for summative evaluations

    b. Students realize their achievement of the objectives is to be assessed for summative evaluations only—not for formative feedback

    c. The objectives are at the *appreciation* rather than at the *willingness-to-try* level

Q. Mr. Matsumota has just inserted a moderately difficult item into his pool for a particular comprehension-level objective. Now, as he attempts to design a hard item for that objective, he thinks, "I'll make this one more difficult by putting in a task that'll require inductive thinking." What reminder do you think Mr. Matsumota needs to hear?

    a. Items requiring inductive reasoning are difficult to design.

    b. Items requiring inductive reasoning are not necessarily more difficult than items requiring only comprehension; the subject matter content also makes a difference.

    c. Items requiring inductive reasoning are normally relevant to conceptualization objectives, not comprehension objectives

R. Out of concern for his students' abilities to read books and articles about science, Mr. Matsumota includes an objective for his students to remember definitions of certain scientific terms in most of his teaching units. During the course he plans to build their reading vocabulary of scientific words. One item he intends to be relevant to one of those objectives is the following:

Task presented to the students:

    Fill in the missing word:

        _____ refers to the force of attraction between the earth and objects.

    Scoring key: +1 for "gravity" only; 0 otherwise

Which one of the following is a weakness of the item?

    a. *Gravity* is not a scientific term.

    b. The item reverses the stimulus–response order of the objective.

    c. The item requires only simple-knowledge cognition.

S. An item with a scoring key designed to reflect which steps in a computation students do or do not remember is most likely to be relevant to which one of the following types of objectives?

    a. simple knowledge

    b. knowledge of a process

    c. application

    d. willingness to try

T. According to the section "Items Relevant to Achievement of Application Objectives," why should at least some items designed to test students' achievement of an *application* objective that specifies the Tenth Amendment to the Constitution confront students with situations in which that amendment does not apply?

    a. The Tenth Amendment is concerned only with rights of individual states; students have broader concerns.

    b. Learning about the first nine amendments is prerequisite to learning about the tenth.

    c. Students need to learn about all aspects of government at the application level, not only the Tenth Amendment.

    d. Achievement of an application objective requires students to discriminate between problems to which the specified content does and doesn't apply.

  U. For items to be relevant to a *creativity* objective, they must _____.

    a. have a scoring key that discriminates between atypical and typical responses

    b. require students to produce a novel product

    c. present students with tasks never previously accomplished

    d. provide students with opportunities for convergent thinking

  Compare your responses to the following A-a, B-b, C-c, D-c, E-b, F-d, G-a, H-b, I-c, J-b, K-c, L-d, M-b, N-a, O-d, P-a, Q-c, R-b, S-b, T-d, U-a.

III. Organize a system for maintaining item pools. Either set up the file from existing software, write the program yourself, or utilize word-processing files to set it up.

IV. In your response to Exercises III and II of the self-assessment exercises for Chapters 2 and 3, respectively, you defined a learning goal with a set of objectives. For *each one* of those objectives, begin developing an item pool by designing at least three items. Make sure that you include both the "task presented to the students" and "scoring key" components of each item.

SUGGESTED READING

ABOUT VALIDITY AND VALIDATING MEASUREMENTS

Cangelosi, J. S. (1982). *Measurement and evaluation: An inductive approach for teachers* (pp. 243–340). Dubuque, IA: Brown.

Thorndike, R. M., Cunningham, G. K., Thorndike, R. L., & Hagen, E. P. (1991). *Measurement and evaluation in psychology and education* (5th ed., pp. 90–156). New York: Macmillan.

ABOUT DESIGNING TESTS

Cangelosi, J. S. (1990b). *Designing tests for evaluating student achievement* (pp. 41–177). New York: Longman.

Ebel, R. L., & Frisbie, D. A. (1986). *Essentials of educational measurement* (pp. 126–201). Englewood Cliffs, NJ: Prentice-Hall.

Tuckman, B. W. (1988). *Testing for teachers* (2nd ed., pp. 51–124). San Diego, CA: Harcourt Brace Jovanovich.

ABOUT INTERPRETING STANDARDIZED TESTS

Cangelosi, J. S. (1990b). *Designing tests for evaluating student achievement* (pp. 178–195). New York: Longman.

Hills, J. R. (1986). *All of Hill's handy hints*. Washington, DC: National Council on Measurement in Education.

Hopkins, K. D., Stanley, J. C., & Hopkins, B. R. (1990). *Educational and psychological measurement and evaluation* (7th ed., pp. 389–481). Englewood Cliffs, NJ: Prentice-Hall.

ABOUT GRADING AND REPORTING

Cangelosi, J. S. (1990b). *Designing tests for evaluating student achievement* (pp. 196–212). New York: Longman.

Gronlund, N. E., & Linn, R. L. (1990) *Measurement and evaluation in teaching* (6th ed., pp. 427–452). New York: Macmillan.

ABOUT EVALUATING TEACHING

Cangelosi, J. S. (1991). *Evaluating classroom instruction*. New York: Longman.
Medley, D. M., Coker, H., & Soar, R. S. (1984). *Measurement-based evaluation of teacher performance: An empirical approach*. New York: Longman.

TAKING WHAT YOU'VE LEARNED TO THE NEXT LEVEL

From your work with Chapter 1 you reflected on the complex art and science of teaching. You formulated ideas for developing curricula consistent with research-based teaching/learning principles. With Chapter 2, you learned to direct your lessons by defining learning goals with objectives. With Chapter 3 you learned how to apply research-based principles for designing lessons according to the type of content and learning level specified by a given objective. You examined ways of managing student behavior and engaging students in various types of learning activities from your work in Chapters 4 and 5. With Chapter 6, you gained ideas and techniques for assessing what students learned from your lessons.

Now, to help you put all of this together into a coherent package that is practical in the reality of today's schools, turn to Chapters 7 and 8. Chapter 7 follows the experiences, thoughts, practices, disappointments, and successes of Dustin Manda as he embarks on, engages in, and completes his first year as an elementary school teacher. Chapter 8 follows a similar pattern with a first year high school teacher, Nancy Fisher. Like you, Mr. Manda and Ms. Fisher studied Chapters 1–6 of this text, and now they are discovering how to put what they learned into practice during their initial experiences in a difficult, but exciting profession.

CHAPTER 7

Theory into Practice:
Dustin Manda, First-Year
Elementary School Teacher

GOAL OF CHAPTER 7

This chapter walks you through Dustin Manda's first year as an elementary school teacher as he learns to put research-based principles and techniques into practice. Chapter 7 will help you

1. anticipate and describe examples of the types of events and problems you are likely to confront while meeting your responsibilities as a teacher in school (*Cognitive: conceptualization*)
2. explain how to integrate the various aspects of instruction (i.e., designing courses, organizing for a school year, managing a classroom, developing teaching units, managing student behavior, engaging students in learning activities, and assessing student achievement) within the role of a professional school teacher during the course of a school year (*Cognitive: application*)
3. given a realistic role description for a teacher in a school, formulate and explain alternative ways of fulfilling that role in a manner consistent with the suggestions in Chapters 1–6 of this text (*Cognitive: application*)

DUSTIN MANDA AND HIS FIRST TEACHING POSITION

Preservice Preparation

Dustin Manda is embarking on his initial year as a professional teacher. Having recently graduated from college with a major in elementary education, he successfully completed scores of courses in the arts and sciences (including mathematics, biology, physical science, art, literature, music, history, and sociology). There were also courses in child psychology, educational psychology, health and physical education, general teaching methods (which used this textbook), special methods in different subject matter areas (e.g., reading, language arts, art, mathematics, social studies, and science), behavior management, special education, measurement and evaluation, and instructional technology. Most of the professional education courses included field-based experiences providing opportunities to work with students in public schools.

He tried out many of the ideas from the coursework in a semester-long student teaching practicum. However, as a student teacher, Dustin tailored his teaching style to the curriculum already established by his cooperating teacher. The cooperating teacher was very supportive of his efforts and immensely helpful in providing learning materials and suggestions for managing behavior and organizing lessons. But opportunities to design complete units were quite limited as he was not involved in planning the courses prior to the opening of the school year.

Although confident in his knowledge of content and pedagogical theory, he worries that he lacks the conceptualization-level and application-level understanding necessary to generate the examples and nonexamples that will engage his students in the kind of learning activities explained in Chapter 3 of this textbook. While enthusiastic about beginning his professional career, Dustin is understandably nervous about succeeding with a full complement of students for which he is solely responsible.

Selecting a Position at Eugene Street Elementary School

Prior to graduation, Dustin discovered that there was considerable demand for persons with his qualifications to work in elementary schools. Opportunities for positions were abundant although not necessarily for the grade level and locations he desired. After interviewing for six positions, and being offered four, he decided to join the faculty of Eugene Street Elementary School as a first-grade teacher. The decision was influenced by such variables as salary, teaching assignment, location, reputation, philosophy, personnel, and administrative style. To assess these variables, he had carefully read literature provided by school district personnel offices, read curriculum guides, counseled with trusted faculty from his college, carefully listened and raised questions at formal interviews with district personnel officials and school administrators, and sought out and conversed informally with potential faculty colleagues. Among his reasons for favoring Eugene Street School were the following:

> He was impressed by the apparent competence and dedication of some of the teachers he met, especially Rita Slater, who seemed quite willing to work cooperatively with him.
>
> Both Rosalie Taylor, primary grade department chairperson, and Principal Ebony Maggio spoke as if the welfare of students is their first priority and the opinions of the faculty are both sought and utilized. They portrayed the attitude reflected in Ms. Maggio's words, "Teachers are here to help students. Administrators and supervisors are here to help teachers help students."
>
> Eugene Street School has a program of instructional and administrative supervision in which all teachers have professional responsibilities to evaluate their own instruction and that of other teachers. (For an extensive treatise on evaluating classroom instruction for purposes of both administrative and instructional supervision see Cangelosi, 1991.)

Many of the clerical and mundane tasks he would be responsible for at other schools where he interviewed (e.g., monitoring the lunch room, bus duty, and collecting lunch fees) are carried out by Eugene Street's staff and paraprofessional personnel.

Although he had imagined himself teaching second or third grade, the assignment to a first-grade class was more in line with his professional goals than teaching upper elementary grades. The other schools offered him positions teaching fifth or sixth grade.

The Assignment

Instructional Responsibilities. When being interviewed for the position, the instructional responsibilities of the position were explained to Dustin by Principal Ebony Maggio. Now it's mid-July, Dustin has already signed his contract as a first-year teacher with "probationary" status (the term this local school district uses for teachers who have not yet received tenure—usually awarded after their third year in the system). Ebony reviews and details the assignment with Dustin:

EBONY: You have total responsibility for one of our three first-grade classes. We designate our class sections by room number; yours is "113." We used to refer to first-grade "A," "B," and "C," but too many people thought that implied some sort of leveling. Then we tried some cutesy names like "the iguanas," but people read all kinds of things into that—including that we were encouraging gangs. Room numbers seem to be as innocuous as we can get.

DUSTIN: You said in the interview that there's no interclass grouping—students are randomly assigned to classes.

EBONY: Yes, you'll have quite a heterogeneous mix. Occasionally, we'll place a student in a particular class if there's some history indicating that the student will work with one teacher better than another, but that's rare. Mostly, we try to keep class sizes about the same and maintain heterogeneity in each class. When we make a special placement, it's a cooperative decision of all the teachers in the relevant department—in your case the primary grade department.

DUSTIN: You said before I should expect between 18 and 24 students.

EBONY: The rolls won't be finalized until the end of the first week, but right now I think you'll have just over 20. We don't allow first grades larger than 24; that's district policy we pushed through six years ago. . . . I want to get back to this grouping business. You're free to establish whatever intra-class grouping patterns that can be justified. Personally, I like flexible grouping—heavy doses of cooperative learning activities in which the subgroup membership changes for different purposes. But you're in charge and you do what you think is best; just make sure you have a sound rationale for your decisions. I don't think any of us can ask ourselves often enough, 'Why am I doing this?' . . .

DUSTIN: What about the schedule—when I teach what and so forth?

EBONY: That's up to you. The only parameters are that you address the minimum standards for each subject area or course—reading, mathematics, writing and speech, social studies, health and physical education, art and music, and science—that's laid out in the district curriculum guide for the first grade. Also, your class has to be in the lunch room at a designated time. Otherwise, the schedule—even recesses for your class—is up to you. Just be able to articulate a rationale for what you decide.

Dustin: I went through the curriculum guide quite carefully. It's not very detailed. Pretty standard stuff like, "The first-grade student will understand base-10 numeration." There's nothing revolutionary in that document—what I'd expect to do anyway. The only thing that bothers me about the guide is that it makes content seem so fragmented. The standards for different courses, which are really learning goals, seem so isolated from one another.

Ebony: I'm not bothered by the fact that the reading, mathematics, science, and other course goals are fragmented in the curriculum guide document because I know the teachers will help their students achieve them using integrative lessons.

Dustin: That's a relief! I plan to integrate the courses so that my students won't clearly distinguish whether at any given moment they're engaged in a science, reading, art, or whatever activity. But in my mind, I've got my objectives clearly delineated so I know what's being targeted in each area. . . . I was afraid, you or some district-level supervisor would walk in my room and worry that what you or the supervisor saw wasn't clearly mathematics or art or whatever was in the curriculum guide.

Ebony: Our philosophy here is that teachers are most effective when they're left to their own devices to organize and teach as they think best—just as long as what they do is professionally tenable and students are making progress toward goals consistent with the curriculum guidelines.

Dustin: You mentioned before that there's a reading resource specialist that would be working with me and some of the other teachers. Won't I have to coordinate at least my reading program with her?

Ebony: Not in a restrictive sense. We're fortunate to have Florence Rice working with all our primary teachers because, as I might have mentioned before, we serve quite a few students from so-called "low-income" communities. Florence's position is paid for from a federal grant for schools that serve such communities. She's here as a *resource* for you and other teachers. She's not here to look over your shoulder, but for you to call on to provide information, ideas, and to help with some of the particularly difficult diagnostic problems in the reading area.

Dustin: And then there's a special education resource person.

Ebony: Actually there are several that serve us and two of our sister schools. You'll probably work mostly with Leonard Socerelli who works with learning-disabled children. How much you need these people will depend on the different special children you have mainstreamed in your class—also on any diagnostic work you request for students you suspect could benefit from special education services.

Dustin: There seems to be more for me to understand that I can absorb right now.

Ebony: You'll be receiving more information between now and the end of August—especially during the faculty orientation sessions. But frankly, it gets so complex that our teachers really learn about this stuff throughout the year—as needs arise.

Dustin: I guess so. Teaching isn't brain surgery; it's a lot more complex.

Other Responsibilities. Besides teaching Dustin is expected to:

take care of some administrative chores related to his class and classroom (e.g., accounting for learning materials and maintaining the student register required by the district office)

serve as a general supervisor of students during school hours, enforcing school rules

assist in the governance of the school by responding to administrators' re-

quests for input and participating in both general faculty and primary department meetings

cooperate in the school's system for both administrative supervision and
instructional supervision of his own teaching and that of other teachers

participate in professional development activities (e.g., by attending inservice
workshops, taking college courses, and being involved in organizations
such as the local affiliate of the Association of Childhood Education, National Association for the Education of Young Children, International
Reading Association, or National Education Association)

represent Eugene Street School as a professional in the community

ORGANIZING FOR THE YEAR

The Givens as of July 15

With the opening day of school about five weeks away, Dustin gets his first look
at room 113. He thinks, "Seven computer stations and three printers for 20 or
so students—I can live with that. But I'll also need one exclusively for myself.
Ebony said I would have access to computers in the faculty work room, but I
can't operate without my own. She said each department also had its own allot-
ment of computers for students' use. I'll check with Rosalie to see if I can get
one more. . . . In any case, I've got some major rearranging to do before this
room is ready for me."

Later that day, Primary Department Chair and kindergarten teacher Rosalie
Taylor and first-grade teacher Rita Slater arrive in room 113 with sets of adopted
curriculum materials for Dustin:

DUSTIN: That's quite a load you've got there. Is all that for me?

ROSALIE: These are your copies of the materials for teachers that go along with the
adopted textbooks for first grade. . . . This is the teacher's kit for the Addison-
Wesley science series we adopted for kindergarten through third grade several
years ago. It has both a teacher's and student edition of the text (Barman, Leyden,
DiSpezio, Mercier, Guthrie, & Ostlund, 1989), blackline masters, transparencies,
idea maps, teacher's edition of a couple of workbooks, activity report pad, unit
posters, science skills guide for teachers, professional information bulletins, and
an outdoor education guide. That takes care of your science course. . . . Now,
for language arts, including reading, we've really got two series here. Why we
have two series is a long story I won't bother you with now, but it leaves you
with one of those 'good-news/bad-news' situations. First, we have this *Changes*
set that has three student books, *Reader's Corner, Writer's Corner,* and *Activity
Book* (Harcourt Brace Jovanovich, 1989). It's a combination reading, writing,
speaking program. . . . Then we've got this Macmillan *Language Arts Today* kit,
it's got quite a bit in here—an audiotape, games, blackline masters, . . . and here's
the text for the students (McCallum, Strong, Thoburn, & Williams, 1990). It's
language arts, but doesn't include a specific reading program so we supplement
it with individual reading books—works out very well.

DUSTIN: What's the "good-bad-news" business?

ROSALIE: The good news is having two different sets of materials to draw from.

RITA: The bad news is we don't have one complete set of student texts for your whole
class. You've got about a dozen of each.

DUSTIN: So, if I have three reading groups, one could be in one program while two are in the other?

RITA: That's one way of doing it. All the student material is duplicable except for the textbooks. You just won't be able to have everyone concurrently doing an assignment out of the same text. If it causes you any real problems, I use *Language Arts Today* with supplemental readers in my class. Martin uses *Changes* in the other first grade; you and I might do some book trading for different activities. But I can't speak for Martin.

DUSTIN: What's the long story?

ROSALIE: It's three-year-old politics.

RITA: It's water under the bridge you don't want to bother with right now—someday over lunch.

DUSTIN: Okay, what else do you have for me?

ROSALIE: Here's your art text (Chapman, 1987) and this *Primary Social Studies Skills* (Nystrom, 1989) has some teacher materials that I've got to locate for you. And here's a teacher's and a student's edition of the math text (Houghton Mifflin, 1991).

DUSTIN: What about mathematical manipulatives and other hands-on materials?

ROSALIE: I'm not sure what we'll have in the budget this year for that, probably in the neighborhood of about two hundred dollars per teacher. Teachers keep their own things, but there's some odds and ends you can find in the storeroom. It's first come, first serve.

RITA: I can help you out in that department. I've got quite a bit we can share.

DUSTIN: Thanks. I've accumulated some stuff; you're welcome to that also. . . . One thing keeps worrying me—I mentioned this to Ebony the other day. I'm familiar with some of these adopted materials and there's an awful lot of good stuff in them. They're really well organized and everything, but following through with each program as it's laid out in these books and kits is going to dictate against the kind of integrated curriculum I had in mind.

ROSALIE: Integrating math with reading with science and all that is great theory, just like inductive teaching. But for these kids' sake, we need to stick with these packaged programs so there's continuity from grade to grade. If we all started doing our own things, kids could never transfer between schools or even from, say, your class to Rita's or Martin's. The second-grade teachers wouldn't know where to pick up when students show up from different first-grade teachers. That's why the primary grade department has adopted the same series for each course for kindergarten through grade three.

RITA: Except for reading and language arts.

ROSALIE: Well that's another story. Also, I wish we could get the upper grade department to use the same series we do. That way, students could follow the same programs from kindergarten through fifth grade, and maybe even into middle school.

Advice from a Colleague

After Rosalie leaves, Rita continues the conversation with Dustin:

RITA: You look a little discouraged.

DUSTIN: It doesn't look like I have as much flexibility developing curricula as my conversation with Ebony led me to believe.

RITA: You probably don't, but you've got a lot more freedom to do your thing than Rosalie suggests.

DUSTIN: Say more words.

RITA: You can use any combination of these adopted materials any way you think best as long as students are progressing toward the goals in the curriculum guidelines and your methods can be defended as professionally acceptable.

DUSTIN: Now you sound like Ebony.

RITA: But, this is your first year as a full-time teacher. It's likely to be the most difficult year of your career, but you're going to learn more than you ever imagined possible. Excuse me, I don't mean to be preaching to you, but you did say, "say more words," and I trust that you'll pick and choose from what I'm saying just like you should from Rosalie, Ebony, and anybody else who shares ideas.

DUSTIN: Okay, if you'll share freely, I promise not to blindly swallow what you say.

RITA: Thanks. In this your first year as a teacher; be conservative and gradually try out your ideas. Start with those things with which you're most confident. If you are confident about how to integrate language arts and mathematics, do so one unit at a time. But if you're unsure about some other things, like integrating music and social studies, hold off until you've gained more experience and become comfortable with what your students can and can't do.

DUSTIN: Are you saying I should do it my way, but tread carefully with experimental ideas?

RITA: Yeah. The easiest thing for you to do is to follow these adopted programs exactly. But that's probably not the best way to teach, at least for you. It may work for Rosalie and some other teachers, but not for you or me. But don't try to teach the "right way" right away! Give yourself some time to develop your talents for teaching the so-called "right way."

DUSTIN: I'm going to spend the next two weeks laying out my overall plan for the year. Do you mind letting me bounce ideas off of you and then critiquing the whole thing when it's done.

RITA: If you hadn't asked, I would've offered. That kind of exchange helps me with my teaching as much as it helps you with yours.

Planning and Organizing the Courses

Unifying Themes. Surrounded by the curriculum materials, the daily time schedule outline shown in Figure 7.1, and the school district calendar, which provides for 180 instructional days including 3 days in the fall and 3 days in the spring for standardized testing, Dustin sits at the computer in room 113 that he's adopted for himself. He ponders the problem of how to integrate content while maintaining enough separation among courses that he can address the curriculum guide's goals and also utilize the adopted texts and programs.

Analyzing various time/course/unit configurations, a climatic moment in his planning occurs when the idea of having periodic themes comes to him. He thinks, "That's it! Every course will focus on a common theme for a week or two at a time. I'll formulate a sequence of topics that would interest the students. The displays in the room and everything would all have something to do with that topic for the week—or maybe the month. . . . Maybe, more time should be spent on some themes than on others. No, I think the period should be the same for all, then the children could anticipate starting and stopping points, that'll lend an

8:30 A.M.	
8:45 A.M.	
9:00 A.M.	
9:15 A.M.	
9:30 A.M.	
9:45 A.M.	
10:00 A.M.	
10:15 A.M.	
10:30 A.M.	
10:45 A.M.	
11:00 A.M.	
11:15 A.M.	
11:30 A.M.	
11:45 A.M.	
12:00 P.M.	
12:15 P.M.	
12:30 P.M.	Lunch and recess
12:45 P.M.	Lunch and recess
1:00 P.M.	Lunch and recess
1:15 P.M.	
1:30 P.M.	
1:45 P.M.	
2:00 P.M.	
2:15 P.M.	
2:30 P.M.	
2:45 P.M.	

Figure 7.1. The Daily Time Frame within Which Dustin Has to Work

air of organization. . . . Whatever the time period is, this'll provide opportunities to integrate across courses without locking me into having to integrate when it isn't practical to do so. Oh, this makes for the perfect compromise between what I think I should do and the concern Rosalie expressed about sticking to the adopted programs. Now I see how I can develop research-based curricula gradually without trying to do too much to soon. That's consistent with Rita's advice. . . . But this is going to take some fancy coordination among the themes and the course units. First I should make a tentative list of themes, but as I do it I should keep the textbook chapters in mind. The mathematics, art, music, and language arts units can be related to almost any theme, but the science and social studies contents are organized around their own themes. I'll look at the sequence of topics from the social studies and science texts. . . . Oh, the reading programs are usually organized into units each focusing on a story that dictates a theme. This may not work out as easily as I first thought!''

Going through chapter titles from the texts stimulates some ideas for themes, but Dustin soon realizes that he's going to have to originate his own theme sequence and just mold the course units to those themes more or less from unit to unit and course to course. He considers a myriad of complex factors that influence his choice of themes and how they should be sequenced. For example, he knows his students represent a wide variety of backgrounds, subcultures, and home environments. He must be careful to select topics that will be of interest to virtually everyone but that will offend hardly anyone. After two more days of thought, he develops the theme sequence for the year that's displayed in Figure 7.2.

Dustin is working with a first-grade class, so he believes the first two weeks must serve as an orientation to the school and the classroom (e.g., establishing rules and procedures and a comfortable, businesslike atmosphere conducive to learning). He wants to immediately involve students in every course during this orientation period. As he developed this theme sequence, he was also developing ideas for the courses and developing titles for units. After several conferences with Rita, he determines some potential grouping and scheduling patterns. Figure 7.3 displays the course unit sequences he formulates during the following week. For each unit he writes a learning goal. However, he only defines the goals for the first two units of each course at this time. Determination of objectives for subsequent goals will depend on his ongoing assessments of student needs. Thus, he plans to specify objectives for each unit one or two weeks before the unit is scheduled to begin.

The Art and Music Course. Dustin decided to include art or music activities every school day but not to designate a daily time slot strictly for this course. Instead he plans to integrate the 19 units listed in Figure 7.3 with units for other courses. Conceiving art and music as modes of communications, the first-graders are to develop their talents to use art and music to illustrate and express what they learn in other courses.

Health and Physical Education. The health and physical education course is organized into the 18 units listed in Figure 7.3. He visualizes drawing on health and physical education problems for conceptualization-level and application-level lessons in mathematics, science, and social studies. In Vignette 5.10, Ms. Bernstein did this in mathematics. For Unit 17 in science, Dustin might raise the question of why they play some team sports in the fall and others in the spring (from health and physical education, units 6, 8, and 13) in an inductive lesson to discover how seasons affect living things. Social studies units on government, peace in the

Figure 7.2. Dustin's Tentative Two-Week Themes to Help Him Integrate His First-Grade Courses

Week	Theme	Week	Theme
1–2	Our School: Eugene Street	19–20	Games
3–4	Where We Live	21–22	Things That Grow
5–6	Friends and Pets	23–24	Birth and Death
7–8	Toys	25–26	Peace
9–10	Wild Animals	27–28	Television
11–12	Our Environment	29–30	Eating and Exercising
13–14	Taking Care of Ourselves	31–32	Technology
15–16	Government	33–34	Looking Back
17–18	Exotic Neighbors	35–36	Looking Forward

Art and Music

1. The Art in Our School
2. The Music in Our School
3. The Art in Our Homes
4. The Music in Our Homes
5. Making Toys
6. Lines That Tell Stories
7. Cutting and Pasting
8. Mixing and Using Colors
9. Music and Art in Nature
10. Drawing People
11. Musical Stories
12. Picture Stories
13. Musical Games
14. Art Games
15. Musical Instruments
16. Choral Singing
17. An Orchestra
18. Happy and Sad Art and Music
19. Our Art and Music Show

Health and Physical Education

1. Playing at Our School
2. Playing for Health at Home
3. Eating for Health
4. Sports Toys
5. Outdoor Recreation
6. Team Sports I
7. How Our Bodies Work I
8. Team Sports II
9. How Our Bodies Work II
10. Fitness Games
11. Growing Up Healthy
12. Things to Avoid
13. Team Sports III
14. Watching Sports on TV
15. Exercising by Ourselves
16. Individual Sports
17. Our Own Olympics I
18. Our Own Olympics II

Mathematics

1. Problem Solving
2. Measuring by Counting
3. Comparisons: $\neq, \approx, >, <, =$
4. Picturing Relationships I
5. Counting and Naming Numbers
6. Multiples
7. Addition on Whole Numbers
8. Subtraction with Whole Numbers
9. Place Value in Addition
10. Place Value in Subtraction
11. Adding Whole Numbers I
12. More about Geometry
13. Adding Whole Numbers II
14. Subtracting Whole Numbers II
15. Numbers between 0 and 1
16. Even More Geometry
17. Picturing Relationships II
18. Geometric Measurements
19. Looking Back
20. Looking Ahead

Reading

1. Reading about School
2. "Get Ready, Get Set, Go!"
3. "Sunny Days" and "I Wonder"
4. "A Place to Live"
5. "The Secret Hiding Place"
6. "I Met a Man"
7. "Teeth, Teeth, Teeth"
8. "Heather's Feathers"
9. "A Boy, a Dog, a Frog"
10. "Toaster Time"
11. "I Wonder Where the Clouds Go" and "Who Has Seen the Wind"
12. "The Little Red Hen and the Grain of Wheat"
13. "The Seasons"
14. "Gilberto and the Wind"
15. "Rainbow Days"
16. "After Supper"
17. "The Gingerbread Man"
18. "The Little Turtle"
19. "The Three Billy Goats Gruff"
20. "What Animals Need"
21. "Where Go the Boats"
22. "Sebastian and the Bee"
23. "Harry the Dirty Dog"
24. "Pets and People"
25. "The Horses"
26. "Okay Everybody!"
27. "The New Baby Calf"
28. "Penguins"
29. "He Bear, She Bear"
30. Looking Back, Looking Forward

(continued)

Figure 7.3. Titles of the Teaching Units Dustin Plans for His First-Grade Courses

Science

1. The Ecology of Our School
2. The Ecology of Your Home
3. Plants
4. How Animals Move
5. How Animals Eat
6. Body Coverings
7. Care of Plants and Animals
8. Comparing Matter
9. Measuring Matter
10. Moving Things
11. Producing Sound
12. Producing Motion
13. Using Machines
14. Rocks
15. Soil
16. Seasons and Weather
17. Seasons and Living Things
18. Our Sun
19. Stars
20. Seeing and Hearing
21. Smelling and Tasting
22. Touching
23. Emotions
24. Inventions
25. Looking Back
26. Looking Forward

Social Studies

1. Our School Community
2. Families
3. Friends
4. Our Neighborhood
5. Our City
6. Government
7. Making Maps
8. Using Maps
9. Our State
10. Our State and Country
11. Other Countries
12. Communities: Birth, Growth, and Death
13. Peace in the World
14. Navigation
15. Communications
16. World Technology
17. Looking Back
18. Looking Forward

Writing and Speaking

1. Listening and Speaking
2. Speaking and Writing
3. Grammar: Sentences
4. Writing: Sentences
5. Grammar: Nouns
6. Writing: A Group Story
7. Grammar: Verbs
8. Writing: A Thank You Letter
9. Grammar: Adjectives
10. Writing: A Paragraph That Describes
11. Grammar: More about Sentences
12. Writing: A Book Report

Figure 7.3. (Continued)

world, and communications (i.e., units 6, 13, and 15) might play on the need to enforce rules, for sportsmanship, and for signals among teammates in team sports.

Mathematics. Because he wanted to emphasize real-life problem solving, Dustin's 20 mathematics units listed in Figure 7.3 don't coincide closely with the textbook's sequence of chapters. Quite confident in his understanding of how mathematics should be taught and in his ability to teach it that way, Dustin plans to deviate from the textbook for many of his conceptualization-level and application-level lessons. He will, however, depend on the text as well as some computer-assisted instruction programs for knowledge-of-a-process lessons and practice exercises.

Leaning heavily on what Rita shared about her own experiences with first-graders, Dustin assumes that by the end of September, he'll have enough diagnostic information on individual students to have them working in three mathematics subgroups similar to Ms. Mills's arrangement in Vignette 5.19. However, although different subgroups may be working on different mathematics units, Dustin plans to have all groups concurrently focusing on the same period theme.

Thus, if at some point, one group is working on Unit 6, a second group on Unit 7, and the third group on Unit 9 and the theme of the time happens to be "Wild Animals," then the first group will do at least some work applying what they're learning about multiples to problems about wild animals while the second relates addition of whole numbers to wild animal problems and the third does the same but for place value in addition.

Reading. Despite, the logistical difficulties posed by not having enough texts for everyone to use at the same time, Dustin decides to follow the *Changes* (Harcourt Brace Jovanovich, 1989) program for reading. After spending the first two weeks with all students working in Unit 1 (see Figure 7.3), he plans to identify three achievement-level groups. All three groups will follow the *Changes* program quite closely, but the pace at which the groups move through the units will vary. He notes that he should continue to collect diagnostic information on individuals and make provisions for reassigning students to groups as warranted by that feedback. Also, he recognizes that all groups are unlikely to matriculate through Unit 29 by the end of the school year; those students will simply get through as many units as reasonably possible. At least one group is likely to complete the sequence ahead of time; he'll develop supplemental units for the advanced group. He does, however, plan to have all students working together on Unit 30 during the final week of school.

Reading and mathematics are the only two courses in which relatively stable grouping patterns will be used.

Science. The 26 science units listed in Figure 7.3 reflect a compromise among attention to the periodic theme sequence, the chapters in the textbook, and the curriculum guidebook goals. Dustin plans to use the text from cover to cover, but to introduce most units by confronting students with problems related to the theme of the moment and to draw on experiences gained in some of the other courses (e.g., refer to one of the stories from the reading text or utilize data collected during health and physical education).

Social Studies. Figure 7.3 lists 18 social studies units. They deviate considerably from the adopted textbook chapter titles. However, he believes his plan still addresses the curriculum guidelines goals.

Writing and Speaking. Although the *Changes* program he's using for the reading courses incorporates writing and speaking activities, Dustin decides to also follow the *Language Arts Today* (McCallum, Strong, Thoburn, & Williams, 1990) program for the writing and speaking course. The 12 units listed in Figure 7.3 reflect that program exactly. Although he anticipates considerable variation among students' writing and speaking achievement levels, he plans to move all students through these units at the same pace. He will individualize by varying assignments within units (e.g., Mr. Fleming's arrangement in Vignette 5.20).

Scheduling the Courses

Based on a rationale similar to the one expressed by Mr. Eicho in Vignette 1.5, Dustin decides to utilize a stable, day-to-day schedule at least for the first half of the school year. Figure 7.4 displays the schedule he determines. He schedules

8:30 A.M.	Community meeting #1
8:45 A.M.	Mathematics (art and music)
9:30 A.M.	Recess
9:40 A.M.	Writing and Speaking (art and music)
10:25 A.M.	Social studies (art and music)
11:00 A.M.	Recess
11:10 A.M.	Science (art and music)
11:55 A.M.	Reading #1 (art and music)
12:30 P.M.	Lunch and recess
1:15 P.M.	Reading #2 (art and music)
1:45 P.M.	Health and physical education (art and music)
2:40 P.M.	Community meeting #2 or individualized work session
3:00 P.M.	Dismissal

Figure 7.4. Dustin's Schedule for His First-Grade Class

daily community meetings to take care of administrative matters and provide time for discussions on how the class is governed; to raise, air, and deal with common-concern problems; to hear suggestions and ideas that don't pertain to any one course; and to deal with general procedural matters. He believes this will help students accept their share of the responsibility for the well-being of the class community. Furthermore, he wants students to clearly discriminate between the business of learning content and administrative and governance classroom tasks.

In devising the schedule, he thinks about how he wants to structure lessons so that intense activities are followed by more relaxed ones, physical inactivity is followed by physical activity, quiet times alternate with noisy ones, and low-appeal activities are followed by high-appeal ones. He plans lessons and organizes days so that the first-graders aren't expected to remain engaged in any one activity for an extended period of time. Also anticipation of an appealing activity helps motivate students to complete a less-appealing one.

Organizing the Classroom

With the courses organized by unit titles and goals and the daily schedule in hand, Dustin is anxious for the opening day of school still two weeks away. To begin organizing his classroom and working out a management plan for the year, he retrieves the textbook you are now reading. Turning to page 135, he carefully responds to each of the 15 questions under "Classroom Organization and Ongoing Routines," to the nine questions under "One-Time Only Tasks," and to the three questions under "Reminders for the First Week's Learning Activities."

After a week of planning and organizing, he has those questions resolved and room 113 arranged to fit his needs. Up to this point, he's been unable to make arrangements for another computer in the room, so for now, he plans to continue with the student computer he adopted leaving six stations for students.

Setting Up the System of Item Pool Files

Dustin sets up his system for maintaining item pool files on the computer. He begins with one disk per course with a file for each unit and a subfile for each objective. He can only begin writing items for the first two units of each course because, at this point, those are the only units for which he has formulated objectives. However, he has the system ready to accept new objectives and new items for every unit as he develops them during the school year. Dustin is pleased to see that he will be able to draw many of the simple knowledge, knowledge-of-process and, comprehension-level items from tests contained in the teacher's supplements accompanying the adopted textbooks. However, he realizes he will have to originate the vast majority of items for the conceptualization, application, creativity, affective, and psychomotor objectives.

Arrangements and Acquisitions

Although much of the week before classes begin is spent in meetings (e.g., a five-hour orientation meeting for all new teachers in the district and meetings of the school faculty and the primary grade department), Dustin finds time to learn Eugene Street School's "ropes" for obtaining supplies and equipment for his classroom. Surprising as it may seem, one of the more frustrating hindrances to their classroom effectiveness faced by first-year teachers is the inability to obtain equipment and supplies for their classrooms (Duke, Cangelosi, & Knight, 1988). Each school seems to have a unique process for teachers expediting such matters as obtaining paper, manipulatives, replacing burned-out projector lamps, gaining access to video recorders, and replacing lost books. Usually, it's a matter of identifying and befriending the right secretary or other staff member who knows how to get things done. Veteran teachers take such matters for granted and don't usually think to inform beginning teachers of this informal network. Fortunately, Dustin asked Rita about the process before wasting time going through formal channels.

Dustin also coordinates plans with other teachers. Rita, Martin, a kindergarten teacher, and a second-grade teacher agree to have their classes participate in a couple of Dustin's class' theme periods (e.g., hold an "Environmental Day" during the eleventh or twelfth week of school). Also, they agreed to participate in Dustin's class' health and physical education olympics and art and music show he's planning. Dustin shows some of the other teachers how to set up a computerized item pool system, and they agree to share test items. With Rita, he works out a plan by which each has the option of sending one or two students at a time to the other's class for temporary supervised "safekeeping." One might exercise this option in cases in which a student's disruptive behavior cannot be conveniently dealt with at the moment and the teacher simply wants to remove the student from the class until there's time for a planned response to the misbehavior.

THE BEGINNING OF AN EVENTFUL SCHOOL YEAR

In preparing for the first week, Dustin carefully considers the principles expressed in the section of Chapter 4 entitled Establishing a Favorable Climate for Learning, paying particular attention to Vignette 4.5. Twenty-four names appear on the preliminary roll he receives just in time for "orientation day," the day before classes begin. He quickly examines the files of the students, noting if and where they attended kindergarten and if any had been previously retained in first grade.

Although, he does not have much confidence in the validity of standardized test scores, he looks at the results of readiness and aptitude tests that are available. He also, reviews any anecdotal records or notes in the files from parents, school administrators, or teachers.

Orientation Day

Students and parents are invited to visit Eugene Street School on orientation day to meet their teachers, become acquainted with the school's physical plant and policies, and have their questions addressed. With the intent of communicating to the first-graders, "Welcome to your classroom! I'm glad you're here and we'll be working together!" Dustin displays Figure 7.5's poster near the entrance to the classroom and, as shown in Figure 7.6, prepares a personalized "storage station" for each student listed on the roll.

Unfortunately, only 16 students visit the school on orientation day, and only 12 of those are accompanied by a parent. Dustin engages in a warm, informative conversation with each student and gives them a letter for their parents. For example:

Figure 7.5. Dustin's Poster Welcoming 24 VIPs

Figure 7.6. A Personalized Storage Station in Room 113

Mr. Manda: Hello, I'm Mr. Manda. (shaking hands) What is your name?

Liu: I'm Liu.

Mr. Manda: I'm so happy to meet you. Please introduce me to this lady who is with you.

Liu: This is my momma.

Ms. Sun-Husan: Hello (shaking hands), I'm Fang Sun-Hasan.

Mr. Manda: Thank you for coming; I'm Dustin Manda, Liu's first-grade teacher. Let's sit down over here by Liu's storage station. . . . Liu, you were in kindergarten at another school. Is that right?

Liu: Yes.

Mr. Manda: What's the name of the school you went to?

Ms. Sun-Husan: He was at Westview; we just moved into this district last month.

Mr. Manda: (turning to Liu) So these are exciting times for you—a new neighborhood, a new place to live, and now a new school! Do you know your new school's name?

Liu: Eugene Street School.

Mr. Manda: Yes it is. And here's a paper for you with the name of the school, my name—Mr. Manda—your room number—113—the names of the other students in your class, and some times and dates for you to go over with your momma later on today. Bring this paper back here with you tomorrow at 8:30 in the morning. . . .

Ms. Sun-Husan: What do you say to your teacher?

Liu: Thank you.

Mr. Manda: You're welcome. Also, here's a letter for your momma; it explains some things about our class and Eugene Street School. . . . Now, let's take a look around the classroom and then you and your mom can tour the building. . . . What do you see against the wall there?

Liu: It's a picture of this room. Why . . .

The conversation continues; the letter for Liu's parents is shown in Figure 7.7. The form letters parents receive appear personalized because of word-processing technology.

Figure 7.7. Initial Letter Dustin Gives to Students' Parents

Eugene Street Elementary School
Southside School District
Ebony Maggio, Principal

Dustin R. Manda

August 29, 1992

Ms. Fang Sun-Husan
Apartment 19
860 Shirley Avenue
Beaverdale, MI

Dear Ms. Sun-Husan:

The beginning of first grade marks a significant event in Liu's life. The year's experiences will influence his (a) attitudes about himself, (b) desire to learn, (c) work habits, (d) social attitudes and skills, (e) self-control, (f) academic abilities and skills, and (g) physical development. As his first-grade teacher, I will strive for Liu's school-related experiences to be as positive as possible. In carrying out this responsibility, my professional preparation should serve me well. However, the success of the endeavor also depends on our working together cooperatively. To this end, we need to routinely communicate about how to most effectively work with Liu.

I will use several means of keeping you informed about our activities for the first-grade students of room 113:

1. Each month, I will send a newsletter to the parents. The letter will have four sections: (a) "Looking Back," summarizing class activities and achievements from the previous month, (b) "This Month," relating upcoming goals and activities, (c) "Looking Forward," previewing what's anticipated for upcoming months, and (d) "From the Students," presenting a sample of students' writings and artwork.

2. With approximately 25 students, I'm unable to contact individual parents as frequently

as I would like. However, by phoning two or three parents each school-day evening, I can converse with a parent once every two weeks. Because of the constraints of work schedules, these periodic phone conferences must not exceed 10 minutes. Although brief, these conversations allow me to apprise you of Liu's progress and enable us to exchange ideas on how we can effectively work with him.

3. The enclosed material includes an academic year calendar for Eugene Street School. Note the four days set aside for parent/teacher conferences. Each time, you, Liu, and I will discuss his end-of-the-term progress report (i.e., the contemporary first-grade equivalent of a "report card").

4. Several times a week, expect Liu to bring home samples of work he's completed in school. Liu needs to share his school accomplishments with you and hear your expressions of interest.

5. I'll assign homework three or four times a week. No more than 30 minutes in any one day should be spent on afterschool homework. Typically, the assignment is for Liu to review a spelling word list with you, collect materials or data to bring to school, or read a brief selection from a book.

6. Occasionally we may need to schedule a conference to cooperatively work out a solution to a problem. The problem may involve helping Liu modify work habits or classroom behaviors. It could also be a pleasant problem such as how to help him nurture some of his special talents.

7. Any time you feel the need to speak with me, please do not hesitate to set up an appointment by calling the school office (phone # 342-4065) between 7:45 A.M. and 4:45 P.M. on any school day. Ms. Sonya Hoyt, school office secretary, maintains a calendar for me and will be happy to take your calls and schedule appointments for us to meet in person or by phone.

8. You are welcome to visit our classroom and observe us in "action" anytime during the school day. Please familiarize yourself with the enclosed "Guidelines for Observers in Room 113" prior to your first visit. Note that school policy requires all visitors to stop by the school office and obtain a building pass before entering the classroom areas. This policy is designed to protect our children from intruders who might compromise the safety and security of the school environment.

Enclosed for your information are the following items:

1. Eugene Street School Academic Year Calendar

2. Daily schedule of courses for the first-grade students of room 113.

3. Course descriptions for art and music, health and physical education, mathematics, reading, science, social studies, and writing and speaking

4. A brief statement of my philosophy of teaching

I am looking forward to working with Liu and you.

Sincerely,

Dustin R. Manda

Dustin R. Manda
First-Grade Teacher
Eugene Street School

enclosures

Figure 7.7. (Continued)

Dustin maintains a high energy level throughout the day, but when the last student is gone and he's finished modifying his plans for opening day (based on ideas that came to him as he met with students and parents), fatigue sets in. He reflects on the day's activities and judges that the meetings were extremely useful to him and for every one of the students and parents who came. The rapport that was established with the students and lines of communications that were opened with parents will pay dividends throughout the year. Having the orientation day go so well heightens Dustin's disappointment that some students and their parents missed the experience. Out of concern for getting the first school day off to a smooth start and sending the message that teaching and learning is *important business*, he attempts to phone parents of the eight students who did not attend but manages to reach only two.

Opening Day

The Plan. Dustin's plans for the first two weeks are directed at initiating the first-graders to the school environment, teaching them fundamental rules and procedures, and establishing a comfortable, businesslike atmosphere conducive to learning and cooperation. But rather than extending orientation day into two days, he decides to get down to the business of learning and into Figure 7.4's schedule from the very beginning. The strategy is to initiate the routine and involve students in coursework while focusing that coursework on the opening theme, "Our School: Eugene Street" (as listed in Figure 7.2).

Although he anticipates being unable to take care of all of the first day's administrative matters during the first scheduled 15-minute community meeting session, he plans to start each course on time according to Figure 7.4's schedule. For each course, he designs a tasksheet (Fig. 7.8) with these purposes:

The students are busy with course-related tasks that also helps orient them to the school environment.

Dustin can easily monitor the activity and cue individuals to be on task.

All students experience success with challenging tasks.

Students begin to develop the following impressions about the course they're starting under Dustin's direction: (a) the content relates to their own individual interests; (b) they are expected to make judgments, and (c) those judgments are valued.

Dustin can utilize student's responses from the tasksheet in subsequent lessons to help them understand course content. For example:

Dustin intends to be conducting a lesson on the concept of *community* during the second week. One of the activities he plans for that lesson is for students to compare their drawings from Figure 7.8's tasksheet to demonstrate how different people in a community view things differently. From that idea, Dustin will conduct a questioning/discussion session leading students to discover that communities need to accommodate differences among their members.

Dustin gains feedback about students' interests and skills that will be valuable for planning subsequent lessons. For example:

As students respond to the tasksheet's items, Dustin will note variations among students' performances in following directions, willingness to draw pictures, and tastes in what they enjoy doing.

These 25 stickers are in an envelope attached to Olga's tasksheet:

Olga Bailey

1.

2.

3.

(continued)

Figure 7.8. Tasksheet Dustin Uses during First Day's Social Studies Period

4.

Oral directions to be explained by the teacher to the students -- one item at a time using an illustrative tasksheet:

1. Pinned to the sheet is an envelope with three kinds of stickers. Take out the stickers and find the one with your name. ··· Now put the others back in the envelope. ··· Thank you. Now stick your name in this first box. ···

2. Now, draw a picture of your teacher -- that's me, Mr. Manda -- right here in this big box. ··· Thank you. I like looking at these pictures of myself.

3. Now, picture in your head what the outside of our school building looks like. ··· Now draw the outside of our school building in this big box. ··· Thank you. I like looking at the different ways you pictured our school.

Figure 7.8. (Continued)

302

4. Now turn to the last page and look at all the pictures. ··· Take
   the rest of the stickers out of your envelope. ··· Put a smiling
   face sticker on each picture that shows something you like to do.
   Put a frowning face sticker on each picture showing something you
   <u>don't</u> like to do. When you're finished, put the leftover stickers
   back in the envelope and raise your hand so I can bring you
   something.

As each student finishes, Dustin exchanges a picture to color for the
completed tasksheet.

Figure 7.8. (Continued)

The Day. Twenty-six students appear on room 113's updated roll Dustin receives at 8 A.M. on the first day. Twenty of those were on his original 24-student roster. In a minor state of panic, he modifies names on the "personalized" storage stations and displays. By 8:30, 19 students are in the room; all 26 are present by 9:30. Having to orient those whom he hadn't met on orientation day and dealing with late-arriving students along with unanticipated administrative tasks interrupts the day's schedule he intended to follow. By 10:25, he's on track and begins the planned social studies lesson by walking students through Figure 7.8's tasksheet. The remainder of the day goes according to plan.

Reflections. Dustin laments the delays and rough beginning due to changes to his roll and late-arriving students. However, he's pleased with how he adjusted and was able to "think on his feet," concurrently managing numerous events. He's amazed at the high energy level he maintained in the presence of the students. They appeared so dependent on him, looking to him for approval and attaching such importance to everything he did. The first time he felt tired at all was during his lunch break beginning at 12:30. But the students seem to reinfect him with their energy when they reappeared at 1:15. His "high" continues beyond the 3 o'clock dismissal, at which time he compulsively works out plans for the next day's activities. The first day's plans for the mathematics and reading and speaking courses will carry over into the second day. Formative feedback suggests that the first day's plans for the other courses may have been too ambitious so he cuts back a little from what he originally had in mind for the second day. At 5:45, his preparations are completed and fatigue sets in.

Learning from Experiences

Becoming More Assertive. The ensuing weeks provide Dustin with the richest learning experiences of his life. Possibly the most important lesson is that he must be assertive to be successful. For example, two reading groups, The "birds" and the "dolphins," are engaged in an independent work session while Dustin is conducting a questioning/discussion session for the "lizards" in preparation for two poems they will soon be reading. Mr. Manda: "Look at the picture on page 37. . . . Where do you think this poem is going to be about, Monica?" Monica: "Outside by the street." Mr. Manda: "Where do you think that street is—" Just then, Ms. Taylor interrupts and says, "Excuse me, Mr. Manda, but I need to see you."

Mr. Manda: "Oh! I didn't see you come in. We're right in the middle of this pre-reading activity. Can't this wait?" Ms. Taylor: "It'll only take a minute." Mr. Manda to the group: "Excuse me, I'll be right back." In room 113's doorway, Rosalie Taylor converses with Dustin for six minutes about ordering equipment for the primary grade department. In the meantime, the lizards find ways to entertain themselves. Other students are encouraged to get off task when they see the lizards no longer working and by the disruption to the classroom routine.

Later in the day, Dustin thinks to himself, "Because of Rosalie's interruption, I didn't get though the pre-reading activity and couldn't assign the poems to the lizards. That was a miserable message to send to the whole class—that the business of learning isn't as important as my business with Ms. department head! I wish she wouldn't do that! . . . Get hold of yourself Dustin! Stop taking your anger out on Rosalie. You're the one who failed to act assertively and take control of your own classroom. You were afraid that if you didn't give in to Rosalie she might not like you as well or maybe you'd lose out on the equipment she's requisitioning. You were passive and now you're resenting her because you didn't take charge. The kids will recover from the experience as long as you display businesslike assertiveness next time something like this comes up."

A few days later, in a similar circumstance (Ms. Taylor's lunch break period is scheduled during Dustin's Reading #1 period), she interrupts a discussion session with, "Mr. Manda, I've got these requisitions for you to look over." Mr. Manda to the group, "Remember what Liu just said; he knows a way rivers and prairies are alike. Everybody silently think about a way rivers and prairies are alike. In 35 seconds I'll be back and we'll see if your way is the same as Liu's." Quickly, he goes to the doorway and tells Ms. Taylor, "I'll look at those during my lunch break between 12:30 and 1:00." Ms. Taylor: "But they have to be in the afternoon mail. Don't you want to approve them?" Mr. Manda: "Yes I do. Leave them on my desk now. I'll be done with them by one. We can discuss them right after school in your room and I'll be happy to run them down to the post office myself before five." Mr. Manda immediately returns to the lizards without looking back at Ms. Taylor to see if she concurs. As she places the papers on his desk, Mr. Manda says to the lizards, "Tell us one way a prairie and a river are like, Oliver. Liu, just shake your head 'yes' or 'no' to tell us if it's the same way you had in mind." Oliver: "Well, a river has plants and . . ."

Similarly, Dustin discovers the need to display assertiveness, not hostility nor passivity, with parents, students, supervisors, and colleagues.

Addressing Behavior Management Problems. It is in meeting his most challenging responsibilities of keeping students on task and responding to off-task behaviors that Dustin finds the greatest need to be assertive. At times, he resents having to constantly work to maintain students' interests and teach students who tend to be off task to be on task. He begins what turns out to be a productive conversation with Rita with an expression of frustration:

> DUSTIN: One day, I'd love to able to just teach my courses without having to worry about Damien harassing Angela about the hair on her face or Margaret trying to paint Olga's ears or Brian fulfilling his role of circus clown!
>
> RITA: So you're having one of *those* days!

DUSTIN: It's just that I'd just gotten Angela to the point where she was about to express one of her opinions in a cooperative group activity, when Damien starts in on her about her mustache. She's such of a gentle little spirit and that bully just doesn't know when to let up on the others!

RITA: What did you do?

DUSTIN: I gave him one of my "shut-up-or-life-as-you-now-know-it-ends" looks. That's always worked in the past. But, of course, I save it for special situations; this was one of those special situations."

RITA: But it didn't work this time?

DUSTIN: Oh, the little coward looked at me and straightened right up. But when I moved on to another group, he was back at it—kept looking at me to see when I was looking—real sneaky!

RITA: What'd you do when you caught him making fun of her again?

DUSTIN: That's what's really got me angry—not at him, but at myself. I know better than to think of students as 'cowards' and 'sneaks,' but I lost it. I told him he had no right to entertain himself at the expense of others. I knew that went over his head, so I asked him if it made him feel like a big-shot to make others feel bad. Not only was that a hostile question; it also suggested to the class that others can hurt their feelings. I know better than that!

RITA: It's natural to act with hostility when you feel out of control.

DUSTIN: I'm afraid I lost some of the things I've worked so hard to build over these first five weeks. The kids saw me out of character.

RITA: So your teaching performance wasn't perfect—big deal. You can fix things. But first, tell me how Damien reacted to your question about if hurting others made him feel better?

DUSTIN: He said he was just kidding and then we went back and forth about "good" and "bad" kidding. But it wasn't a productive exchange; it just escalated the antagonism and wasted a lot of time. If I'd been more assertive, I could've defused the whole incident.

RITA: How?

DUSTIN: By simply separating him from the group and then telling him straight out that he violated classroom rule 2 and to meet me right after he finishes lunch to make plans to prevent him from violating that rule again.

RITA: Okay, that's what you should have done. Are you just going to let it drop and remind yourself to be assertive next time or do you also plan to do something to fix what happened?

DUSTIN: What do you think I should do?

RITA: If these were older students, I'd say take time at one of your community meetings to come clean with them and tell them you thought your own behavior was out of line. But for this age group, you might be better off just communicating this by consistently modeling assertive behavior. They'll realize this was exceptional behavior for you. You're human; it might be good for them to see you make mistakes and then recover.

DUSTIN: I agree. But I know I need to have alternative activities ready so it'll be easier for me to separate misbehaving students, but still keep them busy with coursework. There were examples of teachers using that strategy in this methods book I used in my college days.

See Vignettes 4.23 and 4.26.

Accumulating Ideas and Instructional Materials. While a preservice teacher at his alma mater, Dustin collected a large assortment of unit plans, instructional materials, and ideas for specific learning activities. But after several weeks of in-service teaching, he finds his collection falls far short of what's needed for full-time teaching for a year. As he organizes and prepares course units to fit into a year-long curriculum, he's continually creating and developing ideas and materials. The veteran teachers don't spend nearly as much time as he does preparing because they have built their arsenals from year to year.

Solving Unanticipated Problems. With decreasing frequency since opening day, Dustin encounters problems he had not anticipated when he was developing his organizational plan for the year. For example, when Dustin organized students three groups for the reading course (birds, dolphins, and lizards) and three other groups for the mathematics course ("Euclideans," "Archimedeans," and "Pythagoreans"), he visualized a typical 45-minute class period proceeding as follows:

> For the first 15 minutes, the Euclideans are involved in computer-assisted instruction (CAI) in an independent work session and the Archimedeans are engaged in cooperative group work. While managing to monitor the activities of those two groups, Dustin conducts a questioning/discussion session for the Pythagoreans. In the next 15 minutes, Dustin sits with the Archimedeans discussing the results of the cooperative group work while the Euclideans continue the CAI activity and the Pythagoreans complete a tasksheet in an independent work session. In the final 15 minutes, Dustin conducts an interactive lecture session for the Euclideans while the Archimedeans are involved in a CAI activity and the Pythagoreans compare responses to the tasksheet in a cooperative group session.

What he later discovered was the problem of communicating directions for the group activities to students who have not yet learned to read well enough for him to use tasksheets with written directions. Particularly difficult was directing the groups into the initial activities of the session. If he tried to explain them one at a time to the class as a whole, one group would tend to get off task when the directions were for another. Sometimes students would confuse directions meant for their group with those for another. By first moving them into groups, he could get one group started, then the second, and finally the third, but that proved inefficient. To mitigate the difficulties, Dustin devised the following routine procedure:

1. Each week one student from each group serves as that group's chairperson for the week.
2. During the last three minutes of the period prior to the mathematics or reading periods (see Figure 7.4), Dustin explains the directions for each group's initial activity to that group's chairperson. He also gives the chairperson any materials (e.g., tasksheets) that need to be distributed for the activity.
3. As soon as the mathematics or reading period commences, the chairpersons explain the directions and initiate the sessions as Dustin supervises.

Benefiting from Instructional Supervision. *Instructional supervision* is the art of helping teachers improve their teaching performances (Cangelosi, 1991, pp. 6–7; Cooper, 1984, pp. 1–2). Rita serves as an instructional supervisor for Dustin by sharing ideas on planning, managing student behavior, and other aspects of instruction. Working with Dustin not only helps his classroom effectiveness, it also benefits Rita's teaching because conferring with Dustin forces her to analyze problem situations and reflect on instructional activities more than she would otherwise. As the year progresses and Dustin's confidence soars, Dustin more and more serves as an instructional supervisor for Rita also. Consistent with research findings relative to instructional supervisory practices, Dustin and Rita's cooperative partnerships provide them with the most effective type of help with their teaching (Bang-Jensen, 1986; Brandt, 1989).

Accustomed to sharing ideas with Rita from his first day at Eugene Street, Dustin seeks and comfortably listens to suggestions from other instructional supervisors as well (e.g., other teachers, his department head, principal, and the district primary grade supervisor). Dustin does not always agree with nor take suggestions he receives; however, every one stimulates ideas for everything from coping with individual differences among students to eliciting parents' cooperation.

Dustin's most frustrating problem is finding enough time to do what he considers necessary for optimal classroom effectiveness. The following exchange with Marion Tramonte, fifth-grade teacher, helps:

DUSTIN: There are so many things I ought to be doing, but never get around to!

MARION: Like what?

DUSTIN: I need to develop enrichment materials for some students who are ahead of the rest of the class. And there are parents I should be contacting more often than I do. I haven't been entering items into my item pool file as regularly as I should. I—

MARION: Okay, slow down! I hear you. You have to realize that it's impossible to do everything you want to or should do. Make some difficult decisions and partition your time. Prioritize from what you *must* do—like sleep, eat, and show up in your classroom—to what's critical, down to what you really want to do, but could put off, and then finally to what isn't all that important. Put a high priority on things that will help you save time down the road—like keeping up with that item pool file. Neglect something else instead.

DUSTIN: I try to keep to a schedule, but then students come by and want to talk— they depend on me for strokes all the time. Then time I scheduled for daily planning is gone.

MARION: Don't allow it to happen; take control. You wouldn't drop in on a lawyer or doctor without an appointment. Don't let your clients do that to you.

DUSTIN: What clients?

MARION: Your students are your clients, but also don't let parents, colleagues, or administrators abuse your schedule either.

DUSTIN: But everything can't be scheduled. Unanticipated things have to be taken care of—especially with my students; they're so young.

MARION: Of course they do, but get a calendar anyway and use it as an organizational tool for your convenience—not something you blindly follow.

Dustin: Today is a case in point. I planned to phone a couple of parents right after school, but one of the paraprofessionals on bus duty was absent so Ebony asked me to fill in.

Marion: Those are time when I take a "triage" approach. I decide where my time can be most efficiently spent. Some crises are beyond our reasonable control and others can wait.

Dustin: So now, I have to find the time to schedule my time!

Preparing for Administrative Supervision. Instructional supervision is concerned solely with improving classroom practice. On the other hand, *administrative supervision* is concerned with quality control (Cangelosi, 1991, pp. 163–173). Eugene Street School and district administrators are responsible for determining whether or not Dustin teaches well enough to be retained as a teacher and given incentives to remain on the faculty. The district has an administrative supervisory program in which the classroom instructional practices of each beginning teacher are evaluated three times a year. The outcomes of these evaluations primarily hinge on observational data gathered by a team composed of the school principal, a district supervisor, and a same-grade teacher from another school. Rita helps Dustin prepare for the scheduled visits from his observational team by (a) advising him to use preobservational conferences to apprise team members of the instructional strategies they can anticipate seeing him employ, (b) suggesting that it is appropriate to utilize postobservational conferences, not only for learning from the team's report, but also to express his own needs regarding support services from the administration, and (c) simulating a team visit, with Rita playing the role of the team in a preobservational conference, an in-class observation, and in a postobservational conference.

In anticipation of the team's visits, Dustin is quite nervous. However, after the first few minutes of the first in-class observation he relaxes and learns to enjoy the attention. It helps that he thinks of his visitors as colleagues whose goals of helping students learn are the same as his own. Although he feels the team never saw him at his best, his performances receive better than satisfactory ratings and his confidence continues to rise.

SAMPLE TEACHING UNIT

Designing Mathematics Unit 7

Eight weeks have elapsed since the opening day of school. Presently, the mathematics course is organized into three groups:

The Euclideans (Darlene, Karen, Oliver, Javier, Rodney K., Ty, Margaret) are in the midst of Unit 4, "Picturing Relationships I."

The Archimedeans (Monica, Damien, Angela, Brian, Wang, Lindsay, Roosevelt, Sun, Shelly, Eva) are just beginning Unit 5, "Counting and Naming Numbers."

The Pythagoreans (Cito, Cinny, Liu, Olga, Ivory, Rodney W., Chao-Cui, Evelyn P., Evelyn A.) are just completing Unit 5.

Dustin has already planned Unit 6 for the Pythagoreans. He anticipates they will be ready for Unit 7, "Addition on Whole Numbers," in two weeks. He starts designing Unit 7. It's nearly 9 P.M. as Dustin sits in front of his computer. Nearby are the teacher's edition of the mathematics text, reference books, the district curriculum guide, and his teaching notebook (volumes 1–3). Since August, as ideas occur to him that might be useful in planning lessons, he jots them down in this teaching notebook. Also, there's a section for notes based on formative feedback he's collected during the year and another where he keeps course and unit plans printed from his computer. He reads Unit 7's goal:

> Understand the operation of addition on whole numbers, recall addition facts, and use them for problem solving

He thinks, "I need to define this goal with objectives. If they're ever going to creatively apply addition to real-world problem solving, they'll need to discriminate between concrete addition paradigms and other types of concrete paradigms. That should lead to a process for discovering addition facts. Then they should remember the facts and learn how to apply them. . . ."

To save time in writing the objectives, he copies and displays the file containing the objectives for Unit 6 on the computer screen. Occasionally referring to the notebook, text, and other resources, he "writes over" Unit 6's objectives on the screen as he formulates those for Unit 7. By 9:25 P.M. the goal is defined by the objectives listed in Figure 7.9.

He reflects on the overall unit lesson plan: "So the unit starts with an inquiry lesson that'll stimulate inductive reasoning leading them to discover the concept of whole number addition. That'll require some cleverly devised examples and nonexamples. Fortunately for them, they have a clever teacher! . . . For Objectives B and E we'll have direct instructional lessons and finish off the unit with a deductive lesson for F. I'll integrate the lessons for the comprehension Objectives, C and D, with the lessons for Objectives A and B. They already know how to read numerals and decode '=' and '+.' For this unit, it's only a matter of

Figure 7.9. Objectives Dustin Used to Define Mathematics Unit 7's Learning Goal

Goal: Understand the operation of addition on whole numbers, recall addition facts, and use them for problem solving

Objectives:
- A. Distinguish between concrete paradigms of addition on the set of whole numbers and other concrete paradigms (*Cognitive: conceptualization*)
- B. Given a and b such that a and b are whole numbers each less than 10, figure $a + b$ by selecting two disjoint sets, one with a elements, the other with b elements and counting the elements in the union of those two sets (*Cognitive: knowledge of a process*)
- C. Express the processes specified by Objective B in the form $a + b = c$ where a, b, and c are whole number constants (*Cognitive: comprehension*)
- D. Explain statements in the form $a + b = c$ (such that a, b, and c are whole number constants) in their own words (*Cognitive: comprehension*)
- E. Recite the 100 addition facts ($0 + 0 = 0$ through $9 + 9 = 18$) (*Cognitive: simple knowledge*)
- F. Given a real-life problem, determine if finding the sum of two whole numbers each less than 10 will help solve that problem, and, if so, solve the problem (*Cognitive: application*)

tying together two familiar forms of expressions. Also, I'll make sure they practice with these expressions in the two language arts courses.

"I don't need specific plans for the learning activities yet; I've got to get them through Unit 6 first. But I should at least be pulling together the examples and nonexamples for the first lesson and start thinking about the problems for the last one. Let's see, The Pythagoreans should be done with the unit on multiples sometime in the ninth week, so we should be in the middle of—better check the theme list—"Wild Animals" at that time. So at least some of the examples and nonexamples for the opening lesson better relate to wild animals. By the time they're doing the application lesson, we'll be into the "Our Environment" period. . . . Okay, that'll all fit very nicely."

By 10:45 P.M., he has sketched out the overall plans for the four lessons as shown in Figure 7.10 (including Figure 7.11, p. 312, and Figure 7.12, p. 313). Details will be worked out in daily plans once the unit commences.

Figure 7.10. Dustin's Overall Plans for Mathematics Unit 7 (details to be worked out during daily planning)

For Objective A (from Figure 7.9), a seven-stage conceptualization lesson as follows:

For **task confrontation** and **task work,** students are initially organized into four subgroups. Each subgroup is given a copy of the picture shown in Figure 7.11. The first subgroup is directed to determine (a) the number of animals shown on the ground and (b) the number of animals shown that are above the ground. The second subgroup is to find (a) the number of animals on the ground and (b) the number of animals shown in trees. The third subgroup is to find (a) the combined number of birds and reptiles and (b) the number of mammals. And the fourth subgroup is to find the number of animals to the left of the broken line through the picture and (b) the number of animals to the right of the solid line through the picture.

The copies of the picture are returned to Mr. Manda and then each subgroup reports its pair of numbers to the group as a whole. In a questioning/discussion session, the following question is addressed: "How many altogether appear in the picture?" At this point in the lesson, students may not go back and look at the picture to count all the animals. They will be required to answer the question from the data available from the four subgroups. Manipulatives (e.g., as beads and rods) should be available for constructing sets with element numbers equal to the data points from the subgroups.

For **reflection on work** and **generalization,** Mr. Manda will use inductive questions to lead the students to recognize why the following is true:

The number of animals in the picture can be found by determining either (a) the number that is the total of the first subgroup's number pair or (b) the number that is the total of the third subgroup's number pair. But the number of animals in the picture cannot be found using only data from either the second or fourth subgroup.

The first four stages will be repeated with additional examples and nonexamples as necessary.

For **articulation,** a questioning/discussion session is used to lead students to verbalize (in their own first-grade terms) a statement equivalent to the following (which is stated here in a more sophisticated, precise language than is appropriate for these students):

If a, b are whole numbers, then $a + b$ = the number of elements in the union of sets A and B such that A contains exactly a elements, B contains exactly b elements, and A and B share no common elements.

For **verification,** students will work on an independent or homework assignment using additional examples and nonexamples to test the rule they articulated.

For **refinement,** the verification results will be used in a questioning/discussion session to make any changes in the rule as deemed necessary.

For Objective B, a nine-stage knowledge-of-a-process lesson as follows:

Further **explanation of the purpose of the process** should not be necessary after the process was discovered in the previous conceptualization lesson.

For **explanation and practice on estimating or anticipating outcomes from the process,** very brief independent work, cooperative group, or questioning/discussion sessions will be used to confront students with whole number pairs (abstract, written as numerals, as well as concrete disjoint sets) and demonstrate that the sum can be no less than the larger of the two numbers and no greater than twice the larger. Finer estimates should be demonstrated only for students who are advancing quickly through the unit.

Little time should be needed for the remaining stages of the lesson. A direct learning activity in which students are coached through several exercises and provided corrective feedback should suffice.

For Objectives C and D, comprehension lessons will be integrated with lessons for Objectives A and B and also in concurrent units in the reading and writing and speaking courses.

For Objective E, a five-stage simple knowledge lesson as follows:

For **exposition** and **explication,** students are provided with manipulatives and directed to use the process from Objective **B** to complete their own addition tables (initially up to five) during cooperative group, independent work, or homework sessions.

For **mnemonics,** rules for special cases are pointed out using the tables students developed (e.g., "2 + 1 = 1 + 2"). As part of the integrated art and music course, students will be assigned a whole number for which they make a picture poster illustrating the addition facts for that number (e.g., see Figure 7.12). Also, Mr. Manda will teach students a "catchy" musical tune to which they recite facts.

Monitoring, feedback, and **overlearning** will be effective in two ways: (a) independent work sessions utilizing computer-assisted instruction (CAI) and (b) a continuation of practice exercises and coaching during subsequent lessons and units.

Addition facts for higher numbers (e.g., five through nine tables) are introduced as time permits. Advanced students may complete them in this unit whereas others may not engage in practice activities for the higher facts until subsequent units.

For Objective F, a four-stage application lesson as follows:

During the two **problem confrontation** stages and the **rule articulation** stage, deductive questioning/discussion sessions will be used addressing problems. Here's one possibility related to the theme "Our Environment":

Room 113's first-graders participate in a program in which they collect used glass and metal containers to be sold for about one cent per container to a recycling center for funds for the class treasury. Before storing them in a box in the classroom, students mark each container with either an "O" or "I" depending on whether they found it outside or inside. A special pride is associated with collecting an outside container because there are not only recycling and monetary benefits but also a piece of litter has been removed from the environment.

As part of an application lesson, Mr. Manda directs one subgroup to count and record the number of glass containers in the storage box, another to count and record the number of metal containers, another to count and record the number of outside containers, and another to count and record the inside containers. Mr. Manda then empties the storage box and transports the containers to the recycling center. Payment will be forthcoming. "How much money will we get?" one student asks. Mr. Manda doesn't know, so he asks, "How can we find out? All we have to go by are the data collected by the subgroups."

Extension into subsequent lessons will occur during units following this one.

Figure 7.10. (Continued)

Figure 7.11. Initial Tasksheet for Mathematics Unit 7

Planning for Day One

It's Monday of the tenth week: The Euclideans are involved in Unit 5; the Archimedeans are in the early stages of Unit 6. The Pythagoreans review the results of the Unit 6 mathematics test they took Friday. As a prelude to the lesson for Objective A of Unit 7, Dustin directs each of the Pythagoreans to color only the animals shown in the Figure 7.11's tasksheet.

After school, Dustin plans for Tuesday, He begins with mathematics for the Pythagoreans by looking over the overall plan for mathematics Unit 7 shown in Figure 7.10 as well as his notes on what the Euclideans and Archimedeans should be doing for Units 5 and 6 tomorrow. He thinks, "Okay, I need to get the Euclideans into that cooperative-group stick-bundling activity right away. Let's see . . . , Karen is chairing that group this week; she can get them started first thing with that. I don't need to be with the Archimedeans for the first 15 minutes either. They need to continue working with the three-bean salad they started today. So if necessary, I can spend the first part of the period with the Pythagoreans. . . . I'm glad I thought of having them color the animals for homework. That way, I can at least see that they've all located all the animals before we start with the inductive activity. That'll help things go smoother. . . . Oh-oh! Maybe that wasn't such a smart idea after all! Suppose someone counts the number of animals as they color them. Then there wouldn't be much interest in finding out the total

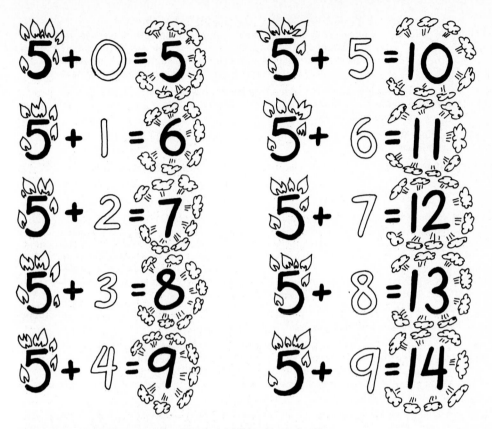

Figure 7.12. A Student's Art Rendition of Addition Facts for Five

from the data pairs after I collect the pictures. . . . Hopefully no one will. If somebody does, I'll play it down and play out the scenario or use my second example/nonexample sooner than I planned. . . . Okay, first I need them in subgroups. Who do I want with whom? . . .''

Soon Dustin has the specifications shown in Figure 7.13 and Figure 7.14 (p. 315) incorporated into his plan for Tuesday.

Day One

Tuesday, 8:47 A.M., the Euclideans are busy in the stick-bundling activity developing principles of numeration, the Archimedeans are completing the three-bean salad exercise using their newly acquired concept of multiples to solve puzzles, and the Pythagoreans are waiting for Mr. Manda with the wild animal pictures stacked on their table. Mr. Manda comments as he looks at the pictures, "The way you colored these pictures makes these animals come alive for me. . . . Look how brightly Chao-Cui colored the snakes. . . . And look at these two. Rodney must have used a light touch to get these soft tones, especially for the bears' fur. Cinny must have pressed harder to get these colors to stand out like this. . . .

Materials needed: • The wild animal pictures they colored for homework (see Figure 7.11) • A set of colored rods for counting • The portable white board • 10 copies of the tasksheet with the subsequent examples and nonexamples (see Figure 7.14) • An audiotape recorder • Each student's mathematics textbook

1. During the transition into the mathematics period, Ivory (this week's chairperson) directs the **Pythagoreans** to stack the wild animal pictures they colored for homework face down on their table and wait for Mr. Manda.

2. (1 minute) Mr. Manda quickly looks through the nine pictures, holding each up and making a descriptive comment about it.

3. (1 minute) Mr. Manda partitions the group into the following four subgroups:

Cito and Rodney W.	Olga, Cinny, and Ivory
Liu and Evelyn P.	Evelyn A. and Chao-Cui

4. (3 minutes) Mr. Manda hands a randomly selected picture to each subgroup directing Cito's subgroup to quietly find and write down the number of animals on the ground and the number of animals above the ground, Olga's subgroup to quietly find and write down the number of animals on the ground and the number of animals in the trees, Liu's subgroup to find and write down the number of birds and reptiles and the number of mammals, and Evelyn A.'s subgroup to quietly find and write down the number of animals shown to the left of the broken line and the number of animals to the right of the solid line.

5. (3 minutes) Mr. Manda collects the pictures and puts them out of sight as the subgroups label and display their data pairs on the portable board.

6. (12 minutes) in a questioning/discussion session, subgroups report their data, then Mr. Manda raises the question about the number of animals in the picture. Inductive questions are used leading the group to determine which data pairs are sufficient for determining the total number of animals. Manipulatives are used as needed to represent the data and combine data points to count.

7. (10 minutes) Mr. Manda distributes and explains the tasksheet with the subsequent examples and nonexamples and the group works on it in an independent work session. In the meantime, Mr. Manda joins the **Euclideans**.

8. (15 minutes) Mr. Manda directs the **Pythagoreans** into a cooperative group session with the task of describing, orally and in pictures on the board, what's **special** about the examples in which they could solve the problem (e.g., how many animals in the picture) that's different from those that they could not solve. Individual roles for the session are as follows: Ivory serves as chair, Cito records the discussion with the tape recorder, Cinny reminds people to stay on task, Liu is the custodian of the manipulatives, Olga serves as the group's official counter—counting out objects as needed, Rodney W. records and labels group findings, Chao-Cui makes illustrations on the board as requested by the group, Evelyn A. determines when the group has reached consensus and should move onto the next task, and Evelyn P. communicates the next task (which is to complete Exercises 1–3 from p. 39 of the textbook and 7–9 from p. 41, and 14–15 from p. 42).

   Before leaving to join the **Archimedeans**, Mr. Manda is to inform the group that the tape recording, illustrations on the board, notes, and textbook exercises are to be reviewed and discussed in class on Wednesday.

9. During the transition into the next period (i.e., recess), Mr. Manda collects the materials and assesses what the group accomplished.

Figure 7.13. Dustin's Agenda for the Pythagoreans' First Day of Mathematics Unit 7

How many baseballs?   How many footballs?   How many balls?

How many animals that fly?   How many birds?   How many animals?

How many shirts?   How many pairs of pants?   How many striped things?

How many bananas?   How many carrots?   How many pieces of fruit?

Tell the story

Tell the story

Select a picture to color from your storage box.

Figure 7.14. Second Tasksheet for Mathematics Unit 7, Second Day

This one doesn't have a name on it, but I'll guess it's Evelyn Prior's. You have a special way of outlining your pictures. Am I right?'' Evelyn P.: ''That's mine.'' Mr. Manda: ''I'm going to display all of these so more people can enjoy them. But first we're going to solve a mystery about them. Cito and Rodney will be partners in finding out two things for us to try to solve the mystery. Walk over here with me and I'll whisper to you the two things to find out. . . . Here, take this picture and quietly find out how many animals are shown on the ground and how many are somewhere above the ground. When you've got the two numbers, write them by your names on the board and return the picture to me. . . . Okay, Liu and Evelyn, come here and I'll tell you what you two are to find out. . . .''

As he relates the tasks to the other three subgroups (as indicated by item 4 of Figure 7.13), Mr. Manda continues to monitor the activities of the whole class, positively reinforcing on-task behaviors and discouraging off-task behaviors as the need arises.

By 8:57 A.M., the four pairs of numbers are on the board, Mr. Manda is back with the Pythagoreans ready to begin item 6 from Figure 7.13. However he is concerned that the 12 minutes allotted for this questioning/discussion session is going to be inadequate, the class is already 4 minutes behind schedule, and the Euclideans appear to be nearly ready for him to join them. Deciding to ''play it by ear,'' he turns to the Pythagoreans and asks, ''How many animals were there in the picture?'' Ivory: ''You didn't tell us to count them all.'' Evelyn A.: ''I counted them when I colored them; there were 20.'' Chao-Cui: ''There were more than that; let's count them for ourselves.'' Mr. Manda: ''We could do that if I hadn't already put the picture away.'' Ivory: ''I can get them.'' Mr. Manda: ''Thanks for offering to help. But let's check Evelyn's answer from the numbers you've put on the board here. Here's some rods to count with. Olga, Cinny, and Ivory counted 7 animals on the ground so count out 7 brown rods for us, Ivory. . . . Thank you. And you said there were 9 animals in the trees. Count those with these green rods, Olga. . . . Super! So, how many animals altogether? Ivory, take over for me here—chair the group—while I go work with the Euclideans for 5 minutes and then get the Archimedeans started with their next task.''

Returning 7 minutes later, he sees that the Pythagoreans have yet to utilize any of the data pairs on the board other than the 7,9 pair from Olga's group— the one to which he initially referred them. At the moment, Chao-Cui and Evelyn A. are attempting to settle their debate by attempting to count animals in the picture from memory. Chao-Cui: ''. . . There was also that mouse on the rock.'' Liu: ''That only makes 11.'' Cito: ''No, we already counted that one.'' Mr. Manda: ''Why don't you use the numbers on the board?'' Ivory: ''They don't work. We counted them out but that's not all the animals.'' Olga: ''Because there was others—more than 16.'' Mr. Manda: ''What about the numbers from your group, Chao-Cui? Here, use the rods. Ivory, you're in charge again until I get back.''

Mr. Manda checks with the Archimedeans, then once again joins the Euclideans. At 9:14, Mr. Manda assesses the classroom situations from his location with the Euclideans and decides to postpone items 7 and 8 from Figure 7.13's agenda until tomorrow. After engaging the other two groups in independent work sessions, he returns to the Pythagoreans for the remainder of the time to complete agenda item 6.

Mr. Manda: "What happened while I was gone, Ivory? Ivory: "We counted 26 rods this time." Mr. Manda: "So you took 15 rods and then 11 rods and put them together." Evelyn A: "And that's 26, but that's not right." Chao-Cui: "Yes it is." Mr. Manda: "Why don't you think there are 26 animals in the picture?" Evelyn A: "Because I counted 20 before." On the board, Mr. Manda draws the picture shown in Figure 7.15 and says pointing to it, "Tell us one more time how you found the numbers 15 and 11." Chao-Cui: "We counted the animals from here . . . to here . . . and then from here . . . to here." Mr. Manda: "Before when we counted 7 and 9, we left out some animals. This time, with the 15 and 11, what went wrong? . . . Anybody? . . . Wasn't there a mama bear right in between these two lines?" Cito: "Oh, I know!" Mr. Manda: "Liu, what do you think Cito just discovered?" Liu: "Those animals count twice." Evelyn P: "Oh, I see it!" Mr. Manda: "Go ahead, Evelyn; tell us." Evelyn P.: "Twenty-six can't be right." Mr. Manda: "Is the right answer greater than or less than 26?" Chao-Cui: "Less." Liu: "And it's bigger than 16." Mr. Manda: "Why did Liu say it's greater than 16, Rodney?" Rodney: "I don't know." Mr. Manda: "Ask him." Rodney W.: "Why?" Liu: "Because when we counted out 7 and 9, that left some birds out." Mr. Manda: "Cito and Rodney, use the rods to get an answer with your 7 and 13. . . . Liu and Evelyn you try it with your 12 and 8. . . . The rest of us will watch you." . . . Olga: "It's 20." Evelyn P.: "We got 20." Evelyn A.: "I told you that!" Mr. Manda: "Who thinks there were 20 animals in the picture? . . . All of us do. Tomorrow, I'll have the pictures on the wall and you can check if 20 is right for sure. Then we need to discuss why some of the number pairs worked and others didn't. It's time to get ready for recess. . . ."

Reflecting on Day One; Planning for Day Two

At 4:45 P.M., Dustin is back in front of his computer going over the day and preparing for tomorrow. He thinks, "That mathematics unit didn't exactly begin for the Pythagoreans as I planned. Evelyn pops up with the 20 right away! It's a

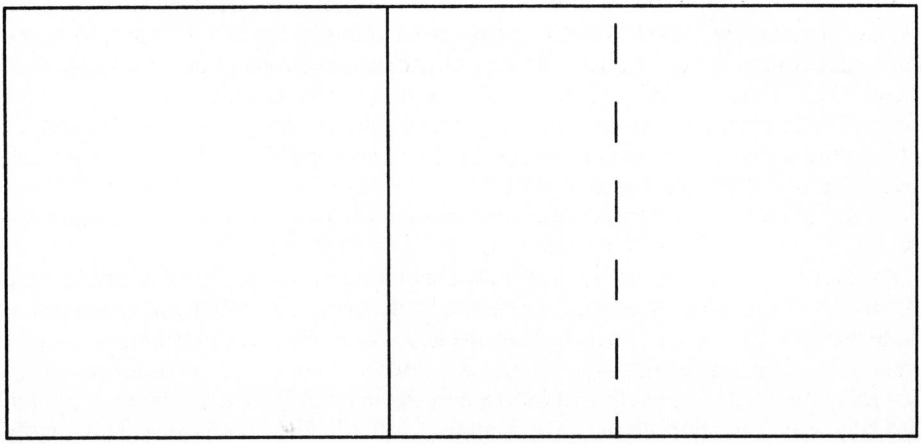

Figure 7.15. Sketch Mr. Manda Put on the Board during Day One's Class

good thing I got those pictures back before they could use them to validate her answer. Actually, it all worked out okay—using the number pairs to check what she said. . . . The big problem stemmed from not enough time. My timing needs work. With another 10 minutes, I'd of had them articulating why two of the pairs worked but not the others. Then another 10 minutes with the subsequent examples and nonexamples on the tasksheet and then another 10 minutes to develop the rule. So I misjudged the time by 30 minutes! . . . So where do we go tomorrow? . . . I really need to be with the Archimedeans at the start of the period. That's okay because I'll just start the Pythagoreans with the tasksheet (Figure 7.14) in an independent work session, then for the second third of the period they can get into the cooperative group session that was planned as item 8 for today (see Figure 7.13)—then finish the period with the Pythagoreans delivering a direct instructional lesson on the process that follows from the relationship they come up with in the cooperative group session. That'll be getting to Objective B (from Figure 7.9). . . . But what if they don't come up with the 'right' relationship? . . . Then, I'll just use that time with an inductive questioning/discussion session and postpone the direct instructional session until Wednesday. . . . Okay, better get this on my disk before I forget. . . .''

Figure 7.16 displays the resulting agenda. Dustin then plans the mathematics period for the Euclideans and the Archimedeans and then for the rest of Wednesday.

Day Two

Wednesday's mathematics period proceeds for the Pythagoreans according to Figure 7.16's agenda. With 15 minutes remaining, Mr. Manda joins the Pythagoreans as Evelyn P. is beginning to explain the textbook assignment, ''Here's the page Mr. Manda marked. Start here . . . and do this one, this one, this one, and over here, Mr. Manda ringed this, this one, 'n this one.'' Cinny: ''What ya' do?'' Mr. Manda: ''Before Evelyn explains how to do these. Let me hear from Rodney to find out what you decided.'' Rodney W. (illustrating his reply with the tasksheet from Figure 7.14): ''Here the balls are the baseballs and footballs. And here the fruit is the bananas 'n peaches.'' Mr. Manda: ''What about this one with the shirts and pants? . . . Or this one with the animals that fly and mammals?'' Liu: ''They're different.'' Mr. Manda: ''How is the shirts-pants one different from the baseballs-footballs one?'' Liu: ''Putting together the shirts and pants is more than the striped things.'' Mr. Manda: ''So what's the rule we're after here? . . . Cinny?'' Cinny: ''Sometimes you can just put them together—not all the time.'' Mr. Manda: ''Oh! Does everyone agree? . . . Everyone does. When does putting two bunches of things together work? . . .''

Mr. Manda begins to perspire recognizing that although these students are nearing the relevant concept, they don't seem to have the verbal skills to express its attributes. He fears that he's turning this into an abstract word game leading nowhere. He thinks, ''I'd better get them to describe what they did and leave it at that rather than try and get them to explain a general rule. After more concrete exercises, this'll go easier. They don't have to do it today or even this week.''

Mr. Manda: ''How many of us are here at this table?'' Cito: ''Nine.'' Evelyn P.: ''No, 10. You didn't count Mr. Manda.'' Mr. Manda: ''Ten of us. How many

Materials needed: • 10 copies of the tasksheet with the subsequent examples and non-examples (see Figure 7.14) • The wild animals pictures displayed on the wall • A set of colored rods for counting • The portable white board • An audiotape recorder • Each student's mathematics textbook

1. During the transition into the mathematics period, Ivory (this week's chairperson) distributes the tasksheets (Figure 7.14) to the **Pythagoreans** and explains the directions to them.

2. (15 minutes) The **Pythagoreans** complete the tasksheets in an independent work session; Mr. Manda is with the **Archimedeans** for this time.

3. (15 minutes) Mr. Manda directs the **Pythagoreans** into a cooperative group session with the task of describing, orally and in pictures on the board, what's **special** about the examples in which they could solve the problem (e.g., from the tasksheet and from yesterday's wild animal picture exercise) that's different from those that they could not solve. Individual roles for the session are as follows: Ivory serves as chair, Cito records the discussion with the tape recorder, Cinny reminds people to stay on task, Liu is the custodian of the manipulatives, Olga serves as the group's official counter—counting out objects as needed, Rodney W. records and labels group findings, Chao-Cui makes illustrations on the board as requested by the group, Evelyn A. determines when the group has reached consensus and should move on to the next task, and Evelyn P. communicates the next task (which is to complete Exercises 1–3 from p. 39 of the textbook and 7–9 from p. 41, and 14–15 from p. 42).

   Before leaving to join the **Euclideans,** Mr. Manda is to inform the group that the illustrations on the board, notes, and textbook exercises are to be reviewed and discussed during the last 15 minutes of the period. The tape recording is to be used if needed to recall something that took place in the meeting.

4. (15 minutes) In a brief questioning/discussion session, the **Pythagoreans** report their conclusions from the cooperative group meeting. If the relationship underlying the process specified by Objective **B** has been discovered by the group, then a direct instructional activity follows in which Mr. Manda explains and illustrates the process using the aforementioned textbook exercises.

   If the relationship was not discovered, then instead of the direct instructional activity, an inductive questioning/discussion session is used to lead the **Pythagoreans** to discover it.

5. During the transition into the next period (i.e., recess), Mr. Manda collects the materials and assesses what the group accomplished.

Figure 7.16. Dustin's Agenda for the Pythagoreans' Second Day of Mathematics Unit 7

at the Euclideans' table right now? . . .'' Chao-Cui: "Seven." Mr. Manda: "Now, pretend all of us went over there and sat with them at their table, how many would be at their table then?" Cito: "Too many; their table's too little." Mr. Manda: "Pretend we all squeezed in." Liu: "Seventeen." Mr. Manda: "Show us why it would be 17 with the rods, Rodney." Rodney W. counts out 10 rods then 7 more, pushes them together, and counts them all again.

Mr. Manda: "How many in our group here, Cinny?" Cinny: "Ten." Mr. Manda: "How many in their group right now, Ivory?" Ivory: "Seven." Mr. Manda: "If we got up and squeezed in with them around their table, how many *girls* would there be around their table?" Olga: "It's—" Mr. Manda: "Don't tell us yet. First, show us with the rods." Olga counts out 10 rods and then 7 more, and says, "It doesn't work. There'd be 8 girls, not 17." Let's look at the shirts and pants one on the sheet. . . . Why didn't that one work? . . .'' Evelyn P.: "Because some of the things don't have stripes." Mr. Manda: "Okay Evelyn, go ahead and finish explaining to us how to do the textbook assignment. Every-

Tell the story. Then add.

15.

$$3 + 2 = \underline{}$$

16.

$$2 + 2 = \underline{}$$

PARTNERS: Make up problems and solve together.

Write the numbers. Then add.

1.

$$\underline{5} + \underline{2} = \underline{7}$$

2.

$$\underline{} + \underline{} = \underline{}$$

Figure 7.17. Skill-Level Exercise (Reprinted with permission from *Mathematics* [pp. 38–39], 1991, Boston: Houghton-Mifflin. Copyright © 1991 by Houghton-Mifflin.)

body open your book to page 39." (See Figure 7.17.) . . . Evelyn P.: "Count these red brushes and get five to write here. Count two yellow ones and put two here. Next count all the brushes and write seven here. . . . Do it over here." Mr. Manda: "Thank you. Evelyn is going to tell you the rest of the textbook assignment to work on until it's time for recess. Tonight, I'm going listen to the tape Cito made of your meeting and we'll work on this some more tomorrow."

Reflecting on Day Two; Planning for Day Three

While supervising the students during recess, Mr. Manda continues to think about that last session with the Pythagoreans. He's disappointed that the students didn't progress toward the articulation stage of the lesson and questions whether or not these first-graders are capable of conceptualizing abstract addition at all. While managing to interact with students as they play, he thinks, "Maybe my whole strategy for teaching mathematics is flawed. The direct lessons for skills go so much smoother than these inquiry ones. If I would've just stuck with the book, I'd be pages ahead! . . . In any case, I can't afford to be thinking about this now. They need my attention and it's almost 9:40, time for speaking and writing. . . ."

By 4:30 P.M., he's had a chance to reflect on the events of the day and since that recess period, enough of his strategies succeeded that he is no longer distressed over his apparent failure to complete that conceptualization lesson. Before designing Thursday's mathematics activities, he reviews the Pythagoreans' work from the textbook exercises and listens to the tape from their cooperative group session. Overall, the students' discussions seemed disjointed with little movement in any one direction. However, Dustin's confidence is buoyed by some of the utterances that indicate higher conceptualization levels than he had perceived when he sat with the group earlier in the day. For example, he hears somebody (possibly Cinny) say, "Bats are like the animals in the middle of that picture." But no one seemed to respond to that and she didn't elaborate any further. So although the discussion didn't build on that statement, it showed that at least some of the students were connecting nonexamples from the wild animal picture from the previous day to nonexamples from today's tasksheet.

Dustin decides to stick with the general strategy of preceding knowledge-level lessons with conceptualization-level lessons. However, for concepts and relationships that are especially difficult for these students to verbalize, he decides not to press for completion of the articulation stage before proceeding to the next objective. Regarding tomorrow's plans for the Pythagoreans' mathematics period, he thinks, "I'll go right into my direct lesson for Objective B but also keep confronting them with nonexamples as well as examples and asking them 'why did the process work that time?' and 'why didn't it work this time?' I won't push for rigorous explanations, just push them to think about it. As they develop more concepts that contrast with addition, such as subtraction, rigorous language will evolve. . . . This means I'll be integrating part of my conceptualization lessons, like the one for Objective A, with knowledge-level lessons, like for Objective B. . . . So, I'll have to supplement skill-level exercises from the text (see, for example, Figure 7.17) with ones that include nonexamples (see, for example, Figure 7.18)"

The agenda he devises for Thursday is given by Figure 7.19 (including Figures 7.20, p. 323, and 7.21, pp. 324–325).

Day Three

Thursday's mathematics period for the Pythagoreans proceeds smoothly according to Figure 7.19's agenda. However, Cito and Rodney are absent. During item 4's questioning/discussion session, Mr. Manda holds up a domino so the Pythagoreans can see only its backside without the spots. "What is this?" he asks. Cinny:

Figure 7.18. One of Dustin's Nonexamples Paralleling the First Exercise from Figure 7.17

"A domino." Mr. Manda: " What's on the front of this domino—the part you can't see right now, Olga?" Olga: "Spots." Mr. Manda: "How many spots does this domino have?" Chao-Cui: "Twelve." Evelyn A.: "No, I say 10." Mr. Manda decides to digress from the planned agenda to seize this opportunity to touch on a relationship from Unit 3; thus, he asks, "Is it possible for Chao-Cui to be correct?" Ivory: "He's just guessing." Liu: "But he might've guessed right."

Figure 7.19. Dustin's Agenda for the Pythagoreans' Third Day of Mathematics Unit 7

Materials needed: • Corrected textbook exercises from yesterday's assignment • A set of colored rods for counting • A set of dominoes • Display board illustrating regular and irregular dominoes (see Figure 7.20) • 10 copies of the tasksheet for today (see Figure 7.21) • Each student's mathematics textbook

1. During the transition into the mathematics period, Ivory supplies each **Pythagorean** with nine red rods and nine blue rods, then tells them Mr. Manda will be with them first and give directions when he arrives.

2. (2 minutes) Mr. Manda returns yesterday's work from the textbook with feedback as needed.

3. (7 minutes) In an interactive lecture session, Mr. Manda reviews the steps the **Pythagoreans** used to complete the textbook exercises and the previous tasksheet examples "that work." He explains how to use manipulatives to find the sum of two whole numbers and walks the group through several examples.

4. (9 minutes) In a questioning/discussion session, Mr. Manda asks a student to describe a domino. Without showing them the domino, he then asks the group to use their rods to tell him how many spots on a domino just from him telling them the number on each side. Students are directed (and coached as needed) to make number sentences expressing what they did. After several more domino examples, Mr. Manda displays a picture of an irregular domino (see Figure 7.20) and asks the students to use the manipulatives to find the number of spots on some hypothetical dominoes only from knowing how many spots are to the left of the one line and how many are to the right of the other. Why the process won't work in this case is discussed.

5. (2 minutes) Mr. Manda distributes and explains the tasksheet (see Figure 7.21) to be completed in an independent work session.

6. (25 minutes) The **Pythagoreans** work on the tasksheet as Mr. Manda joins the **Euclideans** and then the **Archimedeans**.

7. During the transition into the next period (i.e., recess), Mr. Manda collects the materials and assesses what the group accomplished.

Figure 7.20. Dustin's Display of a Domino and an "Irregular" Domino

Olga: "Evelyn might've guessed right too." Mr. Manda: "One of them *might* have guessed the right number. But could *both* guesses be right, Evelyn Prior?" Evelyn P.: "No." Mr. Manda: "Why not, Evelyn?" Evelyn P.: "Because you just can't; that's all." Mr. Manda: "Why not?" Evelyn P.: "You'd count the spots one, two, 'til you stopped and that's only one number." Mr. Manda is tempted to pursue the business about uniqueness further and even introducing an idea related to probabilities, but quickly decides to return to the day's topic. Mr. Manda: "So the number of spots might be 12 or it might be 10, but it can't be both." Ivory: "I think it's another number." Mr. Manda: "What are some other possible numbers?" Ivory: "None—could have no spots." Olga: "Its gotta have a spot—one to a side!" Mr. Manda: "Easy now, . . . yes, Ivory?" Ivory: "I seen a domino that had no spots." Mr. Manda: "Before I show you the front of this one, everybody think of what the front of a domino looks like. . . . Everyone, draw one for me on your paper. . . . Okay, everyone knows what the front of a domino looks like. It's divided into two parts—left and right. Right? . . . Right. . . . Suppose I told you how many dots this domino had on the left side. Would you know for sure how many it has altogether? . . . You're shaking your head 'no.' I'm counting the spots on the left of the little line—1, 2, 3, 4. How many altogether, Liu?" Liu: "You still don't know." Mr. Manda: "Do you know more than you did before?" Olga: "You still don't know." Evelyn A.: "You know there's more than 4." Ivory: "The other side could have no dots." Mr. Manda: "So you now know there's 4 or more dots altogether." Cinny: "How many on the right side?" Mr. Manda: "I though you'd never ask. One, 2—there's 2 on the right side." Evelyn P.: "Five, 6—there's 6 on the front!" Mr. Manda turns the piece over for all to see the 6 spots.

Mr. Manda displays the board shown in Figure 7.20 and says, "Here's a picture of a *regular* domino. But suppose I had an *irregular* domino that looked like this one with three sections. I've got one of those funny *irregular* dominoes in my pocket right now. It doesn't have the same number of spots as this one in the picture." Peeking dramatically at the "irregular domino" in his pocket so no one else can see it, he continues as he demonstrates his words using Figure 7.20's illustration, "I count 6 dots on the left side of this line and 5 dots on the right side of this other line. How—" Cinny: "Eleven! No, that's not right—not as much as 11!" Ivory: "That funny domino doesn't work." Mr. Manda: "Show us why using this picture." . . . Ivory: "You could've counted these ones two times." Mr. Manda: "Could 11 be right?" Olga: "No—11's too much." Ivory: "It could be 11 if there's no spots in this part. . . ."

Convinced that the seven Pythagoreans in attendance today have developed an adequate concept of addition of whole numbers (i.e., Objective A), Mr. Manda cuts this inductive activity short and decides to distribute and explain Figure 7.21's

1. Tell the story then add:

_____ + _____ = _____

2.

_____ + _____ = _____   _____ + _____ = _____

3. Circle the pictures that show 4 + 3 = 7.

Figure 7.21. Tasksheet for Day Three of Mathematics Unit 7

324

4.

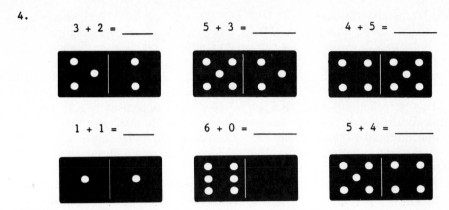

Figure 7.21. (Continued)

tasksheet four minutes ahead of schedule. He thinks to himself, "With the conceptualization-level progress they demonstrated today, I can plan to concentrate on Objectives B and E strictly using direct instructional strategies through the middle of next week. I no longer need to keep coming back to Objective A nearly so often. . . . I just wish Cito and Rodney were here. I'll have to assess where they are when they return."

Day Four through Day Nine

Friday, Dustin meets with the Pythagoreans for the first 15 minutes of the period enumerating and reviewing the steps in the process whereby the students use manipulatives to determine the sum of two whole numbers. Convinced they've satisfactorily achieved Objectives B, C, and D, he has the Pythagoreans work in pairs for the remainder of the period using the process to complete the tasksheet shown in Figure 7.22.

On Monday, Tuesday, and Wednesday, Dustin utilizes five types of direct instructional activities for Objectives C, D, and E—primarily E: (a) Independent work sessions with students practicing addition facts with the aid of CAI on microcomputers, (b) group recitations sessions in which students sing facts to a

Figure 7.22. Tasksheet Pythagoreans Work with in Pairs on Day 9

Directions (explained orally): Use the colored rods to find out the numbers to write in the blanks.

5 + 0 = _____	3 + 1 = 4	5 + 2 = _____	4 + 4 = _____
4 + 5 = 9	3 + 2 = _____	2 + 7 = _____	5 + 4 = _____
2 + 4 = _____	1 + 5 = _____	3 + 4 = _____	1 + 9 = _____
3 + 8 = 11	3 + 7 = _____	5 + 7 = 12	4 + 7 = _____
4 + 8 = _____	3 + 9 = 12	1 + 2 = _____	5 + 5 = _____

"catchy" tune and also respond to flash cards, (c) independent work sessions in which students create illustrations of their "favorite" facts (see, e.g., Figure 7.14), and (d) independent works sessions in which students complete textbook assignments.

Thursday, Dustin stimulates students to reason deductively during a questioning/discussion session for Objective F. Students confront problems such as the one on recycling described in Figure 7.10. Dustin is pleasantly surprised at how quickly the group seems to achieve Objective F. He attributes the success to the concentrated attention to conceptualization in the initial stages of the unit and then the intermittent attention afforded conceptualization during subsequent stages.

Friday is spent reviewing the entire unit with students coaching one another with practice test items relevant to the six objectives. Part of Monday's and part of Tuesday's class periods will be used to administer the unit test to the Pythagoreans.

The Unit Test

Development. Over the weekend, Dustin pulls together the unit test from his item pool file. Figure 7.23 describes the test.

Interpreting and Using the Test Results.

After school on Tuesday, Dustin compiles the results of the test as shown in Table 7.1 (p. 331). He thinks: "Except for Rodney, everyone appears to have performed satisfactorily on all the objectives except for E. Should I delay Unit 8 long enough to squeeze in a few more drill exercises on the addition facts through five? . . . Maybe I should put them back on the computers for those. . . . Naw, tomorrow I'll review the test with them and then get right into Unit 8 on subtraction. We'll integrate drills on addition facts for the rest of the year—especially in units 9, 11, and 13 when they move into adding larger whole numbers. . . . But what about Rodney; he's the only one that seems to have missed the conceptualization objective and that kept him from achieving the application objective. The rest are ready to move on, but Rodney is a different story. I could move him in with the Archimedeans, but they have—let's see. . .—10 in that group now, and I'm not ready to move any of them to either the Pythagoreans or the Euclideans. In fact, there's a good chance Javier will be joining the Archimedeans in a unit or two. . . . Rodney will be okay sticking with the Pythagoreans for now, but when the Archimedeans start Unit 7, I'll have him participate in the initial conceptualization activities. . . .

"What did I learn during this unit that'll help me do a better job when the other two groups get to Unit 7? . . . Don't push too hard for the articulation phase of the conceptualization—at least not until you've built up a variety of hands-on experiences with examples and nonexamples. At least next time I do this unit, I'll be able to build on the examples and nonexamples I formulated for this one. Wouldn't it be nice to only teach units that you've taught before; that means never teaching one for the first time! . . . Okay, Dustin, quit talking to yourself and get tomorrow's plans out of the way. . . ."

There are three parts to the test:

Part I consists of 2 one-to-one interview items each designed to be relevant to Objective A:

1. Task presented to the student:

Mr. Manda displays the following two pictures to the student and says, "Which one of the two pictures shows why 5 + 3 = 8?":

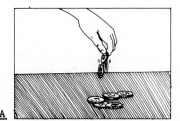 

After the student makes the selection, Mr. Manda says, "Explain to me why that one [the one the student chose] shows 5 + 3 = 8, but the other one doesn't." Mr. Manda does not coach the student toward a correct response, but if necessary, uses probing questions to clarify what the student intends to say.

Scoring key:

+1 if the student selects Picture A and the explanation clearly indicates that she or he identified the attributes of addition on whole numbers that are illustrated by A but not by B

0 if the response does not clearly indicate whether or not the student identified the necessary attributes illustrated by A but not by B

-1 if the response clearly indicates that the student did not identify the necessary attributes illustrated by A but not by B

2. Task presented to the student:

Mr. Manda displays the following two pictures to the student and says, "Which one of the two pictures shows why 2 + 3 = 5?":

(continued)

Figure 7.23. Description of the Mathematics Unit 7 Test Dustin Administers the Pythagoreans

After the student makes the selection, Mr. Manda says, "Explain to me why that one [the one the student chose] shows 2 + 3 = 5, but the other one doesn't." Mr. Manda does not coach the student toward a correct response, but if necessary, uses probing questions to clarify what the student intends to say.

Scoring key:

+1 if the student selects Picture <u>B</u> and the explanation clearly indicates that she or he identified the attributes of addition on whole numbers that are illustrated by <u>B</u> but not by <u>A</u>

0 if the response does not clearly indicate whether or not the student identified the necessary attributes illustrated by <u>B</u> but not by <u>A</u>

-1 if the response clearly indicates that the student did not identify the necessary attributes illustrated by <u>B</u> but not by <u>A</u>

<u>Part II</u> consists of 2 written-response items, the first designed to be relevant to Objective <u>B</u>, the second designed to be relevant to objectives <u>C</u> and <u>D</u>:

1. <u>Task presented to the student</u>:

   The student is provided a set of manipulatives suitable for counting and directed to use them to complete each of the following number sentences (which are indicated sums of whole numbers but exclusive of memorized addition facts):

   $$7 + 5 = \underline{\hspace{1cm}} \qquad 12 + 3 = \underline{\hspace{1cm}}$$

   $$3 + 9 = \underline{\hspace{1cm}} \qquad 4 + 13 = \underline{\hspace{1cm}}$$

   Scoring key:

   (4 points maximum) +1 for each correct response

Figure 7.23. (Continued)

2. Task presented to the student:

The student is directed to draw a line connecting each
addition fact on the left with its matching picture on the
right:

0 + 5 = 5

1 + 7 = 8

3 + 2 = 5

Scoring key:

(3 points maximum) +1 for each correct match

Part III consists of 2 one-to-one interview items, the first
designed to be relevant to Objective E, the second to
Objective F:

1. Task presented to the student:

Twenty-five flash cards (5 randomly selected from each of
the addition tables for 1 through 5) are shuffled and shown
one at a time to the student for two seconds. For each, the
student is allowed one second to respond orally with the
correct sum.

Scoring key:

(25 points maximum) +1 for each on-time correct sum

(continued)

Figure 7.23. (Continued)

2. <u>Task presented to the student</u>:

   Using the accompanying illustrations, Mr. Manda explains the
   following story to the student and asks the questions as
   indicated:

   These people over here in the picture on the left have a
   band. Ted here can play the guitar, Sue the trumpet, and
   Betty here can play the piano and also the drums. How
   many people are in their band? _[ans. <u>A</u>]_ How many
   different <u>kinds</u> of musical instruments can they play
   altogether? _[ans. <u>B</u>]_ Now, over here in this second
   picture is another band. There's Kartina here who can
   play the guitar, Sam who also can play a guitar, Sandra
   who can play the saxophone, and Tim who can play the
   drums. How many people in their band? _[ans. <u>C</u>]_ And
   how many different <u>kinds</u> of musical instruments can they
   play? _[ans. <u>D</u>]_ The two bands decided to join and make
   one band. How many people are now in the new band?
   [ans. <u>E</u>] How many different <u>kinds</u> of instruments can
   the people in the new band play? _[ans. <u>F</u>]_

During the interview, Mr. Manda invites the student to ask
questions to clarify the problem. He should also coach
students to obtain correct answers for <u>A</u>, <u>B</u>, <u>C</u>, and <u>D</u>; but
he may not influence the student's answers or process used
to determine answers for <u>E</u> and <u>F</u>.

<u>Scoring key</u>:

(3 points maximum) Answers for <u>A</u>, <u>B</u>, <u>C</u>, and <u>D</u> are not scored
as their purpose is for Mr. Manda to assess how well the
student comprehends the problem. <u>E</u> is scored as follows:

   +1 if the student attempts to add 3 and 4 and +1 if the
   student's answer is "7"

<u>F</u> is scored as follows:

   +1 if the student's answer is "5"

Part II is administered to the <u>Pythagoreans</u> in a group on Monday while
individual members are administered Part I one at a time. Part III is
administered one at a time on Tuesday while the group is engaged in an
independent work session.

Figure 7.23. (Continued)

TABLE 7.1. Results Dustin Compiled from Administering Figure 7.23's Test to the Pythagoreans

Student	Scores for Items Categorized by Objective				
	Obj. A It. I-1&2 max 2 pt	Obj. B It. II-1 max 4 pt	Obj. C&D It. II-2 max 3 pt	Obj. E It. III-1 max 25 pt	Obj. F It. III-2 max 3 pt
Chao-Cui	2	4	3	23	3
Cinny	2	4	3	19	3
Cito	2	3	3	19	3
Evelyn A.	2	4	3	25	3
Evelyn P.	2	4	3	21	2
Ivory	2	4	3	21	3
Liu	2	4	3	22	3
Olga	2	4	3	16	3
Rodney W.	0	4	2	18	1

INSERVICE OPPORTUNITIES AND PROFESSIONAL CONFERENCES

Throughout the school year, Dustin avails himself of opportunities to improve his teaching performances. Meetings of the local affiliate of the National Association of Young Children and the International Reading Association provide opportunities to share ideas with colleagues and hear professionally relevant presentations. Although they rarely address his particular teaching situation, his creative thinking about teaching is stimulated by a college graduate course he manages to attend one night a week and by several inservice workshops sponsored by the school district. Even though he had enjoyed journals such as *Arithmetic Teacher, Elementary School Journal*, and *The Reading Teacher* for a number of years, he finds the articles even more meaningful now that he has real students and actual courses to teach. His continuous struggle to come up with meaningful examples and real-world problems for his conceptualization and application lessons motivates him to read about art, health and physical fitness, language arts, mathematics, music, science, and social studies more than ever before. The almost constant need to respond to students' queries and thoughts cause him to gain insights into academic content that he never before imagined. He learns from interacting with colleagues and they learn from him. Rita Slater's help is invaluable; even teachers with whom he disagrees on most pedagogical issues (e.g., Rosalie Taylor) stimulate productive thoughts.

In April, Dustin takes three "professional leave days" to attend the annual conference of the International Reading Association. There, he interacts with colleagues from around the world whose goals, problems, frustrations, and successes appear remarkably familiar after eight months in the profession. Even this late in the year, Dustin is energized by the associations with colleagues as well as the conference sessions. Some sessions are "hands-on" activities; others have speakers presenting ideas or research findings. The quality of the sessions varies considerably from very boring to very exciting, but all leave him with thoughts that will improve his classroom effectiveness. At the conference, he reviews exhibits of instructional resources, technology, and publications for teachers.

WINDING DOWN THE SCHOOL YEAR
AND ANTICIPATING NEXT YEAR

The end of May is filled with clerical tasks (e.g., accounting for instructional materials and completing scores of year-end forms and reports required by the district school board). Though feeling exhausted, Dustin is already anticipating his second year. He thinks to himself, "If I had known in August what I know now, my students would've learned so much more! I can't wait until next year to do it right! Now I know what to expect and for what to prepare. This year, I started from scratch. Now, I have a wealth of resources—lesson plans, illustrations, item pools neatly stored on computer disks, and professional colleagues with whom I exchange ideas. That's quite a bit to build on. Although I wasn't perfect, my students learned because of me. They developed intellectually, formed healthy attitudes about learning, and acquired critical skills."

SELF-ASSESSMENT EXERCISES FOR CHAPTER 7

I. With a group of your colleagues who have also read Chapters 1–7, engage in a discussion relative to the following questions or tasks:

A. How important to his success was Dustin's assertive behavior? What might have gone differently if he had not learned to be more assertive?

B. What are the advantages and disadvantages of Dustin's selecting the names Euclideans, Archimedeans, and Pythagoreans for the three first-grade mathematics groups?

C. Following is what Dustin said in response to the question, "Why did you name your mathematics groups Euclideans, Archimedeans, and Pythagoreans?"

"I put a lot of thought into what to call those groups. I wanted to avoid labels that even hinted that one group was better, smarter, or more important than any other one. I had already coded my reading groups with animal names and I wanted the mathematics groups to be different. Color-coding was considered, but that sometimes has racial overtones and there are colors like 'yellow' associated with 'chicken,' and 'green' with 'raw' and so forth. I wanted something that at least sounded equally 'smart' to everyone.

"Historically, of course, Pythagoreans and Euclideans are groups who studied mathematics around 500 B.C. in Greece. As far as I know, there was no group known as the Archimedeans, but I thought if followers of Pythagoras and Elucid could carry their names, my favorite mathematician, Archimedes, could have his group also—just 2,200 years too late! Anyway, I realized such high-sounding, multisyllabic names might seem a bit complex for first-graders. Even worse, such names might suggest that mathematics is more difficult than other subjects. But then I remembered reading Haim Ginott's (1972) wonderful little book, *Teacher and Child*, in which he suggests that adults should expose young children to sophisticated vocabulary. I figured the first-graders might enjoy such high-sounding terms—giving the groups a special air of importance. Also, it would stimulate some discussions on the origins of mathematics.

"It seemed a little risky at first, but now that the year is over, the names seemed to work out well. After a week or so they got comfortable with them, and although I can't say for sure, it might have helped them become more receptive to new vocabulary. Also, they ended up learning more about mathematical history than I ever learned throughout my first eight years in school."

Readdress the question in **B** in light of what Dustin said.

D. What do you think of Dustin's idea of two-week theme periods? How did the themes help him integrate the courses? Critique his selection and sequence of themes.

E. Critique Dustin's initial letter to parents displayed in Figure 7.7. Realizing that it is intended for different parents within a wide range of reading comprehension and interest levels, what do you think of the level of the writing regarding such matters as complexity of the message, paragraphs, and vocabulary? What do you think of his plan to open and maintain lines of communications with parents? Besides establishing lines of communications, what other purposes do you think Dustin had in mind when he composed the letter? If you received such a letter from one of your children's teachers, with what first impressions would it leave you?

F. In light of Figure 7.9's objectives and what you know about the Pythagoreans, critique Figure 7.23's unit test regarding both validity and usability.

G. In light of what you read in the section "Communicating Effectively" beginning on page 140, what do you think of the manner in which Dustin communicated with his students on day one of Mathematics Unit 7 (beginning on p. 313)?

H. No examples of Dustin using games (as suggested in Chapter 5's section "Initiating and Maintaining Student Engagement in Recitation Sessions") are included in this chapter. In light of Figure 7.10's unit plan, where do you think Dustin might have appropriately incorporated games in his lessons?

I. Considering Figure 7.10's unit plan and how Dustin actually conducted Unit 7 for the Pythagoreans, how consistently did Dustin seem to adhere to Chapter 3's suggestions for designing lessons?

J. In what ways did Dustin depend on his own computer and those for students to get things done? What would he have not accomplished as efficiently if he hadn't had ready access to computers?

II. Interview a first-year teacher. Include the following questions: (a) What are some of the more prominent things you've learned since you've started teaching? (b) What to this point in your career has been the most satisfying surprise? (c) What to this point has been the most frustrating surprise?

SUGGESTED READING

Conoley, J. C. (1989). Professional communication and collaboration among educators. In M. C. Reynolds (Ed.), *Knowledge base for the beginning teacher* (pp. 245–254). Oxford: Pergamon Press.

McCarthy, D. J. (1989). The school district: A unique setting. In M. C. Reynolds (Ed.), *Knowledge base for the beginning teacher* (pp. 155–162). Oxford: Pergamon Press.

McCarty, M. M. (1989). Legal rights and responsibilities of public school teachers. In M. C. Reynolds (Ed.), *Knowledge base for the beginning teacher* (pp. 255–266). Oxford: Pergamon Press.

TAKING WHAT YOU'VE LEARNED TO THE NEXT LEVEL

Your ability to apply systematic teaching strategies was enhanced by vicariously experiencing Dustin's first year of teaching. Chapter 8 takes you on a similar journey with another beginning teacher, but this time it is a high school teacher, Nancy Fisher.

CHAPTER 8

Theory into Practice: Nancy Fisher, First-Year High School Teacher

GOAL OF CHAPTER 8

This chapter walks you through Nancy Fisher's first year as a high school teacher as she learns to put research-based principles and techniques into practice. Chapter 8's goal is the same as that for Chapter 7. Acquainting you with the thoughts, strategies, and experiences of another first-year teacher with a different teaching assignment should extend your achievement of that goal.

NANCY FISHER AND HER FIRST TEACHING POSITION

Preservice Preparation

As a teenager, Nancy Fisher developed a desire to help people understand one another. The idea of becoming a social studies teacher first occurred to her while in high school taking a geography course conducted by a dynamic teacher, Benjamin Lancy. She thought, "Mr. Lancy studies people, their environments, and origins and why they do and don't get along with one another. On top of that he makes sure what he learns and how he learns are passed on to the next generation. Teachers live forever through their students!" When Nancy attended college, it was quite natural for her to enroll in a preservice program for secondary teachers with a composite major in social studies.

Besides standard general requirements in the arts, humanities, and sciences, the program included more than a dozen social studies content courses (including economics, history, geography, political science, and sociology). There were also professional education courses (including educational psychology, adolescent psychology, general teaching methods, social and philosophical foundations of education, educational and psychological measurement and evaluation, classroom management, and methods of teaching social studies). Only a few of her university instructors employed the kind of teaching strategies that were recommended in her general teaching methods course—a course that used this textbook. She began her tenure as a student teacher quite confident in her own knowledge-level, intellectual-level, and affective-level development in the field of social studies but worried about being able to help students develop their own skills, abilities, and attitudes. Before her cooperating teacher shifted major responsibilities for the classes to her, she had nightmares about bored students refusing to cooperate with her as she stumbled in full view of the cooperating teacher, supervising professor, and school principal. During the weeks in which she moved from several mini-lessons a day, to one full period a day, to conducting all of her cooperating teachers' classes, the nightmares evaporated and her confidence soared. Though far more time consuming and complex than she had ever before imagined, the satisfaction she derived from working with students during the experience "hooked" her on teaching as she anticipated her first year in the profession.

Selecting a Position at Rainbow High School

As she applies for positions in 30 different school districts, Nancy hopes to be hired at her former high school where she can continue to learn from Mr. Lancy, this time as a colleague. Thus, although the school had not advertised for a social studies teacher, she submits an application to the district where her alma mater, Lynwood High, is located. Late in May shortly before her university graduation, Nancy receives a call from a Lynwood High secretary to set up an interview with Principal Nadia Leinhardt. Nancy enthusiastically meets with the principal:

NADIA: Hello Ms. Fisher, I'm Nadia Leinhardt; it's very nice to meet you. I see by your application that you're a Lynwood graduate.

NANCY: That's right. Mr. Washington was principal then; I see the school is still in good hands.

NADIA: I like to think so; there've been a few changes since you were here.

NANCY: All for the better I hear.

NADIA: As long as we can recruit new teachers like yourself coming out of college with fresh, exciting ideas and energy and retain enough of our veterans to maintain stability, we can't help but improve.

NANCY: Well I'm excited about the possibility of joining the faculty here.

NADIA: Your application file from the district office is quite impressive. You wrote an interesting statement of teaching philosophy—seems to fit right in with what we're all about at Lynwood. Also, Zeke Eskelsen from personnel responded quite positively to your visit with him.

NANCY: Thank you. I was quite impressed with him. But he said he didn't anticipate any openings for social studies teachers in the district.

NADIA: The opening we have here is for a math teacher.

NANCY: But my specialty is social studies.

NADIA: Yes, I know, but we haven't been able to fill all our math positions with math specialists. So our remedial math and beginning algebra are mostly taught by crossover teachers—prepared in health and physical education, social studies, English, and other fields in which more teachers are available.

NANCY: That's terrible!

NADIA: Yes, it is, but we try to move these out-of-field teachers into their specialties as soon as openings for them are available. Some, however, have managed to certify in mathematics through inservice work and they remain math teachers.

NANCY: And you're considering me as a mathematics teacher?

NADIA: And also as a possible women's volleyball coach. Your recommendations are outstanding and I understand you were quite a volleyball player here at Lynwood. . . . You seem like you'd fit right in with our faculty and be good for our students.

NANCY: I'm flattered by your confidence, but I'm not qualified to teach mathematics nor do I have a coaching or physical education background.

NADIA: In this state you may coach without being certified in physical education and we can hire you to teach math under the emergency provision for areas of critical shortage.

NANCY: But I'm a professional social studies teacher.

NADIA: I'd rather hire a professional teacher—even an out-of-field one—who can work with our students than someone who may know the content but doesn't know how to teach.

NANCY: I agree with you; but I'm not ready to teach out of my field.

NADIA: There's an extra $3,000 for coaching volleyball.

NANCY: I really appreciate you considering me, and I would really love to teach here. But in all good conscience, I'm obliged to seek a position teaching social studies. When a social studies position opens up here, I'd be most grateful if you would contact me and allow me to apply for it.

NADIA: I really admire your professional integrity. Be assured that you'll be notified.

NANCY: Thank you. I'll keep my file in the district office current so you'll know how to contact me.

Over the next two months, there are more interviews and several offers but she continues to resist the security of a "job in hand" in pursuit of the "right" position for her. Assessing her situation in late July, Nancy concludes that for now there are no schools in geographical locations she considers desirable that have openings matching her talents and preparation. Thus, she swallows her desire to locate near her home town and decides to begin her career on the faculty of Rainbow High School. Although uncomfortable about the location, she chooses Rainbow High for the following reasons:

Principal Maurice Jones seems committed to a strong social studies program. In the interview, he said, "We consider society and people to be the focal point of Rainbow's curriculum."

Her teaching assignment will include only social studies courses.

The salary is competitive with those of other teaching opportunities.

The opening of school is less than a month away; waiting for another position would not allow her time to organize and prepare courses.

The Assignment

The Teaching Load. Figure 8.1 reflects Nancy's year-long teaching load. Nancy would have preferred a schedule with longer periods so that each course section meets only once every other day. Longer sections she reasons would provide greater flexibility, fewer starting and stopping transitions to manage, and breaks in the monotony of everyday meetings. She plans to initiate a campaign to con-

First- and Second-Semester Schedule

Class	Period	Assignment	Room	Course Credits per Semester
Homeroom	8:10–8:25	Tenth grade—B	203	——
1st	8:30–9:25	U.S. History*	203	0.5
2nd	9:30–10:25	Preparation	——	——
3rd	10:30–11:25	Geography*	203	0.5
4th	11:30–12:25	Geography*	111	0.5
Lunch-A	12:30–12:55	Lunch supervision	lunch room	——
Lunch-B	1:00–1:25	Free	——	——
5th	1:30–2:25	U.S. History*	203	0.5
6th	2:30–3:25	Economics**	203	0.5
Announcements	3:25–3:30	——	203	——

* Two semester course (one group of students both semesters)
** One semester course (different group of students each semester)

Figure 8.1. Nancy Fisher's First-Year Teaching Schedule

vince her colleagues of the advantages of modifying the schedule in this way, but she'll wait until she's an established member of the faculty before suggesting changes in the school's operations.

Other Responsibilities. Besides teaching five classes per semester, Nancy is expected to:

> serve as homeroom monitor and administrator to approximately 25 tenth-graders
>
> serve as a general supervisor of students during school hours, enforcing school rules
>
> while free to eat lunch during Lunch-A period, serve as a lunchroom monitor during that time
>
> assist in the governance of the school by responding to administrators' requests for input and participating in both general faculty and social studies department meetings
>
> cooperate in the school's system for both administrative supervision and instructional supervision of her own teaching
>
> participate in the school's professional exchange program with Francis Parker High School, a school in a neighboring district (Rainbow's teachers serve on summative evaluation teams for teachers at Francis Parker and Francis Parker's teachers do the same for Rainbow's faculty; such programs are described in the professional literature—see, e.g., Cangelosi 1991, pp. 123–126, 161–194)
>
> participate in professional development activities (e.g., by attending inservice workshops, taking college courses, and being involved in organizations such as the state affiliate of the National Council of the Social Studies)
>
> represent Rainbow High as a professional in the community

In conversations with social studies department colleagues Larry Stutler (the department chairperson), and Maxine Wilson, Nancy discusses the possibility of organizing a history club for students.

ORGANIZING FOR THE YEAR

The Givens as of August 1

With the opening day of school about three weeks away, Nancy obtains keys for the building and her "home-base" classroom—room 203, a faculty handbook, a copy of the State Education Office's *Curriculum Guide for Social Studies*, Figure 8.1's schedule, and a teacher's edition of the textbook for each of the assigned courses. As part of her preservice experiences in college, Nancy had conducted numerous lessons, but she had never before been responsible for organizing and preparing entire courses and a classroom for conducting business. She begins by surveying her room (i.e., room 203) and then room 111, the home-base for a biology teacher and the classroom for her fourth-period geography class. She thinks, "No computers available in my room. If I can't get any for students, that'll make it difficult to do the kind of content writing activities that are so valuable. I better make a note to find out what's available for students—I guess people think only mathematics, computer science, business, and writing students need computers. Fortunately, Maurice said he had one for my personal use and I've got my own at home. . . .

"With those fixed lab tables, room 111 is just too inflexible for me to operate! How can I possibly set it up for cooperative group activities. . . . Why can't I use my own room for fourth period? . . . I'll ask Larry if he can work something out and get that switched. . . . For now, I should get my room arranged like I want. . . . But how do I want it arranged? I guess that depends on how I organize the courses—how much students need to move around and how many students each period. Maurice said we won't get class rolls until the first week of school, but that my classes should run between 20 and 30. So, I really need to get a better idea of how I want to organize the courses before worrying much more about the room. Of course, the room will also influence the courses. If there're no computers available and I'm in an inflexible lab fourth period, that's going to limit what I can do.

"Larry said the textbooks are givens for this year, but I'd have a say in the choice of some of the texts next year when there's supposed to be a turnover. . . . Might as well start going through these three texts and see what I've got to work with. . . ."

Over the next few days, Nancy familiarizes herself with the textbooks and state curriculum guide, taking notes to be used in planning the courses. The curriculum guide simply lists goals to be covered in each course; the goals are quite consistent with the topics listed in the textbooks. She judges that the textbooks should be quite useful sources of information and definitions but that she will need to be creative in developing and locating materials for conceptualization and application level lessons. For the U.S. history course the text is titled *History of the United States* (DiBacco, Mason, & Appy, 1991), for geography it is *Earth's Geography and Environment* (Mitsakos, 1991), and for economics it is *McDougal,*

Littell Economics (Watson, 1991). She's pleased that the history text has a rather expansive teacher's edition with suggestions for organizing the course, exercises, and cooperative group activities. There are also supplemental materials including computer software for generating tests and planning lessons. Resource guides with flexible course organizational schemes, exercise sheets, and test items accompany the other two books.

Valuable Help from a Colleague

With Larry Stutler, Nancy raises the issue of scheduling her fourth-period geography class in room 203 instead of room 111. Understanding of Nancy's plight, Larry checks on the matter and finds out that 203 is the only room available fourth period that is large enough to accommodate a drug-abuse awareness class. It seems that due to a new state-mandated requirement, a "double-section" of over 40 students will be using room 203, bringing in extra desks just for fourth period. Room 111 is too inflexible for extra desks to be brought in! Nancy's visions of this fourth-period onslaught on her home-base classroom are upsetting. Larry also informs her that history classrooms are not authorized to house computers for student use. However, there is a computer lab available for students to use an hour before school starts in the morning and after school until 8 P.M.

Resolving to make the best of the room facilities, Nancy begins organizing her courses. She turns to Larry for advice:

> NANCY: I'm having a terrible time getting my courses planned and organized. I've gone through the books, looked at the available materials and facilities, and all that, but I just can't get a handle on the courses from A to Z. . . . I can put together individual lessons, but have trouble fitting the pieces together.
>
> LARRY: I know just what you mean and I have a suggestion. For each course, begin writing a syllabus. Write it for the students to read. Being forced to describe the purposes and organization of a course for students' understanding will get you to organize your thoughts into a coherent whole. Not only does having a syllabi lend a businesslike air to your courses and serve as guides for students, but trying to write them lends structure to the process of organizing and planning the courses.

Planning and Organizing the Courses by Writing Syllabi

Taking Larry's advice, Nancy sits at her computer outlining the course syllabus for her U.S. History course with the aid of a word-processing program. She thinks, "This syllabus needs to be designed so that it sends students the message that this class is serious business, and I'm serious enough about it to have it well organized and planned. The syllabi my college instructors used tended to be full of formal-looking lists of reading references, content, deadlines, and grading criteria. I need some of that here, but I can't be too specific about dates and deadlines until I get into the course and see how things go. In college, there were also a couple of paragraphs providing a rationale for the course. I should have something like that, but I've got to keep in mind that I'm dealing with tenth- and eleventh-graders here—there's the matter of reading level and the danger of turning them off with a long narrative. . . .

"Just what are my purposes for putting a syllabus in their hands? . . . First, it should provide a guide for the course. Second, it needs to give them some ideas about expectations, including things like classroom rules—I don't want to forget that. Then, there's the need of getting the class off to a good start, setting a businesslike tone and building some enthusiasm for history. And fourth, give them the impression I know what I'm doing—seeing a well-organized syllabus will communicate that better than me preaching to them about how important and organized this course is! . . .

"I'll start with an outline of what to include: Name of course, basic information like my name and the room number, a rationale, what the course is all about, a listing of materials they need, classroom rules, an idea of what they'll be doing, goals of the course, and the bases for their grades. . . . Larry is right, writing this thing is going to force me to make some hard decisions that'll get me organizing this course!"

Further thought about how to format the syllabus leads Nancy to an innovative idea. She decides to organize the syllabus around the questions that the document should answer for students—questions she would expect them to raise about the course. After another hour and a few false starts, she works with the following list of questions that will become the headings in the syllabus:

1. WHAT IS THIS COURSE ALL ABOUT?
2. WHAT IS HISTORY?
3. WHY SHOULD YOU LEARN U.S. HISTORY?
4. WITH WHOM WILL YOU BE WORKING IN THIS COURSE?
5. WHERE WILL YOU BE LEARNING U.S. HISTORY?
6. HOW WILL YOU BE EXPECTED TO BEHAVE IN THIS CLASS?
7. WHAT MATERIALS WILL YOU NEED FOR CLASS?
8. WHAT WILL YOU BE DOING FOR THIS CLASS?
9. WHAT WILL YOU LEARN FROM THIS CLASS?
10. HOW WILL YOU KNOW WHEN YOU'VE LEARNED HISTORY?
11. HOW WILL YOUR GRADES FOR THE COURSE BE DETERMINED?

Nancy spends the next day determining how to answer these 11 questions for her students and how to express the answers in the syllabus. The most taxing task is to address the ninth question for which she has to determine the sequence of teaching units for the course and formulate a learning goal for each. She finds the "Chapter Planner" in the teacher's edition of the textbook quite helpful in determining the units and for estimating the number of days and lessons for each. The 22 units about which she ultimately organizes the course rely on but do not completely follow the textbook's 33 chapters.

Once Nancy completes the syllabus, much of her anxiety about teaching U.S. history evaporates and her enthusiasm for the school year intensifies. She feels prepared to go to work. The U.S. history syllabus for the first-period class is displayed in Figure 8.2. In a similar fashion, Nancy develops syllabi for her other courses and sections.

Course Syllabus
for
U.S.History

WHAT IS THIS COURSE ALL ABOUT?

The course is all about the **history of the United States:**
- Journeying through time taking us from the origins of our country to where we are today
- Discovering how to utilize the lessons of history to deal with today's issues and problems

WHAT IS HISTORY?

There are three aspects of history:
- All actual past events
- Methods used by historians to discover and describe past events and explain their causes and influences
- Documented references resulting from the work of historians

WHY SHOULD YOU LEARN U.S. HISTORY?

Everyday of your life you make decisions about how to behave, what to do, where to go, who to see, what to eat, what to wear, and so on and so forth. Those decisions are influenced by your understanding of events in your past life (i.e., your own history). For example, you are more likely to choose to go places you found enjoyable in the past than to places where you were bored. Your understanding of past events help you to control present and future events.

As a world citizen, especially one living in the United States, you have an influence over present and future events in this country. Those events influence your everyday life. Understand events in this country's past and you'll be better able to influence its future.

There are also some more mundane reasons:
- Your success in other courses you take in high school as well as in any vocational school, technical school, or college you might attend depends on your understanding of history.
- A full year credit in U.S. history is required for a high school diploma in this state.
- An understanding of at least some U.S. history is expected of literate citizens in today's society and is needed in many occupations.

WITH WHOM WILL YOU BE WORKING IN THIS COURSE?

You will be working with Nancy Fisher, who is responsible for helping you and your classmates learn U.S. history. You will also be working with your classmates, each of whom will be making a unique contribution to what you get out of this course. In turn, you will contribute to what they learn by sharing your ideas, discoveries, insights, problems, and solutions.

WHERE WILL YOU BE LEARNING U.S. HISTORY?

You will draw your understanding of history from your entire environment whether at home, school, or anywhere else. Your classroom, room 203, at Rainbow High is the place where ideas about history are brought together and formalized. Room 203 is a place of business for learning history.

HOW WILL YOU BE EXPECTED TO BEHAVE IN THIS CLASS?

You and your classmates have the right to go about the business of learning history free from fear of being harmed, intimidated, or embarrassed. Ms. Fisher has the right to go about the business of helping you and your classmates learn history without disruption or interference. Thus, you are expected to follow five rules of conduct:

(continued)

Figure 8.2. Nancy Fisher's Syllabus for Her First-Period U.S. History Course

1. Give yourself a complete opportunity to learn history.
2. Do not interfere with the opportunities of your classmates to learn history.
3. Respect the rights of all members of this class (they include, you, your classmates, and Ms. Fisher).
4. Follow Ms. Fisher's directions for lessons and classroom procedures.
5. Adhere to the rules and policies of Rainbow High as listed on pages 11–15 of the **Student Handbook.**

WHAT MATERIALS WILL YOU NEED FOR CLASS?

Bring the following with you to every class meeting:
- The course textbook:
  DiBacco, T. V., Mason, L. C., & Appy, C. G. (1991). **History of the United States.** Boston: Houghton Mifflin.
- A four-part notebook:
  1. Part 1 is for class notes.
  2. Part 2 is for homework and class assignments.
  3. Part 3 is for saving artifacts from independent and cooperative-group activities.
  4. Part 4 is for maintaining a reference for definitions and facts.
- A scratch pad
- Pencils, pens, and an eraser

You will also need five 5.25″ computer diskettes in a storage case. You will not have to bring these to class every day, but have them available at school (e.g., in your locker).

A textbook has been checked out to you for the school year. You are responsible for maintaining it in good condition and returning it to Ms. Fisher on the last day of class. The other materials can be purchased at the Rainbow High Bookstore or at other retail outlets.

WHAT WILL YOU BE DOING FOR THIS CLASS?

The course is organized into 22 units between one to three weeks each. During each unit you will be:
- Participating in class meetings
  Depending on the agenda for the meetings you will be:
  - Listening to Ms. Fisher speak and seeing her illustrations as you take notes on what is being explained
  - Listening to classmates speak and seeing their illustrations as you take notes on what is being explained
  - Explaining things to the class as your classmates take notes on what you say and show them
  - Asking questions, answering questions, and discussing issues with members of the class during questioning/discussion sessions
  - Working closely with your classmates as part of small task-groups
  - Working independently on assigned exercises
  - Taking brief tests
- Completing homework assignments
- Taking a unit test

WHAT WILL YOU LEARN FROM THIS CLASS?

Each unit will either introduce you to a new historical topic or extend your understanding of a previous topic. During the unit you will:
- Discover an idea or relationship

Figure 8.2. (Continued)

- Add to your ability to use historical methods
- Acquire new information or add depth of understanding to previously acquired information
- Extend your ability to utilize the lessons in history to solve today's problems

Here are the titles of the 22 units:
1. Looking Ahead in Light of Past Lessons; Historical Methods
2. The First Americans, Exploration, and Colonization
3. A New Nation
4. The U.S. Constitution and the New Republic
5. Expansion
6. The Civil War and Reconstruction Eras
7. Emergence of Industrial America, New Frontiers
8. Urban Society and Gilded-Age Politics
9. Protests and the Progressive Movement
10. Expansionism
11. World War I
12. The Roaring Twenties
13. The Great Depression and the New Deal
14. A Search for Peace and World War II
15. A Cold Peace
16. The Politics of Conflict and Hope
17. The Civil Rights Movement
18. The Vietnam War
19. Dirty Politics
20. Toward a Global (and cleaner) Society
21. The New Nationalism
22. Extending What You've Learned into a New Century

Units 1–12 are planned for the first semester, Units 13–22 for the second semester.

HOW WILL YOU KNOW WHEN YOU'VE LEARNED U.S. HISTORY?

Everyone knows at least some history, but no one ever learns it completely. History is being discovered. You will use what you learn in this course to further develop your ability to apply the lessons of history to everyday decision making.

The question is not whether or not you've learned history, but how well you are learning it. During this course, you will be given feedback on your progress through comments Ms. Fisher makes about work you complete, scores you achieve on brief tests, and the grades you achieve based on unit, midsemester, and semester tests.

HOW WILL YOUR GRADES FOR THE COURSE BE DETERMINED?

Your grade for the first semester will be based on 12 unit tests, a midsemester test scheduled between the sixth and seventh units, and a semester test. Your scores on these tests will influence your first semester grade according to the following scale:

- The 12 unit tests .... 60% (5% each)
- The midsemester test 15%
- The semester test 25%

Your grade for the second semester will be based on 10 unit tests, a midsemester test scheduled between the 17th and 18th units, and a semester test. Your scores on these tests will influence your second semester grade according to the following scale:

- The 10 unit tests .... 60% (6% each)
- The midsemester test 15%
- The semester test 25%

Figure 8.2. (Continued)

Organizing the Classroom

With course syllabi in hand, Nancy confidently anticipates meeting her classes. With only a week before opening day, she begins organizing room 203 and working out a management plan for the year. She retrieves the textbook from the teaching methods course she took in college (i.e., the book you are now reading), turns to page 35, and carefully responds to each of the 15 questions under "Classroom Organization and Ongoing Routines," to the nine questions under "One-Time-Only Tasks," and to the three questions under "Reminders for the First Week's Learning Activities." With those questions resolved, she organizes room 203 for efficient transitions between large- and small-group arrangements (e.g., see Figures 1.7 and 1.8). Unfortunately, she has little control over room 111.

Preparations, Arrangements, and Acquisitions

Similar to Dustin Manda's activities described on pages 294–295, Nancy spends the last few days prior to the opening of school setting up her item pool files, learning Rainbow High's "ropes" for obtaining supplies and equipment, and collaborating with other teachers for coordinating units across various content areas and helping one another with potential behavior management problems.

THE BEGINNING OF AN EVENTFUL SCHOOL YEAR

Opening Day

Nancy bases plans for the first day's classes on the model exemplified by Mr. Stockton in Vignette 4.4. However, unlike Mr. Stockton, Nancy does not prepare videotape presentations. For each class, she prepares name cards and a questionnaire/tasksheet for students to work on as soon as they are seated in the classroom. The questionnaire/tasksheet for the U.S. history course is shown in Figure 8.3; she designed the questionnaire/tasksheets with the following purposes in mind:

The students are to immediately get busy working with course content while she takes care of some administrative chores (e.g., distributing textbooks). This, she feels, will help to establish a businesslike classroom learning environment that she read about in Chapter 4 of this text.

The students are both successful and challenged by the tasks. The history students, for example, already know numerous historical events of which no one else in the class is aware (mostly from their own family histories), but they've never before examined how they came to know these things. Also, most of the items involve expressing opinions, describing observations, and reporting about themselves—things everyone *can* do, but require thinking.

The students are to form the following impressions about the course they're starting under Nancy's direction: (a) The content (i.e., history, geography, or economics) they will learn is related to their own individual interests; (b) They are expected to make judgments, and those judgments are valued;

1. What is your name? _____

2. Think of something that happened before you were born that you
   think almost everyone here in this room also knows about. In one
   or two sentences tell what happened.

   _____

   _____

   _____

3. What makes you think what you just wrote actually happened?

   _____

   _____

   _____

4. Think of something that happened before you were born that you
   think no one else in this room (other than yourself) also knows
   about. In one or two sentences tell what happened.

   _____

   _____

   _____

   _____

5. What makes you think what you just wrote actually happened?

   _____

   _____

6. Explain one way in which you have influenced history.

   _____

   _____

   _____

7. Suppose that you are by yourself in this unfamiliar building.
   You're in a hallway and come to a door. Before opening the door,
   you want to know what's on the other side. Fortunately, it's one
   of those old doors with the kind of keyholes you can look through.
   You peek through the keyhole and you see what appears in the
   picture below. Describe exactly what you see through the keyhole
   - only what you can actually see:

                                                        (continued)

Figure 8.3. Questionnaire/Tasksheet Nancy Uses with Her U.S. History Classes on the First Day
   of School

Your description: _____

_____

_____

_____

_____

_____

_____

_____

_____

Now, <u>describe</u> what you would <u>infer</u> the room behind the door looks like based on the limited view you had through the keyhole:

_____

_____

_____

_____

8. Make a list of 10 important questions you're going to have to make a decision about during the next nine months:

A. _____

B. _____

C. _____

D. _____

E. _____

F. _____

G. _____

H. _____

I. _____

J. _____

Figure 8.3. (Continued)

346

(c) They are expected to write about course content; (d) Their experiences in this course will be different from those they've had in previous courses.

Nancy can utilize students' responses to the items in sessions for helping students understand the nature of the course's content. For example, as she "walks" the class through the course syllabus, she will play off their responses while addressing the question "What is history (geography, economics)?" In subsequent lessons, she will occasionally make reference to their responses to this questionnaire/tasksheet.

Nancy can make use of information gained from responses to the last item in planning lessons (e.g., to select topics for problems of interest to students).

Just before each class, she places a name card and a questionnaire/tasksheet on each student's desk. The 55-minute period is spent as follows:

1. She greets students at the door as they enter and directs them to locate the desk with their name card and to begin completing the questionnaire/tasksheet.
2. As students answer the questions and work on the task, Nancy distributes textbooks and course syllabi and takes roll.
3. All students have an opportunity to work on the task, but none gets to complete it before Nancy interrupts the work and "walks" the class through the course syllabus (see Figure 8.2). She uses the sections of the syllabus as an advanced organizer for an interactive lecture session in which she communicates expectations, introduces some classroom procedures, and discusses the nature of the course content. The students' work on the questionnaire/tasksheet is utilized in discussions stimulated by the second section of the syllabus (i.e., What is history (geography, economics)?). For example:

   With the U.S. history classes, Nancy plays off the "peeking-through-a-keyhole task" (i.e., item 7 from Figure 8.3) to explain what she terms the *keyhole logic* of historical method in which we use our intellects to expand what we know beyond what has been actually observed and recorded.

4. Nancy assigns homework that includes the completion of the questionnaire/tasksheet.

Nancy is generally pleased with how the first day went. The students seemed willing to cooperate, the vast majority of them acting friendly and trying to follow directions. After the first few minutes of each period, her nervousness disappeared and she surprised herself by her own glibness—fluently speaking and making the "right" responses to students' questions and behaviors. Her energy level and enthusiasm peaked in the second half of each class.

Many students were reluctant to fill out the questionnaire/tasksheets on their own without seemingly constant explanations and feedback from Nancy, so the administrative duties took longer than she had planned. Thus, no class got through its syllabus and Nancy fears that the students were left "hanging" at the end of the period without understanding course expectations and the meaning of history, geography, or economics. She is especially anxious to meet with them on the second day to finish explaining the syllabi and get back on schedule.

Nancy concludes that teaching in room 111 will be tolerable after all; fourth period went especially well. However, after supervising lunch and arriving back in her own room just prior to fifth period, she discovered that the fourth-period drug-abuse awareness class left room 203 in disarray. Fifth period got off to a rough start and she appeared flustered because she was unable to get the room back in order and the materials laid out by 1:30. The students didn't appear surprised by the disorder nor did they seem to mind it. In fact, some of the students in her other classes were surprised by how well she had things organized.

Learning from Experiences

Becoming More Assertive. Nancy, like Dustin Manda, learned that success depended on being assertive. For example, just before the second day's homeroom period, Nancy visits with Max Forsyth, who teaches the fourth-period drug-abuse awareness class in room 203. Nancy wants to discuss the problem his class created for her yesterday, but she would rather discuss it out of earshot of his homeroom students who are now standing nearby.

Ms. Fisher: Hi, Mr. Forsyth, do you have a minute to talk?

Mr. Forsyth: Of course, Ms. Fisher—there's always time for a colleague! How can I help you?

Ms. Fisher: It's regarding your fourth-period class in room 203. Could we move to an area where we can speak about this privately?

Mr. Forsyth: Oh, don't worry about these kids; they're not interested in what we're saying. What's your problem?

Ms. Fisher: I hate to bother you with this, but—

Mr. Forsyth: No bother at all; we're here to help one another.

Ms. Fisher: Thank you, I appreciate that, but you see, it took me a long time to get the room ready yesterday for my fifth-period history class.

Mr. Forsyth: I thought all you people in history needed was your textbook and lecture notes!

Ms. Fisher: (laughing with Mr. Forsyth): Too many people think that's the way we still do things, but really, I'd appreciate if you could—

Ms. Fisher is interrupted by a student asking Mr. Forsyth a question. He answers the student and they briefly converse as Ms. Fisher waits.

Mr. Forsyth: These kids always have something for us.

Ms. Fisher: I was trying to say that I'd really appreciate it if you could have your students put things back as they were when they came into the room.

Mr. Forsyth: Did we leave any of the extra chairs we brought with us? The kids were supposed to return them to the library.

Ms. Fisher: No, there weren't any chairs left. That wasn't the—

Another student interrupts and starts talking to Mr. Forsyth. Amazed that Mr. Forsyth would allow such rude interruptions and concerned that the bell is about to ring, Ms. Fisher's demeanor turns from passive to hostile as she quips, "I've got to get to my homeroom!" She hurries out, angrily mumbling under her breath as Mr. Forsyth says without turning away from the student, "Thanks for coming by; I'm glad to be of help."

The room is in no better shape when Nancy arrives for fifth period than it was the first day; the problem persists for the remainder of the week. Realizing that she failed to tell Max what she wanted out of fear of stimulating ill feelings, Nancy is angry at herself for not communicating assertively.

Over the weekend she phones Max Forsyth:

MAX: Max Forsyth speaking.

NANCY: Hello, Max, this is Nancy Fisher. We spoke just before your homeroom Tuesday.

MAX: Hello, Nancy. How are you doing?

NANCY: Some things are going well; others aren't. We still have a problem to solve regarding sharing my classroom. I'd really like to meet with you in the room so we can work out a solution.

MAX: What's the matter?

NANCY: It would be best if we met in the classroom where I can show you exactly.

MAX: You want to meet on Monday?

NANCY: It must be a time when students won't be there to interrupt us. I can meet you there any time today or tomorrow. If that's impossible for you, let's meet at 7:30 Monday morning.

MAX: You seem pretty serious, I'd better meet you today. Can you give me an hour?

NANCY: That will be just fine. I'll see you in my room in an hour. Thank you very much. Bye.

MAX: Good-bye, Nancy.

Now that Max understands that Nancy is serious about the two of them solving what he now perceives as his problem as well as Nancy's, he is receptive to Nancy's explanations of just how the room should be left after fourth period. In the classroom working on her "turf," Nancy readily points out exactly what she expects. Nancy is pleased with the agreed-to arrangement and the way Max leaves the room for the rest of the semester.

Nancy also discovers the need to be assertive with parents. For example, one day after school in the hallway, Nancy passes one of her first-period students, Salvador, walking with his father:

MS. FISHER: Hi, Salvador.

SALVADOR: Ms. Fisher, this is my dad.

MS. FISHER: I'm pleased to me you, Mr. Cashio.

MR. CASHIO: And I'm happy to meet you; Sal tells me you're a great history teacher. I'm always telling my boys and girls—they've got to study subjects like history in order to train their memories. Remembering all those names and dates disciplines the mind. Memorizing history makes you smart. Isn't that right, Ms. Fisher? You tell Sal.

Smiling broadly at Mr. Cashio, Nancy thinks to herself, "If only I had stayed in my room 15 seconds longer, I wouldn't be putting up with this right now! This is a tough situation. Mr. Cashio's heart is in the right place; this is his way of encouraging Salvador to study history. I appreciate him trying to support my efforts. But he's sending all the wrong signals about the value of history. I don't want Salvador to swallow that garbage about training the memory, but then I hate to contradict what a father says in front of his child!" Not wanting to appear insulting, Nancy only continues to smile and says, "History is surely important for everyone to learn. I'm so happy to have met you, Mr. Cashio. Thank you for introducing me to your father, Salvador."

In class the following day, Salvador says, "The reason we have to learn history is to train our memories. That's what my dad says, and Ms. Fisher agreed with him yesterday." After diplomatically attempting to correct the record about her beliefs regarding the purpose of studying history, Ms. Fisher resolves to be more assertive in communicating with parents and in responding to misconceived statements about her business.

Nancy's resolve is still fresh in her mind when she meets with Ms. Turner about her daughter Andrea's work in geography:

Ms. TURNER: Andrea just loves your class; she speaks so highly of you! That's why I thought you'd be the one to help her with this problem.

Ms. FISHER: What is the problem?

Ms. TURNER: Andrea's involved with this boy who is older than her. I don't approve of him, but she sees him anyway.

Ms. FISHER: I see that you're concerned.

Ms. TURNER: Since she likes geography so much, I thought we could use that to get her to break it off.

Ms. FISHER: I'm not following you.

Ms. TURNER: Well because geography—you know, studying rocks and stuff is harder for girls, I told her if she kept spending time with this boy, she was going to do bad in your class. Girls don't do as good in science because they're too busy thinking about boys. . . . You see what I mean.

Ms. FISHER: Not really, ma'am, but please go on.

Ms. TURNER: Well, if you could just back me up on this—tell her she'll fail if she doesn't spend more time on geography than with that boy.

Ms. FISHER: I certainly appreciate you sharing your idea with me, and I appreciate your concern for Andrea's best interest. . . . As Andrea's parent, you know more about this situation than I. I'll confine my remarks to what I do know about. First of all, research studies clearly point out that girls to *not* have any more trouble learning geography or science than boys. Many people think that, but women succeed in these areas as well as men.

Ms. TURNER: Well, I'd always heard—of course I know there're exceptions like you.

Ms. FISHER: If you're interested, I can give you some articles that explain the facts about girls and women in academics.

Ms. TURNER: That would be nice.

Ms. FISHER: Secondly, and more to the point here, my responsibility is to teach Andrea and other students geography as professionally and responsibly as possible. I cannot in good conscience base Andrea's grade on anything other than how well she achieves the stated goals of the geography course.

Ms. TURNER: Well, I thought if you just told her, she'd listen.

Ms. Fisher: I'm flattered Andrea has confidence in what I say. But if I lie to her, I'll lose that confidence.

Ms. Turner: I don't mean for you to lie.

Ms. Fisher: I know. You want what's best for your daughter.

Addressing Behavior Management Problems. Consistent with findings of research studies of beginning teachers (Evertson, 1989), Nancy struggles to keep students motivated, on task, and engaged in learning activities. Each school day provides situations she never previously confronted; with each experience she refines the art of managing behavior and winning student cooperation. Prior to the school year, she understood principles and techniques from Chapters 4 and 5 of this text (e.g., using assertive, descriptive, and supportive communications and effective body language; consistently reinforcing on-task behaviors; enforcing rules of conduct; and systematically responding to off-task behaviors utilizing the 12 suggestions explained on pages 157–163. However, her skill applying those principles and techniques are fine-tuned by classroom events and by her reflections on those events.

Benefiting from Supervision. Nancy benefits from instructional supervision and from her preparations for administrative supervision in much the same way as Dustin Manda. However, compared to Eugene Street Elementary School, there are greater opportunities at Rainbow High for teachers to observe one another (e.g., through the professional exchange program with Francis Parker High). Initially Nancy felt nervous about observing and commenting on the instruction of other teachers and was even more nervous having them do the same for her. But after a few times, she found such exchanges so stimulating and helpful that she seized every reasonable opportunity to engage in them. Research studies indicate that both the observers' instructional performances and those of observed teachers benefit from such activities (Allen, Davidson, Hering, & Jesunathadas, 1984).

Self-Assessments and Action Research. Nancy's teaching also benefits from her persistent self-assessments. Routinely, she videotapes her classes and carefully analyzes the tapes in the privacy of her home. To efficiently gain useful formative feedback on her instructional performances, she finds it necessary to focus on one aspect of teaching at a time (e.g., efficiency of transitions or the ratio of intellectual-level questions to knowledge-level questions asked by students) at a time (Cangelosi, 1991, pp. 128–130). She realizes that teaching is a complex art and the classroom environment is too complex for anyone to attempt to absorb a large share of its activities during one observation.

Nancy also conducts a number of action research studies as a means of improving her teaching. Here's an example:

> For most of her interactive lecture sessions, Nancy distributes an outline on which students are to take notes and complete tasks (e.g., see Figure 5.1). She recognizes the value of such forms as advanced organizers for controlling the focus of the sessions. However, Principal Maurice Jones circulates a memo to Rainbow's faculty that they should reduce paper consumption due to budget restraints and Nancy wonders if she should

continue this usage of paper. To assess the value of the outlines, she conducts an experiment in which she delivers an interactive lecture to her
third-period geography class using the form displayed in Figure 8.4. She
then delivers a comparable interactive lecture to her fourth-period geography class but without distributing the form. In fourth period, she raises

Figure 8.4. Outline Nancy Used in an Action Research Project She Conducted in Her
Geography Classes

A. What is a *custom*?

_____

_____

Example of a custom: _____

_____

Example of something that is not a custom: _____

_____

Share:

Modify as you see fit:
What is a *custom*?

_____

_____

Example: _____

_____

Example of way of behaving that is NOT a custom: _____

_____

B. From where do people learn their customs? How do they learn their customs? _____

_____

_____

C. Think of two different groups of people that do not have exactly the same customs:

_____

_____

Describe a difference in those two *societies'* customs.

D. How do cultural changes affect customs?

E. Changes in customs in a particular society occur:

By first: _____

_____

_____

Then by: _____

_____

_____

Either slowly as _____ evolve _____

_____ or more rapidly as needs arise that _____

_____

F. Differences between material and nonmaterial culture:

Figure 8.4. (Continued)

the same questions and directs them to complete the same tasks but with the students taking notes and responding on their own blank paper. The following day, both groups take identical tests over the objectives of the lesson. Not only does the third-period class attain a higher average score on the test, but their comments about the previous day's class session are more positive than those from the fourth-period students. Nancy decides to continue using the structured outlines for interactive lecture sessions even if she has to print them on paper collected from the students.

SAMPLE TEACHING UNIT

Designing U.S. History Unit 17

It is early March; Nancy's first-period U.S. History class is in the final stages of Unit 15, "A Cold Peace." She has completed plans for Unit 16, "The Politics of Conflict and Hope," which she anticipates will be completed within nine calendar days. Sitting at home in front of her computer with her reference materials and notes, she begins designing Unit 17. Nancy reads Unit 17's goal from the course outline she developed in August, "Traces the struggle for human equality in the United States from efforts to end racial segregation and disfranchisement in the 1950s, through the challenges from black power advocates in the late 1960s, to issues faced by minorities in the country today; understands factors influencing the outcome of that struggle and their influence on current events."

She recalls that when she organized the course, she decided to devote an entire unit to the civil rights movement although the topic corresponds to only one 21-page chapter in the textbook; the chapter is "The Civil Rights Movement (1945–1970)." After reviewing the chapter as well as its annotations for teachers, she's quite pleased with the information it presents. She decides to extend the era covered by the chapter by reviewing content from previous chapters that will help students understand the roots of segregation. As with most other units, she will also deal with current issues that are affected by the historical events from the era in question. She thinks, "To define this goal with objectives—first of all, I want the students to conceptualize how segregation both de jure as well as de facto impacts the lives of people—not only those who are the targets of the discrimination, but also members of the so-called "privileged" group. Hopefully, they'll see that everyone loses in such a society. But I'm not going to include any affective objectives here. One or two conceptualization objectives are needed to get them to discover some relationships. If those discoveries happen to influence any attitudes for the better, so be it, but I'm only going to commit myself to assessing cognitive outcomes. . . .

"They'll need to comprehend readings that utilize vocabulary with some nuances that they don't yet understand, so I'll write an objective for targeting some key words. Let's see, . . . there's *segregation*, not only de jure but also . . .

"And then they should be able to recount events to tell the story of the movement past to present; that'll involve comprehension of some historical accounts, recall of processes, and conceptualizations of some relations. . . . This unit's going to have some rather complex objectives. . . ." After an hour of thinking and rethinking, writing and editing, Nancy formulates Objectives A through G in Figure 8.5.

She continues to think, "Now I should assign weights indicating the relative importance of each objective to goal attainment. That'll help me when I have to make out the unit test. There are seven objectives. Where's my calculator? . . . A hundred percent divided by seven is about 14 percent. So if the objectives are equally important, I'd weight each 14 percent. But, let's see . . . I think D and G are the critical ones. Objectives B, C, and E are primarily to enable the students to achieve the others. So, D and G are more than 14 percent each while B, C, and . . ." In a few minutes, Nancy has the objectives weighted as follows: 15 percent for A, 10 percent for B, 10 percent for C, 20 percent for D, 10 percent for E, 15 percent for F, and 20 percent for G.

As she develops general guidelines for the lessons, she thinks, "The way I've organized these objectives, packing content into Objectives B through F, these objectives should be taught in pieces after students have achieved Objective A. Then Objective G is the climax. . . . Okay, I've got to get a grip on the whole picture. . . ."

Goal: Trace the struggle for human equality in the United States from efforts to end racial segregation and disfranchisement in the 1950s, through the challenges from black power advocates in the late 1960s, to issues faced by minorities in the country today; understand factors influencing the outcome of that struggle and their influence on current events

Objectives:
A. Explain how segregation of black people from white people whether de jure segregation in the South or de facto segregation virtually everywhere in the U.S. affected the lives of all citizens both collectively and individually (*Cognitive: conceptualization*)
B. Translate the meaning of the following terms or expressions in the context of communications relative to the civil rights movement: *de jure segregation, de facto segregation, integration, desegregation, states' rights, black urbanization, equality of opportunity, black separatism, black power, role models, white backlash, affirmative action, reverse discrimination, political power, economic power* (*Cognitive: comprehension*)
C. Describe a chronology of the civil rights movement from approximately 1863 to the present (in greater detail after 1950 than prior to 1950) (*Cognitive: knowledge of a process*)
D. Describe the following factors in the civil rights movement as presented in DiBacco, Mason, and Appy (1991) and in other documents and explain the significance of each: Emancipation Proclamation, Thirteenth Amendment to the Constitution, Civil Rights Act of 1866, Fourteenth Amendment to the Constitution, Fifteenth Amendment to the Constitution, *Plessy v. Ferguson*, National Association for the Advancement of Colored People (NAACP), Jim Crow laws, Truman's executive order of 1948, *Brown v. Board of Education of Topeka*, Southern Manifesto, lynching of Emmett Till, Montgomery bus boycott, White Citizens Council, confrontation in Little Rock, Civil Rights Act of 1957, Gandhi's policies of nonviolent resistance, lunch counter sit-ins, protest marches, sleep-ins, boycotts, kneel-ins, wade-ins, Ku Klux Klan (KKK), Southern Christian Leadership Conference (SCLC), Student Nonviolent Coordinating Committee (SNCC), freedom riders, Interstate Commerce Commissions laws, Supreme Court decisions, black urbanization, religion, Constitutional rights, mass media, African independence movements, violence and arrests in the South, the march on Washington, Civil Rights Act of 1964, Freedom Summer Project, Mississippi Freedom Democratic Party (MFDP), Voting Rights Act of 1965, urban violence in the West and North, Black Muslims, black power movement, Black Panther Party, Black Panthers, the Kerner Commission, Civil Rights Act of 1968, white backlash, assassination of Martin Luther King, Jr., American Civil Liberties Union (ACLU), elections of black politicians, extension of strategies used in the struggle against racial prejudice into other movements (e.g., women's rights, environmental protection, consumer action, gay rights activists, etc.) (*Cognitive: comprehension*)
E. Identify the following personalities and their roles in the civil rights movement: Charles Houston, Harry Truman, Thurgood Marshall, Martin Luther King, Jr., Earl Warren, Rosa Parks, Orville Faubus, Dwight Eisenhower, James Lawson, Medgar Evers, James Meredith, Ross Barnett, John Kennedy, George Wallace, Eugene Connor, Lyndon Johnson, Malcom X, Elijah Muhammad, Robert Kennedy, Douglas Wilder, Jesse Jackson (*Cognitive: simple knowledge*)
F. Explain how various stages of the civil rights movement from the early 1950s to today affected or affects the lives of all U.S. citizens both collectively and individually (*Cognitive: conceptualization*)
G. Given a real-life problem or current event, address that problem or interpret that event in light of the lessons of the civil rights movement (*Cognitive: application*)

Figure 8.5. Goal and Objectives for Nancy's Unit on the Civil Rights Movement

She sketches Figure 8.6, breaking Objectives B through F's content into five time periods and continues thinking: "So first we go through an inductive lesson getting them to experience the consequences of a segregated society—that's going to take some creative planning on my part—doing it effectively while avoiding repercussions is going to be a trick. Then there's the next five objectives but only

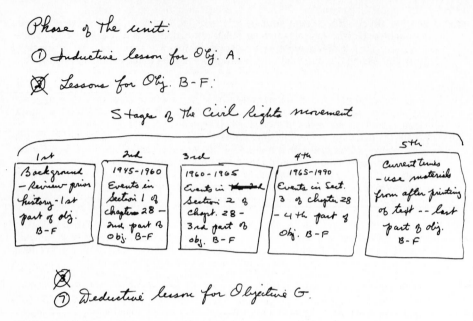

Phase of the unit:

① *Inductive lesson for Obj. A.*

②̶ *Lessons for Obj. B-F.*

Stages of the Civil Rights movement

1st	2nd	3rd	4th	5th
Background – Review prior history – 1st part of obj. B-F	1945-1960 Events in Section 1 of Chapter 28 – 2nd part B obj. B-F	1960-1965 Events in ~~total~~ Section 2 of Chapt. 28 – 3rd part B obj. B-F	1965-1990 Events in Sect. 3 of Chapter 28 – 4th part of Obj. B-F	Current times – use materials from after printing of text -- last part B obj. B-F

②̶
① *Deductive lesson for Objective G.*

Figure 8.6. A Sketch Nancy Made While Planning Unit 17

for background review content to set the stage for the central part of the unit. Then . . . And then we've got to deal with Objectives B through G relative to current times only. Finally, we get to a deductive lesson for Objective G. . . .

"The lessons are pretty much going to follow some things I've done with previous units except for Objective A—that's going to have to be worked out a little more carefully. I just don't think having them see videos and hear and read stories about what it was like to be black in the South or even the North or West in the 1950s is going to do it. They've seen that stuff—and they also need to know what it was like to be white. They need to experience some of the gut-level emotions that go along with arbitrarily sanctioned unfairness—unfairness that's assumed to be simply the way things are. . . . One possibility would be to have my black students role play the dominating group in the segregated society with my white students experiencing the discrimination. . . . But I don't want to emphasize those distinctions in class; some of the black students come from more so-called 'privileged' homes than some of the whites. Then where do I put my native American, Latin, and Eastern students in that scheme? I also don't want to send the message that racial segregation is a problem of only one race—this lesson should not dichotomize the class according to their actual ethnic differences. I need to think of another way of imposing a segregated society—something arbitrary, but on some basis that's clearly obvious to the world—some way that group membership is clearly visible like black and white, but it can't be black and white! . . .

"What about identifying two groups by something they wear—maybe a hat? Hat's won't work because they come off; they'd be sources of disruptions and it needs to be something that's sort of 'stuck' to the body. I've also got to be careful that I don't end up creating a ganglike atmosphere. We've had enough trouble with gangs in this neighborhood without me instigating some insignia or article of clothing for them to rally around! Whatever we try—whatever group designation I come up with has to be confined strictly to the time they're in first-period history. It can't spill out of my classroom or else I'm asking for trouble. In fact, it would be nice if they were only segregated for one class period so animosities aren't carried outside of class where I'm not around to supervise. Maybe the possible repercussions aren't worth attempting something like this. The standard 'what it's like to be black' tapes and stories would surely be a safer route! . . .

"Armbands! Colored armbands would work; I pass them out at the beginning of class—they cling—and I collect them after class—boom, end of segregation! I've got to pick some innocuous colors. Yellow, black, brown, white, red all have some racial associations—blue is probably okay and then some other color that's clearly different but not all that different. I want them to ask themselves, 'What's the difference? Why is this happening to us?' . . . Green, I'll use green. Now how should I split the class, 50–50 or what? I'm the responsible person in the class, so I should be a member of the 'privileged' group. I'll split it close to 50–50, but just tip the numbers in favor of the privileged group. I'll make the assignment of armbands seem random, but I'll make sure that certain students are placed apart to avoid personality conflicts. There're a couple who might be tough to manage in the discriminated-against group and a couple who would be tough to manage if they thought they had power over others. . . .

"Now, what can I do to set up a situation that'll get them to experience a segregated society within a class period? It would be more effective if I could pull it off before they've read any of the textbook pages—before they recognized that the unit is about the civil rights movement. Maybe I could sneak it into the end of Unit 16, while they're still thinking about 'the politics of conflict and hope.' It'd make a nice transition. I could do something on the Unit 16 test—distribute the armbands and administer the test under conditions that favored the "blues" and discriminated against the "greens." The trouble with that is it would contaminate the validity of the test. But then I could always retest after they discover what I was doing. But then I don't have the luxury of the extra days that would take. . . . I've got it! We'll do it on the day we go over the Unit 16 test—the day after the test, but before they know we're actually in Unit 17! Oh, that's beautiful! They'll show up curious about how they did and anxious to go over the test. They're more likely to tolerate my shenanigans when they're looking forward to something like going over a test. . . ."

Excited by her own ideas, Nancy works out the general plan for Objective A as described for the first phase in Figure 8.7. She spent more time planning for Objective A's lesson and described it in greater detail in Figure 8.7's unit plan because the lesson strategy is atypical compared to previous units. The lessons for the other objectives are more similar to numerous ones she's conducted in the past. Thus, as indicated by Figure 8.7, she doesn't describe them in much detail. Details for all lessons will be worked out in her daily plans.

Day One

During homeroom prior to the "segregated" first period, Nancy's students help her rearrange the room so that a large area is designated "for blue only" and a smaller area "for green only." As the first-period students enter, Nancy stands

Course: U.S. History
Unit: 17 out of 22
Title: The Civil Rights Movement
Goal: Trace the struggle for human equality in the United States from efforts to end racial segregation and disfranchisement in the 1950s, through the challenges from black power advocates in the late 1960s, to issues faced by minorities in the country today; understand factors influencing the outcome of that struggle and their influence on current events

Objectives Weighted According to Relative Importance for Goal Achievement (useful in constructing the unit test):

(15%) A. Explain how segregation of black people from white people whether de jure segregation in the South or de facto segregation virtually everywhere in the United States affected the lives of all citizens both collectively and individually (*Cognitive: conceptualization*)

(10%) B. Translate the meaning of the following terms or expressions in the context of communications relative to the civil rights movement: *de jure segregation, de facto segregation, integration, desegregation, states' rights, black urbanization, equality of opportunity, black separatism, black power, role models, white backlash, affirmative action, reverse discrimination, political power, economic power* (*Cognitive: comprehension*)

(10%) C. Describe a chronology of the civil rights movement from approximately 1863 to the present (in greater detail after 1950 than prior to 1950) (*Cognitive: knowledge of a process*)

(20%) D. Describe the following factors in the civil rights movement as presented in DiBacco, Mason, and Appy (1991) and in other documents and explain the significance of each: Emancipation Proclamation, Thirteenth Amendment to the Constitution, Civil Rights Act of 1866, Fourteenth Amendment to the Constitution, Fifteenth Amendment to the Constitution, *Plessy v. Ferguson*, National Association for the Advancement of Colored People (NAACP), Jim Crow laws, Truman's executive order of 1948, *Brown v. Board of Education of Topeka*, Southern Manifesto, lynching of Emmett Till, Montgomery bus boycott, White Citizens Council, confrontation in Little Rock, Civil Rights Act of 1957, Gandhi's policies of nonviolent resistance, lunch counter sit-ins, protest marches, sleep-ins, boycotts, kneel-ins, wade-ins, Ku Klux Klan (KKK), Southern Christian Leadership Conference (SCLC), Student Nonviolent Coordinating Committee (SNCC), freedom riders, Interstate Commerce Commissions laws, Supreme Court decisions, black urbanization, religion, Constitutional rights, mass media, African independence movements, violence and arrests in the South, the march on Washington, Civil Rights Act of 1964, Freedom Summer Project, Mississippi Freedom Democratic Party (MFDP), Voting Rights Act of 1965, urban violence in the West and North, Black Muslims, black power movement, Black Panther Party, Black Panthers, the Kerner Commission, Civil Rights Act of 1968, white backlash, assassination of Martin Luther King, Jr., American Civil Liberties Union (ACLU), elections of black politicians, extension of strategies used in the struggle against racial prejudice into other movements (e.g., women's rights, environmental protection, consumer action, gay rights activists, etc.) (*Cognitive: comprehension*)

(10%) E. Identify the following personalities and their roles in the civil rights movement: Charles Houston, Harry Truman, Thurgood Marshall, Martin Luther King, Jr., Earl Warren, Rosa Parks, Orville Faubus, Dwight Eisenhower, James Lawson, Medgar Evers, James Meredith, Ross Barnett, John Kennedy, George Wallace, Eugene Connor, Lyndon Johnson, Malcolm X, Elijah Muhammad, Robert Kennedy, Douglas Wilder, Jesse Jackson (*Cognitive: simple knowledge*)

(15%) F. Explain how various stages of the civil rights movement from the early 1950s to today affected or affect the lives of all U.S. citizens both collectively and individually (*Cognitive: conceptualization*)

(20%) G. Given a real-life problem or current event, address that problem or interpret that event in light of the lessons of the civil rights movement (*Cognitive: application*)

Figure 8.7. Nancy's Plan for the U.S. History Unit on the Civil Rights Movement

Estimated Number of Class periods: 11

Textbook Page References: 708–729, R-19, R-26, R-28 (unless otherwise indicated, page numbers referred to in the overall lesson plan are from the course textbook (DiBacco, Mason, & Appy, 1991)

Overall Plan for Lessons:
The lessons are to be conducted in seven phases:
1. A lesson for Objective A is to begin the last day of Unit 16, the day in which Ms. Fisher returns and reviews the test for Unit 16 that the class will have taken the previous day. Without announcing the purpose of the exercise, 14 of the 27, as well as Ms. Fisher, wear blue armbands in the classroom during history period. The other 13 students wear green armbands. The classroom is rearranged so that the greens are physically segregated from the blues (but not from Ms. Fisher who is herself a blue). During the period, Ms. Fisher will review the test results with the blues first, responding to their questions while the greens work on some menial task (e.g., sharpening pencils for the blues) while waiting for the test review sessions with the blues to end. The blues are then assigned some thoughtful task (e.g., completing a form critiquing the test—possibly using the pencils that the greens just sharpened) while Ms. Fisher spends the remaining time going over the greens' test results with them. The armbands are turned in at the end of the day's session without further explanation from Ms. Fisher.

   The following day, the armbands are redistributed and the class is again segregated during a brief session in which Ms. Fisher engages the blues in a critique session about the test using the questionnaires to which they responded the previous day. In the meantime, the greens are involved in another menial task. Ms. Fisher halts the session before it "goes too far," collects the armbands, desegregates the groups, and engages the class in a questioning/discussion session relative to their feelings during the simulated segregation.

   The lesson may extend into a third day depending on the direction of the discussion. Possibly, students may be assigned to write an essay expressing their feelings and then sharing them in either large or cooperative group sessions in which they develop hypotheses about the effects of living in a segregated, racially discriminatory society.
2. Lessons for objectives B, C, D, E, and F are conducted relative to events prior to 1945 that established the roots and set the stage for the civil rights movement. The lessons will be integrated with direct instructional strategies for objectives C and E as well as the literal comprehension aspects of objectives B and D. Inquiry instruction will be applied for Objective F as well as for interpretive comprehension aspects of Objectives B and D. Primary emphasis in this phase of the unit will be on relating experiences from Phase 1's lessons to relevant content from previous units (e.g., slavery, Emancipation Proclamation, Thirteenth Amendment, etc.). Readings and videotape programs will be used. One and one-quarter class periods are anticipated for Phase 2.
3. This phase will also pertain to Objectives B, C, D, E, and F except that the content will focus on pertinent events described in Section 1 "Origins of the Civil Rights Movement" (pp. 709–715) of Chapter 28 covering roughly the period between 1945 to 1960. Methods will be similar to that for Phase 2. One and three-quarter class periods are anticipated for Phase 3.
4. This phase will also pertain to Objectives B, C, D, E, and F except that the content will focus on pertinent events described in Section 2 "Freedom Now" (pp. 715–720) of Chapter 28 covering roughly the period between 1960 to 1965. Methods will be similar to that for Phase 2. One and one-half class periods are anticipated for Phase 4.
5. This phase will also pertain to Objectives B, C, D, E, and F except that the content will focus on pertinent events described in Section 3 "High Hopes and Tragic Setbacks" (pp. 721–727) of Chapter 28 covering roughly the period between 1965 to 1990. Methods will be similar to that for Phase 2. Two class periods are anticipated for Phase 5.
6. This phase will also pertain to Objectives B, C, D, E, and F except that the content will focus on pertinent events since 1990 and current events and issues. Methods will be similar to that for Phase 2. One and one-half class periods are anticipated for Phase 6.

(continued)

Figure 8.7. (Continued)

7. In this phase, a deductive lesson will be used to achieve Objective G. The selection of example and nonexample problems raised during this will depend on assessments of students' interests in various issues raised during previous phases. Two class periods are anticipated for Phase 5.

Formative Feedback and Summative Evaluation:
Besides formative feedback throughout, brief tests following homework and individual work assignments will be routine. A day-long unit test will be given at the end of the unit and the results will be reviewed with the class the following day.

Extraordinary Learning Materials and Equipment Needed:
1. Thirteen green and 15 blue armbands
2. Five videotape programs: "Unrecognized Achievement," "Who Looks Like Me?" "I Have a Dream," "Passive Resistance," "Different Perspectives on Affirmative Action"
3. Magazines articles and newspaper clippings from Ms. Fisher's "Civil Rights" file

Figure 8.7. (Continued)

near the door handing each an armband and a slip with directions as she tells them, "Please quietly follow the directions on your slip." Figure 8.8 display the slip for students given blue armbands; the slips for those with green armbands are identical except "green" is substituted for "blue." Students exchange quizzical looks, but past experience has taught them to expect occasional odd behaviors from Ms. Fisher. Tyrone asks, "What's all this about?" But Ms. Fisher gives him one of her silent stares and gestures communicating, "Just follow the directions and don't speak to me right now."

With the greens waiting, Ms. Fisher returns the test papers to the blues as she tells them, "Take five minutes to silently look over your paper, reading my comments. I'll be right back to explain the grading and go over the test with you item-by-item." She then gives each member of the greens a small five-cent pencil sharpener and about 20 assorted pencils and tells them, "Please sharpen these pencils for me so we can use them later on in today's session." Kay: "Ms. Fisher, when will we get our tests back?" Ms. Fisher: "Don't talk right now; you'll get them after I'm through with the blues."

In 30 minutes, Ms. Fisher finishes the test review session with the blues. She has Emma, a blue, distribute questionnaires for critiquing the test to the blues as Ms. Fisher retrieves the freshly sharpened pencils from the greens. Pencils are distributed to the blues and used to express their opinions about the questionnaires. Ms. Fisher returns the greens' test papers. They are graded but not annotated. Only six minutes are spent going over the test with the greens as the

Figure 8.8. Directions Nancy Distributes to "Blue" Students Entering the Room on the First Day of U.S. History Unit 17 and the Last Day of Unit 16

**DIRECTIONS FOR TODAY'S MEETING
IN WHICH WE WILL BE GOING OVER YESTERDAY'S TEST**

1. Please put the armband I gave you on your right arm between your elbow and shoulder.
2. Go directly to the area designated for BLUES and sit quietly in one of the available desks waiting for further directions from me.

blues complete and turn in the questionnaires. Just before the bell ending the period, Ms. Fisher collects the armbands, but she offers no explanations about the day's peculiar activities and refuses to address students' questions as they leave.

Reflecting on Day One and Planning for Day Two

Late that afternoon, Nancy thinks, "First period worked better than I had imagined. If I read their thoughts halfway right, we'll be playing off today's experiences not only for the rest of the unit but also for the rest of the course! It's too bad Lynae and Marcos were absent! I'm sorry I shortchanged the greens on the test review, but I'll make it up to them. They'll be surprised when they find out I made copies of their papers and thoroughly annotated them. I won't give those to them until after tomorrow's discussion and all the students have had a chance to air their feelings about today's discriminatory events. . . . Okay, so where do we go with this tomorrow? . . ."

Nancy formulates and prints from her computer tomorrow's plan shown in Figure 8.9.

Day Two

The second day of the unit proceeds as planned with the class making the transition to Item 5 from Figure 8.9's agenda only 14 minutes into the period. Eagerly students share their thoughts in response to Figure 8.10's tasksheet. During the questioning/discussion session. "Let's cut off discussion for 45 seconds to give everyone time to think about and write an answer to exercise E on the tasksheet," Ms. Fisher says as she begins circulating among the students reading what they write. Forty-nine seconds later, Ms. Fisher: "Let's hear from one of the green people. Okay, Kristine." Kristine: "I didn't like what we were doing; I wanted

Figure 8.9. Nancy's Agenda for the Second Day of the U.S. History Unit 17

1. Transition period redistributing the armbands exactly like yesterday and having students again going to their segregated areas.
2. As the blues wait, Ms. Fisher quickly distributes pencils to the greens to resharpen and gets the greens engaged in that task.
3. While the greens sharpen pencils, Ms. Fisher engages the blues in a discussion session on their opinions about Unit 16's test and their responses to yesterday's questionnaire. In the meantime, Ms. Fisher seems to be ignoring the greens but is actually carefully monitoring their activities, assessing their frustration level as well as the attitudes of the blues. When the time seems right, she is to call a halt to this session and move on to the next agenda item.
4. Transition period in which armbands are returned, class is desegregated, the classroom returned to its usual arrangement, and the tasksheet (shown in Figure 8.10) is distributed.
5. Ms. Fisher engages the whole class in an intellectual-level questioning/discussion session in which students share feelings they experienced during the segregation. They are to develop hypotheses about the effects of such a society on its people. The tasksheet (i.e. Figure 8.10) is to be utilized.
6. Homework assignment: Reread the 13th, 14th, 15th, and 19th Amendments to the Constitution (text pp. 157–161); reread the Emancipation Proclamation (text p. R19); read text pp. 708–710.
7. Transition into third period.

1. Yesterday and earlier today, did you wear a blue or green armband:

2. Describe your feelings when:
   A. You first took your seat yesterday in the rearranged classroom:

   B. During the time Ms. Fisher reviewed the test with the blues:

   C. During the time Ms. Fisher reviewed the test with the greens:

   D. Before today's class whenever you thought about yesterday's class:

   E. At the beginning of today's class when it started off like yesterday's:

3. Make a list of words that come to mind when you think of the kind of community you were part of in yesterday's class and at the very beginning of today's class.

4. Why do you think Ms. Fisher involved you in this experience? What topic of U.S. history do you think we're about to study?

5. Hypotheses:

   Yours   **Others from the Class**

Figure 8.10. Tasksheet for the Second Day of U.S. History Unit 17

it to stop. I knew you were just trying to show us something, but then when we did it again today and you hadn't said anything, I worried you'd turned into some kind of a wush or something." Ms. Fisher: "What's a wush?" Jose: "You know a wush, kinda like a dink or a Nazi." Ms. Fisher: "I'm going to jot those labels on the board for later on today when we start listing words that come to mind when we think of this colored-coded society we created for ourselves yesterday. . . . How do you spell, *wush* and —" Leland: "You don't spell it you just say it!" Ms. Fisher: "You people come up with new words everyday." Marsha:

"You've got to keep up or else you are one." Ms. Fisher: "Are some of you venting hostility built up over the last 24 hours right now? I treated you disrespectfully and now a little resentment is creeping into this conversation. Yes, Eliaja." Eliaja: "But you weren't disrespectful to us who were blue. You were nice to us." Ms. Fisher: "Let's hear from another blue person to comment on what Eliaja just shared with us. Corine." Corine: "I don't think you were fair to the blues either. You deprived us from being with who we wanted. We didn't get to hear what the greens were saying or be in on what they were doing! I felt really stupid being like a teacher's pet or something. I was mad at you for making me look like a wush." Ms. Fisher: "What thoughts does the word *prejudice* bring to mind, R. A.?" R. A.: "Like somebody who doesn't like somebody 'cause they're different." Ms. Fisher: "The word *prejudice* reminds me of *pre-judge*. Corine said I was unfair. Did I pre-judge anybody?" Corine: "No you judged us by our color. That's being prejudiced but it's not prejudging." Ms Fisher: "Well, I guess, I don't know; I'm thinking of prejudging as judging ahead of time. . . ." Ms. Fisher thinks she's made the mistake of deflecting the discussion away from the central issue of feelings and onto semantics. She continues, "I wish I hadn't gotten you off track and into this root of the word *prejudice* business. Let's get back to the question Eliaja and Corine brought to mind—about how the blues were affected by all this. It seems easier for us to agree about the consequences of being green in this society, but let's discuss more about the negative impact of being blue. Joyce, your hand is up?" Joyce: "It's bad even if . . ."

The discussion continues but not particularly focused on the tasksheet items. With six minutes left in the period, Ms. Fisher sees that they will not get to Item 5 of the tasksheet. Thus, she modifies her plans for the homework assignment, directing students to develop 7 to 10 hypotheses about how people's attitudes are affected by living in a segregated society. The reading assignment is postponed.

Reflecting on Day Two; Planning for Subsequent Days

Nancy isn't pleased with the way she handled the discussion in the latter half of the period. She thinks, "At least I made the correct decision by not giving them the reading assignment until they articulated their hypotheses. The readings would sway their thinking. Tomorrow I'll have to spend some time tying up Objective A. Then well start reviewing those relevant amendments, the Emancipation Proclamation and such. Let's see, today is Friday—they'll be working on their statements this weekend. . . . We should be able to get through the second phase of the unit early Tuesday. . . . There's not many textbook pages for them to read but they are packed with events, names, places, relations, vocabulary—a lot of stuff to keep straight and tie together. I'll show them that first video on Monday, it's only . . ."

The Final 10 Days of Unit 17

Seven more class days are spent completing the final six phases of the unit as outlined in Figure 8.7. One day is devoted to administering the in-class part of the unit test and a lively, fruitful exchange occurs when test results are reviewed on the twelfth day. The unit test reflects the level of the unit's lessons. One student's completed test paper is displayed in Figure 8.11; Figure 8.12 (pp. 369–371) shows the scoring sheet that Ms. Fisher returned to that student.

U. S. History *** Unit #17 Test *** The Civil Rights Movement

PART 1: TAKE HOME

NOTE: Please write your responses to the following using the available
space. You may use whatever resources (e.g. books, magazines,
and conferences with classmates and other people) you choose to
prepare your responses. Use whatever sources or suggestions you
want, but ultimately the responses should be your own. In other
words, you make the final decision as what to or not to write.

1. What is your name? *Heiko Baker*

2.(a) Recall the day about two weeks ago when we simulated segregation in
our class. In what ways were the greens' experiences similar to
those of black people living in the South in 1950?

*The greens had to do everything last. Nobody asked them what
they thought. They got crummy jobs. They weren't taught as
good as the blues.*

(b) In what ways were the blues' experiences similar to those of white
people living in the South in 1950?

*They were kept away from the greens. They were treated better
than the greens. They had more chances to do better things.*

(c) In what ways were the greens' experiences similar to those of black
people living in the North in 1970?

*The blacks in the north got angry. The more the class was segregated
the madder the greens got. It wasn't much different than for
1950 in the South except that it didn't happen by law - which made
northern blacks angrier because they couldn't blame it on the law.*

(d) In what ways were the blues' experiences similar to those of white
people living in the North in 1970?

*In class the blues knew discrimination was wrong. By 1970 everyone
was being told that. In our class, the blues would be going against
the authority (the teacher). In the North that wouldn't be true.*

(e) Afterwards, the class discussed different ways green people and
blue people felt while the class was segregated. Describe three of
the ways class members indicated they felt and explain why or
why not those feeling are similar to ways people living in
segregated societies today must feel.

*① Green people got angry at Ms. Fisher because she favored the blues.
Today black people get angry when police bother them more than
white people*

Figure 8.11. Unit 17 as Completed by One of Ms. Fisher's Students, Heiko Baher

② Blue people in class felt funny that they were being treated better than the greens for nothing they did. Some said they were lucky to be blue. That's different from whites today who aren't surprised to have things blacks don't have. But whites don't think they are lucky because blacks are so much better at a lot of things.

③ In our class we knew this was all part of a game. It was going to end. In real-life segregation is real and we never know if it'll stop. But at least it's a lot better than it used to be.

3. Write a scenario in which a hypothetical student, teacher, or administrator here at Rainbow High School commits a crime under civil rights statutes enacted since 1964.

~~The principal tells a student he can't take advanced math because he's black~~ The principal only let's boys in advanced math classes because he says only boys need higher math.

4. Give an example of a human activity that in 1950 was forbidden by laws in South Carolina, but which today in South Carolina is not only legal but also required under civil rights laws now in effect in South Carolina.

A ~~motel owner~~ a land owner rents an apartment to a black family in a white neighborhood. ~~that~~ He could have been arrested for that in S.C. before. Now, if he doesn't he could be arrested.

You have come to the end of the take-home part of this test.

(continued)

Figure 8.11. (Continued)

U. S. History *** Unit #17 Test *** The Civil Rights Movement

<u>PART 2: IN CLASS</u>

NOTE: Unlike the take-home part of this test, you are not to use
      references (e.g., books or notes) or confer with anyone while
      taking Part 2.

5. What is your name? *Heiko Baker*

6. Following is a scrambled list of events. Indicate the
   chronological order of the events by numbering them from 1 through
   5 with "1" being the earliest and "5" being the last.

   _1_ <u>Plessy v. Ferguson</u> Supreme Court decision allowing
        segregation of public facilities

   _2_ <u>Brown v. Board of Education of Topeka</u> Supreme Court
        decision outlawing school segregation

   _4_ Medgar Evers killed

   _5_ January 1, 1970

   _3_ Founding of the NAACP

7. Following is another scrambled list of events. Indicate the
   chronological order of the events as you did for item 4, numbering
   them "1" through "7."

   _4_ Riots in the Watts district of Los Angeles

   _7_ Absolute utopian racial equality

   _6_ January 1, 3000

   _2_ January 1, 1940

   _5_ Civil Rights Act of 1968 prohibiting discrimination in
        housing

   _1_ Presidential order ending segregation in the military

   _3_ Rosa Parks is first arrested

8. Following is another scrambled list of events. Indicate the
   chronological order of the events as you did for item 4, numbering
   them "1" through "6."

   _6_ Civil Rights Act of 1964 outlawing racial, religious, and sex
        discrimination in public places and by employers

   _5_ Martin Luther King, Jr. assassinated

   _2_ March on Washington

   _3_ Signing of the "Southern Manifesto"

Figure 8.11. (Continued)

366

_1_ Formation of the SCLC

_4_ Malcom X assassinated

9. Following is another scrambled list of events. Indicate the
chronological order of the events as you did for item 4, numbering
them "1" through "8."

_7_ Voting Rights Act protected Americans' right to vote

_5_ The Montgomery bus boycott

_8_ Douglas Wilder elected governor of Virginia

_1_ "Emancipation Proclamation"

_3_ U. S. Civil War Between the States

_6_ Martin Luther King, Jr.'s delivers "I Have a Dream" speech

_4_ The lynching of Emmett Till

_2_ Thirteenth Amendment abolishing slavery

10. What is the difference between <u>de jure</u> segregation and <u>de facto</u>
segregation?

_de jure means by law. ~~So So~~ So de jure requires (like in the
South in 1950) the races be separated. de facto makes it
illegal._

11. What is the differences between desegregation and integration?

12. In the 1963, Birmingham, Alabama police officers, under the
direction of Eugene "Bull" Connors responded to nonviolent
protests with brutal arrests. How did such displays of violence
by people (e.g., Bull Connors) who were fighting against the civil
rights movement actually end up helping the cause of civil rights?
What role did the media play in this scenario?

_When they're violent acts against blacks were shown on TV
& in the magazines & videos you showed us, people across
the country saw what was going on and put pressure on the
politicians._

Figure 8.11. (Continued)

(continued)

13. Look at the recent newspaper picture of protesters against the destruction of a northwestern forest. What strategies from the civil rights movement do they appear to be using? Explain how those strategies evolved during the civil rights movement. In your explanation, identify at least two individuals or groups who argued for or used such strategies. Also identify two individuals or groups who spoke against or refused to use such strategies.

Gandi, The black man who went to India, SCLC, Martin L. K., Jr. all believed in "passive resistance". That's what the protesters in the picture or using. Malcom X and Black Panthers were more violent — like The riots in Watts & The protest against unfair arrests in Miami, Florida

14. Attached is an article from this week's newspaper. Explain how the events described in this article are different as a result of the civil rights movement.

The picture with the article shows a black president of a university giving a degree (college) to a white man. That couldn't have happened before. Also the article talks about economic pressure minority groups *The graduation speaker* are using for consumer rights. Before minority groups didn't have enough money to put economic pressure on Companies.

15. Smile, you have come to the end of this test. ☺ How's this ms. Fisher?

Figure 8.11. (Continued)

Item scores for *Heiko Baher*   on the Unit 17 test:

NOTE: For each criterion listed for all items except for 6-9, points
       are awarded as follows:

         +2 if the criterion in question is clearly met
         +1 if it is unclear as to whether or not the criterion is met
         +0 if the criterion is clearly not met

     For items 6-9, the points are awarded as follows:

         +2 if all events are in exact chronological order
         +1 if all but one of the events is in order (adjusting for
            the domino effect)
         +0 if more than one is out of order (even after
            adjusting for the domino effect)

Item 2(a):

Parallels one of the <u>greens'</u> experiences from the
simulated segregation with one for 1950s <u>blacks</u> in the
S. & the parallel is consistent with historical records   0   1   (2)

Parallels another of the <u>greens'</u> experiences from the
simulated segregation with one for 1950s <u>blacks</u> in the
South & the parallel is consistent with historical records   0   1   (2)

Item 2(b):

Parallels one of the <u>blues'</u> experiences from the
simulated segregation with one for 1950s <u>whites</u> in the
S. & the parallel is consistent with historical records   0   1   (2)

Parallels another of the <u>blues'</u> experiences from the
simulated segregation with one for 1950s <u>whites</u> in the
South & the parallel is consistent with historical records   0   (1)   2

Item 2(c):

Parallels one of the <u>greens'</u> experiences from the
simulated segregation with one for 1970s <u>blacks</u> in the
N. & the parallel is consistent with historical records   0   1   (2)

Parallels another of the <u>greens'</u> experiences from the
simulated segregation with one for 1970s <u>blacks</u> in the
North & the parallel is consistent with historical records (0)   1   2

Item 2(d):

Parallels one of the <u>blues'</u> experiences from the
simulated segregation with one for 1970s <u>whites</u> in the
N. & the parallel is consistent with historical records   0   1   (2)

Parallels another of the <u>blues'</u> experiences from the
simulated segregation with one for 1970s <u>whites</u> in the
North & the parallel is consistent with historical records   0   1   (2)

(continued)

Figure 8.12. Ms. Fisher's Scoring Sheet for Heiko Baher's Test Shown in Figure 8.11

Item 2(e):

Parallels one of the feelings expressed in class and provides a tenable explanation as to why that feeling is either simiar or dissimilar to parallel feelings resulting from today's real-world segregated or discriminatory societies   0 ⊗ ②

Parallels another of the feelings expressed in class and provides a tenable explanation as to why that feeling is either similar or dissimilar to parallel feelings resulting from today's real-world segregated or discriminatory soc.   0 1 ②

Parallels yet another of the feelings expressed in class & provides a tenable explanation as to why that feeling is either similar or dissmilar to parallel feelings resulting from today's real-world segregated or discriminatory soc.   0 1 ②

Item 3:

The scenario includes an incident or event in a high school setting   0 1 ②

The scenario includes an incident or event in which one person violates the civil rights of another   0 1 ②

Item 4:

The example is of an activity that was illegal in S. C. in 1950 (e.g., a public swimming pool manager allows blacks and whites to swim in the same pool)   0 1 ②

The example is of an activity that is required by legal statutes in S. C. today as with the swimming pool incident   0 1 ②

Item 6:

2, 3, 4, 5, 1 --- 0 ① 2

Item 7:

4, 7, 6, 1, 5, 2, 3 ------------------------------- 0 ① 2

Item 8:

4, 6, 3, 1, 2, 5 --------------------------------- ⓪ 1 2

Item 9:

7, 5, 8, 2, 1, 6, 4, 3 --------------------------- 0 ① 2

Item 10:

Response indicates both distinguish & separate two groups and that de facto can be de jure, but not necessarily   ⓪ 1 2

de jure is segregation supported by legal statute   0 1 ②

de facto is segregation as a consequence of factors other than legal statute   ⓪ 1 2

Figure 8.12. (Continued)

370

Item 11:

   Response indicates that desegregation is a process by
which either <u>de facto</u> or <u>de jure</u> segregation is reduced   (0)   1   2

   Response indicates that integration is a process by
which two groups mix freely and enjoy the same rights   (0)   1   2

Item 12:

   Response includes a tenable explanation of at least one
way actions of segregationists "backfired" on them   0   1   (2)

   Response at least implicitly alludes to the relation of
violent responses to passive protest & its influence on
the national consciousness   (0)   1   2

   Alludes to the role of media coverage (e.g., national
coverage of brutal replies to nonviolent protests)   0   1   (2)

Item 13:

   Response alludes to the nonviolent protest method pictured   0   1   (2)

   Explanation alludes to the tension between the nonviolence
associated with Gandhi and the more violent methods associated with urban violence & groups e.g., the Black Panthers   (0)   1   2

   Alludes to the role of media coverage (e.g., national
coverage of brutal replies to nonviolent protests)   (0)   1   2

   Identifies at least two groups or individuals associated
with nonviolent methods   0   1   (2)

   Identifies at least two groups or individuals associated
with violent methods   0   1   (2)

Item 14:

   Explains how one event in the article or accompanying
photo was made possible via gains attributable to
the civil rights movement   0   (1)   2

   Explains how a second event in the article or
accompanying photo was made possible via gains
attributable to the civil rights movement   0   (1)   2

   Explains how a third event in the article or
accompanying photo was made possible via gains
attributable to the civil rights movement   0   1   (2)

YOUR SCORE ON THIS TEST IS   <u>   *46*   </u>

Figure 8.12. (Continued)

REFLECTIONS OF THE YEAR

It's June. Nancy thinks, "I can hardly believe it's been less than a year since I joined Rainbow's faculty. I packed more things into this past 10 months than any 10 years of my previous life. It seems like only yesterday that I was preparing for my first class; the school year passed so quickly. I'm at least 20 years wiser than I was a year ago!"

Having assessed her teaching performance throughout the year, Nancy is already preparing for her second year at Rainbow. Although she's identified ways to improve in all areas of her teaching, she is quite pleased with what her students gained in all the courses she taught except for her third-period geography class. She never was comfortable with that group of students; hardly anyone in the class seemed to display the enthusiasm she came to expect from the other classes. She would love to start all over with them armed with the arsenal of instructional materials, ideas, unit plans, daily plans, and test items accumulated over the past 10 months. She was happy to sign a contract in April eager to put her newly acquired "20 years" of experience to work during the next school year.

As with Dustin at Eugene Street Elementary School, Nancy availed herself of numerous inservice opportunities throughout the year (e.g., by participating in workshops and professional meetings and reading professional journals like *Social Education*). Besides her day-to-day experiences working with students, she considers her participation in the professional exchange program for evaluating instruction to be the most significant influence on her professional development. Through the program she observed teachers from both Rainbow and Francis Parker High and they observed her. Utilizing instruments such as the one displayed in Figure 8.13, she learned to analyze her own instructional performances and those of colleagues. Conferences with teachers who completed evaluation questionnaires (e.g., the one shown in Figure 8.14) on her performances as well as with teachers for whom she did the same proved extremely fruitful leading to significant improvements in Nancy's teaching.

Nancy rejected several opportunities to spend her second year at other schools. One reason for the decision to remain at Rainbow was the opportunity to continue in this professional exchange program for evaluation. She vows to use her influence with school administrators and to work through professional organizations (e.g., the local affiliate of the National Education Association) for gaining paid professional time for all teachers to participate in such programs. She reasons, "Our effectiveness in the classroom depends on our preparation outside the classroom. Teachers need to be provided with adequate time away from students in order to maximize the time they spend with students. Six hours interacting with students is too large a share of even a 12-hour workday for adequate instructional preparation and for noninstructional professional responsibilities—such as in conferences with colleagues. Until teachers are given time to provide one another with instructional supervisory services and evaluative feedback, teachers have little control over their own profession!"

Classroom Observation Measurement
for Instructional Methods and Techniques

(Please refer to the attached form as you read these directions.)

Preparing for the Observation

Review the operational definitions and procedures you learned in the training workshop. If it's been a while since you last observed with this instrument, you may want to practice with it in a colleague's class before using it for an actual evaluation of teaching.

The observation should be scheduled with the teacher at least a week in advance. Arrange for the teacher to supply you with a lesson plan that includes a list of the objectives to be targeted by the activities planned for the observation period.

Based on the lesson plan, complete Item 0 prior to the observation period. You will need to refer to it when completing Items 1–3.

For each objective you list for Item 0, label the implied learning level as either (a) memory cognitive, (b) higher cognitive, (c) psychomotor skill, or (d) affective. Use additional descriptors as needed. Separate the objectives by drawing a horizontal line across the page.

Completing the "Description of the Situation" on Page 1 of the Form

Take notes relevant to the "Description of the situation" prior to, during, and immediately after the observations. Compose the narrative from those notes after you have compiled the overall score.

Completing Items 1–3 During the Observation

ITEM 1: For each learning activity, describe what you see or hear that provides any indication as to which objective that activity targets. Clearly indicate which descriptions go with which objectives using horizontal lines across the page.
ITEM 2: Describe any teaching moves that can be classified as either "a" or "b" moves relative to student engagement.
ITEM 3: Describe each learning activity, pointing out those aspects that characterize it as direct teaching, drill and practice, etc. Use horizontal lines to make the associations between objectives and activities clear.

Scoring Items 1–3 Immediately After the Observation

ITEM 1: Based on the descriptive narrative you completed for Item 1 of the form, select the *one and only one true statement* from the following:

  A. There was no indication that any of the learning activities targeted any of stated objectives.
  B. There were indications that some, but not all, of the learning activities targeted stated objectives.
  C. There were indications that each learning activity targeted a stated objective.
  D. There was no evidence to suggest that any one of the above statements is more likely true than either of the other two.

  Score Item 1:

  +0 for selecting statement A, +1 for B, +2 for C, and +1 for D.   (continued)

Figure 8.13. Example of a Classroom Observation Measurement for Instructional Methods and Techniques (Reprinted from *Evaluating Classroom Instruction* [pp. 234–236], by J. S. Cangelosi, 1991, White Plains, NY: Longman.)

ITEM 2: Based on the descriptive narrative you completed for Item 2 of the form, select the *one and only true statement* from the following:

    A. During the observation period, "b" teaching moves (i.e., moves that discourage student engagement) occurred with greater frequency than "a" teaching moves (i.e., moves that encourage student engagement)

    B. There was virtually no difference in the frequency of "a" teaching moves and the frequency of "b" teaching moves during the observation period.

    C. During the observation period, "a" teaching moves occurred with greater frequency than "b" teaching moves.

    D. There was no evidence to suggest that any one of the above statements is more likely true than either of the other two.

Score Item 2:

+0 for selecting statement A, +1 for B, +2 for C, and +1 for D

ITEM 3: The total score for Item 3 should be 0 if the score for Item 1 is 0. Otherwise, based on the descriptive narrative you completed for Item 1 of the form score.

    +2 for each of the following statements that is true.

    +0 for each of the following statements that is false, and

    +1 for each statement on which there is no basis for judging it as true or false.

    A. Either direct teaching or drill and practice methods were used within at least one learning activity that (according to Item 1) targeted either a memory-cognitive or psychomotor-skill level objective.

    B. Systematic inquiry was incorporated in at least one learning activity that (according to Item 1) targeted a higher-level cognitive objective

    C. Either reinforcement theory or strategies for examining alternatives were used within at least one learning activity that (according to Item 1) targeted an affective learning objective.

Compiling the Overall Score

The overall score is the sum of the three item scores. Thus, the maximum possible overall score is 10 (2 + 2 + 6).

Classroom Observation Recording Form for Instructional Methods and Techniques

Teacher's name _____ Observation # _____

Observation date _____ Beginning time _____ Ending time _____

Trained observer's name _____

Description of the situation (identify the class and lesson and explain any special circumstances and factors that should be considered in the interpretation of the observation results):

0. OBJECTIVES FROM THE LESSON PLAN

Obj. ID #	Objective as Stated in the Lesson Plan	Implied Learning Level

Figure 8.13. (Continued)

374

1. ASSOCIATING OBSERVED ACTIVITIES WITH STATED OBJECTIVES *(from "O")*

Obj. ID #	Description of what was observed in the learning activity that made the objective being targeted apparent

2. TEACHING MOVES FOR OBTAINING AND MAINTAINING STUDENT ENGAGEMENT

Description of (a) moves the teacher used to lead students to engage in the learning activity (e.g., proximity to students, eye contact, incorporating students' names in presentations, advanced organizers, wait time for questions) and (b) teacher's moves that discouraged students from being engaged in the learning activity (e.g., judgmental, inane, hostile, or passive comments, flip-flop transitions)

3. TEACHING STRATEGIES AND TECHNIQUES ASSOCIATED WITH OBJECTIVES

Obj. ID #	Description of those aspects of the learning activity that are relevant to the type of teaching model applied

Figure 8.13. (Continued)

Examiner-Opinion Questionaire Used in Hillyard School District's Summative Evaluation Process of Beginning Teachers' Performance

Hillyard School District
Peer Teacher/Examiner Questionaire

1. What is your name? _____
2. Please identify the following with respect to the beginning teacher to whose performance this evaluation pertains:

   Name _____ School _____

   Teacher assignment _____
   _____

3. Explain any special or unusual circumstances or factors that should be taken into consideration as your responses to this questionnaire are being interpreted (e.g., extraordinary [1] events that might have made the observation period particularly stressful for the beginning teacher or personal biases you hold that might influence your responses to these questionnaire items).

4. Please attach the instruments you completed as a result of your (a) classroom observations, (b) interviews, and (c) document examinations.
5. *Regarding organizing and planning for teaching:*
   A. Was the organization of the classroom conducive to learning? Explain.

   B. Was there a systematic and logical connection among (a) the curricula, (b) unit plans, and (c) lesson plans? Explain.

6. *Regarding learning goals and objectives:*
   A. Were the learning goals and objectives made explicit? Explain how.

Figure 8.14. Example of an Examiner-Opinion Questionnaire Used in Summative Evaluation Process of Beginning Teachers' Performances (Reprinted by permission from *Evaluating Classroom Instruction* (p. 243–246) by J. S. Cangelosi, 1991, White Plains, NY: Longman.)

B. How consistent were the learning goals with the prescribed curriculum guide? Explain.

C. Was there a systematic, logical connection between the learning goals and the learning objectives?

D. Did the learning objectives address students' needs (with respect to both content and learning levels)? Explain.

7. *Regarding subject-matter content:*
   A. Was the presentation of content to students organized in a manner consistent with the current thinking of recognized authorities? Identify areas of strength and weakness in how content was organized.

   B. Were the students likely to be left with accurate or inaccurate conceptions regarding subject-matter content? Specify areas where inaccurate impressions may have resulted. Specify areas where especially accurate and insightful impressions may have resulted.

8. *Regarding instructional methods and techniques:*
   A. Were lesson *designs* appropriate to learning objectives? Specify types of objectives (e.g., knowledge level or application level) for which appropriate lessons were designed and types of objectives for which they were not.

   B. Were lessons *conducted* as they were designed? Include examples in your explanation.

   C. What student outcomes, other than those related to stated objectives, may likely be attributed to the teacher's classroom activities? Explain using examples.

(continued)

Figure 8.14. (Continued)

9. *Regarding classroom management:*
   A. How efficient were transition periods? Explain.

   B. Did students tend to be engaged at the beginning of learning activities? Explain.

   C. Did students tend to be engaged throughout learning activities? Explain.

   D. How well did the teacher deal with nondisruptive off-task behaviors? Explain.

   E. How well did the teacher deal with disruptive off-task behaviors? Explain.

10. *Regarding assessment of student achievement:*
    A. Overall, did the teacher generally make accurate summative evaluations of student achievement of learning goals? Explain.

    B. Overall, did the teacher make accurate formative evaluations of student achievement? Explain.

    C. How relevant were the teacher's measurements to student achievement of learning goals? Identify types of objectives (e.g., comprehensive level or affective) that were measured particularly well and types that were not.

    D. How reliable were the achievement tests?

11. Please add any other comments that you think would be helpful to those who will be making a summative evaluation of this teacher's instructional performance.

Figure 8.14. (Continued)

378

SELF-ASSESSMENT EXERCISES FOR CHAPTER 8

I. With a group of your colleagues who have also read Chapters 1–8, engage in a discussion relative to the following questions or tasks:

    A. Critique Nancy's syllabus in Figure 8.2 with respect to readability for high school students, completeness, format, and inclusion of unnecessary material.

    B. Compare the strategies and techniques for establishing a businesslike climate on the opening day of school in the following examples: (a) Mr. Stockton's in Vignette 4.4, (b) Ms. Phegley's Vignette 4.5, (c) Mr. Manda's in Chapter 7, and (d) Ms. Fisher in this chapter. How are the examples similar? In what ways do they differ?

    C. In light of the weighted objectives in her unit plan in Figure 8.7, critique Nancy's unit test displayed in Figures 8.11 and 8.12.

    D. From the examples of the questioning/discussion session described in the section "Day Two," does it appear that Nancy managed to involve a satisfactory number of students in the lessons? Compare her tactics to those of Mr. Landastoy, Ms. Bernstein, and Ms. Rackley in Vignettes 3.8, 5.10, and 5.11, respectively.

    E. Based on the limited description in the section "Sample Teaching Unit," complete Figure 8.13's form for a simulated observation in one of Nancy's classes.

    F. How consistent is Figure 8.7's unit plans with Chapter 3's suggestions for designing lessons?

II. Compare Nancy's first year of teaching to that of the teacher you interviewed when responding to self-assessment Exercise II for Chapter 7.

SUGGESTED READING

Select articles from professional journals for teachers in your area of specialization. Figure 8.15 contains an abbreviated list of journals categorized by teaching specialty.

Figure 8.15. Abbreviated Sample of Professional Journals for Teachers

General to All Teaching Specialties
Educational Leadership
Journal of Classroom Interaction
Kappa Delta Pi Record

Art and Music Education
Art Education
The Journal of Aesthetic Education
Music Educators Journal
The NATS Journal

Business Education
Delta Pi Epsilon Journal
Journal of Business Education
Journal of Education for Business

Career and Vocational Education
Journal of Career Development
Journal Career Planning and Employment
The Journal of Cooperative Education
The Journal of Epsilon Pi Tau
Journal of Studies in Technical Careers

Educational Technology
Educational Technology
Educational Technology Research and Development
Journal of Computer-Based Instruction

Elementary and Early Childhood
Childhood Education
Children Today
Elementary School Journal

English and Literature
English Education
English Journal
The Exercise Exchange
Journal of Teaching Writing
Research in the Teaching of English

Foreign Language
Foreign Language Annals
Language Sciences
Studies in Second Language Acquisition

(continued)

Handicapped and Gifted

The Exceptional Child
The Gifted Child Today
Journal for the Education of the Gifted
*Journal for Vocational Special Needs
 Education*
Journal of Learning Disabilities
Learning Disability Quarterly
Teacher Education and Special Education

Health and Physical Education

Health Education
*Journal of Physical Education, Recreation,
 and Dance*
Journal of School Health
The Physical Educator
Research Quarterly for Exercise and Sports

Home Economics

Home Economics Research Journal
*Journal of Consumer Studies and Home
 Economics*
Journal of Home Economics
*Journal of Vocational Home Economics
 Education*

Mathematics

Arithmetic Teacher
Focus on Learning Problems in Mathematics
*The Journal for Research in Mathematics
 Education*
Mathematics Teacher

Reading

Forum for Reading
Reading Improvement
Reading Research and Instruction
Reading Research Quarterly
The Reading Teacher

Science

Science Activities
Science and Children
Science Education
Science Teacher

Social Studies and Social Science

The History and Social Science Teacher
Journal of Social Studies Research
Social Studies Journal

Figure 8.15. (Continued)

TAKING WHAT YOU'VE LEARNED TO THE NEXT LEVEL

By vicariously experiencing Nancy's and Dustin's initial teaching years, you should gain a step in learning from your direct experiences as you embark on your own teaching career. What is the outlook for your career? You, of course, are the principal factor influencing the answer to that question. Of less, but still significant, importance is how certain issues presently confronting the teaching profession are resolved over the next decade. Those issues are raised in Chapter 9.

CHAPTER 9

Looking Ahead

GOAL OF CHAPTER 9

This chapter is intended to stimulate your thinking about the current movement to reform the way teaching is typically practiced in schools and to reflect on your own professional role in that movement.

A MIXED HISTORY

Exemplary teaching consistent with research-based principles has been success-fully practiced at least since the time of Socrates. The merits of teaching methods based on these principles has been extolled in literary works as early as 1791 when Johann Pestalozzi wrote *Leonard and Gertrude* (Cubberley, 1962, pp. 346–354; Wilds & Lottich, 1961, pp. 292–294). In Bruner's (1960) classic, *The Process of Education*, the fundamental principles by which students achieved intellectual-level objectives are explicated. The efficacy of the model by which inductive lessons lead students to discover content, direct instruction helps them remember and improve their skills with content, comprehension lessons help them utilize communications, and deductive lessons help them apply content is supported by a myriad of research findings (e.g., Dunkin, 1987a; Jones, Palincsar, Ogle, & Carr, 1987; Joyce & Weil, 1986; Resnick & Klopfer, 1989; Reynolds, 1989; Wittrock, 1986). Thousands of teachers, like Dustin Manda and Nancy Fisher, continue to successfully practice these research-based methods within the entire spectrum of elementary, middle, junior high, and senior high school classrooms.

However, such exemplary teaching has never been typical (Bridges, 1986; Jesunathadas, 1990; McLaren, 1989). With an estimated 30,000,000 teachers throughout the world (Peel, 1989), approximately 2,686,000 of the those working in elementary and secondary schools of the United States (Ryan & Cooper, 1988, pp. 34–35), most students never have the opportunity to learn from teachers like Dustin and Nancy. Consequently, the history of professional education is mixed, marked by the crowning achievements of a relatively few and missed opportunities for the masses.

AN IMPENDING REFORMATION

In the minds of some teachers, a question still exists as to whether they should attempt to follow the research-based approaches recommended by the professional literature. They argue that although inquiry instruction may work in theory, it is simply too difficult to implement in realistic classroom situations. While agreeing that their own traditional approaches are unsuccessful with the majority of students, they contend that most people only need fundamental skills and conceptual and application learning is only possible for the "gifted" few. They point to the thousands of successful parents, teachers, academicians, scientists, artists, writers, technicians, humanitarians, politicians, and others who profited from traditional instruction.

In the minds of teachers who successfully implement research-based approaches in their classroom every school day, the research-based approaches are clearly superior to the traditional approaches, not only in theory, but also in practice with virtually every type of student. At this point in time, the most critical issue facing teacher education specialists is not how the art of pedagogy should be practiced but rather how to increase the number of teachers who break from tradition and begin applying the research-based approaches. Teaching is a complex art and science only successfully executed by professionals astute in pedagogy, cognitive science, academic content, behavior management, and evaluation of student achievement, thus reformation of the practices of the majority of teachers is an ambitious goal to say the least.

On the heels of highly publicized reports of failing schools (e.g., Dossey, Mullis, Lindquist, & Chambers, 1988; National Commission on Excellence in Education, 1983; "U.S. Students Again," 1989), the political climate seems ripe to support a reformation. The nations' consciousness has been stirred by media attention to not only the ills of our schools but also to what can be accomplished when competent professional teachers are empowered to implement research-based approaches (e.g., "Learning in America: Schools that Work," 1990). The greatest challenge for professional educators may not be to stimulate the reformation as much as it is to guide the direction of the movement.

There is cause for optimism. A number of high-profile curriculum reform efforts are supported by a solid coalition of learned and professional societies. The National Council of Teachers of Mathematics' (1989) *Curriculum and Evaluation Standards for School Mathematics*, for example, has been endorsed by scores of diverse groups (e.g., the American Federation of Teachers, American Mathematical Society, National Society of Professional Engineers, National School Boards Association, and Association for Supervision and Curriculum Development). With widespread support, similar projects in nearly every content area appear to be influencing K–12 classroom teaching practices (see, e.g., Brandt, 1988).

Although in some influential circles resistance still exists, recent widespread agreement on resolutions to some previously controversial issues should also hasten the reformation in a direction favorable to research-based curricula. First of all, a wealth of proven instructional strategies, techniques, resources, and technologies is now available to help teachers implement research-based approaches that heretofore were either unavailable or untested.

Second, teachers need in-depth preparation in both content areas and teaching methods (which includes cognitive science, behavior management, pedagogical principles, and evaluation of student achievement). In some naive circles, people still contend that to teach, one only needs to be very knowledgeable of subject matter content and there's no value in wasting time with teaching methods. Others, in equally naive circles, argue that teachers do not need to know content beyond the levels they teach to be effective—as long as they practice sound teaching methods (e.g., to teach algebra, you don't need to understand calculus). The systematic teaching strategies employed in the examples throughout this book (e.g., Dustin's and Nancy's design and implementation of mathematics Unit 7 and U.S. history Unit 17, respectively) can succeed only in the hands of teachers who possess sophisticated understandings of subject matter content and teaching methodology. Content and the teaching of content are inextricably related.

Third, teachers should no longer be expected to succeed without appropriate support services of administrators, without competent instructional supervision, and without continuing inservice education. With approximately 2,686,000 teachers conducting courses in the nation's elementary and secondary schools, the reformation can hardly succeed unless inservice as well as preservice teachers are affected. The outmoded model by which teachers collected the tools of their profession (e.g., understanding of content and instructional methods) from their preservice preparation programs in college and then were left unattended to learn how to use the tools during their first inservice years in the classroom has proven ineffectual, at worse, and inefficient, at best (Duke, Cangelosi, & Knight, 1988). In response to such findings, promising models for providing inservice teachers with necessary instructional supervisory support services have been developed and validated (Cangelosi, 1991, pp. 119–159; Harris, 1989, pp. 1–28). With the influence of the Association for Supervision and Curriculum Development, there is considerable hope that the inservice support and education so desperately needed by teachers will become widely available through implementation of these models. Wherever such services are available, they could become a vehicle for guiding teachers toward research-based practices.

Finally, to be truly successful in the classroom, teachers must seize control over their own profession. Nelson, Palonsky, & Carlson (1990) spoke of *empowering teachers to reform schools*:

> Earlier school reforms failed because they did not invite teachers to assume greater authority in the schools. The next agenda for school reform depends on new roles for teachers, in which teachers have responsibilities to improve education as well as opportunities to do so. If schools are to be thoughtful places in which students learn to be informed, creative, productive citizens, the work of teachers needs to be reconsidered and restructured. If students are expected to engage in thoughtful reasoned decision-making, they must see adults in the classroom whose working lives demand and reward such behavior. Defining teachers as mindless factotums of state education policy, publisher whim, or administrative caprice is self-defeating. It is a cynical assessment of teachers' abilities that offers teachers insufficient control over their work. . . .
>
> Research evidence suggests that when teachers are given responsibility for school changes, it is more likely that these changes will be positive and enduring

To Be DISPOSED of,
A Likely Servant Mans Time for 4 Years
who is very well Qualified for a Clerk or to teach
a School, be Reads, Writes, underſtands Arithmetick and
Accompts very well, Enquire of the Printer hereof.

Figure 9.1. Advertisement for a Teacher to Let (American Weekly Mercury, Philadephia, 1735. From Cubberley, Ellwood P., *Public Education in the United States*, Revised Edition. Copyright © 1962 by Houghton Mifflin Company. Used with permission.)

(Roberts & Cawelti, 1984; Sarason, 1982). It is reasonable to predict that if schools are restructured so that teachers assume greater responsibility for essential school processes—from curriculum to staffing—the education afforded students will be improved. (p. 224)

Teachers have begun to overcome attitudes borne from colonial school traditions reflected in Figure 9.1. The message is reaching the public. On a nationally aired television program, Roger Mudd (1990) stated:

From sunup to sundown, school teachers you have seen tonight [on the program "Learning in America: Schools that Work"] work harder than you do no matter what you do. No calling in our society is more demanding than teaching. No calling in our society is more selfless than teaching. No calling in our society is more central to the vitality of our democracy than teaching.

YOUR ROLE

Clearly, the most important variable in determining the future of education is *you* and your colleagues who are also embarking on careers as teachers. How do you influence the success of the profession and the course of the reformation? You begin by teaching as well as you reasonably can. How you practice the complex art and science of teaching impacts the students fortunate enough to be in your tutelage. Sometimes teachers complain, "My students just aren't capable of learning what I'm supposed to teach. With a more capable group, I could succeed, but not with this bunch!" But the capabilities of your students do not influence the success of your teaching performances. Your teaching success depends on how well you lead your students to extend their achievement within their own capabilities. In other words, evaluate how far they reach, not where they reach.

Avail yourself of inservice education opportunities. How well you teach depends on continuing to learn from experiences as well as staying abreast with current research findings. Membership in professional organizations will serve you well in this area.

Our profession is represented by dedicated, highly competent teachers, as well as unethical fools. As a member of the former category, be a protagonist in the reformation of the profession.

SUGGESTED READING

Eraut, M. (1987). Inservice. In M. J. Dunkin (Ed.), *The international encyclopedia of teaching and teacher education* (pp. 730–743). Oxford: Pergamon Press.

Nelson, J. L., Palonsky, S. B., & Carlson, K. (1990). *Critical issues in education*. New York: McGraw-Hill.

Task Force on Teaching as a Profession. (1986). *A nation prepared: Teachers for the 21st Century*. New York: Carnegie Corporation.

TAKING WHAT YOU'VE LEARNED TO THE NEXT LEVEL

The ball is in your court.

References

Allen, R. R. (1988, April). *Mathematics, reform, and excellence—Japan and the U.S.* A presentation at the annual meeting of the National Council of Teachers of Mathematics, Chicago.

Allen, R., Davidson, T., Hering, W., & Jesunathadas, J. (1984). *A study of the conditions of secondary mathematics teacher education.* San Francisco: Far West Laboratory.

Ames, C., & Ames, R. (Eds.). (1985). *Research on motivation in education: Vol 1: Student motivation.* Orlando, FL: Academic Press.

Amundson, H. E. (1969). Percent. In *Historical topics for the mathematics classroom: Thirty-first yearbook* (pp. 146–147). Washington, DC: National Council of Teachers of Mathematics.

Archibald, D. A., & Newman, F. M. (1988). *Beyond standardized testing: Assessing academic achievement in the secondary school.* Reston, VA: National Association of Secondary School Principals.

Arends, R. I. (1988). *Learning to teach.* New York: Random House.

Arnold, D., Atwood, R., & Rogers, V. (1974). Questions and response levels and lapse time intervals. *Journal of Experimental Education, 43,* 11–15.

Azrin, N. H., Hake, D. G., & Hutchinson, R. R. (1965). Motivational aspects of escape from punishment. *Journal of Experimental Analysis of Behavior, 8,* 31–44.

Azrin, N. H., Hutchinson, R. R., & Sallery, R. D. (1964). Pain-aggression toward inanimate objects. *Journal of Experimental Analysis of Behavior, 7,* 223–228.

Ball, D. L. (1988). *The subject matter preparation of prospective mathematics teachers: Challenging the myths* (Research Report No. 88-3). East Lansing: Michigan State University, National Center for Research on Teacher Education.

Bandura, A. (1965). Behavior modification through modeling procedures. In L. Krasner & L. P. Ullman (Eds.), *Research in behavior modification* (pp. 310–340). New York: Holt, Rinehart & Winston.

Bang-Jensen, V. (1986). The view from next door: A look at peer "supervision." In K. K. Zumwalt (Ed.), *Improving teaching* (pp. 51–62). Alexandria, VA: Association for Supervision and Curriculum Development.

Barman, C., Leyden, M. B., DiSpezio, M. A., Mercier, S., Guthrie, V., & Ostlund, K. (1989). *Addison-Wesley Science.* Menlo Park, CA: Addison-Wesley.

Baroody, A. J. (1989). Kindergartners' mental addition with single-digit combinations. *Journal of Research for Mathematics Education, 20,* 159–172.

Becker, W. C. (1986). *Applied psychology for teachers: A behavioral cognitive approach.* Chicago: Science Research Associates.

Berg, F. S. (1987). *Facilitating classroom listening.* Boston: College-Hill Press.

Beyer, B. K. (1987). *Practical strategies for the teaching of thinking.* Boston: Allyn & Bacon.

Biklen, D. (1985). *Achieving the complete school.* New York: Teachers College Press.

Bloom, B. S. (Ed.). (1984). *Taxonomy of educational objectives: The classification of educational goals, book I: Cognitive domain.* New York: Longman.

Bloom, B. S., Hastings, J. T., & Madaus, G. F. (1971). *Handbook on formative and summative evaluation of student learning.* New York: McGraw-Hill.

Bongiovanni, A. F. (1979). An analysis of research on punishment and its relation to the use of corporal punishment in schools. In I. A. Hyman & J. Wise (Eds.), *Corporal punishment in American education* (pp. 351–372). Philadelphia: Temple University Press.

Bos, C. S., & Vaughn, S. (1988). *Strategies for teaching students with learning and behavior problems.* Boston: Allyn & Bacon.

Bourne, L. E., Dominowski, R. L., Loftus, E. F., & Healy, A. F. (1986). *Cognitive processes* (2nd ed.). Englewood Cliffs, NJ: Prentice Hall.

Bowden, R. (1991). *Precision teaching in pre-algebra.* Unpublished doctoral dissertation, Utah State University, Logan.

Brandt, R. S. (Ed.). (1988). *Content of the curriculum: 1988 ASCD yearbook.* Alexandria, VA: Association for Supervision and Curriculum Development.

Brandt, R. S. (1989). A changed professional culture. *Educational Leadership, 46,* 2.

Bridges, E. M. (1986). *The incompetent teacher.* Philadelphia: Falmer Press.

Bruner, J. S. (1960). *The process of education.* New York: Vintage Books.

California State Department of Education. (1987). *Caught in the middle: Educational reform for young adolescents in California public schools.* Sacramento, CA: Author.

Cangelosi, J. S. (1974). Competency based teacher education: A cautionary note. *Contemporary Education, 46,* 124–126.

Cangelosi, J. S. (1980). Four steps to teaching for mathematical application. *Mathematics and Computer Education, 14,* 54–59.

Cangelosi, J. S. (1982). *Measurement and evaluation: An inductive approach for teachers.* Dubuque, IA: Brown.

Canglosi, J. S. (1988a). *Classroom management strategies: Gaining and maintaining students' cooperation.* White Plains, NY: Longman.

Cangelosi, J. S. (1988b). Development and validation of the underprepared mathematics teacher assessment. *Journal for Research in Mathematics Education, 19,* 233–245.

Cangelosi, J. S. (1988c) Language activities that promote awareness of mathematics. *Arithmetic Teacher, 36,* 6–9.

Cangelosi, J. S. (1990a). *Cooperation in the classroom: Students and teachers together* (2nd ed.). Washington, DC: National Education Association.

Cangelosi, J. S. (1990b). *Designing tests for evaluating student achievement.* White Plains, NY: Longman.

Cangelosi, J. S. (1991). *Evaluating classroom instruction.* White Plains, NY: Longman.

Cangelosi, J. S. (1992). *Teaching mathematics in secondary and middle school: Research-based approaches.* New York: Macmillan.

Cangelosi, J. S., Struyk, L. R., Grimes, M. L., & Duke, C. (1988, April). *Classroom management needs of beginning teachers.* Paper presented at the annual meeting of the American Educational Research Association, New Orleans.

Canter, L., & Canter, M. (1976). *Assertive discipline: A take-charge approach for today's educator.* Seal Beach, CA: Canter & Canter Associates.

Chance, P. (1988). *Learning and behavior* (2nd ed.). Belmont, CA: Wadsworth.

Chapman, L. H. (1987). *Discover art 1*. Worcester, MA: Davis.

Charles, C. M. (1989). *Building classroom discipline: From models to practice* (3rd ed.). White Plains, NY: Longman.

Chrisco, I. M. (1989). Peer assistance works. *Educational Leadership, 46*, 31–32.

Christoplos, F., & Valletuttie, P. J. (1990). *Developing children's creative thinking through the arts*. Bloomington, IN: Phi Delta Kappa Educational Foundation.

Clark, C. M., & Peterson, P. L. (1986). Teachers' thought processes. In M. C. Wittrock (Ed.), *Handbook of research on teaching* (3rd ed., pp. 255–296). New York: Macmillan.

Conoley, J. C. (1989). Professional communication and collaboration among educators. In M. C. Reynolds (Ed.), *Knowledge base for the beginning teacher* (pp. 245–254). Oxford: Pergamon Press.

Coolican, J. (1988). Individual differences. In R. McNergney (Ed.), *Guide to classroom teaching* (pp. 211–229). Boston: Allyn & Bacon.

Cooper, H. (1989a). *Homework*. White Plains, NY: Longman.

Cooper, H. (1989b). Synthesis of research on homework. *Educational Leadership, 47*, 85–91.

Cooper, J. M. (1984). Introduction and overview. In J. M. Cooper (Ed.), *Developing skills for instructional supervision* (pp. 1–9). White Plains, NY: Longman.

Coulter, F. (1987). Homework. In M. J. Dunkin (Ed.), *The international encyclopedia of teaching and teacher education* (pp. 272–277). Oxford: Pergamon Press.

Cubberley, E. P. (1962). *Public education in the United States* (rev. ed.). Cambridge, MA: Riverside Press.

Curwin, R., & Mendler, A. (1980). *The discipline book: A comprehensive guide to school and classroom management*. Reston, VA: Reston Publishing.

Davidman, L. (in press). *Teaching with a multicultural perspective across the curriculum: A comprehensive approach to effective instruction*. White Plains, NY: Longman.

Delgado, J. M. R. (1963). Cerebral heterostimulation in a monkey colony. *Science, 141*, 161–163.

DiBacco, T. V., Mason, L. C., & Appy, C. G. (1991). *History of the United States*. Boston: Houghton Mifflin.

Dick, W., & Carey, L. (1985). *The systematic design of instruction* (2nd ed.). Glenview, IL: Scott, Foresman.

Dillon, R. F., & Sternberg, R. J. (Eds.). (1986). *Cognition and instruction*. San Diego, CA: Academic Press.

Dossey, J. A., Mullis, I. V. S., Lindquist, M. M., & Chambers, D. L. (1988). *The mathematics report card: Are we measuring up? Trends and achievement based on the 1986 National Assessment*. Princeton, NJ: Educational Testing Service.

Doyle, W. (1986). Classroom organization and management. In M. C. Wittrock (Ed.), *Handbook of research on teaching* (3rd ed., pp. 392–431). New York: Macmillan.

Dreikurs, R. (1968). *Psychology in the classroom* (2nd ed.). New York: Harper & Row.

Duke, C. R., Cangelosi, J. S., & Knight, R. S. (1988, February). *The Mellon Project: A collaborative effort*. Colloquium presentation at the annual meeting of the American Association of Colleges for Teacher Education, New Orleans.

Dunkin, M. J. (Ed.). (1987a). *The international encyclopedia of teaching and teacher education*. Oxford: Pergamon Press.

Dunkin, M. J. (1987b). Teaching: Art or science? In M. J. Dunkin (Ed.), *The international encyclopedia of teaching and teacher education* (p. 19). Oxford: Pergamon Press.

Ebel, R. L., & Frisbie, D. A. (1986). *Essentials of educational measurement* (4th ed.). Englewood Cliffs, NJ: Prentice Hall.

Edwards, L. (1990, May). *Manipulating math for meaning via calculators, probability, and cooperative learning*. A workshop for elementary school teachers. Logan, UT: Mathematics Teacher Inservice Project.

Elam, S. M. (1989). The second Gallup Phi Delta Kappa Poll of teachers' attitudes toward the public school. *Phi Delta Kappan, 70,* 785–798.

Emmer, E. T., Evertson, C. M., Sanford, J. P., Clements, B. S., & Worsham, M. E. (1989). *Classroom management for secondary teachers* (2nd ed.). Englewood Cliffs, NJ: Prentice Hall.

Engelmann, S. (1971). Does the Piagetian approach imply instruction? In D. R. Green, M. P. Ford, & G. P. Flammer (Eds.), *Measurement and Piaget* (pp. 118–147). New York: McGraw-Hill.

Eraut, M. (1987). Inservice. In M. J. Dunkin (Ed.), *The international encyclopedia of teaching and teacher education* (pp. 730–743). Oxford: Pergamon Press.

Evertson, C. M. (1989). Classroom organization and management. In M. C. Reynolds (Ed.), *Knowledge base for the beginning teacher* (pp. 59–70). Oxford: Pergamon Press.

Farrell, M. A., & Farmer, W. A. (1988). *Secondary mathematics instruction: An integrated approach.* Providence, RI: Janson.

Fisher, C. W., Berliner, D. C., Filby, N. N., Marliave, R., Cahen, L. S., & Dishaw, M. M. (1980). Teaching behaviors, academic learning time, and student achievement: An overview. In C. Denham & A. Lieberman (Eds.), *Time to learn* (pp. 7–32). Washington, DC: National Institute of Education.

Foyle, H. C., & Lyman, L. (1989, March). *Cooperative learning: Research and practice.* Paper presented at the Rocky Mountain Regional Conference for the Social Studies, Phoenix, AZ.

Furth, H. G., & Wachs, H. (1974). *Thinking goes to school.* New York: Oxford University Press.

Gage, N. L. (1985). Hard gains in the soft sciences: The case of pedagogy. *Phi Delta Kappan, 67,* 4–11.

Gagne, E. D. (1985). *The cognitive psychology of school learning.* Boston: Little, Brown.

Garner, R. (1990). When children and adults do not use learning strategies: Toward a theory of setting. *Review of Educational Research, 60,* 517–529.

Ginott, H. G. (1965). *Parent and child.* New York: Avon Books.

Ginott, H. G. (1972). *Teacher and child.* New York: Avon Books.

Glasser, W. (1986). *Control theory in the classroom.* New York: Harper & Row.

Glickman, C. D. (1985). *Supervision of instruction: A developmental approach.* Boston: Allyn & Bacon.

Goodlad, J. I. (1984). *A place called school.* New York: McGraw-Hill.

Gordon, T. (1974). *T.E.T.: Teacher effectiveness training.* New York: Peter H. Wyden.

Gordon, W. J. J. (1961). *Synectics.* New York: Harper & Row.

Gowan, J. C., Demos, G. D., & Torrance, E. P. (1967). *Creativity: Its educational implications.* New York: Wiley.

Grady, M. P. (1990). *Whole brain education.* Bloomington, IN: Phi Delta Kappa Educational Foundation.

Grant, C. A., & Sleeter, C. E. (1989). *Turning on learning: Five approaches for multicultural teaching plans for race, class, gender, and disability.* Columbus, OH: Merrill.

Gronlund, N. E., & Linn, R. L. (1990). *Measurement and evaluation in teaching* (6th ed.). New York: Macmillan.

Guilford, J. P. (1959). *Personality.* New York: McGraw-Hill.

Hambleton R. K., & Swaminathan, H. (1985). *Item response theory.* Boston: Kluwer-Nijhoff Publishing.

Harcourt Brace Jovanovich. (1989). *Changes.* Orlando, FL: Author.

Harris, B. M. (1989): *Inservice education for staff development.* Boston: Allyn & Bacon.

Harris, T. A. (1969). *I'm OK—you're OK: A practical guide to transactional analysis.* New York: Harper & Row.

Harrow, A. J. (1974). *A taxonomy of the psychomotor domain: A guide for developing behavioral objectives.* New York: McKay.

Hilke, E. V. (1990). *Cooperative learning*. Bloomington, IN: Phi Delta Kappa Educational Foundation.

Hills, J. R. (1986). *All of Hill's handy hints*. Washington, DC: National Council on Measurement in Education.

Hoffmann, R. J. (1975). Concept of efficiency in item analysis. *Educational and psychological measurement, 35*, 621–640.

Hopkins, K. D., Stanley, J. C., & Hopkins, B. R. (1990). *Educational and psychological measurement and evaluation* (7th ed.). Englewood Cliffs, NJ: Prentice Hall.

Houghton Mifflin. (1991). *Mathematics*. Boston: Author.

Housner, L. D., & Griffey, D. C. (1985). Teacher cognition: Differences in planning and decision making of experienced and inexperienced teachers. *Research Quarterly for Exercise and Sport, 56*, 45–53.

Houts, P. L. (Ed.). (1977). *The myth of measurability*. New York: Hart Publishing.

Hunkins, F. P. (1989). *Teaching thinking through effective questioning*. Boston: Christopher-Gordon Publishers.

Hyman, I. A., & Wise, J. H. (Eds.). (1979). *Corporal punishment in American education*. Philadelphia: Temple University Press.

Jesunathadas, J. (1990). *Mathematics teachers' instructional activities as a function of academic preparation*. Unpublished doctoral dissertation, Utah State University, Logan.

Johnson, D. W., Johnson, R. T., Tiffany, M., & Zaidman, B. (1984). Cross ethnic relationships: The impact of intergroup cooperation and intergroup competition. *Journal of Educational Research, 78*, 75–79.

Jones, B. F., Palincsar, A. S., Ogle, D. S., & Carr, E. G. (Eds.). (1987). *Strategic teaching and learning: Cognitive instruction in the content areas*. Alexandria, VA: Association for Supervision and Curriculum Development.

Jones, F. H. (1979). The gentle art of classroom discipline. *Principal, 58*, 26–32.

Jones, L. T. (1991). *Strategies for involving parents in their children's education*. Bloomington, IN: Phi Delta Kappa Educational Foundation.

Jones, V. F., & Jones, L. S. (1990). *Comprehensive classroom management: Motivating and managing students* (3rd ed.). Boston: Allyn & Bacon.

Joyce, B., & Weil, M. (1986). *Models of teaching* (3rd ed.). Englewood Cliffs, NJ: Prentice Hall.

Kallen, H. M. (1924). *Culture and democracy in the United States*. New York: Boni & Liveright.

Kayfetz, J. L., & Stice, R. L. (1987). *Academically speaking*. Belmont, CA: Wadsworth.

Kelley, D. (1988). *The art of reasoning*. New York: Norton.

Kohut, S., and Range, D. G. (1979). *Classroom discipline: Case studies and viewpoints*. Washington, DC: National Education Association.

Kouba, V. L. (1989). Children's solutions strategies for equivalent set multiplication and division word problems. *Journal for Research in Mathematics Education, 20*, 147–158.

Kounin, J. (1977). *Discipline and group management in classrooms*. New York: Holt, Rinehart & Winston.

Krathwohl, D., Bloom, B. S., & Masia, B. (1964). *Taxonomy of educational objectives, the classification of educational goals, handbook 2: Affective domain*. White Plains, NY: Longman.

Krug, M. (1976). *The melting of ethnics*. Bloomington, IN: Phi Delta Kappa Educational Foundation.

Kubiszyn, T., & Borich, G. (1987). *Educational testing and measurement: Classroom applications and practice* (2nd ed.). Glenville, IL: Scott, Foresman.

Lamb, R. W., & Thomas, M. D. (1981). The art and science of teacher evaluation. *Principal, 61*, 44–47.

Lanier, J. E., & Little, J. W. (1986). Research on teacher education. In M. C. Wittrock (Ed.), *Handbook of research on teaching* (3rd ed., pp. 527–569). New York: Macmillan.

Learning in America: Schools that work. (1990). [A videotape program]. Alexandria, VA: PBS Videos.

Leedy, P. D. (1985). *Practical research: Planning and design* (3rd ed.). New York: Macmillan.

Linn, R. L. (Ed.). (1989). *Educational measurement* (3rd ed.). New York: American Council on Education/Macmillan.

McCallum, A., Strong, W., Thoburn, T., & Williams, P. (1990). *Macmillan language arts today.* New York: Macmillan.

McCarthy, D. J. (1989). The school district: A unique setting. In M. C. Reynolds (Ed.), *Knowledge base for the beginning teacher* (pp. 155–162). Oxford: Pergamon Press.

McCarty, M. M. (1989). Legal rights and responsibilities of public school teachers. In M. C. Reynolds (Ed.), *Knowledge base for the beginning teacher* (pp. 255–266). Oxford: Pergamon Press.

McDiarmid, G. W., Ball, D. L., & Anderson, C. W. (1987). Why staying one chapter ahead doesn't really work: Subject-specific pedagogy. In M. J. Dunkin (Ed.), *The international encyclopedia of teaching and teacher education* (pp. 193–205). Oxford: Pergamon Press.

McLaren, P. (1989). *Life in schools: An introduction to critical pedagogy in the foundations of education.* White Plains, NY: Longman.

McNeil, J. D., (1990). *Curriculum: A comprehensive introduction* (4th ed.). Glenview, IL: Scott, Foresman/Little, Brown.

Medley, D. M., Coker, H., & Soar, R. S. (1984). *Measurement-based evaluation of teacher performance: An empirical approach.* White Plains, NY: Longman.

Meeks, L., & Heit, P. (1990). *Merrill health: Focus on you.* Columbus, OH: Merrill.

Merriam-Webster Inc. (1986). *Webster's Third New International Dictionary.* Chicago: Author.

Mitsakos, C. L. (1991). *Earth's geography and environment.* Evanston, IL: McDougal, Littell.

Mudd, R. (1990). [Editorial comment on video program *Learning in America: Schools that work*]. Alexandria, VA: PBS Videos.

Myers, D. G. (1986). *Psychology.* New York: Worth Publishers.

National Commission on Excellence in Education. (1983). *A nation at risk: The imperative for educational reform.* Washington, DC: U.S. Government Printing Office.

National Council of Teachers of Mathematics. (1989). *Curriculum and evaluation standards for school mathematics.* Reston, VA: Author.

National Council of Teachers of Mathematics. (1991). *Professional standards for teaching mathematics.* Reston, VA: Author.

National Education Association. (1972). *Report on the task force on corporal punishment.* Washington, DC: Author.

Nelson, J. L., Palonsky, S. B., & Carlson, K. (1990). *Critical issues in education.* New York: McGraw-Hill.

Nystrom. (1989). *Primary social studies skills.* Chicago: Author.

Ornstein, A. C. (1990). *Strategies for effective teaching.* New York: Harper & Row.

Peel, E. A. (1989). Teaching. In *The new encyclopedia Britannica* (Vol. 28, pp. 433–450). Chicago: Britannica.

Popham, W. J. (1988). *Educational evaluation* (2nd ed.). Englewood Cliffs, NJ: Prentice Hall.

Popham, W. J. (1990). *Modern educational measurement: A practitioner's perspective* (2nd ed.). Englewood Cliffs, NJ: Prentice Hall.

Posamentier, A. S., & Stepelman, J. (1990). *Teaching secondary school mathematics: Techniques and enrichment units* (3rd ed.). Columbus, OH: Merrill.

Quina, J. (1989). *Effective secondary teaching: Going beyond the bell curve.* New York: Harper & Row.

Random House, Inc. (1984). *The Random House college dictionary* (rev. ed.). New York: Author.

Raney, P., & Robbins, P. (1989). Professional growth and support through peer coaching. *Educational Leadership, 46,* 35–38.

Resnick, L. B., & Klopfer, L. E. (Eds.). (1989). *Toward the thinking curriculum: Current cognitive research: 1989 ASCD yearbook.* Alexandria, VA: Association for Supervision and Curriculum Development.

Reynolds, M. C. (Ed.). (1989). *Knowledge base for the beginning teacher.* Oxford: Pergamon Press.

Roberts, A. D., & Cawelti, G. (1984). *Redefining general education in the American high school.* Alexandria, VA: Association for Supervision and Curriculum Development.

Robbins, A. (1987, May). *Skills of power seminar.* Seminar presentation of the Robbins Research Institute, Detroit.

Rogers, R. L., & McMillin, S. C. (1989). *Freeing someone you love from alcohol and other drugs: A step-by-step plan starting today!* Los Angeles: Body Press.

Rose, T. L. (1984). Current uses of corporal punishment in American public schools. *Journal of Educational Psychology, 76,* 427–441.

Rosenshine, B. (1987). Direct instruction. In M. J. Dunkin (Ed.), *The international encyclopedia of teaching and teacher education* (pp. 257–262). Oxford: Pergamon Press.

Ruetten, M. K. (1986). *Comprehending academic lectures.* New York: Macmillan.

Rust, J. O., & Kinnard, K. Q. (1983). Personality characteristics of the users of corporal punishment in the schools. *Journal of School Psychology, 21,* 91–105.

Ryan, K., & Cooper, J. M. (1988). *Those who can, teach* (5th ed.). Boston: Houghton-Mifflin.

Sabornie, E. J. (1985). Social mainstreaming of handicapped students: Facing an unpleasant reality. *Remedial and Special Education, 6,* 12–16.

Santrock, J. W. (1984). *Adolescence* (2nd ed.). Dubuque, IA: W. C. Brown.

Sarason, S. B. (1982). *The culture of the school and the problem of change* (2nd ed.). Boston: Allyn & Bacon.

Schoenfeld, A. H. (1985). *Mathematical problem solving.* San Diego, CA: Academic Press.

Schoenfeld, A. H. (1988). When good teaching leads to bad results: The disasters of "well-taught" mathematics courses. *Educational Psychologist, 23,* 145–166.

Shuell, T. J. (1990). Phases of meaningful learning. *Review of Educational Research, 60,* 531–547.

Slavin, R. E. (1988). Cooperative learning and student achievement. *Educational Leadership, 46,* 31–33.

Slavin, R. E. (1991). Synthesis of research on cooperative learning. *Educational Leadership, 48,* 71–82.

Sleeter, C., & Grant, C. (1987). An analysis of multicultural education in the United States. *Harvard Educational Review, 57,* 421–444.

Smedslund, J. (1977). Symposium: Practical and theoretical issues in Piagetian psychology III—Piaget's psychology in practice. *British Journal of Educational Psychology, 47,* 1–6.

Smith, B. O. (1987). Teaching: Definitions of teaching. In M. J. Dunkin (Ed.), *The international encyclopedia of teaching and teacher education* (pp. 11–15). Oxford: Pergamon Press.

Soar, R. S., Medley, D. M., & Coker, H. (1983). Teacher evaluation: A critique of currently used methods. *Phi Delta Kappan, 65,* 239–246.

Stallings, J. A., & Stipek, D. (1986). Research on early childhood and elementary school teaching programs. In M. C. Wittrock (Ed.), *Handbook of research on teaching* (3rd ed., pp. 727–753). New York: Macmillan.

Stallion, B. K. (1988, April). *Classroom management intervention: The effects of mentoring relationships on the inductee teacher's behavior.* Paper presented at the annual meeting of the American Educational Research Association, New Orleans.

Stanley, S. J., & Popham, W. J. (Eds.). (1988) *Teacher evaluation: Six prescriptions for success.* Alexandria, VA: Association for Curriculum and Supervision.

Steere, B. F. (1988). *Becoming an effective classroom manager: A resource for teachers.* Albany, NY: State University of New York Press.

Stiggins, R. J. (1988). Revitalizing classroom assessment: The highest instructional priority. *Phi Delta Kappan, 69,* 363–368.

Stiggins, R. J., Conklin, N. K., and Bridgeford, N. J. (1986). Classroom assessment: A key to effective education. *Educational Measurement: Issues and Practices, 5,* 5–17.

Stiggins, R. J., & Duke, D. (1988). *The case for commitment to teacher growth: Research on teacher evaluation.* Albany: State University of New York Press.

Strike, K., & Soltis, J. (1986). Who broke the fish tank? And other ethical dilemmas. *Instructor, 95,* 36–39.

Strom, R. D. (1969). *Psychology for the classroom.* Englewood Cliffs, NJ: Prentice Hall.

Sulzer-Azaroff, B., & Mayer, G. R. (1977). *Applying behavior analysis procedures with children and youth.* New York: Holt, Rinehart & Winston.

Swartz, R. J., & Perkins, D. N. (1990). *Teaching thinking: Issues and approaches* (rev. ed.). Pacific Grove, CA: Midwest Publications.

Task Force on Teaching as a Profession. (1986). *A nation prepared: Teachers for the 21st century.* New York: Carnegie Corporation.

Tauber, R. T. (1990). *Classroom management from A to Z.* Fort Worth, TX: Holt, Rinehart & Winston.

TenBrink, T. D. (1990). Instructional objectives. In J. M. Cooper (Ed.), *Classroom teaching skills* (4th ed., pp. 51–83). Lexington, MA: Heath.

Thorndike, R. M., Cunningham, G. K., Thorndike, R. L., & Hagen, E. P. (1991). *Measurement and evaluation in psychology and education* (5th ed., pp. 90–156). New York: Macmillan.

Torrance, E. P. (1962). *Guiding creative talent.* Englewood Cliffs, NJ: Prentice Hall.

Torrance, E. P. (1966). Fostering creative behavior. In R. D. Strom (Ed.), *The inner-city classroom: Teacher behavior* (pp. 57–74). Columbus, OH: Merrill.

Towers, R. L. (1987). *How schools can help combat student drug and alcohol abuse.* Washington, DC: National Education Association.

Towers, R. L. (in press). *Children of alcoholics/addicts.* Washington, DC: National Education Association.

Tuckman, B. W. (1988). *Testing for teachers* (2nd ed.). San Diego, CA: Harcourt Brace Jovanovich.

Ulrich, R. E., & Azrin, N. H. (1962). Reflexive fighting in response to aversive stimulation. *Journal of Experimental Analysis of Behavior, 5,* 511–520.

U.S. students again rank near bottom in math and science. (1989). *Report on educational research, 23*(2), 1–4.

U.S. teens lag behind in math, science. (1989). *Education USA, 31,* 153 + .

Van Dyke, H. T. (1984). Corporal punishment in our schools. *The Clearing House, 57,* 296–300.

Van Horn, K. L. (1982, April). *The Utah pupil/teacher self-concept program: Teacher strategies that invite improvement of pupil and teacher self-concept.* Paper presented at the annual meeting of the American Educational Research Association, New York.

Voorhies, R. (1989). Cooperative learning: What is it? *Social Studies Review, 28,* 7–10.

Watson, G. G. (1991). *McDougal, Littell economics.* Evanston, IL: McDougal, Littell.

Weber, W. A. (1986). Classroom management. In J. M. Cooper (Ed.), *Classroom teaching skills* (3rd ed., pp. 271–357). Lexington, MA: Heath.

Welsh, R. S. (1985). Spanking: A grand old American tradition? *Children Today, 14*, 25–29.

Wilds, E. H., & Lottich, K. V. (1961). *The foundations of modern education* (3rd ed.). New York: Holt, Rinehart & Winston.

Winitzky, N. (1988). Developing multicultural and mainstreamed classrooms. In R. I. Arends, *Learning to teach* (pp. 202–209). New York: Random House.

Wittrock, M. C. (Ed.). (1986). *Handbook of research on teaching* (3rd ed.). New York: Macmillan.

Wolery, M., Bailey, D. B., Jr., & Sugai, G. M. (1988). *Effective teaching: Principles and procedures of applied behavioral analysis with exceptional students*. Boston: Allyn & Bacon.

Wolman, B. B. (Ed.). (1989). *Dictionary of behavioral science* (2nd ed.). San Diego, CA: Academic Press.

Wolpe, J., & Lazarus, A. A. (1966). *Behavior therapy techniques: A guide to the treatment of neuroses*. Oxford: Pergamon Press.

Wood, F. H. (1982). The influence of public opinion and social custom on the use of corporal punishment in schools. In F. H. Wood & K. C. Lakin (Eds.), *Punishment and aversive stimulation in special education: Legal, theoretical and practical issues in their use with emotionally disturbed children and youth* (pp. 29–30). Reston, VA: Council for Exceptional Children.

Worthen, B. R., & Sanders, J. R. (1987). *Educational evaluation: Alternative approaches and practical guidelines*. White Plains, NY: Longman.

Zumwalt, K. K. (Ed.). (1986). *Improving teaching: 1986 ASCD yearbook*. Alexandria, VA: Association for Supervision and Curriculum Development.

Index